System Innovation and the Transition to Sustainability

Transition at the societal level
↑ = A system innovation.

System Innovation and the Transition to Sustainability

Theory, Evidence and Policy

Edited by

Boelie Elzen

Senior Researcher, School of Business, Public Administration and Technology, University of Twente, The Netherlands

Frank W. Geels

Assistant Professor, Department of Technology Management, Eindhoven University of Technology, The Netherlands

Ken Green

Professor of Environmental Innovation Management, Manchester Business School, University of Manchester, UK

Edward Elgar
Cheltenham, UK • Northampton, MA, USA

Published by
Edward Elgar Publishing Limited
Glensanda House
Montpellier Parade
Cheltenham
Glos GL50 1UA
UK

Edward Elgar Publishing, Inc.
136 West Street
Suite 202
Northampton
Massachusetts 01060
USA

A catalogue record for this book
is available from the British Library

Library of Congress Cataloguing in Publication Data

System innovation and the transition to sustainability : theory, evidence and
    policy / edited by Boelie Elzen, Frank W. Geels, Ken Green.
        p. cm.
    Includes index.
    1. Sustainable development. 2. Environmental policy. 3. System theory.
    I. Elzen, Boelie, 1953– II. Geels, Frank W., 1971– III. Green, Kenneth.

HC79.E5S967   2004
338.9'27–dc22

ISBN 1 84376 683 3   2004047069

Printed and bound in Great Britain by MPG Books Ltd, Bodmin, Cornwall

Contents

Figures

Tables

Contributors

Frank-Martin Belz is Professor of Brewery and Food Industry Management at the Technical University of Munich. He is located at the Centre of Life and Food Sciences in Weihenstephan. Frank-Martin Belz studied Business Administration at the universities of Giessen and Mannheim (Germany), majoring in marketing/consumption. In 1995 he received his PhD at the University of St Gallen (Switzerland). His main interests of research are sustainability marketing and consumption. Over the past decade he focused these efforts on the domains of food/eating, houses/living and mobility/moving, participating in various interdisciplinary and international research projects.

Luca Berchicci is a PhD researcher at Delft University of Technology in the department of the Design for Sustainability programme. His research focuses on environmental product development within networks and entrepreneurial firms. He graduated at Urbino University in Geology and after a period working in geophysical and geological matters he decided to go back to study joining the EAEME postgraduate course in Environmental Management at Polytechnic University of Athens and at Erasmus University of Rotterdam. On that occasion during the Ecodesign lectures he had the opportunity to meet Professor Brezet and J.C. Diehl, and shortly afterwards became a research fellow in their department.

Frans Berkhout is director of the ESRC Sustainable Technologies Programme, and Senior Fellow and Head of the Environment and Energy Programme at SPRU – Science and Technology Policy Research – at the University of Sussex. He has extensive research and research management experience across a number of fields. His early research was concerned with the economic, political and security aspects of the nuclear fuel cycle and radioactive waste management, with special emphasis on the international control of fissile materials (plutonium and highly enriched uranium). More recent work has been concerned with technology, policy and sustainability, with special emphasis on the links between technological innovation and environmental performance in firms, the measurement of sustainability performance, futures scenarios studies, business adaptation to environmental change, and policy frameworks for innovation and the environment.

Halina Szejnwald Brown is Professor of Environmental Health and Policy at Clark University, Worcester, MA, USA. She received a PhD degree in chemistry from New York University. Prior to joining Clark University, Brown was a chief toxicologist for the Massachusetts Department of Environmental Protection. Brown's research focuses on environmental regulatory regimes in the USA and Europe, the use of science and information in public policy, and social learning through technological innovation for sustainability. Brown has authored over 40 articles and two books and served on numerous state and national advisory panels, including the National Academy of Science, Environmental Protection Agency, the Massachusetts Toxic Use Reduction Institute, National Science Foundation, and the American Association for the Advancement of Science. She is Fellow of the Society for Risk Analysis, and Fellow of the American Association for the Advancement of Science.

Aad Correljé is Associate Professor at the Section Economics of Infrastructures of the Faculty of Technology, Policy and Management of the Delft University of Technology. He is a research fellow with the Clingendael International Energy Programme (CIEP). After studying Political Science (International Relations and European Law) at the University of Amsterdam, he wrote a PhD thesis at the Centre for International Energy Studies (EURICES) at the Erasmus University in Rotterdam. Correljé has been involved in academic research, teaching and advising on many energy-related issues, including oil and gas markets, economic restructuring and (sustainable) energy policy.

Jurian Edelenbos is assistant professor at the Centre for Public Management, Erasmus University, Rotterdam, the Netherlands. He has published on interactive governance, process management, public–private partnership, transition management, and trust in complex interorganizational cooperation. He does research mainly in the domain of urban planning and infrastructure.

Boelie Elzen is senior researcher at the School of Business, Public Administration and Technology, University of Twente, Enschede, the Netherlands. His general research interest is in understanding the dynamics of socio-technical change and using these insights to develop suggestions on how to tackle the societal problems related to these change processes. Over the past decade he has focused these efforts on the domain of passenger mobility, worked on various relevant EU research projects and acted as consultant to various institutions in the field, in the Netherlands as well as abroad.

Frank W. Geels is Assistant Professor at the Department of Technology Management, Eindhoven University of Technology, the Netherlands. His general research interest is in understanding the dynamics of technological transitions and system innovations. To understand these dynamics he has developed a conceptual perspective, using insights from innovation studies and the sociology of technology. He also does case-studies from different domains (for example, transport, manufacturing, hygiene), mainly historical, to test and refine the perspective. He has also done prospective work on socio-technical scenarios, using the same perspective.

Ken Green is Professor of Environmental Innovation Management in the Manchester Business School at the University of Manchester. He teaches and researches in technology and innovation management, with a strong interest in environmental issues. He is director of the school's Centre for Research on Organisations, Management and Technical Change (CROMTEC). He is also a director of the newly-formed Institute of Innovation Research and is associated with the Tyndall Centre for Climate Change Research. Professor Green's current research interests are in the socio-economic analysis of technological development, especially with regard to environmental influences on innovation. Current research contracts are with the Tyndall Centre, on the influence of long-term technological change on greenhouse gas emissions, and the ESRC, on sustainability in food systems.

Peter S. Hofman is a senior research associate of the Center for Clean Technology and Environmental Policy at the University of Twente in Enschede, the Netherlands. His research centres on the role of policy and innovation in transition paths towards more sustainable production and consumption. He currently holds a post-doctoral position, funded by NWO (the Dutch national science foundation), in which he is involved in analysis of socio-technical change related to the energy system and the development of socio-technical scenarios.

René Kemp is senior research fellow at Maastricht Economic Research Institute on Innovation and Technology (MERIT) from Maastricht University and senior advisor of TNO-STB. He is an expert on the topic of innovation for the environment, about which he has published several books and articles (see www.meritbbs.unimaas.nl/rkemp). His current work is on transitions to sustainability, focusing on how these transitions may be managed. He has been consultant for the European Commission, OECD and Dutch government and can be contacted at r.kemp@merit.unimaas.nl.

Sirkku Kivisaari is senior researcher at VTT Technology Studies, VTT Technical Research Centre of Finland. Her research relates to future-oriented technology assessment and especially to developing the approach of societal embedding for promoting dialogue between producers, users and societal actors in shaping new health services and technologies. Her current work focuses on facilitating public–private partnerships for developing and introducing innovations provoked by societal concerns for wellbeing of the ageing society and for a cleaner environment.

Raimo Lovio is Professor of Innovation and Environmental Management at the Department of Management, the Helsinki School of Economics, Finland. In recent years he has studied energy sector development and innovations from the point of view of climate change. In addition, his current work focuses on the globalization of large Finnish companies in terms of innovation activities and corporate responsibility, and the role of environmental management systems and reporting in improving the environmental performance of business organizations.

Jan Rotmans is one of the founders of Integrated Assessment (IA), and has outstanding experience in IA modeling, scenario-building, uncertainty management and transition management. During the past 15 years he has led a diversity of innovative projects in the field of climate change, global change, sustainable development and transitions. Since 1992 Jan Rotmans has had a professorship at Maastricht University, and since 1998 a full professorship on 'Integrated Assessment'. He is founder and director of the International Centre for Integrative Studies (ICIS) (1998) at Maastricht University. He is Vice-Chairman of the European Forum on Integrated Environmental Assessment (EFIEA), Vice-President of the Integrated Assessment Society (TIAS), and founder of the Dutch Knowledge Network on System Innovations: transitions towards a sustainable society (KSI).

Elizabeth Shove is a reader in the Department of Sociology at Lancaster University. She has worked on different aspects of environmental sociology, from energy and buildings to the domestic freezer. Her recent book, *Comfort, Cleanliness and Convenience: the Social Organization of Normality*, takes these ideas forward with reference to key areas of everyday life and ordinary consumption. Elizabeth is currently working on projects relating to the kitchen, the bathroom and the future of comfort, these being important arenas in which to explore images, practices and technologies, and the dynamic relation between them.

Adrian Smith is a social scientist who analyses relationships between technology, society and sustainable development. He has done research for a variety of public and non-governmental organizations, including the Economic and Social Research Council, the European Commission, the Environment Agency, the Department of the Environment, the Department of Trade and Industry, the Sustainable Development Commission and the Institute for Prospective Technological Studies. He is a member of the editorial board for two journals: *Sustainable Development*; and *Theomai – Revista de Sociedad, Naturaleza y Desarrollo*. He also sits on the advisory board of the International Bibliography of the Social Sciences.

Andy Stirling is a senior lecturer at SPRU – science and technology policy research, at the University of Sussex. He has a background in astrophysics, a Masters in social anthropology and archaeology (Edinburgh) and a DPhil in technology policy (Sussex). Formerly working for Greenpeace International, he later served on their Board. His research focuses on technological risk and technology choice in areas spanning the nuclear, energy, chemicals, medical and biotechnology sectors. In particular, he is actively involved in developing more 'participatory' and 'precautionary' approaches in technology policy and in the analysis of strategic issues like flexibility, resilience and diversity. He has served on a number of UK and EU policy advisory committees, including the EU's Energy Policy Consultative Committee, the UK Advisory Committee on Toxic Substances and the UK GM Science Review Panel.

Geert R. Teisman is Professor in Decision Making and Complexity Theory and Chair of the Centre for Public Management at the Erasmus University in Rotterdam. His research topics are intergovermental cooperation, public–private partnership and management of joint decision making, mainly in the areas of transport, spatial and economic developments and environmental affairs.

Erja Väyrynen is researcher at VTT Technology Studies, VTT Technical Research Centre of Finland. Her areas of expertise are technology foresight and societal embedding of innovations. Her earlier activities have ranged from urban planning to environmental impact assessment. She has lately been involved in developing Finnish technology foresight practices on the basis of European experience. In her recent study on ageing of the population as a challenge for technology foresight and innovations, she also discusses the role of national innovation policy in developing social innovations.

Geert Verbong is Associate Professor in Technology and Sustainability Studies, Department of Technology Management, Eindhoven University of Technology (EUT). His main area of research is on system innovations, in particular energy systems, and on implementation strategies for renewable energy technologies. He has been an editor and researcher in large projects on the history of technology in the Netherlands in the nineteenth and twentieth centuries. Currently his research focuses on electricity systems in Europe and on biomass. He teaches Technology Assessment, System Innovations and Strategic Niche Management in the STS programme of EUT, the MSc programme Sustainable Energy Technologies and other EUT engineering programmes.

Professor Philip J. Vergragt is a visiting senior fellow at Tellus Institute, presently on leave from Delft University of Technology in the Netherlands where he holds a professorship. His research focuses on societal transitions towards sustainable mobility and sustainable consumption, with special interest in the questions of infrastructure, culture, stakeholder perspectives and participation, and social learning. He facilitates visioning and backcasting workshops, by a methodology developed in the STD (Sustainable Technological Development) Programme, and the SusHouse project.

Abbreviations

ANT	Actor-Network Theory
ANWB	(Dutch) motoring association
AT	Appropriate/Alternative Technology
AVG	Automatic Vehicle Guidance
BCM	billion cubic metres
BOM	Brabant Development Corporation
BPM	Bataafse Petroleum Maatschappij (subsidiary of Shell in the Netherlands)
BSTE	Bounded Sociotechnical Experiments
CEV	city electric vehicles
CIEP	Clingendael International Energy Programme
CMS	City Mobility System
CROMTEC	Centre for Research on Organizations Management and Technical Change, Manchester Business School, (UK)
DSM	Dutch State Mines
DFS	Design for Sustainability
DTO	Sustainable Technology Development programme (Dutch)
EAEME	postgraduate course in Environmental Management at the Polytechnic University of Athens and Erasmus University of Amsterdam
ECMT	European Conference of Ministers of Transport
EFIEA	European Forum on Integrated Environmental Assessment
ESCO	Energy Service Company
EURICES	Centre for International Energy Studies, Erasmus University, Rotterdam
EUT	Eindhoven University of Technology
FCB	Fuel cell bus
GPS	Global Positioning System
HEV	hybrid electric vehicle
IA	Integrated Assessment
ICIS	International Centre for Integrative Studies, Maastricht University, Netherlands
ICT	Information and Communication Technology

IHDP	International Human Dimensions Programme
IRA	increasing returns to adoption
KNV	freight transport organization in the Netherlands
KSI	(Dutch) Knowledge Network on System Innovations
LDV	long-distance vehicle
LTS	Large Technical Systems
MC	Mobility Centre
MERIT	Maastricht Economic Research Institute on Innovation and Technology, Maastricht University, Netherlands
MTI	Ministry for Trade and Industry (Finland)
NAM	Nederlandse Aardolie Maatschappij, partnership of BPM (Shell) and Standard Oil Company of New Jersey
NEPP	National Environmental Policy Plan (Netherlands)
NS	National Rail Company, Netherlands
NVVP	National Plan for Traffic and Transport, Netherlands
NWO	Dutch Research Council
pkt	passenger kilometres travelled
RAI, BOVAG	represent car dealers and garages in the Netherlands
SCOT	Social Construction of Technology
SGB	State Gas Company (Netherlands)
SMEC	Social Management of Environmental Change
SNAM	Società Nazionale Metanodotti (National Methane Company), Italy
SNM	Strategic Niche Management
SPRU	Science and Technology Policy Research, University of Sussex
SROG	Commission Cooperation Regional Organizations Gas Supply
STF	Sustainable Texel Foundation
STSc	Socio-technical Scenario
STS	Science, Technology and Society
TBM	Faculty of Technology Policy and Management, University of Delft
TEMO	Texel Own Mobility System
TEP	Technoeconomic paradigm
3VO	traffic safety organization in the Netherlands
TIAS	The Integrated Assessment Society (Netherlands)
TNO	Organization for applied research in technological innovation in industry
V&W	Ministry of Transport, Public Works and Water Management (the Netherlands)
VEGIN	United gas companies in the Netherlands

VROM	Ministry of Housing, Spatial Planning and the Environment, Netherlands
VSN	regional transport providers in the Netherlands
VTT	Technical Research Centre of Finland

Preface

Since the publication of the Brundtland report in 1987, the goal of sustainability has increasingly gained the attention of a variety of societal actors, including public authorities, NGOs, consumer groups and industrial firms as well as researchers in a wide range of disciplines. At the general level, there is widespread consensus that various characteristics of modern societies are not sustainable and should change. When things get more prescriptive, however, many feel that the goals of sustainability seem to clash with other vital societal interests.

In recent decades, impressive results have been achieved in the environmental aspect of sustainability, for example by curbing the emissions of a variety of pollutants. Nonetheless, many feel that achieving the broader goals of sustainability is still remote since many problems appear extremely difficult to tackle, such as obtaining large reductions in the emission of greenhouse gases. Furthermore, the scope of the term of sustainability has become broadened to include a variety of goals, including a healthy environment, a healthy society and a healthy economy. To achieve this multitude of targets we seem to need fundamental changes, and these changes are denoted by terms like system innovation, transition and industrial transformation.

Across the world, researchers from different disciplinary backgrounds have begun to try to understand the processes underlying these changes and policy makers have begun to use these insights. In the Netherlands, for example, various ministries have set up so-called 'transition teams' who wrestle with the issue of how to set in motion fundamental changes towards achieving sustainability. This suggests a need to exchange insights, experiences and views between a divergent research community and policy makers.

This led to a Dutch initiative to organize an international workshop on 'Transitions Towards Sustainability Through System Innovation', held at the University of Twente in the summer of 2002. The workshop was funded by the RMNO (The Dutch Advisory Council for Research on Nature and Environment), the Dutch National Council for Agricultural Research (Innovatienetwerk Groene Ruimte en Agrocluster), the Dutch Ministry of Housing, Spatial Planning and the Environment, the Industrial Transformation Project of the International Human Dimensions

Programme (IHDP IT), the Greening of Industry Network, the Dutch National Initiative for Sustainable Development (NIDO) and the University of Twente.

The workshop was organized by an international steering committee and selected participants came from ten different countries. They included researchers with various disciplinary backgrounds as well as policy makers. The main goal of the workshop was to seek some common ground amongst the heterogeneity of approaches, and define an agenda for further work. This book contains a selection of ten papers that were prepared for the workshop and fuelled the discussions; it includes a general introduction and a conclusion that teases out some general findings.

We would very much like to thank our sponsors for making it possible to organize this workshop and all participants for their contributions as either authors or commentators and for their participation in the discussions making the workshop a success.

Boelie Elzen
Frank W. Geels
Ken Green

WORKSHOP PARTICIPANTS

Colette Alma, Peter Aubert, Theo Beckers, Frank-Martin Belz, Frans Berkhout, Halina Brown, Tine Bruland, Joske Bunders, Maurits Butter, Aad Correljé, Frans Duijnhouwer, Boelie Elzen, Gertjan Fonk, Frank Geels, Ken Green, John Grin, Rob Hoppe, Jorge Islas, Klaus Jacob, Ulrik Jørgensen, René Kemp, Sirkku Kivisaari, Derk Loorbach, Rob Maas, Arie Rip, Harald Rohracher, Jan Rotmans, Johan Schot, Elizabeth Shove, Ruud Smits, Geert Teisman, Andrew Tylecote, Pier Vellinga, Geert Verbong, Frans Vollenbroek, Matthias Weber, Anna Wieczorek, Jan de Wilt.

Foreword

On behalf of the sponsors of the international workshop on 'Transitions Towards Sustainability Through System Innovation' I am happy to recommend to you the edited volume of the most interesting research results and ideas presented at this workshop.

Global environmental change poses an unprecedented international challenge for 21st century societies since it requires a radical change in the way human needs in the field of energy, food, water and mobility are met. It calls for a transformation of our current consumption and production patterns as well as a transformation of incentive structures and the institutions that shape the relationship between the two. Such a proactive approach is based on the understandings of system analysis, system being defined as a set of inter-related economic activities and actors and flows of goods and services. For system change to be effective, it needs attention in all aspects of life: technology, institutions, economy, and the socio-cultural sphere. Because of this complexity, it is not surprising that a change to a more sustainable system will require a long time – at least one generation.

For that reason, research into societal transformations that have the potential to decouple economic development from environmental burden has become the focus of many research institutes worldwide. Two types of research activities can be distinguished: one is focused on understanding the dynamics of past transitions that, very often, occurred without deliberate planning; the second type of research focuses on the possibilities of steering societal changes towards sustainability.

This book is one of the first to present the state of the art in knowledge of transitions towards sustainability through system innovation. Even though knowledge in this field is still in its infancy, we are starting to recognize the foundation of a new field of research with a new set of definitions and approaches. I very much hope this book will serve as a good starting point for those who want to further expand this field. The book is primarily meant for those who are curious about how transformations take place and what problems societies face when they want to steer these great changes in a desired direction.

Pier Vellinga

Chair of the Scientific Steering Committee of the Industrial Transformation Project of the International Human Dimensions Programme on Global Environmental Change (IHDP IT)

1. General introduction: system innovation and transitions to sustainability

Frank W. Geels, Boelie Elzen, Ken Green

Modern societies face structural problems in several sectors. In the energy sector there are problems related to oil dependency, reliability, and CO_2 and NO_x emissions. The transport system suffers from congestion, air pollution (particulates, NO_x), energy use and CO_2 emissions. Cattle farming suffers from manure disposal problems, ammonia emissions and diseases like BSE and foot and mouth disease. These problems are deeply rooted in social production and consumption patterns.

Since the 1980s, much effort has been made to solve problems with product and process innovations. Cleaner products and processes have been developed alongside the application of end-of-pipe solutions. Sometimes these innovations have led to substantial improvements in environmental efficiency, such as in the case of automobile catalysts which greatly reduced tailpipe-emissions of pollutants. The focus in these cases has been on changing some technological artefact.

Substantial improvements in environmental efficiency (a 'Factor 2' is a general average) may still be possible with innovations of an 'incremental' kind. But larger jumps in environmental efficiency (possibly by a 'Factor 10') may only be possible with system innovations. The promise of transitions to sustainability via system innovations is schematically represented in Figure 1.1. Such transitions to sustainability require changes from, for example, one transport system to another or from one energy system to another. Such system innovations not only involve new technological artefacts, but also new markets, user practices, regulations, infrastructures and cultural meanings.

Because of its sustainability potential there is increasing interest from policy makers, NGOs and large firms in transitions and system innovations. The Stockholm Environment Institute, for instance, has published a book on the *Great Transition* (Raskin *et al.*, 2002). The American National Research Council (1999) and the Dutch Research Council

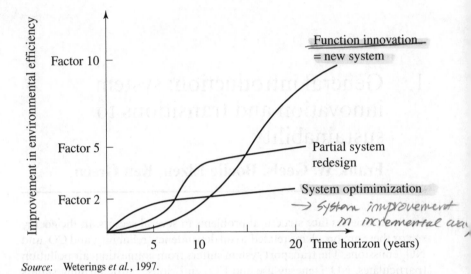

Source: Weterings *et al.*, 1997.

Figure 1.1.   System optimization versus system innovation

(NWO) have made the study of transitions part of their research portfolio. The IHDP research programme (International Human Dimensions
Programme on Global Environmental Change) has a Project on 'Industrial
Transformation' (similar in meaning to 'transitions'). The Dutch government gave transitions a central place in its fourth National Environmental
Policy Plan (VROM, 2001) and has established 'transition teams' within
various ministries.

To link with and to feed this growing interest, this book explores how
system innovations come about and how policymakers might influence
them.

DELINEATING THE TOPIC OF ANALYSIS: TRANSITIONS AND SYSTEM INNOVATIONS

In *Webster's Dictionary* the term 'transition' is defined as a 'passage from
one state, stage, subject, or place to another' or 'a movement, development,
or evolution from one form, stage, or style to another'. The states/forms
have certain internal characteristics, which give them coherence and stability. The notion of a transition also has the connotation of rapid change, a
'jump' from one state to another.

Transitions can occur on different levels, depending on the unit of analysis. An example at the level of society as a whole is the transition from

hunter-gatherer society to urban society. Another example is the transition from rural to industrial society. At a lower level, there are transitions in societal functions such as transport, communication, housing, feeding, energy supply and use, and recreation. Examples are the transition in transport systems from horse-and-carriage to automobile, or the transition from telegraph to telephone. There are also transitions at the level of organizations and firms, for example the transition from punched card machines to computers within IBM (Chandler, 2001) or the transition of DSM (Dutch State Mines) from coal mining via bulk chemicals to fine chemicals. This book focuses on a specific type of transition, notably transition at the level of societal functions.

What is it that changes at this level during transitions? In the way we use the term, these transitions involve changes in *socio-technical systems*. These comprise a cluster of elements, including technology, regulations, user practices and markets, cultural meanings, infrastructure, maintenance networks and supply networks. Technology plays an important role in fulfilling societal functions, but its functioning depends upon its relationship to the other elements. Technologies realize functionalities in concrete user contexts, which are made up of users, their competencies, preferences, cultural values and interpretations. User contexts are also shaped by a variety of existing artefacts and infrastructures (for example, road infrastructures, electricity networks), and regulations.

Technologies also need to be produced, distributed and 'tuned' with existing user contexts. This requires aspects such as technological knowledge, machines, skilled labour, capital, natural resources and components, and distribution networks. Although these supply and demand aspects can be distinguished analytically, they are mutually dependent in practice. To highlight this interrelatedness, we use the term 'socio-technical systems'. Transitions at the societal level then involve a change from one socio-technical system to another, that is a *system innovation*.

This way of delineating the unit of analysis has several implications. Firstly, it means that the focus is wider than just an industry or a sectoral system of innovation. There has been some attention paid in the past to the emergence of new industries (Van de Ven and Garud, 1989), how industries coevolve with government and universities in so-called triple helix dynamics (Etzkowitz and Leydesdorff, 2000), and how firms, public authorities and universities work together in innovation systems or innovation communities (Breschi and Malerba, 1997; Malerba, 2002; Lynn *et al.*, 1996). These approaches, however, mainly look at the supply-side and the production of innovations. They take the user side for granted or narrow it down to 'the market' which functions as a neutral selection environment.

There is another body of literature which shows that users do more than just buy and adopt (new) technologies. Cultural studies and social studies of technology have found that users have to 'domesticate' new technologies to fit existing user contexts. This involves symbolic and practical work, in which users integrate the artefact into their user practices, and cognitive work, which includes learning about the artefact (Lie and Sørensen, 1996; Du Gay *et al.*, 1997). This fits an emerging trend in innovation studies and science and technology studies, in which more attention is paid to the role of users in innovation and technological development (see Schwartz-Cowan, 1987; Kline and Pinch, 1996; Eggerton, 1999; Coombs *et al.*, 2001; Oudshoorn and Pinch, 2003). These observations imply that system innovations not only involve changes in industries, firms and technical knowledge, but also changes in user contexts and symbolic meanings.

This book acknowledges this and aims to bring together two bodies of literature which have remained relatively separate so far: on the one hand evolutionary economics, innovation studies and innovation system approaches and, on the other hand, cultural studies, and science and technology studies.

A second implication is that system innovations appear as a particular kind of innovation. To illustrate this, we use the innovation typology of Abernathy and Clark (1985), but widen it. They distinguish two dimensions. The first dimension consists of linkages between a firm and its customers, including channels of distribution and service, customer applications and customer knowledge. The second dimension relates to the technological and production competences of a firm, including production systems, skills, technical knowledge and supplier relations. Combining these two dimensions results in four types of innovations (see Figure 1.2):

1. architectural: disrupts existing technology and linkages with users;
2. niche creation: conserves existing technology but breaks linkages with users; new markets are explored with existing products;
3. incremental: conserves both existing technology and users;
4. revolutionary: disrupts technology but conserves user linkages (same markets).

Abernathy and Clark developed their innovation typology primarily to determine the consequences of different kinds of innovations for firms. While their point about linkages and alignments between elements is important, their focus on firms is too limited for our purposes as disruptions occur on a much wider scale during system innovations. Hence, system innovations

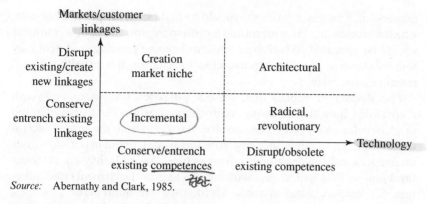

Source: Abernathy and Clark, 1985.

Figure 1.2. Typology of innovations

can be described as architectural innovations 'writ large', because they involve substantial changes on the supply side and on the user side. The term also highlights that system innovations are not about component changes, but about changes in the entire architecture or structure of socio-technical systems. Without changes on the user side, technological discontinuities are better described as 'technological revolutions', which do not change functionalities.

A third implication is that system innovations are multi-actor processes. This not only denotes interactions between actors *within* a societal group (for example, industry, user group, scientific community, policy community), but also interactions *between* societal groups. A range of societal groups or stakeholders is involved in system innovations: firms, suppliers, universities and knowledge institutes, public authorities, public interest groups, users. Their activities create and maintain elements of socio-technical systems. The societal groups have their own perceptions of the future, values and preferences, strategies, and resources (money, knowledge, contacts). Although these societal groups have some degree of autonomy, they are also related to each other and interpenetrate each other (Stankiewicz, 1992).

Their activities are to some degree aligned, and it is this that gives socio-technical systems their stability and a recognizable state or form. Within systems, innovations still take place but they are usually of an incremental nature, leading to trajectories in technical development, policies, infrastructures and demand. As long as these trajectories are aligned, socio-technical systems are stable. This stability is not the result of an overarching rationality or force by an all-powerful actor. Instead, stability is the emergent outcome of many activities of many actors. Stability need not be harmonious. There may be tensions and conflicts of opinion about a range of matters, such as which problems should be highest on the problem agenda, which directions are most promising for solving a problem, or how resources should be allocated. When these tensions become pressing, a system may lose its stability, creating opportunities for change. But usually tensions remain manageable.

This discussion implies that, for our purposes, transitions or system innovations have the following main characteristics. First, they develop in a 'coevolutionary' way. They involve changes in both the supply side (in technology, knowledge, industry structures) and the demand side (user preferences, cultural meaning, infrastructure). Second, they are architectural innovations writ large, involving changes in the elements and structure of socio-technical systems. Third, they are multi-actor processes, involving a wide range of societal groups. A fourth characteristic that follows from a wide range of historical studies is that they unfold within a long timescale, possibly of the order of several decades (see Geels, 2002).

ACADEMIC RELEVANCE

Given the specifics of our interest in system innovation as described above, we identify three gaps in existing bodies of literature. The first gap concerns the 'systems of innovation' approach, which has emerged in the last decade. This approach investigates at different analytical levels how innovations emerge from the coevolution of a range of elements. The levels are national systems of innovation, regional systems of innovation or sectoral innovation systems. The main focus in the system of innovation approach is on the *functioning* of systems rather than the *change* of systems. For instance, at the national level these studies lead to a static or comparative analysis of the innovative performance of different countries. In a recent overview of sectoral systems of innovation, it was noted that 'one of the key questions that need to be explored in-depth is: how do new sectoral systems emerge, and what is the link with the previous sectoral system?' (Malerba, 2002; 262). This means that the topic of system innovation as we use it is under-addressed in this literature.

A second gap stems from the literature on 'path dependence' and 'lock-in'. In evolutionary economics, David (1985) and Arthur (1988) have shown that path dependence plays an important role in the case of two competing technologies. Once one of the technologies has gained a lead, it benefits from increasing returns to adoption and creates a dominant path. Several mechanisms cause increasing returns, such as economies of scale, leading to lower cost, learning-by-using, network externalities, informational increasing returns, and technological interrelatedness. Because of these increasing returns a certain technology becomes entrenched while there is no guarantee it is the 'best' one from a broader societal perspective. Other economists have widened the analysis, adding institutional aspects and user routines to the lock-in analysis (Cowan, 1990; Cowan and Gunby, 1996).

Research from other disciplines has added more reasons why existing systems are characterized by stability, inertia and lock-in. Established systems may be stabilized by legally binding contracts (Walker, 2000). Actors and organizations are embedded in interdependent networks (with suppliers or users), which represent a kind of 'organizational capital', and create stability through mutual role expectations. Cognitive routines make engineers and designers look in particular directions and not in others (Nelson and Winter, 1982; Dosi, 1982). This can make them 'blind' to developments outside their focus. Core capabilities can thus turn into core rigidities (Leonard-Barton, 1995). Firms have sunk investments and built-up capital, which they do not want to write-off (examples are investments in machines and production tools, skills and knowledge). It is difficult for established firms to switch to competence-destroying breakthroughs (Tushman and Anderson, 1986; Christensen, 1997).

Existing systems are also stable because they are embedded in society. People adapt their lifestyles to them, favourable institutional arrangements and formal regulations are created, and accompanying infrastructures are set up. The alignment between these heterogeneous elements leads to 'technological momentum' (Hughes, 1994). The importance of these alignments between heterogeneous elements is highlighted in such concepts as the 'techno-institutional complex' (Unruh, 2000) and 'techno-economic networks' (Callon, 1991). All these approaches highlight aspects of the stability of existing systems but none of them addresses the issue of change and transition from one system to another. Given all these explanations of stability, it is a mystery how and why transitions occur. Path-dependency literatures may help us understand lock-in, but how can we understand 'lock-out'?

A third gap relates to recent academic sustainability debates. There has been a widening in recent years of the analytical focus, from clean products to sustainable systems (Schot *et al.*, 1994; Vellinga and Herb, 1999; Unruh, 2000; Jacobsson and Johnson, 2000; Berkhout, 2002). In transport, energy and other systems there are promising new technologies with better environmental performance. But many of these new technologies are not (yet) taken up. This is partly for economic reasons, but there are also social, cultural, infrastructural and regulatory reasons. Existing systems seem to be 'locked in' on many dimensions. Implementation of promising new environmental technologies may require other changes in user practices, regulation or infrastructure. Although the importance of system innovations is increasingly emphasized in sustainability debates, there is not yet much known about how system innovations occur and how policy makers may influence them.

see Durant !

GOVERNANCE

Transitions are complex, uncertain and involve multiple societal groups or stakeholders. Hence, policymakers and other decision-makers puzzle over how to influence system innovations and how to identify possible and promising directions for transitions. This is complicated by the awareness that the state is not an all-powerful and all-knowing actor in this matter. Public authorities are just one societal group among several others. Like other groups, they have limited power, a limited cognitive perspective and limited resources to influence system dynamics.

This observation caused a shift in policy studies from a focus on 'government' to 'governance' (e.g. Kooiman, 1993; Rhodes, 1997; Kohler-Koch and Eising, 2000; Van Heffen *et al.*, 2000). Governance means that there is directionality and coordination at the systems level, but that it has an emergent character, arising from the interaction between multiple societal groups. Public authorities may try to influence this emergent directionality, but cannot steer it at will. This emerging governance paradigm emphasizes aspects such as policy networks, interaction between multiple societal groups and learning processes.

This is not the only relevant policy paradigm. In policy science, three general policy paradigms are distinguished (see Table 1.1): (i) the traditional top-down model with a central role for (national) government and hierarchical relations, (ii) a bottom-up or market model with a large degree of autonomy for local actors, and (iii) a governance or policy network model with shared rule-making and agreements between interdependent actors with diverging values and beliefs. These three policy paradigms differ not only in their basic philosophy, but also in their instruments. Formal rules and regulations are common in the command-and-control paradigm, subsidies, taxes and (financial) incentives in the market model, and network management, learning processes, experiments and interactive policymaking in the third paradigm.

These policy paradigms coexist in all democratic societies with varying degrees of emphasis on each of them. This variety of paradigms and instruments complicates the issue of governing transitions and system

Table 1.1   Different policy paradigms

	Classic steering paradigm (top-down, command-and-control)	Market model (bottom up)	Policy networks (processes and networks)
Level of analysis	Relationship is between principal and agent	Relationship is between principal and local actors	Network of actors
Perspective	Centralized, hierarchical organization	Local actors	Interactions between actors
Characterization of relationships	Hierarchical	Autonomous	Mutually dependent
Characterization of interaction processes	Neutral implementation of formulated goals	Self organization on the basis of autonomous decisions	Interaction processes in which information and resources are exchanged
Foundation scientific disciplines	Classic political science	Neo-classical economy	Sociology, innovation studies, neo-institutional political science
Governance instruments	Formal rules, regulations and laws	Financial incentives (subsidies, taxes)	Learning processes, network management through seminars and strategic conferences, experiments, vision building at scenario workshops, public debates

Source: Based on De Bruijn *et al.*, 1993: 22.

innovations. It raises questions such as these: is one policy paradigm best suited to influence transitions or is a mix of paradigms and instruments needed? In the latter case, what should this mix look like? Is the optimal mix dependent upon specific circumstances and, if so, which ones?

RESEARCH QUESTIONS AND LEVEL OF AMBITION

Given our dual ambition to enhance the understanding of transitions and to stimulate the formulation of policies that guide transitions towards sustainability there are two main research questions that drive this book:

1. How do system innovations or transitions come about? What theories can be used to conceptualize (part of) their dynamics and what gaps exist in those theories? What can we learn from historical examples of transitions?
2. How can transitions or system innovations be influenced by actors, in particular by public authorities? What instruments and tools exist and how should they be used?

Although this book aims high, it is not our ambition to provide the ultimate answers to these questions. Instead, we want to create a signpost into this uncharted territory. System innovations are a complex topic, involving many kinds of actors and issues. In this book, authors from different disciplines make their own distinctive interventions into the topic, coming at it from different angles and with different intellectual frameworks: innovation studies, sociology of technology, institutional economics, history of technology, policy studies, including studies of network governance, learning and the impact of regulation, innovation management and governance approaches, organizational studies and management of structural change and leadership. This grouping of different disciplinary backgrounds around a particular topic creates variety and space for interdisciplinary discussion. Although different disciplines highlight different aspects of system innovations, they do share a common view on human actors as boundedly rational and embedded in social networks and institutions. This means transitions are not and cannot be planned in advance in a rational manner but emerge as actors navigate their way through multiple uncertainties. These shared views provide common ground between different authors.

BOOK STRUCTURE

The book is in two sections, addressing the two main research questions. The first section is on 'Understanding Transitions', with one part focusing on theoretical explorations (Chapters 2, 3 and 4), and one on empirical examples (Chapters 5 and 6). The second section deals with 'Inducing Transitions'; it also consists of two parts, the first on transition management in general (Chapters 7 and 8) and the second on tools for transition management (Chapters 9, 10 and 11).

Part I: Theoretical Explorations of Transitions

Chapter 2 by Frank Geels addresses the general question of how system innovations come about. Geels reviews a broad range of relevant literatures, concluding that they do not add up to an integrated perspective on system innovations. He offers a pragmatic synthesis in the form of a 'multi level perspective' (MLP) to analyse and explain transition processes. These levels are (i) *technological niches* where novelties are developed, (ii) *socio-technical regimes* and (iii) *socio-technical landscape*, which comprises a range of exogenous developments which influence regimes and niches. The main argument is that system innovations result from linkages between processes at these multiple levels. This means that system innovations are not caused by a change in a single factor or 'driver', but are the result of the interplay of many processes and activities.

Chapter 3 by Frans Berkhout, Adrian Smith and Andy Stirling also looks at the general level of system innovations. They take aim at the multi-level perspective, arguing that this approach places too much emphasis on the role of technological niches as the principal locus for regime change. Instead, they argue, there is a range of different *transition contexts* in which regime change can take place. They argue that there is a greater plurality of possible transformation pathways than suggested by the multi-level perspective notion. They develop a four-fold typology of transition contexts, which they illustrate with brief examples.

Chapter 4 by Elizabeth Shove has a more specific focus on users and consumption. She sees much of the current work on transitions as socio-technical in its orientation as it acknowledges the institutional and political processes required in support. She argues, however, that the agenda remains lopsided, skewed around provision rather than consumption and around the diffusion rather than the use of technological systems, tools and techniques. She seeks to recover some of that missing ground. Using the case of laundering, she argues that it is necessary to think more systematically about the relation between consumption, provision and practice. She suggests that shared understandings of 'normality' are important in this respect. Notions of what it is to be a normal and acceptable member of society have far reaching environmental implications. They carry in their wake a trail of resource requirements like those associated with daily showering, with wearing freshly laundered clothing, with not having a siesta, with eating imported food or with having foreign holidays.

Part II: Empirical Examples of Transitions

Chapter 5 by Frank Belz presents a historical analysis of changes in the Swiss agri-food chain over the past three decades. He describes a shift away from the industrialized form of agriculture, a form which creates major sustainability problems. The shift is not yet completed but has progressed a long way. Switzerland is one of the leading Western countries in sustainable agriculture, balancing economic, ecological and social dimensions. In this transition two new forms of agriculture play a role. Organic farming takes a holistic stance, respecting the principles of nature, by seeking to maintain long-term fertility and biological activity of soils using locally adapted biological and mechanical methods as opposed to reliance on external inputs. Integrated production is a third way between organic farming and industrialized agriculture. In his analysis, Belz proposes a number of additions to Geels's multi-level perspective.

In Chapter 6, Aad Correljé and Geert Verbong describe the transition to the use of natural gas in the Netherlands in the 1950s and 1960s. The discovery of a large deposit of natural gas in 1959 caused a shock to the energy system based on coal and coal-based gas. They distinguish three dimensions of the gas regime, notably (i) the material network, (ii) the institutional framework and (iii) the market for energy. They show that the transition to a new system required a process of interrelated changes on these three dimensions. They also show the transition cannot be understood without taking note of earlier developments that took place in the 1950s. The authors analyse in detail the strategies, visions and activities of relevant actors, and show the struggles and negotiations that took place.

Part III: Transition Policy

In Chapter 7, René Kemp and Jan Rotmans present a general framework for transition management. They argue that policy interventions should target not just economic conditions (through taxes and regulations) but also beliefs, expectations and institutional factors. They propose a management strategy based on modulation of ongoing dynamics rather than planning and control. The overall steering philosophy is to embark on a process of 'learning-by-doing'. This involves articulation of future visions, setting up experiments to learn about the feasibility of visions, and the evaluation and adjustments of visions. Transition management is not a one-off exercise but involves several policy cycles of adjustment and learning. In that sense it is goal-oriented incrementalism. The authors apply their ideas to the domain of transport and mobility. They show what the first step of transition management might look like for a transition towards sustainable transport.

In Chapter 8 Geert Teisman and Jurian Edelenbos argue that 'management of transitions requires a transition of management', that is, a transition from hierarchical steering to interactive forms of governance. This requires institutional change because, as they state it, 'the best way to kill a new idea is to put it in an old organization'. The authors identify three barriers which hinder transition management: (i) missing links between interactive processes and formal decision-making; (ii) fragmented departmental structures of governmental organizations frustrating productive and innovative interactions; and (iii) the reluctance of public actors to share responsibility and accountability with each other and with private actors or societal actors. They discuss several experiments as possible forerunners for new democratic governance systems: parallel democracy, hybrid democracy and participatory democracy. In current Dutch practice, the first form is advocated as a model for system innovation. The authors argue that this is not sufficient and that a change should take place towards a hybrid democracy or participatory democracy. This requires a redefinition of the role of various actors, especially at various levels of government.

Part IV: Tools for Transition Policy and Empirical Illustrations

In Chapter 9 Halina Brown, Philip Vergragt, Ken Green and Luca Berchicci discuss 'bounded socio-technical experiments' (BSTE) as attempts to introduce a new technology, service, or social arrangement on a small scale. Based on insights from theories of organizational learning, policy-oriented learning and diffusion of innovation, the authors identify two types of learning: technical single-loop learning, and higher-order social learning. The first type of learning occurs among the participants in the experiment and their immediate professional networks. The second type occurs in society at large. The authors argue that both types play a key role in a transition towards sustainable mobility systems. They analyse two Dutch experiments in personal mobility, the development of a three-wheeled 'bike-plus' vehicle called Mitka and an attempt to solve mobility problems on the island of Texel. The cases show that the first type of learning took place to a considerable extent and that it can be facilitated by deployment of structured visioning exercises, by diffusion of ideas among related BSTEs, by innovative couplings of problems and solutions, and by creating links among related experiments. The cases also show that the second type of learning was more difficult. The authors provide recommendations on how both kinds of learning could be organized, stressing the importance of visions and vision-building processes.

In Chapter 10 Sirkku Kivisaari, Raimo Lovio and Erja Väyrynen take as a starting point that experimenting with alternatives to an existing system can play a crucial role in broader transition processes because they provide the seeds for change. They use the so-called 'societal embedding of innovations' approach to analyse management of experiments. This approach has been designed to enhance commercialization of innovations that yield financial profit as well as contribute to sustainable development. It has been geared especially towards supporting collaboration between public and private actors in cases where there is a considerable public interest in finding innovative solutions to societal issues. The chapter discusses two Finnish experiments, which can be perceived as pilots of system innovations. The first deals with a new energy service company concept in Finnish municipalities and the second with development of a new diabetes self-management system. Combining findings from both cases, they discuss how the management of these experiments can be strengthened so that their results can indeed form the seeds for a transition.

In Chapter 11 Boelie Elzen, Frank Geels, Peter Hofman and Ken Green present a new scenario method to explore future system innovations and support transition management. In a strict sense, transitions cannot be steered, because of their complex nature, but it is possible to stimulate developments in more sustainable directions over a longer period of time. This requires a vision of which directions that might be, that is which combination(s) of technologies and their societal embedding might contribute to a sustainable system. To help develop such visions, scenario studies or other foresight methods can be used. Although many such methods exist, the authors argue that they have limitations for exploring system innovations and transitions. Hence, they present a new scenario method, called 'Socio-Technical Scenarios'. The chapter describes the main features of the method and illustrates it by describing two short scenarios for the passenger mobility domain. The authors thus provide a concrete tool to help develop guiding visions.

In Chapter 12 the editors take stock of the findings of the book, and suggest a research agenda for the future.

REFERENCES

Abernathy, W.J., and K.B. Clark (1985), 'Innovation: mapping the winds of creative destruction', *Research Policy*, **14**, 3–22.

Arthur, Brian (1988), 'Competing technologies: an overview', in Giovanni Dosi, Chris Freeman, Richard Nelson, Gerald Silverberg and Luc Soete (eds), *Technical Change and Economic Theory*, London: Pinter, pp. 590–607.

Berkhout, F. (2002), 'Technological regimes, path dependency and the environment', *Global Environmental Change*, **12**, 1–4.

Breschi, Stefano, and Franco Malerba (1997), 'Sectoral innovation systems: technological regimes, Schumpeterian dynamics, and spatial boundaries', in Charles Edquist (ed.), *Systems of Innovation: Technologies, Institutions and Organizations*, London and Washington, DC: Pinter, pp. 130–56.

Callon, Michel (1991), 'Techno-economic networks and irreversibility', in John Law (ed.), *A Sociology of Monsters, Essays on Power, Technology and Domination*, London: Routledge, pp. 132–61.

Chandler, Alfred D. (2001), *Inventing the Electronic Century: The Epic Story of the Consumer Electronics and Computer Industries*, New York: The Free Press.

Christensen, Clay (1997), *The Innovator's Dilemma: When New Technologies Cause Great Firms to Fail*, Boston, MA: Harvard Business School Press.

Coombs, Rod, Ken Green, Albert Richards and Vivian Walsh (eds) (2001), *Technology and the Market: Demand, and Innovation*, Cheltenham, UK: Edward Elgar.

Cowan, R. (1990), 'Nuclear power reactors: a study in technological lock-in', *Journal of Economic History*, **50**, 541–67.

Cowan, R., and P. Gunby (1996), 'Sprayed to death: path dependence, lock-in and pest control strategies', *Economic Journal*, **106**, 521–42.

David, P.A. (1985), 'Clio and the economics of QWERTY', *American Economic Review* **75**, 332–37.

De Bruijn, Johan A., Walter J.M. Kickert and Johannes F.M. Koppenjan (1993), 'Inleiding: Beleidsnetwerken en overheidssturing', in Johannes F.M. Koppenjan, Johan A. De Bruijn and Willem J.M. Kickert (eds), *Netwerkmanagement in het openbaar bestuur*, The Hague: Vuga, pp. 11–30.

Dosi, G. (1982), 'Technological paradigms and technological trajectories: a suggested interpretation of the determinants and directions of technical change', *Research Policy*, **6**, 147–62.

Du Gay, Paul, Stuart Hall, Linda Janes, Hugh MacKay and Keith Negus (1997), *Doing Cultural Studies: The Story of the Sony Walkman*, London: Sage Publications.

Eggerton, D. (1999), 'From innovation to use: ten eclectic theses on the historiography of technology', *History and Technology*, **16**, 111–36.

Etzkowitz, H., and L. Leydesdorff (2000), 'The dynamics of innovation: from national systems and "Mode 2" to a triple helix of University–Industry–Government relations', *Research Policy*, **29**(2), 109–23.

Geels, F.W. (2002), 'Technological transitions as evolutionary reconfiguration processes: A multi-level perspective and a case-study', *Research Policy*, **31**, 1257–74.

Hughes, Thomas P. (1994), 'Technological momentum', in Merrit R. Smith and Leo Marx (eds), *Does Technology Drive History? The Dilemma of Technological Determinism*, Cambridge, MA: The MIT Press, pp. 101–13.

Jacobbson, S., and A. Johnson (2000), 'The diffusion of renewable energy technology: an analytical framework and key issues for research', *Energy Policy*, **28**, 625–40.

Kline, R., and T. Pinch (1996), 'Users as agents of technological change: the social construction of the automobile in the rural United States', *Technology and Culture*, **37**, 763–95.

Kohler-Koch, Beate, and Rainer Eising (eds) (2000), *The Transformation of Governance in the European Union*, London and New York: Routledge.

Kooiman, Jan (ed.) (1993), *Modern Governance: New Government–Society Interactions*, London: Sage.

Leonard-Barton, Dorothy (1995), *Wellsprings of Knowledge: Building and Sustaining the Sources of Innovation*, Boston, MA: Harvard Business School Press.

Lie, Merete, and Knut H. Sørensen (eds) (1996), *Making Technology Our Own: Domesticating Technology into Everyday Life*, Oslo: Scandinavian University Press.

Lynn, L.H., N.M. Reddy and J.D. Aram (1996), 'Linking technology and institutions: The innovation community framework', *Research Policy*, **25**, 91–106.

Malerba, F. (2002), 'Sectoral systems of innovation', *Research Policy*, **31**(2), 247–64.

National Research Council (1999), *Our Common Journey. A Transition Toward Sustainability*, Washington, DC: National Academy Press.

Nelson, Richard R., and Sidney G. Winter (1982), *An Evolutionary Theory of Economic Change*, Cambridge (MA): Bellknap Press.

Oudshoorn, Nelly, and Trevor Pinch (eds) (2003), *How Users Matter: The Co-Construction of Users and Technology*, Cambridge, MA: MIT Press.

Raskin, Paul, Tariq Banuri, Gilberto Gallopin, Pablo Butman, Al Hammond, Robert Kates and Rob Swart (2002), *Great Transition. The Promise and Lure of the Times Ahead*, Boston: Stockholm Environment Institute and Global Scenario Group.

Rhodes, Ron A.W. (1997), *Understanding Governance: Policy Networks, Governance, Reflexivity and Accountability*, Buckingham: Open University Press.

Schot, J., R. Hoogma and B. Elzen (1994), 'Strategies for shifting technological systems. The case of the automobile system', *Futures*, **26**, 1060–76.

Schwartz-Cowan, Ruth (1987), 'The consumption junction: a proposal for research strategies in the sociology of technology', in Wiebe E. Bijker, P. Hughes Thomas and Trevor Pinch (eds), *The Social Construction of Technological Systems: New Directions in the Sociology and History of Technology*, Cambridge, MA: The MIT Press, pp. 261–80.

Stankiewicz, Robert (1992), 'Technology as an autonomous socio-cognitive system', in Harold Grupp (ed.), *Dynamics of Science-Based Innovation*, Berlin: Springer-Verlag, pp.19–44.

Tushman, M., and P. Anderson (1986), 'Technological discontinuities and organization environments', *Administrative Science Quarterly*, **31**, 493–65.

Unruh, G.C. (2000), 'Understanding carbon lock-in', *Energy Policy*, **28**, 817–30.

Van de Ven, Andrew H., and Raghu Garud (1989), 'A framework for understanding the emergence of new industries', in Richard Rosenbloom and Robert Burgelman (eds), *Research on Technological Innovation, Management and Policy*, Greenwich, CT: JAI Press, pp. 195–225.

Van Heffen, Oscar, Walter J.M. Kickert and Jacques J.A. Thomassen (eds) (2000), *Governance in Modern Societies: Effects, Change and Formation of Government Institutions*, Dordrecht: Kluwer Academic Publishers.

Vellinga, Pier, and Nadia Herb (eds) (1999), 'Industrial transformation science plan', International Human Dimensions Programme report no. 12.

VROM (2001), *Een wereld en een wil, werken aan duurzaamheid, Nationaal Milieubeleidsplan 4*, Dutch Environmental Policy Plan 4, established by nine Dutch departments under the coordination of VROM (The Department of Housing, Spatial Planning and Environment), The Hague: VROM.

Walker, W. (2000), 'Entrapment in large technology systems: institutional commitments and power relations', *Research Policy*, **29**, 833–46.

Weterings, Rob, Jan Kuijper, Erik Smeets, Gert J. Annokkée and Bert Minne (1997), *81 Mogelijkheden, Technologie voor Duurzame Ontwikkeling. Eindrapport van de milieugerichte technologieverkenning*, The Hague: VROM (Department of Housing, Spatial Planning and Environment).

PART I

Theoretical explorations of transitions

2. Understanding system innovations: a critical literature review and a conceptual synthesis

Frank W. Geels

INTRODUCTION

System innovations are defined as large-scale transformations in the way societal functions such as transportation, communication, housing, feeding, are fulfilled. Technology plays an important role in fulfilling societal functions. Artefacts by themselves have no power, they do nothing. Only in association with human agency and social structures and organizations do artefacts fulfil functions. In real-life situations (for example, organizations, firms, houses) we never encounter artefacts per se, but artefacts-in-context. For the analysis of working/functioning artefacts in context, it is the combination of the social and the technical that is the appropriate unit of analysis (Fleck, 1993, 2000). From the perspective of science and technology studies two basic notions of technology are important: (i) technology is heterogeneous, not just a material contraption (engineers know this, their work is heterogeneous engineering); (ii) the functioning of technologies involves linkages between heterogeneous elements. Hughes (1987) coined the metaphor of a seamless web to indicate how physical artefacts, organizations (for example, manufacturing firms, investment banks, research and development laboratories), natural resources, scientific elements (that is, books, articles), legislative artefacts (laws) are combined in order to achieve functionalities. From these considerations it follows that societal functions are fulfilled by socio-technical systems. Socio-technical systems consist of a cluster of elements, including technology, regulation, user practices and markets, cultural meaning, infrastructure, maintenance networks, supply networks (see Figure 2.1 for an example for land-based transportation).

In this conceptualization, a system innovation can be understood as a change from one socio-technical system to another. One aspect of a system innovation is *technological substitution,* which comprises three sub-processes: (i) emergence of new technologies, (ii) diffusion of new

19

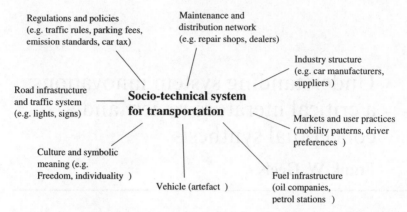

Figure 2.1   Socio-technical system for modern car-based transportation

technologies, (iii) replacement of old by new technology. The second aspect is *coevolution*. System innovations not only involve technological substitutions, but also changes in elements such as user practices, regulation, industrial networks, infrastructure, and cultural meaning. The third aspect is the *emergence of new functionalities*. When radical innovations have particular technical properties, this may enable the articulation of new functional characteristics. Radical innovations may then introduce new functionalities and change the way in which performance is measured (Abernathy and Clark, 1985; Utterback, 1994; Christensen, 1997).

This chapter addresses the following question: how do major changes in socio-technical systems occur?

LITERATURE REVIEW AND CRITICAL EVALUATION

There are few literatures which discuss all aspects of system innovations. Literatures typically focus on one or two aspects, but make simplistic assumptions about other aspects. Thus literatures provide bits and pieces which can be used as building blocks for a more integrative perspective. I take technological substitution as the entry point for the literature review, and discuss the other aspects when I discuss existing literatures. In the literatures there are large differences about what it is that changes during technological substitution, and the kind of change process. I will describe and critically evaluate a range of sociological, economic and socio-technical literatures. I distinguish three basic approaches on system innovations in these literatures: point-source approaches, replacement

approaches, and transformation approaches. Point-source approaches typi-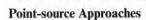
cally focus on emergence and diffusion of (radical) novelties, but say little
about replacement. Replacement approaches focus on the competition
between old and new technologies, but typically make simplistic assumptions about the emergence and diffusion of novelties. Transformation
approaches focus mainly on emergence of novelties, and how rules and perceptions of novelties gradually change. Each of these approaches has interesting insights and weaknesses.

Point-source Approaches

Literatures in these approaches focus on the emergence and diffusion of new
technologies but do not say much about replacement. Change begins as a
point source, initiated by the emergence of a (radical) novelty. Subsequently,
the novelty conquers the world.

Technology life cycle approach
In technology life cycle approaches several phases are distinguished. The
main focus is on the market shares of technologies, firm strategies and
market structures.

In the first phase (birth, childhood) a new technology is born. The new
technology exists as a variety of products, and has low production volumes
and market shares. There is technological uncertainty, and uncertainty
about user preferences. Learning processes are targeted towards product
innovation. The industry structure is fluid, consisting of many small firms,
and high rates of entry and exit.

In the second phase (adolescence), the initial diversity gives way to standardization, leading to a dominant design. The rate of product innovation
slows down. Process innovations become more important to lower costs,
and conquer higher market shares. Concentration and shake-out occur and
the industry structure stabilizes.

In the third phase (maturity) growth rates slow down as markets become
saturated and improvements face diminishing returns. The market becomes
concentrated in the hands of a few producers, leading to an oligopolistic
industry structure. Producers try to squeeze out the last marginal cost
improvements from scale economies.

Economic path-dependency theories
In economic path-dependency theories the market share of technologies is
also what changes. The focus is on self-reinforcing processes, leading to
increasing returns of adoptions (David, 1985; Arthur, 1988). This means
that the more a particular technology is used, the greater its attractiveness

relative to its competitors. Arthur (1988: 591) identified five sources of increasing returns to adoption (IRA): (i) learning by using: the more a technology is used, the more is learned about it, the more it is improved; (ii) network externalities: the more a technology is used by other users, the larger the availability and variety of (related) products that become available and are adapted to the product; (iii) scale economies in production, allowing the price per unit to go down; (iv) informational increasing returns: the more a technology is used, the more attention it receives, stimulating others to adopt; (v) technological interrelatedness: the more a technology is used, the more complementary technologies are developed.

Although these five mechanisms of IRA are certainly relevant for the diffusion of new technologies, they do not say much about emergence and replacement. Path dependency literature is unconcerned with questions relating either to the existence of prior technologies, or to the way in which new technologies are able to displace older technologies.

Science and technology studies: SCOT, ANT and LTS

An influential approach in science and technology studies is SCOT (Social Construction of Technology). In the early, SCOT1 approach (Pinch and Bijker, 1987; Kline and Pinch, 1996) the focus is on sociocognitive processes (meaning and interpretation in social groups). The main aim is to understand the form and function of new technologies. Why do new technologies stabilize into a particular form, and how are they used? To answer this question, the focus is on the relevant social groups which are involved in the development process, such as engineers, users, policy makers, societal groups, and so on. These social groups may have different ideas about problems, solutions and meanings of the artefact. There is interpretative flexibility. Gradually a consensus emerges about the dominant meaning of an artefact, leading to stabilization. Selection is thus seen as a sociocognitive process (closure and stabilization of one interpretation in social groups). The later SCOT2 approach (for example, Bijker, 1995) gave the analysis a more structuralist flavour by adding the notion of a technological frame to look at structural social, cognitive and material elements. The technological frame comprises elements such as: goals, key problems, problem-solving strategies (heuristics), requirements to be met by solutions to problems, current theories, tacit knowledge, testing procedures, and design methods and criteria. The SCOT analysis stops when the artefact, social groups and technological frame have stabilized. SCOT does not say much about wider diffusion of new technologies. The replacement of old technologies is not dealt with in the framework.

In the research approaches of Large Technical Systems (LTS) and actor-network theory (ANT) the focus is on linkages in and around emerging technologies. In both perspectives the dynamic is that heterogeneous elements are gradually linked together, emphasizing coevolution.

In LTS research the emergence and development of large technical systems is loosely described as life-cycle (Hughes, 1983, 1987; Mayntz and Hughes, 1988). Several types of system builder (inventor, inventor-entrepreneur, manager-entrepreneurs, financier-entrepreneurs) are active in different phases: invention, development, innovation, growth, competition and consolidation, momentum. System builders like Thomas Edison are heterogeneous engineers, working not only on physical materials, but also on people, texts, devices, city councils, economics and so on. Hughes coined the term 'seamless web' to indicate the heterogeneous character of LTS. In the early phases, the web and its linkages were fragile, requiring Edison to put in a lot of work to uphold it. As the electricity network grew and stabilized, it gained momentum and began to have coordinating effects. A reversal occured as the technology shifted from flexibility to dynamic rigidity (Staudenmaier, 1989). The technology shifts roles from a possible social option to a culture-shaping and highly specified social force.

The perspective of socio-technical linkages is most consistently developed in ANT (Latour, 1987, 1991, 1992, 1993; Callon, Law and Rip, 1986; Callon, 1991; Callon *et al.*, 1992). New technologies emerge from the start as heterogeneous configurations. In the early phase of a new technology, the network consists of few elements and linkages. Innovation is about the accumulation of elements and linking them together in a working configuration. As the network is expanded and more elements are tied together, a technology 'becomes more real'. Diffusion is also a process of creating socio-technical linkages. The diffusion of an artefact across time and space needs to be accompanied by an expansion of linkages in which the artefact can function, such as, test apparatus, spare parts, maintenance networks, and infrastructure. 'Thousands of people are at work, hundreds of thousands of new actors are mobilized' (Latour, 1987: 135).

These different point-source literatures are useful because they distinguish patterns or phases in the emergence and diffusion of new technologies. They do not say much, however, about technological replacement. Because of their focus on new technologies, they tend to neglect the existence of old technologies.

Replacement Approaches

Literatures in these approaches focus mainly on economic competition and substitution. The focus is on technologies which compete with each other in markets on the basis of cost and performance. The emergence of new technologies is often conceptualized in a simplistic way, for example as a stochastic process, driven by individual genius.

Technological and economic substitution approaches
Technological and economic substitution approaches understand replacement as a market-based process, in which new technologies replace incumbent technologies, because of higher performance and lower price.

Grübler (1991, 1998) and Nakićenović (1986, 1991) have initiated a particular approach to long-term technological replacements. Their basic assumption is that the replacement of an old technology by a new technology proceeds along the logistic substitution curve: $f/(1-f) = e^{(a.t + b)}$, in which t is the independent variable representing some unit of time, a and b are constants, f is the fractional market share of the new competitor and $(1-f)$ is the fractional market share of the old one. Logistic curve models are entirely descriptive, and do not explain why curves behave as they do.

The competitive dynamic is made more explicit in neo-classical economic approaches. Buyers compare price and performance of rival technologies. Users are represented as having a fixed set of user preferences. A new technology replaces an old technology, if its performance characteristics have a better fit with the user preferences and users buy more of it. The user is represented as a rational actor, who has some kind of formula in his head to make optimal adoption choices.

To describe developments in price and performance over time, the concept of learning curves was developed. The performance of technologies increases as organizations and individuals gain experience with them, that is, organizational and individual learning by doing and learning by using (Arrow, 1962; Rosenberg, 1982). Learning depends on the actual accumulation of experience. Learning curves are generally described in the form of a power function, measured as cumulative output: $Y = a \cdot X^{-b}$, where y is the cost or performance of the xth unit, a is the cost associated with the first unit, and b is a parameter measuring the cost reductions for each doubling of cumulative output (that is, the learning rate). If the learning rate of new technologies is higher than that of established technologies then the former will eventually replace the latter.

A first criticism is that replacement approaches assume that new technologies compete in the same markets as the old technologies. This assumption can be questioned with regard to the early phases of new technologies. The first automobiles did not compete with horse-and-carriages. Instead they were used for pleasure and adventure, in racing and touring. Similarly, the first steamships did not compete with merchant sailing ships, but were used for auxiliary functions, such a tow boats or pirate hunters (Geels,

2002a). More generally, substitution approaches are unclear about the emergence of new technologies.

A second criticism is that substitution approaches suggest that old and new technologies always have a relationship of competitive struggle. Although competition certainly plays a role in the life cycle of new technologies, it is not necessarily true for the early phases. Railroads did not immediately compete with canals and water transportation, but were used as feeders to them (Rosenberg, 1976: 197). New technologies may also form technical hybridizations with old technologies. Steam engines were first used as additional power sources on sailing ships to be used when there was no wind.

Third, the conceptualization of the demand side is static (fixed user preferences). Although user preferences may be assumed relatively stable in the short-run, they definitely change over longer time periods. Particularly with very new technologies, users may develop new preferences, practices and new cognitive categories. The evolution of consumer preferences is an underdeveloped area in economics, but is recently being taken up in innovation studies and technology studies. Consumption acts are nested into cognitive categories and mental models of the actors (Aversi *et al.*, 1999). Furthermore, adoption is not a passive act, because a product has to be integrated in user practices. These domestication processes may involve innovations in organization routines, work practices, management styles, symbolic meaning (Lie and Sørensen, 1996).

Punctuated equilibria and technology cycles approach
In technology management and industrial economics the concepts of punctuated equilibria and technology cycles have been coined (Tushman and Anderson, 1986; Anderson and Tushman, 1990; Rosenkopf and Tushman, 1994; Tushman and Murmann, 1998). It is argued that technological development constitutes an evolutionary process punctuated by discontinuous change. For long periods of time technological change is relatively stable, proceeding incrementally down design hierarchies and technical trajectories. These periods of incremental change are punctuated by brief periods of rapid change. An era of ferment is triggered by the emergence of a technological breakthrough, which is 'relatively rare and tends to be driven by individual genius' (Tushman and Anderson, 1986: 440). Because a revolutionary innovation is crude, different design options are tried, creating uncertainty about which design will win. The period of ferment is closed by the emergence of a dominant design. A period of incremental technical change then follows, until it is broken by the next technological discontinuity.

One problem is that the punctuated-equilibrium analysis is implicit about technological substitution and competition. This stems from their definition of technological discontinuities, as offering 'sharp price-performance improvements over existing technologies' (Tushman and Anderson, 1986: 441). Competition between old and new technologies is thus simply defined away. But technological discontinuities do not emerge as superior alternatives with their performance characteristics ready. Instead they emerge as hopeful monstrosities, which cannot readily compete with the established technology (Mokyr, 1990: 291–2).

A second problem is the appearance of radical novelty, which is presented as discontinuous and 'driven by individual genius'. The process of invention is black-boxed and mystified. If we look at technical success (the *outcome* of activities), then a discontinuity can be found. But if we look at the underlying *activities* of invention, then invention is more gradual and continuous.

A third problem is the suggestion that the era of ferment is short. This suggestion neglects that there may be a substantial time period between invention (technical feasibility) and innovation (economic feasibility). One reason for delay between invention and innovation is the wider context. As long as the wider context (markets, regulations, cultural preferences) is not appropriate, new technologies may not be picked up and further developed.

A fourth problem is the suggestion of stability *until* a technical discontinuity appears. The appearance of a discontinuity is said to 'trigger' a period of ferment. This representation runs the risk of technological determinism. Technical discontinuity may also appear as a *reaction* to political, institutional, cultural and market developments. On these dimensions, there may already be ferment *before* the emergence of a technical discontinuity.

Evolutionary economics
Given the interest in technological discontinuities of founding father Schumpeter, neo-Schumpetaria evolutionary economists have paid surprisingly little attention to the topic. Some exceptions are Nelson and Winter (1982) and Dosi (1982) who take seriously what engineers and designers actually do. Nelson and Winter see human beings as having limited cognitive capacities. Hence, human beings use rules and cognitive frameworks to make sense of the world. These rules and frameworks are shared within groups and organizations, providing coordination and stability. Nelson and Winter develop a new theory of the firm, based on bounded rationality and routines, which guide actions. Organizational and cognitive routines play a role in organizational (inter)actions, and also with regard to innovation. Search activities of engineers are guided by cognitive heuristics. Instead of searching in all directions, engineers and research and development (R&D) managers typically expect to find better results in certain directions. Because their search activities are focused in particular directions, they add up to technical trajectories. Routines are the basis of path dependency and stability over time.

In so far as firms differ in their organizational and cognitive routines, there is variation in their technological search directions and the resulting products. The products (and the underlying routines and the firms which carry them) are selected in markets. Successful products (and firms) continue their routines, while less successful firms die out (survival of the fittest). When different firms share particular routines, these routines make up a technological regime or paradigm. The shared routines and cognitive beliefs may result in natural trajectories on a sectoral level because engineers in different firms work in the same direction:

> Natural trajectories are specific to a particular technology or broadly defined technological regime. (. . .) Our concept is more cognitive, relating to technicians' beliefs about what is feasible or at least worth attempting. For example, the advent of the DC-3 in the 1930s defined a particular technological regime: metal skin, low wing, piston-powered planes. Engineers had notions regarding the potential of this regime. For more than two decades innovation in aircraft design essentially involved better exploitation of this potential: improving the engines, enlarging the planes, making them more efficient. (Nelson and Winter, 1982: 258–9)

Technological regimes create stability, because they provide a direction for incremental technical development. This analysis of the persistence of established technologies is a useful antidote to those approaches which too easily assume that new technologies simply replace old technologies. While Nelson, Winter and Dosi give much attention to stability at firm and sector level, they do not say much about major technological substitutions, that is, about how stable routines are overcome. They also do not say much about how technological regimes come into being.

Long-wave theory
Long-wave theory is a particular stream of evolutionary economics, aiming to understand long-term technological changes on the level of the entire economy, so-called shifts in technoeconomic paradigms (TEP). Freeman and Perez (1988) distinguish four such historical clusters: (i) the first industrial revolution, (ii) steam power and iron, (iii) electricity and heavy engineering (the second industrial revolution), (iv) oil, automobiles, plastics. Information technology and biotechnology may be the fifth cycle. In each TEP there is a particular key factor which has low and falling relative cost, and which has potential for use in many products or processes. The key factor of the fourth TEP was oil; it was steel in the third, and coal in the second.

With regard to system innovations, Freeman and Perez make several interesting points. First, 'a new paradigm emerges in a world still dominated by an old paradigm and begins to demonstrate its comparative advantages at first in one or a few sectors' (p. 58).

Second, the emergence of innovations is explained as a reaction to problems in the existing TEP. Innovations 'are the result of an active and prolonged search in response to perceived limits or diminishing returns' (p. 58). As long as the existing TEP is stable and not in crisis, new technologies are held back because they do not fit with the institutional and social framework. Initially there will be a degree of mismatch between the technoeconomic subsystem and the old socio-institutional framework.

Third, diffusion takes place as a (cross-sectoral) clustering of innovations (Ayres, 1989). For instance, it was the combination of steel, gasoline and the internal combustion engine which made large-scale production of the automobile possible. Emerging technologies can positively influence each other, having positive feedbacks and catalytic effects (Grübler and Nakićenović, 1991: 337).

Fourth, diffusion of a new TEP is accompanied by deep structural changes to overcome the initial mismatch, involving: organizational forms in the firm and at plant level, new skill profile in labour force, new product mix, wave of infrastructural investment, new pattern of consumption of goods and services; new types of distribution and consumer behaviour.

A problem with long-wave theories is that they treat the process of technological change rather superficially. There is no detailed attention to what engineers really do and think. Technological development is understood as functionalistic and linear, because it is explained as reaction to macroelements such as key factors, limits and bottlenecks. But such macroelements need to be picked up by engineers and put on the problem agenda of technical communities in order to have effects. Long-wave theories do not describe how new technologies emerge. Not enough use is made of insights in innovation studies, evolutionary economics and the sociology of technology, which emphasize learning processes, social networks, uncertainty, and so on. Macro-aspects should be combined with processes at the micro-level and real-life activities of actors involved in developing new technologies.

A second problem is that long-wave theories suffer from deterministic overtones. The suggested causality is that technoeconomic forces do the initial *acting* and the socio-institutional framework the eventual *reacting*. The socioinstitutional seems subordinate to the technoeconomic. Insufficient room is made for social innovations which co-exist alongside technical ones. A socio-technical system may be changing on political, institutional and market dimensions *before* the emergence of a new radical technology.

Steam power appears to be not a technological driving force in the early nineteenth century British economy, but rather a component of a much wider change, involving incremental technological shifts, and social and organisational changes. (. . .) All of this fits into a wider process of social change which comprises industrialization: the emergence of finance sources, of disciplined work forces, of distribution systems for products, and so on. These things, of course, do not just emerge: they were created via long-term processes of social and institutional change. These changes were not simply effects of some prior process of radical technological breakthrough; in fact it would be more plausible to argue that *they were the preconditions for technological change, rather than its effect*. (Bruland and Smith, 2000: 18; my italics)

In a recent contribution, Freeman and Louçã (2001) focused on interactions between five sub-systems: science, technology, economy, politics and culture, each with their own development lines. They explicitly distanced themselves from technological determinism. With regard to transitions they argue that: 'It is essential to study both the relatively independent development of each stream of history and their interdependencies, their loss of integration, and their reintegration' (p. 127). This notion of streams or development lines, and match and mismatch seems fruitful.

Transformation Approaches

Literatures in these approaches see system innovations as a transformation process. They tend to focus on the early phases of technological development, and show how future states unfold from existing ones; the new is perceived as growing out of the old.

Sociological literatures
In sociological literatures the focus is on actor groups, their activities, perceptions and rules and routines which guide perceptions (such as search heuristics, cognitive categories, problem agendas, exemplars). People think and act on the basis of a cognitive frame. This frame does not shift suddenly, but step by step. Hence, system innovations can be seen as a transformation process. New knowledge and practices develop stepwise. Form and function of new technologies are first perceived with concepts related to the old technology (see box 2.1 below). As engineers, users and others build experience with the new technology, they gradually develop new understandings and practices; frames are modified on the basis of concrete experience, leading to new technical forms and new functionalities. Because these new understandings and practices are improvised out of old ones, the dynamic is one of transformation. This is how the *computer* regime grew out of the *computing* regime (Van den Ende and Kemp, 1999).

BOX 2.1   HISTORICAL EXAMPLES OF USING
          'OLD' CONCEPTS TO INTERPRET NEW
          TECHNOLOGIES

'(. . .) Edison put his electric mains underground, explaining: "why,
don't you lift water pipes and gas pipes up on stilts." (. . .)
Just as gas meters were installed at each residence, Edison
demanded residential electric meters for his system. (. . .)
Edison also drew comparisons between electrical and gas
pressure as he explained the resistance to flow encountered
in wires and pipes'. (Basalla, 1988: 47–8)

Whenever a new technology is born, few see its ultimate
place in society. The inventors of radio did not foresee its
use for broadcasting entertainment, sports and news; they
saw it as a telegraph without wires. The early builders of
automobiles did not see an age of 'automobility'; they saw
a 'horseless carriage'. Likewise, the computer's inventors
perceived its role in society in terms of the functions it was
specifically replacing in contemporary society. The predic-
tions that they made about potential applications for the
new invention had to come from the context of 'computing'
that they knew. Though they recognized the electronic
computer's novelty, they did not see how it would permit
operations fundamentally different from those performed by
human computers. (Ceruzzi, 1986: 196)

When experience is limited, the customer's search for understanding is dominated by attempts to relate the new product
to existing concepts. (. . .) In the early stages, the new product
is defined largely in terms of the old; as learning occurs, it
develops a meaning and definition of its own. (. . .) It was,
thus, no accident that early customer decisions about automobiles were framed in terms of a choice between a 'horseless carriage' and a 'carriage with a horse'. (Clark, 1985: 245)

Socio-technical theories

In socio-technical literatures the focus is on networks of heterogeneous elements. The linkages and the elements are not automatic, but require continuous reproduction, maintenance and repair work. System innovations/
transitions are conceptualized as transformations in seamless webs.

Large Technical System

Some authors in the LTS approach addressed the issue of changes in large technical systems, in particular Summerton (1994). They argue that transitions in LTS occur via gradual transformation. Von Meier (1994) sketches a possible future transformation of the electricity system, in which certain sustainable technologies are first introduced into the system to deal with particular problems, but will subsequently lead to further gradual changes, because of particular functional characteristics (such as more flexibility, decentralized operation). Many incremental changes may add up to major reconfigurations.

Transformation approaches see continuity between old and new technologies. New technologies emerge in the context of old technologies, and gradually grow into their own (with distinct design communities, knowledge base, technical trajectories) through a transformation process, including specialization and differentiation.

The transformation approaches focus mainly on the early phases of new technologies and on the warm situations, when cognitive frameworks, perceptions and practices are in flux. They pay less attention to what happens in cold situations. In particular they do not say much about technological diffusion. Economic aspects (like performance, prices, market shares) are underexposed.

Conclusion

One conclusion is that different literatures have interesting things to say about system innovations, but that these are still too much in bits and pieces, which do not add up. Different approaches and literatures make different cross-sections of socio-technical systems. Economic, sociological and socio-technical aspects all play a role in system innovations. The challenge is to integrate the different approaches.

Another conclusion is about how literatures can be integrated. A first heuristic for integration is to distinguish phases in system innovations. Point-source approaches and transformation approaches focus on the emergence and diffusion of new technologies. These approaches often have a sociological or socio-technical perspective, looking at actors, their activities and perceptions, and the emerging web of linkages between heterogeneous elements. Replacement approaches focus more on economic competition between old and new technologies. Price, performance and user preferences are important variables in substitution.

The second heuristic is to distinguish levels of analysis. Some theories worked on a meso-level (such as technology life cycle, evolutionary economics, punctuated equilibria, economic path dependence theories). Long-wave theories focus on the macro-level of entire economies. And innovation studies and science and technology studies highlight the micro-level and real-life activities and perceptions of actors. Thus, an integrative framework needs to encompass different phases and different levels. In the next section a perspective will be presented which uses these heuristics to integrate different literatures discussed above.

INTEGRATION IN AN EVOLUTIONARY MULTI-LEVEL PERSPECTIVE

Sociological and Socio-technical Approaches as Integrative Frame

There is a wider call in the literature for an integration of perspectives. Many of these authors see a combination of evolutionary economics, approaches from STS and sociology as promising (e.g. MacKenzie, 1992; Coombs, Saviotti and Walsh, 1992; Weber, 1997; Rip and Kemp, 1998. For instance Weber thinks that:

> A major convergence can be identified between evolutionary economics and the sociology of technology. Although they have very different roots, the basic understanding of the process of technological change is quite similar, and – even more important – sufficiently open to introduce elements of the other perspective. (. . .) What is still missing is the actual integration in a single framework which would allow to investigate different cases from a wider perspective, and to bridge explicitly between economics and sociology with regard to technology studies. (Weber, 1997: 83)

I understand economic processes (that is, rational calculations aimed at optimization) as embedded in sociological processes (social networks, shared perceptions). Neo-classical economics is useful for short time periods, characterized by stability, allowing (rational) calculations to be made. But for longer time periods perceptions, cognitions, user practices, and so on, cannot be assumed to be fixed. In stable situations, perceptions, cognitive frames and rules as well as the socio-technical linkages are back-grounded, forming a frame or context for economic action. Economic action and rational calculations are possible because of a stable frame (Callon, 1998). In situations in flux, perceptions and rules are changing and transforming. Because of these changes in frames, there is much uncertainty. There is much room for subjective interpretation and strategic manoevring, creating new social networks, and so on. Once the situation begins to cool down, rules and cognitive frames become more stable, providing a basis for (economic) calculation.

This basic conceptualization means that rules, perceptions and socio-technical linkages provide a context for human action. During periods of flux, learning processes, experimentation, interaction are important. But in stable situations, economic considerations (e.g. costs, performance, optimizing calculations) are important.

An Integrative Multi-level Perspective

Given these considerations there is a conceptual framework which is promising for the integration of different approaches, the multi-level framework which sprouts from a combination of sociology of technology and evolutionary economics (Kemp, 1994; Schot, Hoogma and Elzen, 1994; Rip and Kemp, 1998; Kemp *et al.*, 1998, 2001; Van den Ende and Kemp, 1999; Rip, 2000; Geels, 2002a, 2002b). Three levels are distinguished, which are not ontological descriptions of 'reality', but analytical and heuristic concepts to understand the complex dynamics of socio-technical change.

Socio-technical regimes

The elements and linkages in socio-technical systems are the result of activities of social groups which (re)produce them. The activities of these different groups are aligned to each other and coordinated. To understand this coordination, I introduce the concept 'socio-technical regime', which builds upon Nelson and Winter's (1982) technological regimes, but includes more actors and a wider set of rules. Rip and Kemp (1998) widened the technological regime concept defining it with the sociological category of rules:

> A technological regime is the rule-set or grammar embedded in a complex of engineering practices, production process technologies, product characteristics, skills and procedures, ways of handling relevant artefacts and persons, ways of defining problems; all of them embedded in institutions and infrastructures.
> (Rip and Kemp, 1998: 340)

While Nelson and Winter's cognitive routines are embedded in the minds of engineers, rules are embedded much more widely. This widening also means that more social groups are taken on board than engineering communities. Technical trajectories are not only influenced by engineers, but also by users, policy makers, societal groups, suppliers, scientists, banks etc. (Figure 2.2).

I propose the term socio-technical regimes to refer to the semi-coherent set of rules carried by different social groups. By providing orientation and coordination to the activities of relevant actor groups, socio-technical regimes account for the stability of socio-technical systems. This stability is of a dynamic kind, meaning that innovation still occurs but is of an

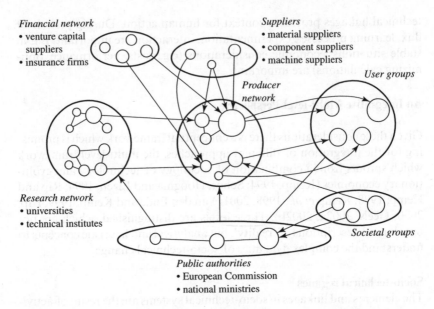

Figure 2.2   The multi-actor network involved in socio-technical systems

incremental nature. This leads to interlinked trajectories on multiple dimensions of socio-technical systems, such as technology, scientific knowledge, markets, infrastructure, culture and symbolic meaning, industry networks and sectoral policy (see Figure 2.3).

Usually the different trajectories are aligned and go in similar directions, creating stability and resilience. At times, however, trajectories may diverge resulting in maladjustments and tensions (see also Freeman and Louça, 2001). When the activities of different social groups and the resulting trajectories go in different directions, this leads to misalignment and instability in socio-technical regimes.

Socio-technical landscape
Technological trajectories are situated in a *socio-technical landscape*, consisting of a set of deep structural trends. The landscape metaphor is chosen because of the connotation of relative stability and the material context of society, that is, the material and spatial arrangements of cities, factories, highways, and electricity infrastructures. The socio-technical landscape contains a set of heterogeneous, slow-changing factors such as cultural and normative values, broad political coalitions, long-term economic developments, accumulating environmental problems growth, emigration. But it also contains shocks and surprises, such as wars, rapidly rising oil prices.

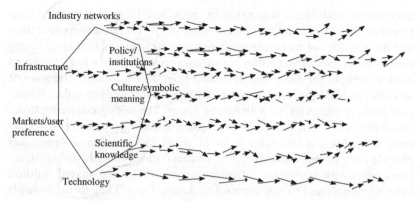

Figure 2.3   Alignment of trajectories in socio-technical regimes

The main point is that the landscape is an external context for actors in niches and regimes. While regimes can be changed (to some extent) by actors in the regime, it is more difficult to change landscape factors.

Technological niches

While regimes generate incremental innovations, radical innovations are generated in niches. Because these niches are protected from normal market selection, they act as incubation rooms for radical novelties (Schot, 1998). Radically new technologies need such protection because they usually emerge as hopeful monstrosities (Mokyr, 1990). They have relatively low technical performance, are often cumbersome and expensive. Niches offer protection for novelties because the selection criteria are very different from those in general use. An example is the army, which has stimulated many radical innovations in their early phases (such as digital computer, jet engines, radar). Niches are important, because they provide locations for learning processes, such as learning by doing, learning by using and learning by interacting (Rosenberg, 1982; Von Hippel, 1988; Lundvall, 1988). Niches also provide space to build the social networks which support innovations, like supply chains and user–producer relationships. These internal niche processes have been analysed and described under the heading of strategic niche management (Kemp, Schot and Hoogma, 1998; Kemp, Rip, and Schot, 2001; Hoogma, 2000; Hoogma *et al.*, 2002).

The sociological characteristics of the three levels: different kinds of structuration

The (socio)logic of the three levels is that they provide different kinds of structuration of activities in local practices. In *technological niches* there is only vague and loose structuration, provided for instance by diffuse promises about potential uses (Van Lente, 1993). There is experimentation and the activities of niche-actors go in many directions. There is no strong coordination. Social networks are precarious, and actors have to put in work to uphold the niche and articulate rules. In *regimes* structuration of activities in local practices is much stronger. The rules are stable, having coordinating effects on the activities of actors. The rules guide perceptions, role expectations and actions in social communities. It is possible to deviate from the rules, but this takes a lot of effort. *Socio-technical landscapes* provide even stronger structuration. Material environments (urban structures, electricity networks, infrastructures) and widely shared cultural beliefs, symbols and values are hard to deviate from. They form gradients for action.

Nested hierarchy
The relation between the three concepts can be understood as a nested hierarchy (Figure 2.4). The nested character of these levels means that regimes are embedded within landscapes and niches within regimes. In Figure 2.4 the novelties in niches are represented with arrows, because they are often geared to the problems of existing regimes. Figure 2.4 also schematically portrays linkages and elements of existing socio-technical systems. The linkages between the elements provide socio-technical systems with stability, making it hard for novelties to break through.

   Actors in the social network which support the niche, hope that novel-

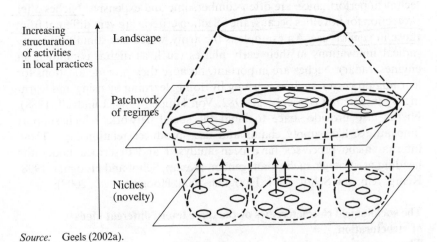

Source: Geels (2002a).

Figure 2.4   Multiple levels as a nested hierarchy

ties will eventually be used in the regime or even replace it. This is not easy, however, because the existing regime is entrenched in many ways (institutionally, organizationally, economically, and culturally). Radical novelties may have a mismatch with the existing regime (Freeman and Perez, 1988), preventing their breakthrough. Nevertheless, niches are crucial for system innovations, because they provide the seeds for change. In the multi-level perspective the following aspects are characteristic for the dynamics of technological transitions.

Novelties emerge in technological niches. The radical potential of novelties is not always immediately clear. Novelties start insignificant, often contributing to solving problems in the existing regime. In the niche, actors learn about radical innovations. This learning does not involve just technical elements, but also user preferences, regulations, symbolic meanings and so on. These different elements need to be aligned to create a functioning configuration. Because a dominant design has not yet stabilized, the efforts go many directions, leading to a variety in designs. Radical innovations may gradually stabilize into a dominant design, represented with arrows growing longer and fatter (Figure 2.5).

Diffusion and breakthrough of new technologies occurs as the outcome of linkages between developments at multiple levels. Radical innovations can break from the niche-level when the external circumstances are right, that is, when ongoing processes at the levels of regime and landscape create a window of opportunity.

Once the innovation breaks through into mass markets it enters competition with the existing regime, and may eventually replace it. This will be accompanied by changes on the wider dimensions of the socio-technical regime. System innovations thus not only involve technology and market shares but also changes in regulation, infrastructure, symbolic meaning, and industrial networks. The new regime may eventually influence wider landscape developments.

System innovations are seldom about the breakthrough of one radical technology, but come about by the linking and clustering of multiple technologies. The multi-level perspective can be seen as a conceptual combination of two kinds of explanations: a) external circumstances and b) internal drivers.

External circumstances Ongoing processes in socio-technical regimes and landscape provide windows of opportunity for novelties. These windows emerge when tensions occur between elements in the socio-technical regime, that is, when the activities of social groups are misaligned. There may be multiple reasons for such destabilization.

One reason may be that changes on the landscape level put pressure on the regime. Climate change, for instance, is nowadays putting pressure on

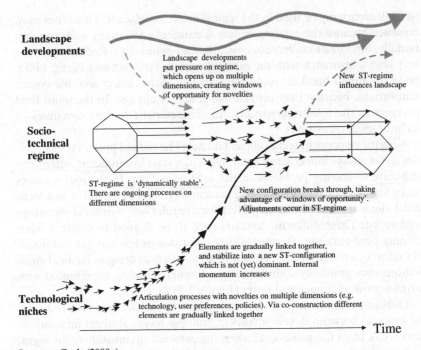

Landscape developments

Landscape developments
put pressure on regime,
which opens up on multiple
dimensions, creating windows
of opportunity for novelties

New ST-regime
influences landscape

Socio-technical regime

ST-regime is 'dynamically stable'.
There are ongoing processes on
different dimensions

New configuration breaks through, taking
advantage of 'windows of opportunity'.
Adjustments occur in ST-regime

Elements are gradually linked together,
and stabilize into a new ST-configuration
which is not (yet) dominant. Internal
momentum increases

Technological niches

Articulation processes with novelties on multiple dimensions (e.g.
technology, user preferences, policies). Via co-construction different
elements are gradually linked together

Time

Source: Geels (2000a).

Figure 2.5   A dynamic multi-level perspective on system innovations

energy and transport sectors. Broad cultural changes in values and ideologies, or change in political coalitions, may also create pressure.

A second reason is that internal technical problems in the existing regime can create opportunities for novelties. Examples are bottlenecks (Rosenberg, 1976), reverse salients (Hughes, 1987), diminishing returns of existing technology (Freeman and Perez, 1988), expected problems and presumptive anomalies (Constant, 1980).

A third reason is that negative externalities may create pressure on the regime. The externalities are often picked up and problematized by outsiders, e.g. societal pressure groups, external engineering and scientific professionals, or outside firms (Van de Poel, 2000). To get negative externalities on the technical agenda of regime actors, consumer pressures and regulatory measures may be required.

A fourth reason is that changing user preferences may lead to tensions when established technologies have difficulties in meeting them. Changing user preferences may also lead to new markets with which new technologies may link up. User preferences may change for many reasons, for example, concern about negative externalities, wide cultural changes, changes in relative prices, policy measures such as taxes. User preferences may also change endogenously, as users interact with new technologies, and discover new functionalities.

A fifth reason is that strategic and competitive games between firms may open up the regime. New technologies are one way in which companies try to get a competitive advantage. Although most R&D investments go towards incremental improvements, some are spent on the exploration of radical innovations. Because companies react to each other's moves, strategic games may emerge which suddenly accelerate the development of new technologies leading to domino and bandwagon effects.

Internal drivers Besides such external circumstances at the regime-level, there are also internal drivers which stimulate diffusion of innovations and technological substitution. Economic perspectives highlight the improvement of price and performance, via technical improvements or increasing returns to adoption (Arthur, 1988). In socio-technical perspectives diffusion is understood as a process of creating linkages between heterogeneous elements (actor-network theory). Diffusion takes place because more elements are linked together, leading to momentum (Hughes, 1987; 1994; Staudenmaier, 1989). The increase of linkages leads to irreversibility, mutual dependencies, lock-in and path dependence. In sociological and technology-dynamics literatures we find contributions which note the importance of mechanisms in the diffusion process (such as bandwagon effects, acceleration because of strategic games). The diffusion process is crooked, proceeding with fits and bursts, accelerating and slowing down.

Via this pragmatic combination of explanations, I claim that the multi-level perspective is able to encompass and integrate insights from different literatures. This is schematically represented in Figure 2.6.

Different Phases in Transitions

I propose four phases in the innovation journey of a new technology (see also Rotmans et al., 2001). In the first two phases, the emphasis is on perceptions and rules. In the last two phases, economic competition and socio-technical linkages play a more important role. Economic competition and technological replacement thus appear as a particular phase in system innovations, embedded in sociological and socio-technical frames.

First phase: emergence of novelty in an existing context
A new technology is not born in an empty world, but within existing regimes, often to solve local problems. Initially, the novelty is confined to

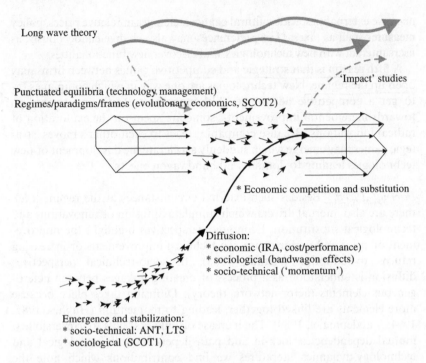

Figure 2.6   Integration of different literatures in the multi-level perspective

technological niches and small market niches, with limited visibility at the regime level. There is much uncertainty about design and functionality. Both the technical form and ideas about functionality are strongly shaped by the existing regime (see Box 2.1). Actors improvise, engage in experiments to work out the best design and find out what users want. As long as their activities continue, the novelty may smoulder below the surface.

A particular mechanism in this phase is *technological add-on* and *hybridization*. Novelties may link up with existing technologies as an auxiliary add-on to improve their functioning. In that case old and new technologies do not immediately compete head on, but form some sort of symbiosis. The steam engine, for instance, entered sailing ships as an auxiliary device to be used when there were no winds.

Second phase: technical specialization in market niches and exploration of new functionalities
As niche-actors continue to interact, socialization and institutionalization processes lead to the emergence of a dedicated community of people who know each other. Professional associations and special journals are created,

as well as new conferences where engineers and designers can meet and discuss problem agendas, promising findings and search heuristics. Learning experiences are exchanged, best practices established, and the new technology is gradually improved. It gradually develops a technical trajectory of its own, with its own set of rules. The emergence of rules is important for the wide diffusion of new technologies and economic competition.

> In order for commerce to grow in any uncharted territory there need to be rules. Not regulation necessarily, or even governments, just rules. There need to be property rights, for example, and some sense of contracts. In higher technology areas there need to be rules for intellectual property (who owns the operating system? Under what terms?) and provisions for standardisation (how do different products work together? Which technical platform becomes the norm?). Without these rules, commerce may still emerge, but it will not flourish. (Spar, 2001: xviii)

As users interact with the new technology, they build up experience with it, and gradually explore new functionalities. They develop new cognitions and concepts to make sense of the technology.

> It is important to note that concept development is based in experience, and that it occurs through a sequence of interactions between the product and the user. Those interactions provide information about the new product's relationship to other products and to the customer's needs. (Clark, 1985: 243)

Emergence of new functionalities and technical specialization occur gradually through 'probing and learning' (Lynn *et al.*, 1996), working outward from established practices to explore new ways. 'New practices do not so much flow directly from technologies that inspire them as they are improvised out of old practices that no longer work in new settings' (Marvin, 1988: 5). This phase results in a stabilization of rules, such as design rules observed in specialized technical communities, user preferences, rules which constitute markets.

Third phase: wide diffusion, breakthrough of new technology and competition with established regime.

Once the new technology and the basic rules have stabilized, wider diffusion can occur. Wider diffusion depends on external opportunities, improvements in the price/performance ratio and the increasing number of linkages between elements. Diffusion gives the new technology more visibility. As the new technology enters mainstream markets it enters a competitive relationship with the established regime. Economic considerations about price and performance play an important role. Economic calculations are possible because a stable frame has been formed. Network externalities, economies of scale and complementary technologies may lead to increasing returns to adoption. There may also be hypes and bandwagon effects, and firms can become entangled in an innovation race, investing in new technologies because they do not want to fall behind competitors.

Fourth phase: gradual replacement of established regime, wider transformations

The new technology replaces the old technology. There are several reasons why this often happens in a gradual fashion. First, incremental innovations lead to gradual improvements in the cost/performance ratio of the new technology. Second, when the societal domains consist of many market niches with different selection criteria, it takes time to conquer them all. A third reason is that creating wider dimensions in the socio-technical regime takes time, involving new infrastructures, new user practices, new policies, new organizations. A fourth reason is that incumbents tend to stick to old technologies, because of vested interests and sunk investments. Incumbents will switch to new technologies once investments are written off. The incumbents also tend to defend themselves, for example by improving the existing technology (sailing ship effect), political lobbying or evasion to other markets.

CONCLUSIONS

How do system innovations come about? Different literatures offer interesting bits and pieces, but these do not add up to a coherent perspective. I offered a pragmatic integration of literatures in a multi-level perspective, distinguishing different levels and different phases. With this perspective the following answers can be given regarding technological transitions.

1. System innovations start in technological niches. The technical form and functionality are strongly shaped by concepts, rules and problem agendas in the existing regime.
2. Diffusion and breakthrough of new technologies occurs as the outcome of linkages between developments at multiple levels. In empirical studies of system innovations, one should not just look at promising novelties, but also at ongoing processes in the regime and landscape. The existing regime should not just be analysed as a barrier. Ongoing processes in the regime can also provide opportunities for novelties to link up with.

3. System innovations come about by the linking of multiple technologies.
4. System innovations do not only involve technology and market shares but also changes of wider dimensions such as regulation, infrastructure, symbolic meaning, and industrial networks.

The multi-level perspective can be characterized as working 'from the outside in', describing, mapping and analysing the entire long-term process. The explanation of the emergence of new regimes is that multiple developments gradually link up and reinforce each other. The explanation is thus located in the alignment and interlocking of different processes. Hence, the multi-level perspective is a structuralist process approach, which provides an overall framework to analyse transitions. The approach needs to be complemented, however, with an actor-oriented approach working 'from the inside out'. Such an approach would look at how actors try to navigate transitions, how they develop visions and adapt them through searching and learning.

The answers in this chapter are conceptual. To make them more robust, empirical studies on transitions need to be done.

REFERENCES

Abernathy, W.J., and K.B. Clark (1985), 'Innovation: mapping the winds of creative destruction', *Research Policy*, **14**, 3–22.

Anderson, P., and M. Tushman (1990), 'Technological discontinuities and dominant designs: a cyclical model of technological change', *Administrative Science Quarterly*, **35**, 604–33.

Arrow, K. (1962), 'The economic implications of learning by doing', *Review of Economic Studies*, **29**, 155–73.

Arthur, Brian (1988), 'Competing technologies: an overview', in Giovanni Dosi, Chris Freeman, Richard Nelson, Gerald Silverberg and Luc Soete (eds), *Technical Change and Economic Theory*, London: Pinter, pp. 590–607.

Aversi, R., G. Dosi, G. Fagiolo, M. Meacci and C. Olivetti (1999), 'Demand dynamics with socially evolving preferences', *Industrial and Corporate Change*, **8**, 353–408.

Ayres, Robert (1989), 'Technological transformations and long waves', International Institute for Applied Systems Analysis research report 89-1, Laxenburg: IIASA.

Basalla, George (1988), *The Evolution of Technology*, Cambridge: Cambridge University Press.

Bijker, Wiebe E. (1995), *Of Bicycles, Bakelites and Bulbs: Towards a Theory of Sociotechnical Change*, Cambridge, MA and London: MIT Press.

Bruland, K., and K. Smith (2000), 'Technological transitions in history and theory', unpublished paper.

Callon, Michel (1991), 'Techno-economic networks and irreversibility', in John Law (ed.), *A Sociology of Monsters: Essays on Power, Technology and Domination*, London: Routledge, pp. 132–61.

Callon, Michel (ed.) (1998), *The Laws of the Market*, Oxford: Blackwell.
Callon, Michel, P. Laredo and V. Rabeharisoa (1992), 'The management and evaluation of technological programs and the dynamics of techno-economic networks: the case of the AFME', *Research Policy*, **21**, 215–36
Callon, Michel, John Law and Arie Rip (1986), *Mapping the Dynamics of Science and Technology*, London: The Macmillan Press Ltd.
Ceruzzi, Paul (1986), 'An unforeseen revolution: computers and expectations, 1935–80', in Joseph J. Corn (ed.), *Imagining Tomorrow: History, Technology and the American Future*, Cambridge, MA: MIT Press, pp. 188–201.
Christensen, Clay (1997), *The Innovator's Dilemma: When New Technologies Cause Great Firms to Fail*, Boston, MA: Harvard Business School Press.
Clark, K.B. (1985), 'The interaction of design hierarchies and market concepts in technological evolution', *Research Policy*, **14**(1985), 23–33.
Constant, Edward W. (1980), *The Origins of the Turbojet Revolution*, Baltimore and London: The John Hopkins University Press.
Coombs, Rod, Paolo Saviotti and Vivian Walsh, (1992), 'Technology and the firm: the convergence of economic and sociological approaches', in Rod Coombs, Paolo Saviotti and Vivian Walsh (eds), *Technological Change and Company Strategies: Economic and Sociological Perspectives*, London: Academic Press, pp. 1–24.
David, P.A. (1985), 'Clio and the economics of QWERTY', *American Economic Review* **75**, 332–7.
Dosi, G. (1982), 'Technological paradigms and technological trajectories: a suggested interpretation of the determinants and directions of technical change', *Research Policy*, **6**, 147–62.
Fleck, J. (1993), 'Configurations: crystallizing contingency', *The International Journal of Human Factors in Manufacturing*, **3**, 15–36.
Fleck, Jamie (2000), 'Artefact ← → activity: the coevolution of artefacts, knowledge and organization in technological innovation', in John Ziman (ed.), *Technological Innovation as an Evolutionary Process*, Cambridge: Cambridge University Press, pp. 248–66.
Freeman, Chris, and Carlotta Perez (1988), 'Structural crisis of adjustment, business cycles and investment behaviour', in Giovanni Dosi, Chris Freeman, Richard Nelson, Gerald Silverberg and Luc Soete (eds), *Technical Change and Economic Theory*, London: Pinter, pp. 38–66.
Freeman, Chris, and Francisco Louçã (2001), *As Time Goes By: From the Industrial Revolutions to the Information Revolution*, Oxford: Oxford University Press.
Geels, F.W. (2002a), 'Technological transitions as evolutionary reconfiguration processes: a multi-level perspective and a case-study', *Research Policy*, **31**(2002), 1257–74.
Geels, F.W. (2002b), 'Understanding the dynamics of technological transitions', PhD thesis, Twente University, Enschede, the Netherlands.
Grübler, A. (1991), 'Diffusion: long-term patterns and discontinuities', *Technological Forecasting and Social Change*, **39**, 159–80.
Grübler, Arnold, and Nebosja Nakićenović (1991), 'Long waves, technology diffusion, and substitution', International Institute for Applied Systems Analysis research report 91-17, Laxenburg: IIASA.
Grübler, Arnold (1998), *Technology and Global Change*, Cambridge: Cambridge University Press.
Hoogma, Remco (2000), 'Exploiting technological niches: strategies for experimen-

tal introduction of electric vehicles', PhD thesis, Twente University, Enschede, the Netherlands.

Hoogma, Remco, René Kemp, Johan Schot and Bernard Truffer (2002), *Experimenting for Sustainable Transport: the Approach of Strategic Niche Management*, London and New York: Spon Press.

Hughes, Thomas P. (1983), *Networks of Power Electrification in Western Society, 1880–1930*, Baltimore, MD: Johns Hopkins University Press.

Hughes, Thomas P. (1987), 'The evolution of large technological systems', in Wiebe E. Bijker, Thomas P. Hughes and Trevor Pinch (eds), *The Social Construction of Technological Systems: New Directions in the Sociology and History of Technology*, Cambridge, MA: MIT Press, pp. 51–82.

Hughes, Thomas P. (1994), 'Technological momentum', in Merrit R. Smith and Leo Marx (eds), *Does Technology Drive History? The Dilemma of Technological Determinism*, Cambridge, MA: MIT Press, pp. 101–13.

Kemp, R. (1994), 'Technology and the transition to environmental sustainability. The problem of technological regime shifts', *Futures*, **26**, 1023–46.

Kemp, R., J. Schot and R. Hoogma (1998), 'Regime shifts to sustainability through processes of niche formation: the approach of strategic niche management', *Technology Analysis and Strategic Management*, **10**, 175–96.

Kemp, René, Arie Rip and Johan Schot (2001), 'Constructing transition paths through the management of niches', in Raghu Garud and Peter Karnoe (eds), *Path Dependence and Creation*, Mahwah, NJ: Lawrence Erlbaum Associates Publishers, pp. 269–99.

Kline, R., and T. Pinch (1996), 'Users as agents of technological change: the social construction of the automobile in the rural United States', *Technology and Culture*, **37**, 763–95.

Latour, Bruno (1987), *Science in Action*, Cambridge, MA: Harvard University Press.

Latour, Bruno (1991), 'Society is technology made durable', in John Law (ed.), *A Sociology of Monsters: Essays on Power, Technology and Domination*, London: Routledge, pp. 103–31.

Latour, Bruno (1992), 'Where are the missing masses? The sociology of a few mundane artefacts', in Wiebe E. Bijker and John Law (eds), *Shaping Technology / Building Society*, Cambridge, MA and London, UK: MIT Press, pp. 205–24.

Latour, Bruno (1993), *La clef de Berlin et autres lecons d'un amateur de sciences*, Paris: Editions la Decouverte.

Lie, M., and K.H. Sørensen, (eds), 1996, *Making Technology Our Own: Domesticating Technology into Everyday Life*, Oslo: Scandinavian University Press.

Lundvall, Bengt A. (1988), 'Innovation as an interactive process: from user-producer interaction to the national system of innovation', in Giovanni Dosi, Chris Freeman, Richard Nelson, Gerald Silverberg and Luc Soete (eds), *Technical Change and Economic Theory*, London: Pinter, pp. 349–69.

Lynn, G.S., J.G. Morone and A.S. Paulson (1996), 'Marketing and discontinuous innovation: the probe and learn process', *California Management Review*, **38**, 8–37.

MacKenzie, Donald (1992), 'Economic and sociological explanations of technical change', in: Rod Coombs, Paolo Saviotti and Vivian Walsh (eds), *Technological Change and Company Strategies: Economic and Sociological Perspectives*, London: Academic Press, pp. 25–48.

Marvin, Carolyn (1988), *When Old Technologies Were New: Thinking About Electric Communication in the Late Nineteenth Century*, Oxford: Oxford University Press.

Mayntz, Renate, and Thomas P. Hughes (eds) (1988), *The Development of Large Technical Systems*, Frankfurt: Campus Verlag; and Boulder, CO: Westview Press.

Mokyr, Joel (1990), *The Lever of Riches*, New York: Oxford University Press.

Nakićenović, N. (1986), 'The automobile road to technological change: diffusion of the automobile as a process of technological substitution', *Technological Forecasting and Social Change*, **29**, 309–40.

Nakićenović, N. (1991), 'Diffusion of pervasive systems: a case of transport infrastructures', *Technological Forecasting and Social Change*, **39**, 181–200.

Nelson, Richard R., and Sidney G. Winter (1982), *An Evolutionary Theory of Economic Change*, Cambridge (MA): Bellknap Press.

Pinch, Trevor J., and Wiebe E. Bijker (1987), 'The social construction of facts and artifacts: or how the sociology of science and the sociology of technology might benefit each other', in Wiebe E. Bijker, Thomas P. Hughes and Trevor J. Pinch, (eds): *The Social Construction of Technological Systems: New Directions in the Sociology and History of Technology,* Cambridge, MA: MIT Press, pp. 17–50.

Rip, Arie (2000), 'There's no turn like the empirical turn', in Peter Kroes, Anthonie Meijers and Carl Mitcham (eds), *The Empirical Turn in the Philosophy of Technology*, Amsterdam: Elsevier Science, pp. 3–17.

Rip, Arie, and René Kemp (1998), 'Technological change', in Steven Rayner and Elly L. Malone (eds), *Human Choice and Climate Change,* Columbus, OH: Battelle Press. Volume 2, pp. 327–99.

Rosenberg, Nathan (1976), *Perspectives on Technology,* Cambridge, UK: Cambridge University Press.

Rosenberg, Nathan (1982), *Inside the Black Box: Technology and Economics,* Cambridge: Cambridge University Press.

Rosenkopf, Lori, and Michael L. Tushman (1994), 'The coevolution of technology and organization', in Joel Baum and Jitendra Singh (eds), *Evolutionary Dynamics of Organizations,* Oxford: Oxford University Press, pp. 403–24.

Rotmans, J., R. Kemp and M. van Asselt (2001), 'More evolution than revolution: transition management in public policy', *Foresight*, 3, 15–31.

Schot, J. (1998), 'The usefulness of evolutionary models for explaining innovation. The case of the Netherlands in the Nineteenth century', *History of Technology,* **14**, 173–200.

Schot, J., R. Hoogma and B. Elzen (1994), 'Strategies for shifting technological systems. The case of the automobile system', *Futures,* **26**, 1060–76.

Spar, Debora (2001), *Pirates, Prophets and Pioneers: Business and Politics along the Technological Frontier,* London: Random House.

Staudenmaier, John M. (1989), 'The politics of successful technologies', in S.H. Cutliffe and R.C. Post (eds), *In Context: History and the History of Technology: Essays in Honor of Melvin Kranzberg,* Bethlehem, PA: Lehigh University Press, pp. 150–71.

Summerton, Jane (ed.) (1994), *Changing Large Technical Systems,* Boulder, San Francisco, Oxford: Westview Press.

Tushman, M., and P. Anderson (1986), 'Technological discontinuities and organization environments', *Administrative Science Quarterly,* **31**, 493–65.

Tushman, M.L., and J.P. Murmann (1998), 'Dominant designs, technology cycles, and organizational outcomes', *Research in Organizational Behaviour,* **20**, 231–66

Tushman, M.L., and L. Rosenkopf (1992), 'Organizational determinants of technological change: towards a sociology of technical evolution', in L.L. Cummings and B.M. Staw (eds): *Research in Organizational Behavior,* **14**, pp. 311–47.

Utterback, James M. (1994), *Mastering the Dynamics of Innovation*, Boston, MA: Harvard Business School Press.

Van den Ende, J., and R. Kemp (1999), 'Technological transformations in history: how the computer regime grew out of existing computing regimes', *Research Policy*, **28**, 833–51.

Van de Poel, I. (2000), 'On the role of outsiders in technical development', *Technology Analysis & Strategic Management*, **12**, 383–97.

Van Lente, Harro (1993), 'Promising technology: the dynamics of expectations in technological development', PhD thesis, Twente University, Delft, the Netherlands.

Von Hippel, Eric (1988), *The Sources of Innovation*, Oxford: Oxford University Press.

Von Meier, Alexandra (1994), 'Integrating supple technologies into utility power systems: possibilities for reconfiguration', in Jane Summerton (ed.), *Changing Large Technical Systems*, Boulder, San Francisco, Oxford: Westview Press, pp. 211–30.

Weber, Mathias (1997), 'Innovation diffusion and political control of energy technologies: a comparison of combined heat and power generation in the UK and Germany', PhD thesis, Institut für Sozialforschung der Universität Stuttgart, Germany.

3. Socio-technological regimes and transition contexts

Frans Berkhout, Adrian Smith and Andy Stirling

INTRODUCTION

This chapter is concerned with processes of change and transformation in socio-technical regimes – patterns of artefacts, institutions, rules and norms assembled and maintained to perform economic and social activities. The discussion addresses recent theory in understanding the regime transformation process. We argue that these approaches place too much emphasis on the role of technological 'niches' as the principal locus for regime change. Instead, we argue that there is a range of different 'transition contexts' in which regime change can take place.

Niches are protected 'experimental settings' (Rip and Kemp, 1998) where norms and practices are developed which depart from those of an incumbent technological regime. According to niche-based understandings, regime changes begin when practices and norms developed in the niche become adopted more widely. Their influence grows and gathers momentum, until eventually the wider technological regime becomes completely transformed by the configurations originally nurtured within the niche. This is an elegant and plausible model, supported by a rich body of historical empirical evidence. However, there is a danger that attention to this particular mechanism may have inhibited complementary and more multidimensional understandings of regime change. In this chapter, we pose the question as to whether there may be a greater plurality of possible transformation pathways. We discuss the possibility of a number of specific alternative contexts and drivers for regime change, with significant implications for both research and policy analysis.

This chapter has two objectives: to develop a critique of the niche-based model; and to set out an alternative 'transition contexts' approach to the explanation of regime change processes. We begin by documenting the recent emergence of niche-based ideas of 'transition management' as a means to inform public policy promoting technological change. We discuss salient characteristics of the niche-based model and identify a number of unresolved conceptual and practical limitations. Whilst the niche-based model has contributed a great deal to our understanding of regime change, we propose that this work now be carried forward through a clearer analysis of the variety of transition contexts underlying regime change. In order to transcend present preoccupations with niche-based processes, we develop, as a heuristic exercise, a four-fold typology of transition contexts. This suggests certain insights and prompts a series of questions that we hope may contribute to the continuing academic and policy debate about transition management.

REGIME SHIFTS AND TRANSITION MANAGEMENT

Why is it so important to understand better the transformation of technological regimes? One answer is rooted in long-standing questions about the public effects of technology beyond the immediate production and use relationship. Policymakers and other social groups have a history of seeking to control the deleterious affects of new technologies and/or to encourage technologies with wider social benefits (Bauer, 1995). Aspirations to more effective social control of technology are longstanding concerns, even predating industrialization (Leiss, 1990). Yet, whilst the concerns are perennial, the particular ways in which civil society and public bodies have sought to understand and affect technological change have varied over the years, as has the record of success.

There are many reasons why different interest groups have sought to influence at a systemic level the direction of technological innovation. Political aspirations such as social equity (Elliot and Elliot, 1976), gender equality (Wajcman, 1996), reduced unemployment (Freeman and Soete, 1987) and nuclear and conventional disarmament (MacKenzie, 1990; Kaldor, 1983) have all in various ways been used to justify normative influence on technology policy. In the present European context, issues such as social inclusion, ageing, the 'knowledge society', global competitiveness and community enlargement all compete for attention as potential rationales for efforts to manage transformations in technological regimes.

However, the most intense efforts at deliberate social management of technological change currently lie in the environmental field. Since the advent in the mid-1980s of 'sustainable development' as a policy-making objective, political attention to environmental challenges has grown at national, regional and international level. In few other areas is the two edged nature of technological development more pronounced, the ambitions more transcendent, and the conflicts more acute.

Here, policy interest in system innovation mirrors a change in the analytical focus of academic literature on technology and the environment. In the 1990s, attempts to improve the environmental performance of technologies tended to emphasize processes of innovation associated with individual technologies. The focus tended to be on switches from more polluting to less polluting processes and products. The primary aims were to develop appraisal and valuation techniques that could inform a choice between different technologies, and to understand how switches were being helped or hindered by regulatory, market, political and institutional drivers (e.g. Clayton *et al.*, 1999). This perspective served as a means to promote the development of individual 'cleaner' technologies, such as emissions control, process management and the use of recycled inputs.

But solutions to many regional and global environmental problems such as climate change, groundwater contamination, urban congestion and waste management appear to require deeper changes across technological systems. The response of analysts, including those developing niche-based models, has been to extend attention to processes of change across interconnected systems of artefacts, institutions, rules and norms. Their interest has been to understand how to foster innovation and diffusion of new technological configurations that deliver goods and services with greater environmental efficiency (Berkhout, 2002). More ambitiously, their aim is to transform the structural characteristics of technological regimes so that they are more responsive to environmental signals and ecological principles, reshaping entire trajectories of technological innovation developed within them (van de Poel, 2002).

This focus on transforming entire technological regimes, rather than separately analysing and promoting specific artefacts or practices, has variously been labelled 'regime shift', 'strategic niche management', 'systems innovation' and 'transition management' in the literature (Kemp, Schot and Hoogma, 1998; Kemp and Rotmans, 2001; Kemp, Rip and Schot, 2001; Rotmans, Kemp and van Asselt, 2001). At the heart of these transition management arguments sits the niche-based model of regime transformation. In this model, transition managers support what they hold to be desirable technological configurations by promoting protected institutional and market niches in which favoured configurations are supported and allowed to prosper, enabling them either to replace or transform dominant, unsustainable regimes. Thus experiments within the niche 'seed' processes of transformation within the existing technological regime. So, for example, recommendations are made for creating protected niches that develop car-sharing or low emission bus fleets, using zero emissions technologies, with the aim of learning and building institutional capacity for wider transformations of the entire personal transportation regime (Weber *et al.*, 1999; Hoogma *et al.*, 2002).

Although drawing on broader inputs, much of the formative academic and policy activity promoting the development of a transition management approach has taken place in the Netherlands. Here, the conjunction of a sophisticated, but pragmatic interdisciplinary community of practitioners in the field of technology studies, an established tradition of collaborative cross-institutional engagement in innovation systems and a strong national policy agenda prioritizing environmental sustainability have provided fertile conditions for the growth of the transition management approach. As a result, transition management is promoted in the Netherlands as a policy alternative both to hands-off, market-driven technological change and to more classical technology policy approaches ('picking winners'). Quite assertive claims are made about the potential utility of the approach:

> . . . strategic niche management is not just a useful addition to a spectrum of policy instruments . . . it may be the only feasible way to transform environmentally unsustainable regimes. (Kemp, Schot and Hoogma, 1998: 191)

Whilst acknowledging the manifest significance and value of the transition management approach, we will examine in the sections that follow, the extent to which such assertions and aspirations are sustained by the present status of the niche-based model of regime transformation.

NICHES, REGIMES AND LANDSCAPES: ANALYSIS OR DESCRIPTION?

Drawing on an earlier tradition in the social studies of technology (especially Bijker, Hughes and Pinch, 1987), transition management theorists have developed a sociologically and historically well-informed analysis. They employ a concept of 'technology' that is much broader than the individual 'artefact', or even the associated 'technique' (Ellul, 1964; Winner, 1981; Hughes, 1983; Callon, 1987; Bijker, 1995; MacKenzie, 2001). Technologies in this sense are seen as being formed by, and embedded within, particular economic, social, cultural and institutional structures and systems of beliefs. Conversely, technological configurations themselves constitute, order and change the nature of these encompassing structures. An intimate and dynamic process of 'structuration' of technologies and their social context is seen to be at work, confirmed by case studies and examples from the history of technology (Giddens, 1984). In short, technologies are seen as 'socially shaped and society shaping' (Hughes, 1987).

However, the transition management programme also draws on ideas and analysis from the field of evolutionary and institutional economics. In this tradition, the term 'technology' tends to be used in a somewhat narrower sense (Nelson and Winter, 1977; Dosi 1982; Freeman, 1994). To emphasize and handle more explicitly the breadth and complexity of the more encompassing notion of technology, transition management theorists have introduced the concept of *socio-technical configurations* (Rip and Kemp, 1998). This is defined to include the social relations (such as the interests, values and behaviours of people and organizations) that link, use and make sense of technological artefacts (that is, tools and machines). The resulting operational mix of 'software' and 'hardware' is encapsulated in the elegant formulation that technologies are 'configurations that work' (ibid: 330).

In order to accommodate the role of human agency on the part of innovators and entrepreneurs producing new knowledge and artefacts, while also doing justice to the ways in which contexts shape and are shaped by novelty, transition management theorists have developed a multi-level approach (see Geels in this volume). The socio-technical regime occupies an intermediate or meso-level position between the micro-level niches and a macro-level 'socio-technical landscape'. This multi-level model has already been influential in a number of ways. It has helped move forward notions of the wider institutional adjustments that are associated with major technical discontinuities. It has drawn continued attention to the importance of the interplay between the macro-level and meso- and micro-level changes in the unfolding of socio-technical change. And it has furnished a rich body of examples to illustrate these accounts, so helping to develop a set of fertile concepts and ideas.

Each of the levels is associated with a particular socio-technical arrangement:

- Niches: '. . . protected spaces for the development and use of promising technologies by means of experimentation, with the aim of 1) learning about the desirability of the new technology, and 2) enhancing the further development and the rate of application of the new technology' (Kemp *et al.*, 1998: 186).
- Regimes: '. . . the rule set . . . embedded in a complex of engineering practices, production process technologies, product characteristics, skills and procedures, ways of handling relevant artefacts and persons, ways of defining problems; all of them embedded in institutions and infrastructures' (Rip and Kemp, 1998: 340). Analysts suggest regimes can be characterized along seven dimensions:

technology; user practices and application domains; symbolic meanings of technology; infrastructures; industry structure; policy; and knowledge (Geels, 2002; Schot, 1998). This is a wide-ranging list.
- Landscapes: '. . . background variables such as the material infrastructure, political culture and coalitions, social values, worldviews and paradigms, the macro economy, demography and the natural environment which channel transition processes and change themselves slowly in an autonomous way' (Kemp and Rotmans, 2001: 7).

Configurations *that might work* become 'configurations that work' as they move in a trajectory from the micro-level of niches to the macro-level of landscapes, gradually representing larger assemblages of practices, technologies, skills, ideologies, norms and expectations, imposing larger-scale impacts on their landscapes until they become constitutive and emblematic of them. Throughout this journey the socio-technical configuration becomes better adapted to its context, becomes more stable (both technically and institutionally) and exhibits growing irreversibility.

The predominantly descriptive nature of this approach creates a risk that, by drawing on past examples of socio-technical transformations, and by developing historical narratives of systems change, future transitions come to be treated teleologically. The impression may be given that there is a degree of inevitability about the process whereby tentative, mobile and elastic socio-technical configurations are seen to lead inexorably to lasting and increasingly large-scale changes in a socio-technical regime. In practice, very few local configurations developed in niches are successful in seeding regime transformation. Why and how some niches set in motion transformational change at wider scales, while others fail, remains a matter for analysis.

The remaining sections suggest ways of developing a more robust analytical framework for understanding change in socio-technical regimes. We argue for consideration of a more differentiated notion of transition. In particular, we propose a taxonomy of four 'ideal types' of transition, as a way of marking out the ways in which regime changes appear to unfold: *endogenous renewal; reorientation of trajectories; emergent transformation; and purposive transitions*.

We argue that not all transitions are alike. Indeed, it may be more correct to say that each transition displays unique characteristics, dynamics and history. A model of transition processes will always be an abstraction of processes of change that are local and specific, and where chance and agency play an important role. Our taxonomy of four ideal types is intended to provide a heuristic to aid the work of constructing a more generalized model.

Before discussing the taxonomy, we will address a series of issues that arise from the niche-based transition management research agenda. These are:

- inconsistencies in the mapping of conceptual onto empirical levels in socio-technical regimes;
- ambiguities in the relationship between the niche and the wider regime;
- problems in the notion of the guiding vision; and
- the possibility of top-down, as well as bottom-up, processes of regime change.

Conceptual and Empirical Levels

We understand each conceptual level in the socio-technical hierarchy to be increasingly structural and therefore less amenable to exclusive control by particular groups of social actors. Thus the defining characteristic of the socio-technical landscape is that it tends not to be open to unilateral change from actors within single socio-technical regimes (Geels, 2002). Landscape processes operate on a wider scale. However, it is unclear how these different conceptual levels should be applied empirically. By this we mean that a socio-technical regime could be defined at one of several empirical levels.

Take as an example socio-technical change in agriculture. The displacement of DDT by less persistent, less toxic and more targeted pesticides based on innovative biochemical mechanisms was made possible by research undertaken as what might be recognized as a niche activity. The substitution of DDT might be labelled a regime shift since it involved changes in regulatory systems, technologies, consumer attitudes and the practices of producers and consumers. However, looked at from the higher empirical level of general agricultural regimes, one would hardly call this switching of pesticides a regime shift. Crop production remains heavily based on chemical inputs, with key structural features of the regime relatively undisturbed. Moreover, where the 'high input' agricultural regime is seen to be in competition with an expanding 'organic' agricultural niche, developments in either may transform the relative positions of each (that is, the regime may influence the niche).

This example shows the need for greater precision in describing the level of analysis implied by the notion of a socio-technical regime. Other examples might focus on whether a regime in the electricity sector might best be understood to lie at the level of the primary fuel (coal, gas, oil or nuclear), or in the general configuration of the power generation and distribution system (high voltage transmission from large centralized steam-cycle plant, or low voltage distribution from small-scale micro-generation). Such examples suggest that contending notions of the socio-technical regime can typically be nested empirically. What looks like a regime shift at one level may be viewed merely as an incremental change in inputs for a wider regime. Or alternatively, a regime shift at a lower empirical level might be seen as a niche activity with regime transforming potential within a higher-level regime. This theoretical ambiguity brings us back to the way transition management understands transformation mechanisms to flow upwards through a widening stream of changes.

From Niches to Regimes?

The transition management literature suggests that niche-based experiments can transform regimes by nurturing socio-technical configurations, which grow and transform incumbent regime activities. Determinants of the growth of novel configurations include the effectiveness with which they are protected and nurtured within the niche, the intrinsic developmental potential of the niche, the scope for applying niche technologies in new settings, and the niche's compatibility with the incumbent regime (Weber *et al.*, 1999). Yet the 'regime compatibility' criterion for success implies that niches which are radically divergent from the incumbent regime may struggle to seed transformation successfully. The corollary – that more compatible niches may more readily lead to transformations – raises questions over the degree of change that would constitute a 'transformation'.

Alternatively, Geels (2002), in a study of the transition from sail to steam shipping, suggests that elements of a niche can seed transformation by 'linking up' with the incumbent regime. Niche activities (such as steamships) break through when they successfully link up and resolve aspects of the incumbent regime that have come 'under tension' (such as the irregularity of sailing ships). Here the determinants of success lie not so much in the general 'compatibilities' of one configuration with another, but in the efficacy with which the new configuration resolves a 'bottleneck' in the incumbent regime. Given the many uncertainties that may exist over the compatibility or efficacy of a solution to a bottleneck, expectations of performance may be as important as evidence of performance (Basalla, 1988; Schot, 1998). Either way, some component of the niche activity potentially resolves a 'bottleneck' that has hitherto constrained further development of the incumbent regime. The niche-derived solution now pushes regime development along a new trajectory (Geels, 2002).

This kind of 'linking' can occur across the different aspects of a socio-technical regime (Geels, 2002; Schot, 1998). In other words, links may be made with the hardware or software of the technologies themselves, associated user practices or application domains, their symbolic meanings, industry structures, infrastructures or associated bodies of knowledge and policy making. If links are successfully forged between the niche and the wider regime, then a process of 'reconfiguration' may trigger changes across the regime.[1] However, this process is understood to be 'haphazard and co-incidental' (Geels, 2002; Schot, 1998). We still do not have a theory of 'linking' that could help us understand how to harness niches to the deliberate purpose of transition management.

The notion of 'tensions' within particular dimensions of a dominant regime and the identification of corresponding opportunities for linking to niche-based experimental configurations suggests a further, hitherto neglected, line of enquiry. But how do these tensions arise? Geels identifies changes in the socio-technical landscape as the source of important tensions in embedded regimes. Broad economic and demographic change, for example, drove millions to leave Europe for the Americas in the 19th and early 20th centuries, thus increasing demand for trans-Atlantic passenger shipping. This demand was then met by fast and reliable steel steam-powered ships. Causation went in the other direction as well, with lower cost passenger transport making the journey affordable to greater numbers of people.

Today, it is the negative consequences of the exploitation of natural resources and environmental services that are introducing analogous tensions to many socio-technical regimes. The carbon-intensity of the energy and transport sectors is an example, as is chemicals-intensity in agriculture. These observations imply that certain processes of regime transformation operate in a top-down fashion, acting from the landscape downwards into the regime. The important possibility is raised that 'top-down' processes may play a crucial role in generating 'bottom-up' opportunities for 'linking'.

Guiding Visions

Transition management seeks to direct the widening process of socio-technical change, and stabilization around a new regime. The objective for transition management is to steer bottom-up, niche-to-regime processes of transformation towards a pre-defined goal or 'vision' (Kemp and Rotmans, 2001: 4). Examples of such visions might be a low-carbon energy infrastructure, or a cleaner chemical production-and-use regime based on principles of industrial ecology. The point to note is that the starting point for the management process is the articulation of the vision. Niche experiments with novel socio-technical configurations create conditions for learning about the viability of a vision and the pathways towards its realization. Lessons from experiments should then inform and possibly revise the vision. Promising niches are further diffused by active policy intervention. Competencies and new skills are built up. New markets are created and consumer demand promoted. The position of the new configuration is strengthened and a normatively-desirable transformation of the regime is moved on. At all times, however, the touchstone is the vision – always under review, but always driving the transition management process.

It is at this point that we find a disjuncture between the historically-informed niche-based model of regime transformation and the normative policy aspirations of transition management. The niche-based model is illustrated with a number of examples in which an overarching, consensual vision of the future socio-technical regime was largely absent (van de Ven *et al.*, 1989) – certainly in the sense anticipated for transition management. In cases such as the advent of radio communications, television broadcasting, electronic computing, the turbojet in air transport and the gas turbine in the electricity system, the formative 'guiding visions' were typically significantly more modest and less widely shared than the eventual uses and impacts would suggest (Rosenberg, 1994). Conversely, examples abound of over-ambition in guiding visions, as with the development of successive innovations in space flight, nuclear propulsion, nuclear explosives in civil engineering, supersonic air transport and satellite-based mobile telephony. Of course, there are also examples of guiding visions which matched the potential of the configurations in question, as perhaps in the case of the automobile, geo-synchronous satellites and terrestrial mobile telephony. There appears to be no necessary correlation between the character of a particular guiding vision and the scale of the ambitions that are actually realized. Transition management takes historical observations of key features of successful transitions and calls for ambitious normative visions. Implicit are assumptions that a guiding vision is functional to regime change and that it is possible to identify *ex ante* a vision which may then be followed with real prospects of success. Both components of this assumption are problematic.

Right at the outset, there are serious difficulties in determining whether any given guiding vision is socially viable, or is desirable from the perspective of society as a whole. The transition management literature has developed a picture of an iterative and reflective process, providing for reviews of both guiding visions and the emerging configurations. This involves coordination between the contending perspectives of a variety of social actors. It remains unclear precisely how it can be ensured that the particular set of actors engaged in the development of any given niche do indeed reflect an appropriate range of social interests and perspectives. It is perhaps more likely that in competitive market conditions, profoundly differing visions continue to be promoted by different interests.

Although somewhat neglected in the transition management literature itself, the question of how to be more inclusive in the engagement of diverse social actors in the regime innovation process is a central concern of the closely related literature on 'constructive technology assessment'

(Rip, 1995; Rip *et al.*, 1996; Schot and Rip, 1997; Grin *et al.*, 1997; Schot, 2001). For all its sophistication, this literature also displays a tendency to treat as unproblematic the feasibility and desirability of aspirations to societal consensus aimed at identifying some determinate 'public interest'.

This is not an abstract or trivial problem. It strikes right at the heart of the normative character and public policy aspirations of the transition management project. In short, decades of work in the field of social choice has shown that there cannot, whether in principle or in practice, be a definitive means to integrate divergent perspectives, interests and preferences, such as to yield a single coherent ordering of technological (or other policy) options (Arrow, 1963; Bezembinder, 1989). Such managerial aspirations are confounded by the incommensurable dimensions of technological performance, strongly divergent socio-political interests and perspectives (Brown *et al.*, 2000), recursive interrelationships between the social and evaluative context, and the profound and ever-present exposure to surprise (Wynne, 1992; Stirling, 2003). Further serious issues are raised concerning the role of power (Lukes, 1974; Eagleton, 1991) and the nature of effective social deliberation (Habermas, 1996; Munton, 2003) in the formation of 'guiding visions'. In the main cases of interest involving dominant socio-technological regimes with high political and economic stakes in complex plural societies, not only is the process of consensus building, but the very notion of public interest itself, often highly problematic.

Unqualified and unproblematized notions of 'societal consensus' or 'public interest' can therefore often represent little more than rhetorical resources. Where the underlying assumptions, processes and limitations are not made explicit and examined, such concepts lend themselves to deliberate manipulation by socio-political interests on all sides of any debate on technological change. This blurs the distinction between emergent and historically-contingent processes of regime change, and the normatively-driven concept of transition management. It raises the prospect that the implementation, design, and even the very notion of transition management itself, might simply constitute further political resources and arenas for the interplay of the contending interests embodied in competing socio-technical regimes.

That different socio-political constituencies often disagree profoundly about the best way forward is especially true in the context of technology policy for sustainable development. Here researchers have noted a vast array of competing definitions and interpretations (Pearce, 1989). To some, this all-things-to-all-people quality is a fundamental weakness in the sustainable development vision: one that makes any realistic hope of sustainable development sheer folly (Beckerman, 1994). To others, including the present authors, the contested nature of the sustainable development 'vision' can be seen as a strength since it creates debate, necessitates continuing reflection, requires us to sift evidence from rhetoric, emphasizing the importance of being explicit about what is being sustained, for whom it is being sustained, how it will be sustained, and why it should be sustained (Jacobs, 1999; Dobson, 1998).

Either way, the real value of the notion of the 'guiding vision' in transition management does not lie, as is often implied, in its apparently unproblematic normative policy credentials. Quite the contrary: by focusing on the role of guiding visions, attention is concentrated on the importance of legitimate and effective deliberation and learning, and on the crucial role of providing for plurality, reversibility and sustained dissent. This raises issues concerning the diversity and resilience of wider social commitments to different technological trajectories and the extent to which particular commitments might be withdrawn (Brooks, 1986; Wynne, 1992; Stirling, 2003). It is acknowledged in transition management that the building of support and expectations around a vision is a necessary first step in attracting the resources and constituency of interests vital for carving out protective niches (Geels and Smit, 2000). The important lesson is that there is a need to be more reflective, explicit and specific about the role of divergent interests and power in this essential first step in the transition management process.

Bottom-up or Top-down?

It is at the meso-level where transition management objectives are most closely targeted: a vision for a new socio-technical regime. The niche-based model deliberately uses the term 'socio-technical regime' in place of the longer-standing term 'technological regime' in order to address more explicitly a wider set of social, political and institutional influences in technical change (Kemp *et al.*, 1998). As has been mentioned, in its original setting of institutional economics, the notion of the 'technological regime' implies a narrower set of norms and procedures at the core of the innovation process (Nelson and Winter, 1982). Analysts have studied the way such engineering-based regimes channel innovations along particular trajectories (Sahal, 1981; Dosi, 1988). The concept of socio-technical regime includes these more technical dimensions but embeds them in a wider set of sociological and economic relations. Indeed, transition management advocates the involvement in niche experiments of actors normally excluded from policy decisions about technological developments. Strategic niche management is the 'collective endeavour' of 'state policymakers, a regulatory agency, local authorities (such as a development agency), non-governmental organizations, a citizen group, a private company, an industry organization, a special interest group or an independent individual'

(Kemp *et al.*, 1998: 188). Issues of widespread socio-technical change opens transition management to include a set of actors beyond innovating firms and their immediate locus between suppliers and customers.

As already pointed out, networks of actors from the wider society with an interest in a socio-technical configuration will have differing 'visions' for sustainable development and the associated changes required of different socio-technical regimes. Beyond the general issues already discussed, this presents a rather specific difficulty for the niche-based model. Socially-based demands for more sustainable paths of development, for instance, may arise in specific social niches such as civil society organizations and networks, or protest movements. Yet these are only rarely directly articulated at the micro-level in ways that can be translated into technological innovation. It is even rarer that such direct micro-level articulation yields innovations of a form that would be recognized retrospectively as being decisive in the emergence of a particular technological transition. Instead, social aspirations that are becoming embedded in an institutional order typically first need to engage at the macro-level of the landscape of general opinion, legislation and so on, before they can become effective in seeding a transition. At this macro-level they are more likely to be translated into a form that can be channelled into market and regulatory signals that may in turn influence the emergence and adoption of socio-technical novelty, initially at the micro-level.

In the context of sustainable development, perhaps only the Appropriate or Alternative Technology (AT) social movement has sought a process of change that resonates with the niche-based model. The AT movement is part of the wider environmental movement that advocated its vision for sustainable development through the creation of practical examples on the ground (Willoughby, 1990). The wider membership of the environment movement has tended to engage in more overtly political action and sought directly to change the higher-level socio-technical landscape of institutions and economic structures. Rather than create sustainable niches from below, environmentalists have lobbied, boycotted, occupied, demonstrated and undertaken 'direct action'. Activists have sought to seed transformations from above (Doherty, 2002; Smith, 2003).

It is important to note that this form of change is different to those, identified in the preceding section, which brought regimes into 'tension' more generally. In the latter instance, changes in the landscape are not specifically directed at a particular regime, yet they nevertheless put that regime under some tension and induce change. Thus the changing demographic profile of a society or economic reform can have repercussions for a socio-technical regime without this being the motive for landscape changes. In contrast, more overtly political attempts by social groups to change landscape variables do tend to have one or more regimes in mind as targets while making their demands. Environmental campaigns over waste management are directed toward policymakers at the macro-level (for example, reforming tax regimes, introducing targets) which campaigners believe will induce changes to socio-technical regimes addressing, for instance, packaging systems, material use, waste collection or resource recovery.

Engagement by social actors may also be focused directly at the incumbent regimes themselves. Since the 1970s, environmentalists have targeted the nuclear industry as a socio-technical regime in its own right, engaging with all the regime dimensions noted in the transition management literature. Activities have challenged the iconic 'progressive' status of the technology (symbolism), the basis for investment founded in energy demand projections (policy), the favoured terms of regulation and financing (industry structure), the credibility of the science underlying the safety case (knowledge) and the viability and legitimacy of associated activities of fuel production and waste management (infrastructures) (Greenpeace, 1990). Indeed, although much of this activity was motivated by the aim of establishing alternative renewable energy technologies on a widespread basis, the main sociopolitical actors considered their efforts to be more productively targeted at undermining the incumbent regime than at nurturing its potential successor.

One does not need to agree with these aims in order to appreciate the effectiveness of this kind of strategy. Indeed, this is explicitly acknowledged on all sides of the nuclear debate (Patterson, 1985), and is reflected in the subsequent history of policy attention to renewable energy as an alternative 'low carbon' option. In many ways, the nuclear case can be viewed as a paradigmatic exemplar of engagement by social interest groups in socio-technical regime change. Yet numerous similar examples may be found: the deliberate targeting of waste incineration at sea by specially designed ships, followed by terrestrial toxic waste incineration (as a means to foster 'cleaner technology'); campaigns focusing on chemical intensive agriculture (to promote organic production); and the use of paper (to promote chlorine-free bleaching and recycling). Niche-focused activities by environmental pressure groups also exist, especially in recent years. Examples such as the hydrocarbon refrigerator and the promotion of consumer photovoltaics provide case studies for the transition management literature (van de Poel, 2002). In most cases, however, concerted (and often successful) regime-changing engagement by social actors has targeted the incumbent regime, rather than its potential successor. This represents a direct antithesis of the bottom-up niche-based model.

The lesson appears to be that attempts at normatively-driven socio-technical transitions (that is, those forms most pertinent to the transition management project) do not follow exclusively the pattern described by the niche-based model, but instead imply much greater attention to macro-level processes (public opinion, government policy, the structure and scope of markets) and their capacity to influence and induce innovations at the micro- and meso-level. Here the landscape is actively seeking to act on and influence the regime, not the other way around.

Such an observation opens up the possibility that transitions will not follow the single path envisaged in the niche-based model. In certain contexts, the bottom-up niche-to-regime transformation may indeed generate a novel way of fulfilling (and constituting) an existing or new social function. Yet in other contexts, it may be changes at the macro-level, in the institutional, economic, political, or cultural settings of the landscape, that drive a transformation from the top-down. Since drivers of change originate from both within and beyond the socio-technical regime it becomes important to understand their origins and how social actors adapt to such pressures. There emerges a clear need for greater acknowledgement and understanding of different transition contexts.

Where does this critique leave us? Although applauding the achievements gained through the current focus on a niche-based model of regime change, we have raised a series of concerns over the limits and idiosyncrasies of the resulting debate. In particular, we argue that current approaches to descriptive and normative discussions of regime change display what might be summarized as three key characteristics:

- They are *unilinear* in that they tend unduly to emphasize processes of regime change which begin within niches and work up, at the expense of those which directly address the various dimensions of the socio-technical regime or those which operate 'downwards' from general features of the socio-technical landscape.
- They are *univalent* in that they underplay the problematic nature of political intentionality and social choice when faced with multiple perspectives and interests. This leads to a tendency to reify notions of consensus and public interest, neglecting consideration of power and the benefits of strategic properties such as diversity and reversibility.
- They are *unidimensional*, in that they underdiscriminate between different transition contexts, such as those associated with drivers for change which are alternatively internal or external to the socio-technical regime, or which differentiate between changes that happen due to historic contingency and those that are the result of the deliberate exercise of agency.

Our proposal is that efforts be made towards constructing understandings of processes of regime change that are more *multilineal, multivalent* and *multidimensional* in the above senses. This reveals the importance of recognizing the multi-level nature of the nested socio-technical hierarchy running from the niche to the landscape, in that (depending on the perspective and the context) one can identify a continuum of regimes at successively higher levels of socio-technical aggregation, any one of which might serve as a focus for different kinds of transition management strategy. There exists considerable scope for further research in revealing the nature of the different processes and strategies implied by these different levels of aggregation.

REGIME STABILITY AND CHANGE

Theories of change in technological and socio-technical systems stress the stability and continuity of these systems, and the rarity of systems innovations. A range of explanations for processes of technological channelling, path dependence, 'lock in' and 'lock out' have been proposed. Dosi (1988), using the term 'technological paradigm', defined technological regimes as '. . . a pattern for solution of selected techno-economic problems based on highly selected principles . . .' In this analysis, the choice of technical problems is defined by prevailing knowledge and problem-solving heuristics that '. . . restrict the actual combinations in a notional characteristics space to a certain number of prototypical bundles'. Arthur (1989) argued that learning effects and increasing returns to economic scale would lead to a process of technological 'lock in' that would systematically exclude competing and possibly superior (in some dimensions) technologies. David (1985) in his famous, though controversial, example of the QWERTY keyboard argued for three factors leading to path dependency in technological change: technical interrelatedness; economies of scale; and quasi-irreversibility. The first and the last of these relate to the 'switching costs' involved in moving from one technological regime to another. A number of other well-known studies use different cases to make similar arguments (Cowan and Gunby, 1996). Finally, Walker (2000) stresses the importance of embedded institutional, political and economic commitments to a particular technological regime identified with a long-term need (maintaining nuclear fuel cycle capabilities in this case). He argues that this process of institutional 'entrapment' is ubiquitous in large technical systems.

The literature therefore places emphasis on the persistence of change along well-defined pathways. Innovation and novelty are seen as being bounded by working assumptions, institutional commitments and capital endowments inherent to a given regime. Technologies and their institutional context therefore interact to guide change along well-defined channels and form barriers preventing switching to alternative regimes. As with many 'structural' accounts, the problem with this picture is that it says very little about the conditions under which change occurs, or about the switches that may occur between regimes. Regime shifts or successions clearly have occurred in the past. The horse-drawn carriage was replaced by the tram as the principal means of passenger mobility in cities, and the telegraph by the telephone. We can expect similar transitions to occur in the future.

We therefore take it as axiomatic that, while regimes exhibit a high degree of stability and coherence, they are also dynamic and challenged by alternatives. The stability and path dependency of regimes is relative. Regimes are continually subject to competitive selection pressures exerted by other regimes and by new socio-technical configurations in niches. Often these pressures are weak and incoherent, but at other times they become stronger. Some regimes have the capacity to respond more readily to these selection pressures than others. To give two simple examples, the disposable diaper regime (competing with the reusable diaper) has been able to respond to selection pressure on environmental grounds during the last ten years, while the chemical film regime appears likely, for most applications, eventually to be replaced by digital photography.

This feature of technological regimes we term its 'adaptive capacity'. In simple terms, the adaptive capacity of a regime is related to its ability to recognize its vulnerability to competitive threats (frequently a collective task of regime members); and to reduce its vulnerability to these threats (perhaps through competitive innovation, through reconfiguration, or by influencing the regulatory environment to exclude the new entrant). The greater the adaptive capacity of the regime, the more resilient it will be in the face of competitive selection pressures.

Another way of characterizing adaptive capacity is by reference to the 'functions' of technological systems as defined in the innovation systems literature. In an extensive review of this literature, Jacobbson and Johnson (2000) identify five such functions performed by technological systems:

1. Creation of new knowledge: the main source of variety in technological systems.
2. Influence over the direction of search processes among users and suppliers of technology: the articulation of supply and demand is seen as critical to the perceived costs and benefits of regime switching.
3. Supply of resources: These include capital, competences and input materials as well as political resources that support the legitimacy of a regime.
4. Creation of positive external economies: This is a pivotal characteristic. An example is the formation of socio-technical networks that

provide 'spillover' effects by reducing uncertainty, reducing the cost of information, accessing tacit knowledge and sharing costs.
5. Formation of markets: Innovations rarely find ready-made markets, which therefore need to be stimulated or created afresh. Market formation is related to the marketing efforts of firms, as well as the regulatory and other influences on the shape of markets.

More adaptive regimes would be those that are able to perform these functions effectively. Over time, we would normally expect more adaptive regimes to succeed and those with less adaptive capacity to be subsumed or substituted.

Having established that socio-technical regimes face competitive selection pressures to which they must respond and adapt, the next question concerns the source and configuration of the selection pressure. Such competition may emerge in a number of different ways:

- The creation of novel socio-technical configurations for meeting a social function within niches (for example, the application of membrane technology for municipal wastewater treatment).
- An innovation that seeds a transformation in a higher-level regime (such as the impact of high levels of wind turbine capacity on the structure and operation of the electricity system).
- The spur to innovation felt through competition from another socio-technical regime serving the same or overlapping markets or social functions (such as competition between the different electricity technological regimes: coal; gas; oil; nuclear and renewables).
- The competition between different 'visions' for the future held by a variety of social actors, some of whom are more directly embedded within the regime than others; and the different power resources they have to pursue these visions (for example, current contention over the use of conventional risk assessment versus more 'precautionary' approaches to chemicals regulation).
- The generation of changes in the socio-technical landscape that put the regime in tension (for example, the liberalization of energy markets in the EU).
- Politically motivated change in the landscape targeted at changing a range of problematic socio-technical regimes (such as current public debates over genetically modified foods in the EU).

Looking at this list of competitive pressures, we can draw some general conclusions relevant to research about transition contexts and regime transformations. First, selection pressures act on socio-technical regimes at different levels. The magnitude and form of these pressures and the capacity of the regime to respond to them will have consequences for the pattern and direction of the transformation process. Thus the prevalence of a strong downward pressure deriving from landscape change may tend to drive transformation differently to the growing success and expansion of a niche-based alternative. A bottom-up process may transform the dominant socio-technical configuration, or it may fail to do so; while a top-down process may only prompt incremental changes that relieve tensions in the incumbent regime. In other instances, selection pressures may converge – top-down tensions creating opportunities for niches to link into and change the incumbent regime. These top-down and bottom-up drivers play out amidst underpinning economic pressures on firms concerning competitiveness, market share, profitability, investor returns and reputation. It is shifts in the relative strength of these selection pressures that generate opportunities for change. The art in transition management must lie in recognizing which driver offers the best leverage for change at which point.

Second, some selection pressures are consciously and purposefully targeted at regime transformation, while others emerge contingently. This distinction between what was intended and what emerged unintended is partly accounted for in the debate about the relative importance of agency and structure in explaining change. To the extent that entrepreneurs and other advocates are always necessary for a new technological configuration to come to life and be diffused, the changes motivated by innovation are always attributable to agency. But regime transformations are often explained as unintended outcomes of small technical and other adjustments. The Kondratiev-Freeman long-wave theory of technological and institutional transformations is expressed as unintended outcomes of processes that early innovators could not have imagined, let alone guided and managed (Freeman and Louça, 2001). All transformations include a mixture of the intended and the unintended, but the degree to which they are either one or the other may be a way of differentiating transition contexts.

TRANSITION CONTEXTS: THE COORDINATION AND LOCUS OF RESOURCES

In summary, we argue that specific configurations of selection pressures on the socio-technical regime will account for specific, historically-situated transformation processes. Relating the context of transformation to transformation processes must become a starting point for analysis, particularly for transition management advocates seeking the purposive steering of regime change.

As a first step, we suggest that transition contexts can be mapped using two differentiating factors. The first dimension relates to whether change is

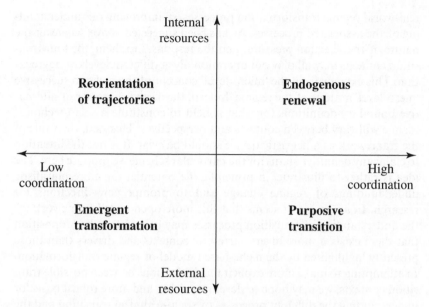

Figure 3.1   Four transition contexts and transformation processes

envisaged and coordinated at the level of the regime, or whether it is the emergent outcome of the normal behaviour of agents within the regime (involving no new mechanisms of coordination).[2] This dimension seeks to distinguish between regime transformations that are intended and those that are the unintended outcomes of historical processes.

The second dimension concerns the degree to which the response to selection pressure is based on resources available within the regime (or which can be coopted by the regime), or depends on resources that are only available from outside the regime. Relevant resources would be those needed to carry out the regime functions listed above. The *locus* of the resources to innovate and adapt is therefore important to the nature of the transformation process. If the resources to adapt are available internally, then change is likely to be more incremental and structural relationships within the regime are less likely to be overturned. If the capacity to adapt is highly constrained by the lack of resources internally then the opportunity for major structural change exists. This coordination of actors/locus of resources framework gives rise to a fourfold mapping of transition contexts (see Figure 3.1).

The four quadrants represent schematic 'ideal types'. Comparisons and contrasts between the elements of each transformation can be made against real-world regime transformation processes, so improving our understanding of the associated processes. As has been suggested above, whatever the nature of the selection pressures and the responses to them, the four transition contexts may all play out operationally at different levels of aggregation. This extends from the 'micro-level' concept of the niche to successive 'meso-level' notions of the regime. Indeed, the nested character of alternative boundary definitions for what is held to constitute a socio-technical regime will vary between contexts and perspectives. This said, the value of the framework as a heuristic device should be clear. It is not the intention to claim any definitive status for the particular scheme we propose here. The idea is rather to illustrate, in principle, the potential for more pluralistic understandings of regime change and to prompt new directions for research. In any event, it seems that this more open-ended framework for the understanding of transition processes may help to test the proposition that there exists a more diverse array of contexts and drivers than those presently highlighted by the niche-based model of regime transformation. In attempting to make more explicit the distinctions between possible transition contexts, we may hope to develop a richer and more robust basis for understanding the different processes of socio-technical transition and the associated opportunities for normative policy intervention.

As a first step towards this aim, each of the transition contexts introduced above are briefly characterized below. A series of stylized examples – emphasizing the energy sector for the purposes of effective comparison – are used to provide more concrete illustration.

1. Endogenous renewal: This arises in the context of socio-technical regime actors (firms, supply chains, customers, regulators) making conscious efforts to find ways of responding to a perceived competitive threat to the regime. In terms of our typology, the pressure to change the regime is a result of high coordination. Responses are based on resources originating within the regime. However, given that innovative activity is shaped from within the regime itself, it will tend to be steered by the prevailing values, cognitive structures and problem-solving routines of the incumbent regime. Decisions over future technological choices will be guided by past experience. Thus the transformation process will tend to be incremental. Looking back over a long period of time the transformation can appear radical, but it will have come about through an alignment of smaller changes.

    An example of this kind of process may be found in the progressive scaling up of the thermal capacity of steam-generating plant over the course of the 20th century. Constituted by a multitude of individually minor organizational and engineering innovations, the result was a radical transformation in the character of the electricity regime (Hughes, 1987). Likewise, investment in flue gas desulphurization plant as a response to concerns over acid emissions (Boehmer-Christiansen and Skea, 1991), or the development of carbon sequestration techniques might also be taken as examples of endogenous renewal. In either case, the long-term implications, were the processes of change to be deep-seated and sustained, would be one of incremental regime transition.

2. Reorientation of trajectories: Some socio-technical regimes exhibit an intrinsic property of 'systemness' (Rosenberg, 1994: 216–17) in their processes of change while at the same time being highly unpredictable. In these regimes, trajectories of change may be radically altered by internal processes without being associated with discontinuities in the actors, networks or institutions involved in the regime. The stimulus for such radical reorientation is a shock, originating either inside or outside the incumbent regime. The response, however, is formed within the regime. In the electricity sector, an example of this kind of regime change might be seen with the advent of wide-scale adoption of combined cycle gas turbines, especially in the UK (Islas, 1997). This radical transformation in the technical and operational characteristics of generation systems was not widely anticipated or intended, but arose through the conjunction of a series of uncoordinated technological opportunities, changes in market regulation and obstacles facing alternatives such as coal and nuclear generation. However, the adoption of gas turbines was managed within the dominant electricity generation regime, rather than being a development imposed from without.

3. Emergent transformation: Many classical regime transitions have an apparently autonomous (though socially-contingent) logic. In our typology, this type of transformation arises from uncoordinated pressures for change and responses formed beyond the incumbent regime. The major technological cycles described in Kondratiev's long waves have this kind of dependency on complex, pervasive social and economic processes. Likewise, many of the more specific examples in the technological transitions literature have this form (Christensen, 1997). Their origin is typically in scientific activity often carried out in universities and small firms operating outside existing industries (Dosi, 1988). These transitions can be observed, but there is sometimes little basis *ex ante* to distinguish between those alternatives that will 'catch on' (Mokyr, 1991: 276) and those that will not. In the energy sector, a long term example is provided by the series of 'energy successions' governing the dominance of different 'primary fuels' running over a period of three centuries or so from wood, through coal, to oil and gas. Other examples of such technologies with major disruptive potential include

information and genetic-modification technology. The impacts of these technologies have of course been across many different technological regimes – in this sense it is incorrect to speak of a single transition, but of many parallel transitions stimulated from a common technological basis and shaped by regime-specific configurations of interests and goals. It is also clear from the GM example that the environmental impacts (as perceived by key actors and institutions) of these emergent transitions may remain quite uncertain even some way down the process of path creation.

4. Purposive transitions: While emergent transitions have an autonomous quality, we seek to distinguish these from purposive transitions which have in some senses been intended and pursued to reflect the expectations of a broad and effective set of interests, largely located outside the regimes in question. A good example of this type of transition is the history of civil nuclear power in the industrialized world, and the possible partial transition to the greater use of renewable energy technologies. Nuclear power was widely regarded in the 1950s and 1960s as a critical technology with the potential to generate broad economic and political (military) benefits. A common narrative was developed which involved a series of technological transitions from uranium to plutonium fuel cycles. Scientific, policy and industrial interests were coopted to this vision to form a powerful interest grouping which was typically in strong contention with established interests within the incumbent regime of the electricity system itself. This latter example shows that this form of transition – imagined, planned and partially executed – does not necessarily generate social and environmental benefits.

Transition management is the transformation of a socio-technical regime guided primarily by negotiation between social actors from beyond the regime. Key to the transition management programme is that these social actors have a greater role in forming the socio-technical response to the coordinated pressure for change. Obviously, this demand for change has to be mediated by the regime actors. Transition management is also the outcome of a deliberate attempt to change the regime. Thus, in terms of our scheme, the transformation process is most likely to be that of purposive transition. The historical transformations used to exemplify the niche-based model of transformation tended to be the result of many contingencies and were managed through changes internal to the regime, i.e. emergent transition. Of course, the transition context for any given socio-technical regime need not be fixed. Contexts may change, and the proposition in this chapter is that any change in context may influence the pattern of regime transition.

CONCLUSION: TOWARDS A RESEARCH AGENDA

We have sought to argue a need to be more explicit and specific about the relationships between contexts and processes of change in socio-technical regimes. We suggest a heuristic and schematic distinction based on the degree of coordination of regime change between actors, networks and institutions, and the locus of resources required to respond to selection pressures acting on the regime. This framework produces four different contexts for regime change, distinguishing between 'purposive transitions' (deliberate change caused by outside actors), 'endogenous renewal' (deliberate change fostered by regime members), 're-orientation of trajectories' (spontaneous change resulting from relationships and dynamics within a regime) and 'emergent transformations' (the unintended consequence of changes wrought outside prevailing regimes). Taken together, this picture suggests a rich conceptual arena for the interplay of different forms of selection pressure, different configurations of actors, networks and institutions, and different resources to respond to pressures for change, all operating at various levels in the socio-technical continuum.

The typology is a first attempt at a heuristic based on ideal types. If it has any utility then this will arise through its further application and elaboration. The following are a few research challenges that might constitute such development:

- The notion of selection pressures operating at the level of a socio-technical regime needs to be further elaborated and grounded in theory. Selection pressures are typically thought of as operating at the level of firms and discrete technologies, rather than at the more macro regime level.
- Assessments are needed of regime function (following Jacobbson and Johnson's typology) and of 'adaptive capacity' based on comparative measures, so providing the basis for a more analytical (less descriptive) approach to regime transitions. Critical to this will be the analysis of the resources that are needed to respond to selection pressures.
- Further elaboration is needed of the ideas of coordination of change and the locus of resources to enable change. Again, approaches and measures for characterising these two dimensions of regime transformations need to be developed, and the conjectures we have made about transition contexts need to be tested.

The imperatives are clear for improved understanding of what determines successful technological transitions. More pluralistic notions of the relationships between transition context and regime transformation may aid such understanding and so help foster more robust and deliberate social choice in this crucial area.

ACKNOWLEDGEMENTS

An earlier version of this chapter was presented at a workshop on 'Transitions and System Innovations' held at the University of Twente, Enschede, 4–6 July 2002. We acknowledge the comments of workshop participants and are grateful for comments from our colleagues Staffan Jacobbson, Ed Steinmuller and Frank Geels. Thanks also to Michelle Harris for chasing up references.

NOTES

1. In fact, the reconfiguration may also involve the old regime retreating into niches of its own. It is ironic that one of the final niches for sailboats was transporting coal to the ports around the world so that steamboats would have a ready supply of fuel (Gruebler, 1990). Old technologies often continue to coexist alongside the new technologies, although their market-share declines.
2. In making this distinction between low and high levels of coordination we want to move beyond a simple planned/market-based dichotomy, to take account of more complex processes of the social regulation of technologies that involve not just the state, but also other social actors including civil society organizations and consumers.

REFERENCES

Arrow, K. (1963), *Social Choice and Individual Values*, New Haven, CT: Yale University Press.

Arthur, W. (1989), 'Competing technologies, increasing returns and lock-in by historical events', *The Economics Journal*, **99**, 116–31.

Basalla, G. (1988), *The Evolution of New Technology*, Cambridge: Cambridge University Press.

Bauer, M. (1995), *Resistance to New Technology*, Cambridge: Cambridge University Press.

Beckerman, W. (1994), 'Sustainable development: is it a useful concept?', *Environmental Values*, **3**, 191–209.

Berkhout, F. (2002), 'Technological regimes, path dependency and the environment', *Global Environmental Change*, **12** (1), 1–4.

Bezembinder, T. (1989), 'Social choice theory and practice', in C. Vlek and T. Cvetkovitch (eds), *Social Decision Methodology for Technological Projects*, Dordrecht: Kluwer.

Bijker, W. (1995), *Of Bicycles, Bakelites and Bulbs. Toward a Theory of Sociotechnical Change*, Cambridge, MA: MIT Press.

Bijker, W., T. Hughes and T. Pinch (eds) (1987), *The Social Construction of Technological Systems: New Directions in the Sociology and History of Technology*, Cambridge, MA: MIT Press.
Boehmer-Christiansen, S., and J. Skea (1991), *Acid Politics: Environmental and Energy Policies in Britain and Germany*, London: Belhaven Press.
Brooks, H. (1986), 'The typology of surprises in technology, institution and development', in W.C. Clark and R.E. Munn (eds), *Sustainable Development of the Biosphere*, New York: Cambridge University Press, pp. 325–48.
Brown, N., B. Rappert and A. Webster (eds) (2000), *Contested Futures: A Sociology of Prospective Technoscience*, Aldershot: Ashgate.
Callon, M. (1987), 'Society in the making: the study of technology as a tool for sociological analysis', in W. Bijker, T. Hughes and T. Pinch (eds), *The Social Construction of Technological Systems. New Directions in the Sociology and History of Technology*, Cambridge, MA and London: MIT Press, pp. 83–103.
Christensen, C.M. (1997), *The Innovator's Dilemma: When New Technologies Cause Great Firms to Fail*, Boston, MA: Harvard Business School Press.
Clayton, A., G. Spinardi and R. Williams (1999), *Policies for Cleaner Technology: A New Agenda for Government and Industry*, London: Earthscan.
Cowan, R., and P. Gunby (1996), 'Sprayed to death: path dependence, lock-in and pest control strategies', *Economic Journal*, **106**, 521–42.
David, P.A. (1985), 'Clio and the Economics of QWERTY', *American Economic Review*, **76**, 332–7.
Dobson, A. (1998), *Justice and the Environment*, London: Routledge.
Doherty, B. (2002), *Ideas and Actions in the Green Movement*, London: Routledge.
Dosi, G. (1982), 'Technological paradigms and technological trajectories: a suggested interpretation of the determinants and directions of technical change', *Research Policy*, **6**, 147–62.
Dosi, G. (1988), 'The nature of the innovative process', in G. Dosi, C. Freeman, R. Nelson, G. Silverberg and L. Soete (eds), *Technical Change and Economic Theory*, London: Pinter, pp. 221–38.
Eagleton, T. (1991), *Ideology: An Introduction*, London: Verso.
Elliot, D., and R. Elliot (1976), *The Control of Technology*, London: Chapman and Hall.
Ellul, J. (1964), *The Technological Society*, translation by J. Wilkinson, New York: Knopf.
Freeman, C. (1994), 'Technical change and technological regimes', in G. Hodgson, W. Samuels and M. Tool (eds), *The Elgar Companion to Institutional and Evolutionary Economics*, Cheltenham: Edward Elgar, pp. 309–15.
Freeman, C., and L. Soete (1987), *Technical Change and Full Employment*, Oxford: Basil Blackwell.
Freeman, C., and F. Louçá (2001), *As Time Goes By*, Oxford: Oxford University Press.
Geels, F. (2002), 'Technological transitions as evolutionary reconfiguration processes: a multi-level perspective and case study', *Research Policy*, **31**, 1257–74.
Geels, F., and W. Smit (2000), 'Failed technology futures: pitfalls and lessons from a historical survey', *Futures*, **32**, 867–85.
Giddens, A. (1984), *The Constitution of Society: Outline of the Theory of Structuration*, Cambridge: Polity.
Greenpeace International (1990), 'Questions and answers on nuclear energy', briefing paper, London, April 1989.

Grin, J., H. van de Graaf and R. Hoppe (1997), *Technology Assessment Through Interaction: A Guide*, The Hague: Rathenau Institute.

Gruebler, A. (1990), *The Rise and Fall of Infrastructures*, Heidelberg: Physica-Verlag.

Habermas, J. (1996), 'Popular sovereignty as procedure', in J. Habermas, *Between Facts and Norms: Contributions to a Discourse Theory of Law and Democracy*, Cambridge, MA: MIT Press, 463–90.

Hoogma, R., R. Kemp, J. Schot and B. Truffer (2002), *Experimenting for Sustainable Transport: The Approach of Strategic Niche Management*, London: Spno Press.

Hughes, T. (1983), *Networks of Power Electrification in Western Society, 1880–1930*, Baltimore, MD: Johns Hopkins University Press.

Hughes, T. (1987), 'The evolution of large technical systems', in W. Bijker, T. Hughes and T. Pinch (eds), *The Social Construction of Technological Systems: New Directions in the Sociology and History of Technology*, Cambridge, MA: MIT Press, 51–82.

Islas, J. (1997), 'Getting round the lock-in in electricity generating systems: the example of the gas turbine', *Research Policy*, **26** (1), 49–66.

Jacobs, M. (1999), 'Sustainable development as a contested concept', in A. Dobson (ed.), *Fairness and Futurity*, London: Routledge.

Jacobbson, S., and A. Johnson (2000), 'The diffusion of renewable energy technology: an analytical framework and key issues for research', *Energy Policy,* **28**, 625–40.

Kaldor, M. (1983), *The Baroque Arsenal*, London: Abacus.

Kemp, R., A. Rip and J. Schot (2001), 'Constructing transition paths through the management of niches', in R. Garud and P. Karnoe (eds), *Path Dependence and Creation*, Mahwah, NJ: Lawrence Erlbaum Associates Publishers, pp. 269–99.

Kemp, R., and J. Rotmans (2001), 'The management of the co-evolution of technical, environmental and social systems', paper presented to the International Conference Towards Environmental Innovation Systems, Garmisch-Partenkirchen, September.

Kemp, R., J. Schot and R. Hoogma (1998), 'Regime shifts to sustainability through processes of niche formation: the approach of strategic niche management', *Technology Analysis and Strategic Management*, **10** (2), 175–95.

Leiss, W. (1990), *Under Technology's Thumb*, Montreal: McGill-Queen's University Press.

Lukes, S. (1974), *Power: A Radical View*, London: Macmillan.

MacKenzie, D. (1990), *Inventing Accuracy: A Historical Sociology of Nuclear Missile Guidance*, Cambridge, MA: MIT Press.

MacKenzie, D. (2001), *Knowing Machines: Essays on Technical Change*, Cambridge, MA: MIT Press.

Mokyr, J. (1991), *The Lever to Riches: Technological Creativity and Economic Progress*, Oxford: Oxford University Press.

Munton, R. (2003), 'Deliberative democracy and environmental decision-making', in F. Berkhout, M. Leach and I. Scoones (eds), *Negotiating Environmental Change*, Cheltenham: Edward Elgar, pp. 109–36.

Nelson, R., and S. Winter, (1977), 'In search of useful theory of innovation', *Research Policy*, **6**, 36–76.

Nelson, R., and S. Winter (1982), *An Evolutionary Theory of Economic Change*, Cambridge, MA: Harvard University Press.

Patterson, W.C. (1985), *Going Critical: An Unofficial History of British Nuclear Power*, London: Paladin.

Pearce, D. (1989), *Blueprint for a Green Economy*, London: Earthscan.

Rip, A. (1995), 'Introduction of new technology: making use of recent insights from sociology and economics of technology', *Technology Analysis & Strategic Management*, **7** (4), 417–31.

Rip, A., and R. Kemp (1998), 'Technological change', in S. Rayner and E. Malone (eds), *Human Choices and Climate Change 2*, Columbus, OH: Battelle.

Rip, A., T. Misa and J. Schot (1996), *Managing Technology in Society*, London: Pinter.

Rosenberg, N.J. (1994), *Explaining the Black Box*, Cambridge: Cambridge University Press.

Rotmans, J., R. Kemp and M. van Asselt (2001), 'More evolution than revolution: transition management in public policy', *Foresight*, **3** (1), 15–31.

Sahal, D. (1981), *Patterns of Technological Innovation*, Reading, MA: Addison-Wesley.

Schot, J. (1998), 'The usefulness of evolutionary models for explaining innovation. The case of the Netherlands in the 19th century', *History and Technology*, **14**, 173–200.

Schot, J. (2001), 'Towards new forms of participatory technology development', *Technology Analysis and Strategic Management*, **13** (1), 39–52.

Schot, J., and A. Rip (1997), 'The past and future of constructive technology assessment', *Technological Forecasting and Social Change*, **54**, 251–68.

Smith, A. (2003), 'Transforming technological regimes for sustainable development: a role for appropriate technology niches?', *Science & Public Policy*, **30** (2), April.

Stirling, A. (2003), 'Risk, uncertainty and precaution: some instrumental implications from the social sciences', in F. Berkhout, M. Leach and I. Scoones (eds), *Negotiating Environmental Change*, Cheltenham: Edward Elgar, pp. 33–76.

van de Poel, I. (2002), 'The transformation of technological regimes', *Research Policy*, **32** (1), 49–68.

van de Ven, A., H. Angle and M. Poole (1989), *Research on the Management of Innovation: The Minnesota Studies*, New York: Harper & Row.

Wajcman, J. (1996), *Feminism Confronts Technology*, Cambridge: Polity Press.

Walker, W. (2000), 'Entrapment in large technology systems: institutional commitments and power relations', *Research Policy*, **29** (7–8), 833–46.

Weber, M., R. Hoogma, B. Lane and J. Schot (1999), *Experimenting with Sustainable Transport Innovations: A Workbook for Strategic Niche Management*, Twente: University of Twente Press.

Willoughby, K. (1990), *Technology Choice: A Critique of the Appropriate Technology Movement*, London: Intermediate Technology Development Group.

Winner, L. (1981), *Autonomous Technology: Technics Out of Control as a Theme in Political Thought*, Cambridge, MA: MIT Press.

Wynne, B. (1992), 'Uncertainty and environmental learning: reconceiving science and policy in the preventive paradigm', *Global Environmental Change*, **2** (2), 111–27.

4. Sustainability, system innovation and the laundry

Elizabeth Shove

Few would disagree that the challenge of sustainability is one of moving toward less resource-intensive ways of life built around new regimes of mobility, renewable energy or localized systems of food production. In understanding how shifts of this kind might be realized and in trying to engender them, environmentalists have much to gain from the careful analysis of comparable, large-scale transitions in the past. Following Hughes's (1983) path breaking study of the social and technical construction of networks of electrical power, it is by now usual to document the 'seamless webs' from which technological transitions like that from sail to steam, or from horse to car, have been woven and to acknowledge the institutional and political processes required in support. In this sense, much contemporary debate is genuinely 'socio-technical' in its orientation. However, there is another sense in which the agenda remains lopsided, skewed around provision rather than consumption and around the diffusion rather than the use of technological systems, tools and techniques. This chapter seeks to recover some of that missing ground and in the process develop and enrich 'transition theories' that have grown out of science and technology studies and the analysis of innovation.

The simple step of starting with convention and practice generates a substantially new menu of questions about the dynamics of system innovation. Approached in this way, the challenge is not only one of conceptualizing and steering pathways of infrastructural development like those associated with energy supply, but of also understanding the transformation of demand and the institutionalization of energy consuming services like lighting, cooling or central heating. This means thinking about the ideas and expectations that lie behind the fact that around half of domestic energy consumption in the UK is now devoted to heating and cooling. It means asking how is it that personal bathing and laundry currently account for around a third of domestic water consumption and that demand for water has risen by 70 per cent in the UK over the last 30 years (Environment Agency, 2002). Likewise, when considering mobility, the central question is how social obligations have come to require the forms of co-presence that they do. Taken for granted patterns of daily life are surely not static, nor are they free from commercial and government influence or from the scripts embedded in specific devices or in more encompassing regimes and socio-technical landscapes. But in analysing the creep of conventions that sustain what are ultimately unsustainable ways of life, it is, I argue, necessary to push the agenda on and to think more systematically and more systemically about the relation between consumption, provision and practice. This is an important step if theories of transition are to conceptualize the transformation of 'demand'.

Although I want to consider the reconfiguration of consumption and practice and although I take this to be crucial when contemplating transitions to a more sustainable society, I do not want to fall back on simplistic models in which change is attributed to the beliefs and actions of self-consciously green consumers (Hobson, 2001). Nor do I take the job to be one of topping up on human agency, of slotting consumers into the frame alongside recognized system builders and institutions, giving free reign to consumer oriented design, or enhancing opportunities for (presumably green) citizen-consumer involvement in the shaping of provision (Spaargaren, 1997).

Following a different route, I suggest that shared understandings of 'normality' matter more. This is so because notions of what it is to be a normal and acceptable member of society have far reaching environmental implications: they carry in their wake a trail of inescapable resource requirements like those associated with daily showering, with wearing freshly laundered clothing, with not having a siesta, with eating imported food or with having foreign holidays. There are, of course, important social divisions in what constitutes 'normality' and persistent differences between nations, social classes and sub-cultures. Equally, there are observable currents of convergence about which I will say more in due course. For present purposes, I take normal practices to be those in which collective identities are anchored (Douglas and Isherwood, 1996; Bourdieu, 1984), which constitute a form of social glue, and which are, at any one point in time and in any one culture, seen to be obligatory, non-negotiable conditions of everyday life.

CHALLENGES FOR TRANSITION THEORY

There are good environmental reasons for seeking to understand transitions in service and practice as well as in the resources and technologies of provision. However, such an exercise presents a number of generic challenges for transition theory as it has developed this far. In what follows

I focus on three such questions and suggest that each can be addressed by drawing in and drawing upon other fields of social theory.

The first concerns the boundaries and phases of system development. It is clear that definitions of normal and appropriate standards (for example of housing, mobility, comfort, personal hygiene or laundry) have changed over time, but can we discern distinctive moments equivalent to those of exploration, diffusion and stabilization? And if not, what then is the relation between unfolding concepts of service and the 'careers' of technological systems on which service provision depends?

Second, when analysing the respecification of convention it is as important to consider convergence between societies – perhaps fuelled by common reliance on similar technologies – as it is to detail movement between sociotechnical niches, regimes and landscapes within any one society. For example, how is it that people in Singapore and Denmark have come to expect the same indoor climate and the same conditions of 'comfort' all year round (de Dear, 1994)? By switching attention from transitions in energy systems to systems of comfort it becomes possible, and indeed necessary, to track the global circulation of tools and skills, and the migration of sociotechnically configured expectations and practices. This move prompts us to re-engage with questions about what sustainable ways of life might actually involve as well as about how necessary transitions might be achieved. From this perspective, the redefinition of societal functions is at least as important as the means through which they are fulfilled.

Third, the effective accomplishment of everyday life depends upon the active integration of a vast array of rules, resources and socio-technical complexes. Since the reconfiguration of 'normal' ways of doing things (cooking, washing, moving around and so on) often involves new ways of 'assembling' the ingredients of daily life, mechanisms of coordination deserve attention in their own right. Although central to any analysis of changing habit, questions about the relation between coexisting socio-technical systems are not routinely addressed by those who study bounded domains of innovation and who analyse the unfolding of such developments within specific national or social contexts.

Although challenging, these are not entirely unfamiliar issues. On the first point, there is continuing discussion about how to represent the steps and stages of innovation given what we know about 'innofusion' and the constant repositioning of technology in practice. Likewise, anthropologists, perhaps more than scholars of science and technology, have long been interested in the circulation and cross-cultural appropriation of material objects. Even more obviously, much effort has been invested in making and remaking the point that systems and technologies do not exist in isolation. It is none the less the case that the dominant concern has been to explain how new technologies are assimilated in practice, rather than to understand how practices and conventions themselves (co)evolve.

SYSTEM INNOVATION AND THE LAUNDRY

In shifting the focus of enquiry and stepping outside the normal repertoire of cases and examples, I want to explore ways of extending transition theory so as to address the dynamics of consumption and practice.

At first sight, laundering is a curiously mundane example to take. It has not required significant public or private sector investment; it does not revolve around a clearly identifiable technological complex; it has not obviously passed through discrete phases of development nor are there any recognizable system builders. One might therefore conclude that it does not really qualify as a case of system innovation as that term has come to be understood. On the other hand, the reconfiguration of laundering has all the necessary features: it involves a wide range of actors, including firms, consumers, knowledge producers, NGOs and governments and is the result of an interplay between many factors and actors that influence each other. It also implies change at various levels: at the micro-level of individual actions, at the meso-level of structuring paradigms and rules and at the macro-level of structural trends.

Over the last century, techniques and habits of clothes washing have changed significantly, with long-term consequences for domestic electricity and water demand. In Western European countries and in the USA, something like 20 per cent of household water consumption now relates to the production of clean clothing and, in combination, the main appliances involved (the washing machine and the dryer) account for a still significant fraction of domestic energy use (DEFRA, 2000; American Water Works Association, 1999). These figures reflect a five-fold increase in the frequency with which the laundry is done. No longer a weekly activity, the average number of laundry cycles (that is the number of times that washing machines are run per year) is 274 in the UK (DEFRA, 2000), and 392 in America (Biermeyer, 2001).

At the same time, what it means to wash well has been redefined. Not so long ago, boiling was deemed essential in order to get things really clean. Now less than 7 per cent of the (UK) wash is done at 90° C (DEFRA, 2000). Mainly because of this, the energy efficiency of American washing machines increased by 50 per cent between 1981 and 1999 (Association of Home Appliance Manufacturers, 2000: 35). These developments in the meaning and practice of laundry have direct but contradictory implications for resource consumption and the case is interesting precisely because this is an area in which increasingly efficient technologies sustain more demanding concepts of service (Shove, 2003).

In addition, and as the example of the laundry also illustrates, innovation in the way that 'societal functions' like the production of clean clothing are defined and fulfilled depends upon the practical integration of a variety of what seem to be self-contained systems. The size and content of the laundry basket is, for instance, closely related to the textile and fashion industries and the mass production of clothing. Meanwhile, the design of domestic washing machines relates to the range of fabrics in circulation, to the availability of detergent and to contemporary concepts of cleanliness and social/moral order. In so far as laundering is about cleanliness it is relevant to acknowledge the work of those who argue that boundary-making activities of this kind are, at heart, expressions and reproductions of social order. This points to an entirely different way of thinking about the dynamics of transition. As Mary Douglas has famously observed, 'dirt is essentially disorder' (Douglas, 1984: 2): it is matter out of place. Understood in these terms, washing is part of a more encompassing system of social order with the effect that transitions in practice match developments in the specification and policing of social–symbolic boundaries and distinctions. It is also the case that however people define standards of cleanliness, maintaining them is an important part of another kind of system, namely that of self identity. Kaufmann puts it this way: 'there can be no construction of identity without the affirmation of cleanliness: to be oneself, to be a self-respecting individual, is to be clean' (Kaufmann, 1998: 16).

As these few observations suggest, the exercise of placing the production of 'appropriately' laundered clothing centre stage, and of viewing laundering as a system or, more accurately, a system of systems in transition, has the conceptually useful effect of broadening what are becoming 'orthodox' discussions grounded in studies of bounded, supply oriented, domains like those of energy, water, food or mobility. I therefore use laundering – and the intellectual resources of a variety of disciplines – to elaborate on the three challenges identified above. First, what are the units of system innovation, how are system boundaries conceptualized and what does this mean for the representation of phases of system development? Second, how do systems unfold *between* as well as within societies? In other words, what are the 'horizontal' as well as the 'vertical' dynamics at play in the formation of socio-technical regimes and landscapes? Third, what are the modes and mechanisms of system integration, and how do these influence transitions in what people take to be normal and appropriate practice? In the final section I take stock of what this discussion means for transition theory and for environmental policy.

SYSTEM BOUNDARIES AND PHASES OF DEVELOPMENT

Hughes (1983) and others have written about the typical phases of system development including those of initial exploration, take-off, diffusion, and stabilization. This framework has given shape to historical studies that have sought to capture the institutional dynamics of each 'stage' (see, for instance, Kaijser (2003) and Summerton (1994)). It is easy to see the relevance of this approach when documenting the development of infrastructural arrangements like those of electric power, mains water, telecommunications or networks of road and rail. But what about the laundry?

It is not too difficult to describe what laundering involves. As currently configured, it consists of a sequence of interdependent steps: sorting clothes, putting them in a machine, adding detergent, drying (on a line or in a tumble dryer), ironing, folding and putting away. But as a socio-technical system, it is harder to pin down. To what extent is it defined by what there is to launder, by when and why laundering is undertaken or by the tools and competencies involved? Although all these features change, there are no system builders in sight and no obviously unifying or transparently dominant forces in play. Partly because of this, it is hard to discern or describe specific states and stages of transition.

While laundering has a history, it is not one built around the sequential construction of a readily identifiable system. Some commentators claim that laundry standards have increased over time (Cowan, 1983; Forty, 1986), but there is no clear metric of progression. Looking back, the history of washing clothes is marked by sometimes substantial shifts in what the process is thought to be about and in how it is evaluated. As a result there are different ways of characterizing 'phases' of innovation. One option is to track the history of ideas. Taking this route, Vigarello (1998) distinguishes between periods in which laundering was understood as a means of cleaning the body (changing the shirt reputedly took the place of refreshing and washing oneself in mid-16th-century France (Vigarello, 1998: 58)) or conceptualized as a form of clothing care (in which case, the purpose is to restore clothing that has been contaminated through contact with the body or the outside world (Sams, 2001)). Other histories focus on what there is to wash. Bode (2000), for example, highlights the practical consequences of the transition from linen to cotton while Handley (1999) documents the development of synthetic fabrics and what this entails for the wash (see also Anson, 1988). In detailing the rise and fall of the steam laundry and the privatization of a once collective practice, Mohun (1999) takes yet another approach, this time focusing on the allocation and management of laundry as a form of work. Although the careers of specific devices – the domestic

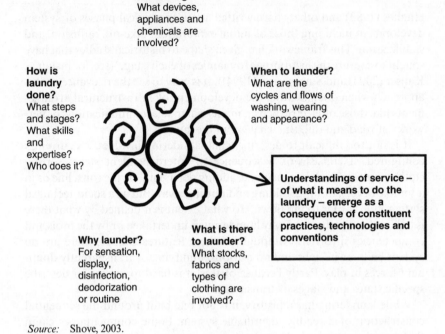

What are the tools of laundering?
What devices, appliances and chemicals are involved?

How is laundry done?
What steps and stages?
What skills and expertise?
Who does it?

When to launder?
What are the cycles and flows of washing, wearing and appearance?

Why launder?
For sensation, display, disinfection, deodorization or routine

What is there to launder?
What stocks, fabrics and types of clothing are involved?

Understandings of service – of what it means to do the laundry – emerge as a consequence of constituent practices, technologies and conventions

Source: Shove, 2003.

Figure 4.1 Laundering as a system of systems

washing machine, the electric iron or the tumble dryer – can be described and analysed in terms of their development, introduction and establishment (Strasser, 1982; Cowan, 1983; Parr, 1999), this terminology does not work for laundering as a whole.

There is no sense in which laundering has become more embedded or entrenched, or in which the practice has stabilized. Instead, the picture is one of a more or less continual de- and restabilization of the different elements that together make up the enterprise as a whole. In fact, one might even conclude that it is this interaction between contributory systems that generates transitions and transformations in the meaning and practice of washing well.

Figure 4.1 illustrates these points, showing laundry to be a system of systems defined and energized by changing relationships between one whorl and another.

Patterns of conceptual and technical path dependency mean that certain features set the scene in which others do (and do not) develop and in practice the contributory whorls are unlikely to be of unequal weight. However, the central point is that we need to analyse the transformation not of one part of the system or another, but of the concepts and understandings of service that emerge through and from the integrative practice of 'doing' the laundry.

In this section I have argued that it is inappropriate to think about the development of laundering, as a whole, in terms of phases and stages of innovation. Other ideas are needed to describe the transformation of what amounts to a system of systems. One possible solution is to position and analyse emergent concepts of service and normal practice in terms of the levels and layers of innovation.

LEVELS AND LAYERS OF INNOVATION

Rip and Kemp (1998) and Rip and Groen (2001) consider the dynamics of innovation with the help of a three-layered model in which the development of novel arrangements and configurations structures and is structured by a patchwork of socio-technical regimes that defines and is in turn defined by the contours of a macro-level socio-technical landscape. This tiered model promises to be of real value in analysing the socio-technical coevolution of what people take to be normal and necessary forms of laundering. In other words, composite concepts of service – of what it is to wash well – appear to have a comfortable and intelligible home at the meso-level plane of the socio-technical regime.

The layered scheme is, for sure, useful in analysing the relationship between developments in washing technology and in users' and consumers' understandings of cleanliness. Framed in this way, an historical review of reports from the British Consumers' Association (from 1957 to 2001) and from the American Consumers Union (from 1937 to 2000) shows how washing machine manufacturers have redefined cleanliness as whiteness rather than an absence of bacteria, and how they and the appliances and categories they produce, have reconstructed laundering around new concepts of freshness and sensation (Shove, 2003). In this respect novel technologies have evidently reconfigured important aspects of the laundry regime.

Other writers describe how new laundry-related technologies are accommodated and appropriated within existing regimes or maybe even landscapes of convention and social order. In the course of her research, Joy Parr found that 'many who owned dryers continued to use their lines regularly even after they had invested in a machine' (Parr, 1999: 264). Rather than replacing the line, the dryer offered distinctive qualities of its own; hence its adoption was not just a matter of trading between convenience, speed, fragrance, texture and ease of ironing. Instead, users' rationales and actions demonstrated the positioning of both devices (and attendant practices) within highly elaborate systems of personal and domestic propriety.

As the preceding paragraphs indicate, it is possible and useful to position and analyse emergent practices of laundering in terms of the 'vertical' interaction between novel configurations, niches, regimes, and landscapes.

But in environmental terms, such an approach misses a hugely important part of the picture. Just seven manufacturers (Weiss and Gross, 1995) make around 70 per cent of all laundry appliances. Although machines are customized and detergents coloured to suit the traditions and preferences of different markets, the mechanisms through which commercial interests colonize meanings of cleanliness are much the same. In the UK, over 90 per cent of households own a washing machine (DEFRA, 2000) and, as hinted at above, those who use such devices are bought into an increasingly dominant technological repertoire. Since similar machines are used and sold around the world, these technologies exert a powerful force for cross-cultural convergence, slicing across what are routinely, if implicitly, analysed as nationally or at least culturally bounded socio-technical regimes and landscapes.

Consistent with its roots in innovation studies, the three-tiered model represents the trajectories of novel arrangements born of and diffused through self-contained environments. But what happens when something like a fully formed washing machine, complete with inscribed concepts of cleanliness, comes crashing into such a scene, as it does in parts of Brazil today? How does the vocabulary of niche, regime and landscape help in making sense of the consequent standardization of laundering and the convergence of attendant notions of service (and resource demand)? Likewise, how might these ideas be used in explaining other codetermining parts of the laundry system like the global proliferation of lightweight machine washable clothing or the valuing of some but not other fragrances (Corbin, 1986)?

These questions remind us that system-relevant, regime-shaping ingredients (that is ideas and/or technologies) circulate between societies. In thinking about innovations of service it is important to analyse processes of cross-cultural regime formation, and the details of configuration and appropriation. In other words, how are standardized washing machines, automobiles, and convenience foods in fact deployed in different societies? As the laundry example suggests, regimes and even landscapes may converge between societies (with potentially damaging environmental consequences) despite exhibiting and being held in place by distinctive, locally and historically-specific path dependencies. Transition theorists have concentrated on specifying movement in the vertical dimension, that is between one level and the next. Partly because of this, they have much less to say about 'horizontal' developments of the type illustrated in Figure 4.2.

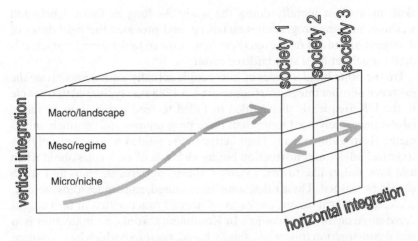

Figure 4.2   Horizontal and vertical dimensions of socio-technical change

As this figure suggests, technological systems carry concepts, classifications, scripts and framings of problems between socio-technical regimes and landscapes. That said, the cultural and environmental ramifications of horizontal trends, like the mass marketing of identical washing machines, are inherently unpredictable given that local contexts of appropriation are of defining importance (Miller, 1998). Writing about the arrival of these appliances in Soweto, Meintjes makes the point that their symbolic and practical significance varies depending upon how they are positioned in terms of existing regimes of cleanliness, gender, identity and propriety (Meintjes, 2001). There is more that could be said about the relation between the horizontal and vertical dimensions of system innovation but for present purposes I want to underline the point that transitions toward sustainability depend partly on system innovation but also on system *integration*.

SYSTEMS OF SYSTEMS AND MODES OF INTEGRATION

What is it that holds systems of laundering together and do modes of integration themselves differ over time and between one society and another?

In some cases there are clear patterns of interdependence. For example, washing machines are currently designed to cope with a contemporary diet of machine washable clothing. As international 'fabric care' symbols indicate, textiles and garments are in turn designed to be machine-washed. These networks of technical coherence have arguably absorbed much of the skill involved in literally doing the wash. As long as fabric labels and washing machine programmes match up, and provided the right doses of detergent are added (and even these now come in tablet form), the scene is pretty much set for a standardized result.

On the other hand, studies of how people actually wash demonstrate the existence of other integrative frameworks. A 1988 survey showed that people in the UK frequently disregarded or failed to read instructions or fabric labels: they rarely used more than three programmes and routinely mixed materials in a single load. Their actions were guided not (or not only) by technical advice and instruction but by all kinds of tacit rules about when and how things like towels, pyjamas, sheets, underwear, jeans and shirts should be washed. These rules, sometimes shared, sometimes idiosyncratic, coalesced to form unique packages of normal practice that in turn engendered an array of 'injunctions'. In Kaufmann's words, an injunction is 'a social construction (historical, family based, personal) which has produced the framework of assumptions triggering the action – the thing that simply has to be done' (Kaufmann, 1998: 21). Triggers like those that prompt people to wash their hair, have a shower, change their shirt or water the lawn are located within the realm of what Giddens (1984) describes as practical consciousness: they are done without further thought or reflection. In arguing that that rules and resources (structures) are sustained and recreated through just such routine accomplishments, Giddens claims that 'the structural properties of social systems are both medium and outcome of the practices they recursively organize' (1984: 25). By implication, transition theorists need to think about how systems are transformed at the level of practical consciousness. Exactly how do new injunctions break through layers of engrained habit and how are novel arrangements normalized?

The notion that people have a 'way' of doing things is useful in conceptualizing the coexistence of stability and change (Lie and Sørensen, 1996; Silverstone *et al.*, 1992). To return to laundering, the very complexity of the system – what is to be washed, when and why – permits extensive customization of practice around a range of standardized products and appliances. Although washing machines are running at an increasingly uniform 40°C all around Britain, each is positioned within a relatively distinctive domestic regime of sequence, timing, purpose, performance, hygiene, freshness and appearance.

What counts as appropriately laundered clothing depends, in this analysis, on the coordination of socio-technical arrangements (in what was earlier described as a 'system of systems') and on their integration through also coordinative frameworks of meaning and practice. Figure 4.3 illustrates some of these features. It shows how technologies and practices are combined in the course of everyday life and it positions personal and

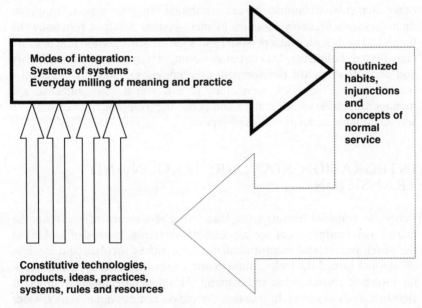

Modes of integration:
Systems of systems
Everyday milling of meaning and practice

Routinized habits, injunctions and concepts of normal service

Constitutive technologies, products, ideas, practices, systems, rules and resources

Source: Shove, 2003.

Figure 4.3 Modes of integration

societal concepts of normal service as the outcome of these integrative processes.

In figuring out how concepts of normal service change, the key questions have to do with how suites of technology interact and how they are actively deployed together. For all its power and relevance, Giddens's theory of structuration takes little heed of the material world or of the tools and technologies of daily life. In Latour's terms, the masses are indeed missing (1992). In trying to fit them back into the scheme, and so find a way of relating technological transitions to transitions of practice and service, I have made much of the notion of integration. I have also distinguished, somewhat tentatively, between two modes: one that has to do with the interdependence of socio-technical systems and another that relates to the way in which things (machines, materials, etc.) are fitted together in the course of daily life. Before drawing this section to a close I want to make one further point.

Washing machines are now positioned as normal and necessary appliances and it is commonly accepted that whatever emerges from them is clean. The washing machine therefore operates as a kind of meta-device: not only is it something to be integrated, it is also something that influences how other elements of laundering are combined. In this respect, appliance manufacturers arguably function as meta-system builders, providing the terms and tools with which personal and societal concepts and practices are constructed. Following this kind of reasoning it may be possible to identify and perhaps shape the development of other comparably pivotal entities (sometimes technologies, sometimes ideas), which also influence the manner and mode of integration and hence the (re)production of more or less sustainable understandings of service.

INTEGRATION, STANDARDIZATION AND TRANSITION

I chose to consider transitions in laundering as a means of exploring the qualities and properties of service-related innovation. Instead of looking at the development and institutionalization of infrastructures and systems of supply I turned the tables round in order to consider the systemic reconfiguration of consumption and demand. This meant dealing with different elements and questions. In practice, people do not consume energy, water or gas. Instead, units of consumption and change relate to the specification and reproduction of normal conventions like those of comfort, copresence or cleanliness. From this perspective, the transition to a more sustainable society is not just a matter of fulfilling stable and taken for granted needs in a more efficient manner. It is, in addition, a question of understanding what people take to be the necessary conditions of everyday life and of understanding how these concepts change and how they are sociotechnically configured.

In this final section I reflect on what this exercise has revealed and what it has added to the discussion of system innovation. I also comment on how policymakers and others might intervene to shape transitions in systems of service and convention.

Taking a long-term view, it is clear that firmly held concepts of normal practice are immensely malleable. A few hundred years ago it was quite common for the children of certain social groups to be sewn into their clothes for the winter. Less than a hundred years ago, 'boiling was considered essential for getting the wash really clean and germ-free' (Zmroczek, 1992: 176). Laundering is today represented as a process of freshening up tired or stale clothing, and who knows what it might become tomorrow. In environmental terms, this essential fluidity is encouraging. There is no inescapable logic of escalatory pressure and no unremittingly path dependent narrative of increasing demand.

At the same time, this apparent lack of path dependency is something of a puzzle. If infrastructures can be usefully analysed with reference to phases of emergence, development and stabilization, how is it that conventions and practices, which might be expected to coevolve with systems of provision, do not fit these frameworks? This was one of the three questions with which I began. Part of the answer lies in the fact that meanings of what it is to wash well are generated through the intersection of a number of interdependent yet relatively self-contained systems. Even if we agree that the details of laundering are but the expression of another 'higher level' system of social order (Douglas, 1984), it is still relevant to notice the changing tools and materials through which distinctions are made real. More than that, it is important to acknowledge that laundering is not only about cleaning and that other contributory 'systems' (of gender, textiles or temporal order) are also involved. As I have described it, laundering is best understood as a system of systems that has an emergent dynamic of its own. Is it then the case that the enterprise of laundering only 'exists' or can only be analysed at the meso- or regime-level, as defined by transition theory? And if so, is this also true of other composite practices? These questions suggest the need for further analysis of distinctively 'regime level' dynamics across different sectors.

When thinking about transitions of service and practice and about forms of regime-level change it is necessary to think about how relatively self-contained systems relate to each other and how they are related together in the course of everyday life. While various authors have written about the 'appropriation' of new technologies within the domestic sphere, few have explicitly attended to the modes and forms of integration that lie behind what people talk of as 'their way' of doing things. This is a significant omission and an important opportunity. For Reckwitz (2002) and Schatski (1996), the existence of a practice depends on the specific interconnectedness of many elements – forms of bodily activities, mental activities, things and their use, background knowledge in the form of understanding, know-how and notions of competence, states of emotion and motivational knowledge (Hand *et al.,* 2003). And for Giddens, the practical consciousness and knowledge of all competent members of society is not 'incidental to the persistent patterning of social life but is integral to it' (1984: 27). Framed in this way, the very business of doing the laundry is a process of temporarily stabilizing and reproducing something like a regime (in terms of transition theory) or society (for Giddens). In emphasizing the constitutive and essentially integrative nature of enterprises like 'laundering', theories of practice have much to offer those interested in the making and breaking of resource-intensive ways of life. What is missing, but what might easily be included, is a more explicit recognition that the contemporary reproduction of routine goes on with and within an also stabilizing, also integrative, environment of coexisting socio-technical systems. In short, a selective blending of theories of practice and of technological transition promises to be of real value in describing and analysing the transformation of entire complexes of activity.

In my brief review of laundering I also noticed the cross-cultural standardization of technologies (and attendant scripts), and the multiple contexts and conditions in which devices and ideas are appropriated. Although theories of technological transition have yet to deal with 'horizontal' mechanisms of regime or landscape-level convergence between societies, similar themes have been addressed by writers interested in the globalization (or Americanization) of commodities and values and in 'local' processes of customization and adaptation (Hannertz, 1996; Burke, 1996). These debates are of some significance when contemplating the possibility of local, national or international transitions toward more sustainable forms of 'normal' practice. This, then, is another arena in which the reach and range of transition theory might be extended.

Re-read in terms of environmental strategy, my discussion of clothes washing generates a number of practical, policy relevant insights. The first concerns the relation between resource and service. Governments and environmental groups typically focus on efficiency and patterns of *resource* consumption, for instance, introducing energy labelling schemes, offering consumer advice, setting technical regulations, fostering the development of more efficient appliance standards, facilitating investment in renewable energy and so on. Meanwhile, commercial activity revolves around the construction of new concepts of *service*: new ideas of hygiene, new concepts of 'freshly laundered' clothing, new visions of domesticity and propriety.

This split between resource and service has important implications for the types of actors involved in different forms of system innovation. Though willing to advise consumers to wash a full load at a time, national policymakers rarely venture into the domain of fashion, appearance and body odour. That is not to say that governments have no interest in the provision and social construction of cleanliness. As histories of sanitation and public health reveal (Melosi, 2000; Ogle, 1996; Tomes, 1998), such institutions have been extremely important in promoting technologies and ideologies that, in combination, sustain what Cowan describes as the 'senseless tyranny of spotless shirts' (Cowan, 1983: 216). Even so, contemporary policymakers are unlikely to get involved in directly specifying the 'sniff test' despite the fact that this measure influences the amount of washing done and hence the consumption of energy and water. Because of this reluctance, a good part of the potential for system innovation lies beyond their normal reach.

On the other hand, there is some connection between the definition of service and how it is achieved. The fact that boiling laundry is no longer normal practice, and that the majority of UK laundry is now done at 40°C is a good example. Since washing machines have never been able to sustain a prolonged simmering of the kind traditionally required for a 'proper' wash, the first manufacturers introduced and established other criteria of cleanliness, measures of whiteness being the most common. With whiteness, not heat, as the point of reference a more environmentally benign, or at least energy efficient, range of technological options came into view, including those that depend on the use of detergents designed to operate at low temperatures. Because manufacturers have been obliged and able to dissociate laundering from disinfection, governments have been able to push for more resource efficiency. In this instance, resource efficiencies have gone hand in hand with the redefinition of normal practice.

It is none the less clear that commercial rather than government organizations dominate the specification of service. This has further consequences for the scope and scale of possible intervention. Major appliance manufacturers and detergent producers concentrate on constructing and developing mass markets around the world. That is the lateral arena in which they operate. By comparison, resource-based initiatives are generally national, or at best European. This is important in considering the type of effort that might be made to introduce and engender new practice. There is a tendency to think about ways of engineering and managing *resource-*based system transition through the careful cultivation of socio-technical experiments located within protected spaces and strategic niches. Approached in this way, the policy challenge is to build the networks and alliances required to gradually embed novel arrangements into the regimes and landscapes of wider society.

But in so far as new concepts of *service* are deliberately fabricated, their development appears to involve the rapid diffusion of convention leaping, culture defying commodities, use of which draws consumers into new paradigms (in this case of laundering). What part do policymakers have to play in this alternative dynamic of typically transnational service specification? Do they contribute at all to the formation of collective conventions of ordinary practice and if so, how? Never mind government involvement in steering modes of provision, or in managing markets and forms of system innovation, how do national and international modes of policy making shape and structure the formation of routinized and taken for granted expectations, conventions and habits? Following this question through, and doing so with respect to mobility, to diet, to personal hygiene or to laundering, would help determine both the limits and possibilities of engendering regime and landscape-level transitions toward sustainability.

REFERENCES

American Water Works Association (1999), *Residential End Uses of Water*, Denver, CO: American Water Works Association, extracts available at http://www. waterwiser.org/template.cfm?page1=awwarf/wateruse&page2=books_menu2, accessed 21 March, 2001.

Anson, R. (1988), 'Know your labels', *Manufacturing Clothier*, **69** (11), November, 47–52.

Association of Home Appliance Manufacturers (AHAM) (2000), *Fact Book 2000*, Washington, DC: AHAM.

Biermeyer, P. (2001), 'Coming changes in the U.S. clothes washer market', Lawrence Berkeley National Laboratory, unpublished paper, Berkeley, CA.

Bode, M. (2000), 'Clothing Care Function: Germany', Faculty of Technology Policy and Management, Delft University of Technology, *SusHouse Project final report*.

Bourdieu, P. (1984), *Distinction: A Social Critique of Judgement and Taste*, London: Routledge.

Burke, T. (1996), *Lifebuoy Men, Lux Women: Commodification, Consumption and Cleanliness in Modern Zimbabwe*, London: Leicester University Press.

Corbin, A. (1986), *The Foul and the Fragrant*, Leamington Spa: Berg.

Cowan, R.S. (1983), *More Work for Mother: The Ironies of Household Technology from the Open Hearth to the Microwave*, New York: Basic Books.

de Dear, R. (1994), 'Outdoor climatic influences on indoor thermal comfort requirements', in N. Oseland and M. Humphreys (eds), *Thermal Comfort: Past, Present and Future*, Watford: Building Research Establishment.

Department of the Environment, Transport and the Regions (DEFRA) (2000), 'Washing machines in the United Kingdom: a sector review paper on projected energy consumption for the Department of the Environment, Transport and the Regions', WTWM4031, October 2000, http://www.mtprog.com/wet/wash_mach/wtwmdown4031.pdf (accessed 14 April, 2002).

Douglas, M. (1984), *Purity and Danger: An Analysis of the Concepts of Pollution and Taboo*, London: Routledge.

Douglas, M., and B. Isherwood (1996), *The World of Goods: Towards an Anthropology of Consumption*, London: Routledge.

Environment Agency (2002), 'Using Water Wisely', http://www.doingyourbit.org.uk/yourbit/index.html.

Forty, A. (1986), *Objects of Desire: Design and Society Since 1750*, London: Thames and Hudson.

Giddens, A. (1984), *The Constitution of Society*, Cambridge: Polity Press.

Hand, M., E. Shove and D. Southerton (2003), 'Explaining daily showering: a discussion of policy and practice', ESRC Sustainable Technologies Programme working paper series, available at http://www.sustainabletechnologies.ac.uk/PDF/Working%20papers/105a.pdf.

Handley, S. (1999), *Nylon: The Manmade Fashion Revolution*, London: Bloomsbury.

Hannerz, U. (1996), *Transnational Connections*, London: Routledge.

Hobson, K. (2001), 'Sustainable lifestyles: rethinking barriers and behaviour change', in M. Cohen and J. Murphy (eds), *Exploring Sustainable Consumption: Environmental Policy and the Social Sciences*, Amsterdam: Pergamon.

Hughes T.P. (1983), *Networks of Power*, Baltimore, MD: John Hopkins University Press.

Kaijser, A. (2003), 'Redirecting infrasystems towards sustainability. What can we learn from History?' in A. Biel, B. Hansson and M. Martensson (eds), *Individual and Structural Determinants of Environmental Practice*, Aldershot: Ashgate Environmental Policy and Practice.

Kaufmann, J.C. (1998), *Dirty Linen: Couples and Their Laundry*, London: Middlesex University Press.

Latour, B. (1992), 'Where are the missing masses? The sociology of a few mundane artifacts', in W. Bijker and J. Law (eds), *Shaping Technology/Building Society*, Cambridge, MA: MIT Press.

Lie, M., and K. Sørensen (1996), *Making Technology Our Own? Domesticating Technology into Everyday Life*, Oslo: Scandinavian University Press.

Meintjes, H. (2001), 'Washing machines make lazy women: domestic appliances and the negotiation of women's propriety in Soweto', *Journal of Material Culture*, **6** (3), 345–63.

Melosi, M. (2000), *The Sanitary City: Urban Infrastructure in America from Colonial Times to The Present*, Baltimore, MD: Johns Hopkins University Press.

Miller, D. (1998), 'Coca-Cola: a black sweet drink from Trinidad', in D. Miller (ed.), *Material Cultures: Why Some Things Matter*, London: UCL Press.

Mohun, A. (1999), *Steam Laundries*, Baltimore, MD: Johns Hopkins University Press.

Ogle, M. (1996), *All the Modern Conveniences: American Household Plumbing 1840–1890*, Baltimore, MD: Johns Hopkins University Press.

Parr, J. (1999), *Domestic Goods: The Material, the Moral, and the Economic in the Postwar Years*, Toronto: University of Toronto Press.

Reckwitz, A. (2002), 'Toward a theory of social practices: a development in culturalist theorizing', *European Journal of Social Theory*, **5** (2), 243–63.

Rip, A., and A. Groen (2001), 'Many visible hands', in R. Coombs, K. Green, V. Walsh and A. Richards (eds), *Technology and the Market: Demands, Users and Innovation*, Cheltenham: Edward Elgar.

Rip, A., and R. Kemp (1998), 'Technological change', in S. Rayner and E. Malone (eds), *Human Choice and Climate Change: Resources and Technology*, vol 2, Columbus, OH: Battelle Press.

Sams, P. (2001), 'Clothes care – sending the right signals', presentation to the International Appliance Technical Conference, Columbus, OH, 27 March.

Schatski, T. (1996), *Social Practices: a Wittgensteinian Approach to Human Activity and the Social*, Cambridge: Cambridge University Press.

Shove, E. (2003), *Comfort, Cleanliness and Convenience: The Social Organization of Normality*, Oxford: Berg.

Silverstone, R., E. Hirsch and D. Morley (1992), 'Introduction', in R. Silverstone and E. Hirsch (eds), *Consuming Technologies*, London: Routledge.

Spaargaren, G. (1997), *The Ecological Modernisation of Production and Consumption: Essays in Environmental Sociology*, Wageningen: Landbouw Universitiet.

Strasser, S. (1982), *Never Done*, New York: Pantheon.

Summerton, J. (1994), *Changing Large Technical Systems*, Boulder, CO: Westview Press.

Tomes, N. (1998), *The Gospel of Germs: Men, Women, and the Microbe in American Life*, Cambridge, MA: Harvard University Press.

Vigarello, G. (1998), *Concepts of Cleanliness: Changing Attitudes in France Since the Middle Ages*, Cambridge: Cambridge University Press.

Weiss, D., and A. Gross (1995), 'Industry corner: major household appliances in Western Europe', *Business Economics*, July **30** (3), 67–72.
Zmroczek, C. (1992), 'Dirty linen: Women, class and washing machines, 1920s–1960s', *Women's Studies International Forum*, **15** (2), 173–85.

PART II

Empirical examples of transitions

5. A transition towards sustainability in the Swiss agri-food chain (1970–2000): using and improving the multi-level perspective

Frank-Martin Belz

INTRODUCTION[1]

This chapter presents a case study of transitions, namely the shift from industrialized agriculture to sustainable agriculture in Switzerland in the period 1970–2000. This shift is not yet completed, but has progressed a long way. In the beginning of the 21st century, Switzerland is one of the leading Western countries in sustainable agriculture, balancing economic, ecological and social dimensions. Most of the arable land is cultivated according to ecological criteria, a large proportion according to integrated production and organic farming (see Figure 5.1). I will briefly describe the contrast between the three agricultural practices as a first mapping of the transition.

The industrialization of agriculture began in the first half of the 20th century and spread all over Western countries after the Second World War. In *industrialized agriculture* much use is made of agrochemicals (fertilizers, pesticides) and mechanization, which maximize yield per acre and revenues. In order to reduce cost there is a high degree of specialization (for example, plant production, animal farms) and labour is substituted with technology. Agricultural products are supplied to cooperatives or to food retail chains. There is hardly any direct contact between the producer and the consumer.

Organic farming takes a holistic point of view and respects the principles of nature. The main aim of organic farming is to maintain and increase long-term fertility and biological activity of soils using locally adapted biological and mechanical methods as opposed to reliance on external inputs. Another aim is to maintain and encourage agricultural and natural biodiversity on the farm and surroundings, and to promote the sustainable use of water and all life therein. The guiding principle is to work compatibly

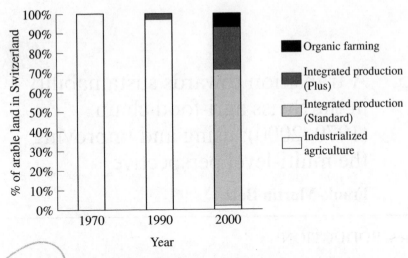

Figure 5.1   *A transition in the Swiss agri-food chain, 1970–2000*

with natural cycles and processes in soil, plants and animals. A characteristic of organic farming is that the use of chemical fertilizers and pesticides
is not allowed. The yield per acre is not maximized but optimized under
special consideration of ecological aspects. In general, organic farming is
more labour-intensive than industrialized agriculture. Another characteristic is that organic farming is primarily local or national, both in production and distribution. Organic food products are sold via various channels.
Direct marketing, that is, the contact between producers and consumers,
plays an important role.

    Integrated production (IP) is a 'third way' between industrialized agri-
culture and organic farming. There are two standards, which can be
differentiated: high ecological standards (IP plus) and minimum ecological
standards (IP standard). Generally, integrated production pursues
ecological objectives in an economically viable way. Similar to organic
farming, integrated production aims at maintaining and increasing long-
term fertility and biological activity of soils using biological and mechanical methods as opposed to reliance on inputs. However, integrated
production allows a limited use of selected chemical fertilizers and pesticides according to the motto: 'As little as possible and as much as necessary'. Prior to any use of fertilizers and pesticides the fertility of the soil is
analysed. Restrictive rules for different plant cultivations like wheat, pota-
toes and rape have to be followed (such as mechanical instead of chemical
weed control). Integrated production is more labour-intensive than industrialized agriculture but less so than organic farming.

Comparative life cycle and soil analysis show that integrated production and organic farming are superior to industrialized agriculture from an ecological point of view (Niggli *et al.*, 1995; Jungbluth, 2000). Organic farming is better than integrated production in ecological terms, but the difference is not so great, especially with IP plus.

This brief description indicates that the (ongoing) transition involves changes in user practices, guiding principles, social networks of production, distribution and use. The main question of the chapter is the following: how did the transition towards sustainability in the Swiss agri-food chain come about?

To describe and analyse this transition, the multi-level perspective is used as described by Geels in Chapter 2. At the end of the chapter I will make additions to this perspective. The empirical case study mainly focuses on the first stage of the agri-food chain, that is, sustainable innovations in agriculture. Processing, packaging, transportation and consumption of food products are discussed in connection with organic farming and integrated production. The focus is on the period between 1970 and 2000, when major changes took place in Swiss agriculture. The case study deals with domestic food products and does not include food imports.[2] The empirical data are based on several sources: semi-structured, open interviews with experts, written documents, archival records, physical artefacts, and participatory as well as non-participatory observations.

The following section briefly sketches the multi-level perspective, which will be used. Then two subsequent sections describe the transition according to two periods (1970–1990 and 1990–2000). In the final section the empirical case study is analysed and discussed.

THE MULTI-LEVEL PERSPECTIVE

I will only briefly sketch the multi-level perspective, because it has been described elsewhere in further detail (Chapter 2 in this book; Rip and Kemp, 1998; Kemp, Rip and Schot, 2001; Geels, 2002). The multi-level perspective distinguishes three levels. The *meso-level* of *socio-technical regimes* accounts for stability of existing systems. It includes technologies, user practices, social networks, regulations, infrastructure, techno-scientific knowledge and cultural values and guiding principles. The regime is carried by a range of actors and social groups, such as scientists, manufacturers/producers, suppliers, policymakers, users, distribution networks. The socio-technical regime is stable because the multiple dimensions and activities of multiple groups are aligned. The *micro-level* of *technological niches* is the locus for radical innovations. Because radical innovations cannot immediately survive in the mainstream market, they need some protection. This can be in the form of government subsidies, by market niches with special selection criteria or by support by a dedicated group of people (enthusiasts, amateurs, pioneers). Niches thus form incubation rooms for radical innovations. As long as the radical innovation has not stabilized, all kinds of learning and articulation processes take place in the niche, about technical specifications, user preferences, symbolic meaning, supply and distribution networks. There is also a *macro-level*, the *socio-technical landscape*, consisting of external factors, which influence dynamics in regimes and niches (e.g. culture, macropolitics, macroeconomics).

The nested character of these levels means that regimes are embedded within landscapes and niches within regimes. New technologies and practices are initially developed within the framework of the existing regime and landscape, but often face a mismatch with the established economic, social and/or political dimensions (Freeman and Perez, 1988). Niches play a crucial role in transitions, in the sense that they form the seeds for change. The crux of the multi-level perspective is that transitions come about through the interplay between dynamics at multiple levels and in several phases.

In the first phase, radical novelties emerge in niches in the context of existing regime and landscape developments, with their specific problems, rules and capabilities. The novelty links up with values at the landscape-level or with small problems in regimes. Actors improvise, engage in experiments to work out the best design and find out what users want.

In the second phase the novelty is used in small market niches. Gradually a dedicated community emerges, directing their activities to the improvement of the new technology and practice. Members of the community meet at conferences, discuss problem agendas, promising findings and search heuristics. This phase results in a stabilization of rules, such as a dominant design, an articulation of user preferences. The new technology and practice gradually improve, as a result of learning processes.

The third phase is characterized by wide diffusion, breakthrough of new technology and competition with the established regime. There will be internal drivers for such breakthrough. For instance, actors with interests may push for further expansion of the technology (strategic games). Or price/performance dimensions gradually improve. But the key point of the multi-level perspective is that transitions occur as the outcome of linkages between developments at multiple levels. Radical innovations can break from the niche-level when ongoing processes at regime and landscape levels create a window of opportunity. There may be changes at the landscape level, which put pressure on the regime. There may be internal problems in the regime, which cannot be met with the available technology. There may be negative externalities, which are placed on the problem agenda by 'outsiders', such as societal pressure groups. Or there may be tensions within the existing regime, because of changing user preferences or stricter regulations. Changing user preferences may lead to new markets, to which new technologies may link up. In sum, the breakthrough of radical innovations depends both on internal drivers and niche-processes and on external developments in regimes and landscapes.

In the fourth phase the new technology replaces the old regime. The creation of a new socio-technical regime takes time. Incumbent actors may stick to the old technologies, or try to defend themselves, for example, by improving the existing technology, political lobbying or evasion to other markets.

I will use the multi-level perspective to describe and analyse the transition in Swiss agriculture. In each empirical section I will first describe the existing regime, and then turn to the niches. Landscape developments will be mixed in to highlight their influence on niche- and regime-dynamics.

First Phase in the Transition (1970–90): Emergence of Niches in a Stable Regime

Industrialized agriculture had been the dominant socio-technical regime in Swiss agriculture. It was formed after the Second World War when a high degree of self-sufficiency and low dependency on food imports were important objectives of Swiss agricultural policy. To provide the Swiss population with a sufficient amount of healthy nutrition, the government was willing to pay income subsidies for farmers and guarantee fixed minimum prices for agricultural products. The subsidies and fixed prices formed strong economic incentives for the farmers to increase productivity by means of chemical fertilizers and pesticides as well as modern technology. These developments were widely supported by the Swiss population, because they were in line with the common beliefs of economic growth, material wealth and technological development. In the 1970s and 1980s, some problems emerged in the regime. The maximization of yields and profits resulted in overproduction on the one hand and negative ecological and social side effects on the other. Attention for negative ecological effects was stimulated by a wider landscape development, namely the emergence of the environmental movement. For instance, the book *Silent Spring* (Carson, 1962) received much attention and caused societal concern. It was also in the 1960s that the *Konsumentinnen-Forum*, an important Swiss consumer organization, started an information campaign on the excessive use of chemical fertilizers and pesticides in Swiss agriculture. They broke a 'taboo' and were criticized by Swiss farmers and politicians. However, the bad publicity put pressure on the dominant socio-technological regime. Negative social effects took the form of a decrease in the numbers of farmers and the loss of (agri)cultural heritage. The landscape developments and the criticism on industrialized agriculture created windows of opportunities for the emergence of two niches: organic farming and integrated production.

The niche of organic farming had already existed since the first half of the 20th century, but it was very small. The anthroposophist Rudolf Steiner (1861–1925) was an early critic of the industrialization of agriculture. His anthroposophist ideas and concepts were the philosophical background of biological-dynamic farming. The politician Hans Müller (1894–1965) gave impetus to organic-biological farming in Switzerland during the 1930s and 1940s. After the Second World War, organic farming was not given any attention by Swiss policy makers and the wider public. Organic farming was contrary to the main principles of economic growth and technological development. However, in the 1970s organic farming became attractive for the alternative youth and counter-culture. A number of idealists moved to the rural areas to fulfil their alternative lifestyle in communes and started with organic farming. In 1973 organic farmers, critical scientists and politicians set up a special research institute of organic farming to find and articulate best practices, and make knowledge more widely accessible. They also formulated written principles and rules for organic farming, based on practical experiences by the early pioneers. Additionally the institute did scientific research and developed new rules for the breeding, production, processing and packaging of organic food products. The aims, principles and measures were not decided in a top-down fashion, but rather in a process of trial and error, learning and negotiation.

At that time, organic farmers were still a small social network. Many organic farmers in Switzerland knew each other personally. In 1980 formalization and professionalization occurred with the founding of the association of Swiss organic farming organizations, later called Bio Suisse. This association represented and promoted the interests of organic farmers. During the 1980s a slow, but steady growth of organic farming took place. But the niche still remained small. In 1990 there were around 900 Swiss organic farmers as compared to approximately 90 000 farmers in industrialized agriculture (1 per cent). Until the end of the 1980s the Swiss organic farmers and their organizations did not get any formal support or subsidies from the Swiss government. The niche was carried out mainly by pioneers and enthusiasts. Organic farmers were considered as outsiders by the majority of politicians and population. Not just the producers, but also the consumers of organic food products were regarded as 'strange' and 'sectarian'. This symbolic image and cultural interpretation hindered further diffusion. Organic food products were not available in conventional food stores. Direct marketing played an important role in organic farming, for example, sales ex-farm, weekly markets in towns and cities, as well as home delivery. The personal contact between the farmers and consumers built up trust, which was important in the context of organic food products.[3] Organic food stores, third world stores and reform stores were other distribution channels for organic farmers. For these distribution channels it was essential to prove that the agricultural products were indeed organic. In 1981 Bio Suisse introduced the 'bud' as the official label for certified organic food products in Switzerland, which helped potential buyers to recognize organic food products and differentiate between certified organic food products and fraud ones. During the 1980s the 'bud' was only known to a small amount of green consumers. In general, the prices of organic food products were (much) higher than the prices of conventional food. But a small group of people had a willingness to pay premium prices for organic products. Often the supply of organic food products was limited due to seasonality and region.

Another emerging niche was integrated production, which was mainly set up by Migros, the largest Swiss food retailer, and a cooperative with a long-term commitment for social and ecological issues. A large proportion of Swiss households are members of the cooperative. The membership is free of charge and has some benefits like the weekly magazine 'Brückenbauer' and special offers. In 1970 the Migros household members voted in favour of a petition for healthy food, which was free of chemical residuals. The Migros management took the concern of their members seriously. One option for them was to support and enhance organic farming. However, back in 1970 there was just a small number of organic farmers, who were tied up in local networks and could not provide the quantities of food Migros needed. Besides, organic farming had an alternative symbolic image, which deterred Migros.

Another option was to develop a new kind of agriculture, which used as few chemicals as possible and as much as necessary. The Migros management went for the latter option and decided to build their own network of consultants, rules and programme to avoid wearisome never-ending discussions with independent specialists in the area of agricultural production and research (Gugelmann, 1988: 16). In the beginning of the 1970s Migros hired agricultural experts to set up standards for integrated production in cooperation with a selected number of farmers, which were willing to participate in the so-called 'M-Sano-programme'.[4] This approach was innovative in the sense that Migros took responsibility for the whole agri-food chain and set up new standards, which were quite different from industrialized agriculture. Important aims of the Migros engagement were to reduce the use of chemicals, to integrate ecological criteria into the whole agri-food chain, and to provide the customer with high-quality, healthy food. The Migros agricultural experts advised the M-Sano-farmers and controlled them on a regular basis. In 1974 the first M-Sano-products were introduced in the market. During the 1970s and 1980s Migros continuously expanded the M-Sano-programme for vegetables and fruits. In 1990 there were around 1 800 M-Sano-producers, double the amount of organic farmers, but still a small number compared to the total of 90 000 conventional farmers.

In sum, by 1990 the dominant socio-technological regime of industrialized agriculture was still stable, but under the surface, new practices had emerged in niches. The new practices did not yet break through. The two niches had low visibility, but some degree of stabilization had already occurred. All kinds of rules had been articulated (such as quality labels, certificates, best practices) and social networks for production, distribution and use had been formed. While organic farming was rooted in social movements and followed a bottom-up approach, integrated production was initiated and put forth by a single actor in a top-down fashion with some cooperative elements, that is, close cooperation with selected M-Sano farmers.

Second Phase in the Transition (1990–2000): Breakthrough of Niches and Transformation of the Regime

In 1986 two major events happened, which changed the landscape on the macro level. One event was the Chernobyl disaster, which shook popular belief in the safety of nuclear plants and modern technology. The second incident was the Sandoz accident in Schweizerhalle, which released poisonous gases into the air and agro-chemicals into the river Rhine. The two ecological disasters led to a significant change in cultural values, namely a rise in environmental consciousness in the Swiss population. These macro-developments put pressure on the established agricultural regime. Actors who had upheld the industrial production regime began to change their perceptions, preferences and strategies. The Swiss population was no longer willing to subsidize a kind of agriculture which led to overproduction and ecological problems (Schweizerischer Bundesrat, 1992: 283–92). For example, in 1986 the Swiss population rejected a law to support the domestic sugar production. For the first time in the history of Switzerland, the population did not vote in favour of supporting industrialized farmers. The long-term social contract between the Swiss population and the farmers began to fall apart (Bundesamt für Umwelt, Wald und Landschaft 2002: 196).

The macro-change in cultural values led to a change in user preferences in the agricultural regime. Picking up on these new consumer markets, large retailers and production firms began to change their strategies towards ecological food products. For instance, Toni Basle launched Bio-yoghurt and Baer the 'Eco-Tomme' (Belz, 1995: 104–5). Both the Bio-yoghurt and the

Bio-soft cheese were distributed and marketed via organic farms retailers and speciality shops as well as conventional food retailers (Migros, Coop and independent food retailers). The introduction of organic food products by a well-known, highly reputed company and brand like Baer had a great influence on the perceptions of Swiss consumers, decision makers in Swiss retailing, agriculture and agricultural politics. Organic production gradually was taken more seriously.

On the international level there were also two other developments, which put pressure on the existing regime: the European integration and the Uruguay negotiations of GATT, which demanded the reduction of the agricultural subsidies and the stepwise liberalization of the agricultural and food markets (Schweizerischer Bundesrat, 1992: 292–318). In the beginning of the 1990s it became obvious that a change in Swiss agricultural policy was badly needed. The question was the direction and the intensity of the change in Swiss agriculture. The issue was widely discussed and two different initiatives were put forward. Such bottom-up initiatives are characteristic of Swiss democratic culture.[5]

The first was the Popular Initiative for an Ecological and Productive Rural Agriculture, put forward in February 1990 by the Swiss union of farmers. The initiative purported to embody the multiple functions of agriculture and corresponding measures in the Swiss constitution. The main concern of the initiative was the jeopardy of the existence of Swiss farmers due to national and international pressures. The second initiative was 'Farmers and Consumers – For an Ecological Agriculture', launched in December 1991 by a committee of 23 different consumer, environmental and animal organizations. The main concern of the initiative was the natural environment. Moreover, the initiative suggested social measures to balance the income differences in Swiss agriculture.

Both initiatives were discussed in the national parliament and an alternative suggestion was made. Since Swiss agriculture would not be able to compete on prices in the international markets, parliament and the government proposed to pursue a high quality strategy and make a transformation from industrialized to ecological agriculture. Key elements were the reduction of income subsidies in line with GATT and financial compensations for ecological contributions. In a plebiscite the Swiss population rejected the two initiatives and accepted the proposal made by the government. This can be seen as a new social contract between Swiss farmers and the population, aimed at sustainability. As a result of these changes, the socio-technological regime of industrial production destabilized, creating opportunities for the breakthrough of niches.

A new agricultural law was implemented in 1993, which supported ecological forms of agriculture, namely organic farming and integrated production. According to article 31b of the new agriculture law, compensation was paid to these two forms of agriculture. The ecological compensation supported farmers who already practised organic farming and integrated production and was an economic incentive for conventional farmers to convert, something which most of them did in subsequent years. Some conventional farmers shifted to organic farming, but most of them began to practise integrated production. Some of the latter used their new experiences to make a further shift to organic farming. The ecological compensation for organic farming was higher than for integrated farming. But integrated production as defined by the government had lower standards of integrated production as implemented by Migros in the M-Sano-programme. This resulted in three different kinds of ecological farming: (i) organic farming as the highest ecological standard, (ii) integrated production set up by Migros as a high ecological standard (IP plus), (iii) integrated production as defined by the government as a minimum ecological standard (IP standard).

The disintegration of the industrial production regime created opportunities for the niches of integration production and organic farming. These niches became part of strategic games and alliances between actors. Food retail chains became especially involved in strategic positioning regarding both niches. This positioning also involved finding answers to further questions. How should the new kind of food products be positioned; in the high-quality segment with premium prices, or in the upper-middle segment with higher prices? What would be the value added? How should it be communicated? Which kind of and how much information did the consumers need? Such questions were answered through trial and error and muddling through. On the one hand the involvement of more actors in the niches created complications, but, on the other it led to stronger social networks, bandwagon effects and wider diffusion of the niches.

The niche of integrated production grew considerably during the 1990s. One of the main reasons for its rise was that Swiss farmers had to fulfil the minimum standards of integrated production according to article 31b of the agricultural law to receive compensation. That was a strong incentive for the large majority of farmers to switch to this form of integrated production. In 2000 around 50 000 farmers (70 per cent) cultivated their arable land according to the minimum standards of integrated production (IP standard), another 15 000 farmers (20 per cent) to the higher standards of integrated production (IP plus) as defined by IP Suisse, which was founded in 1994. A problem for this niche was that the moderate use of chemicals and the different kinds of integrated production were difficult to communicate to the consumer. In that respect organic farming is more logical and easier to communicate. Besides, organic farmers were controlled and certified by an independent third party, which contributed to the high credibility of the 'bud' and organic farming in Switzerland.

The unclear legal situation contributed to the confusion of Swiss consumers. In the mid-1990s many consumers confused organic farming and integrated production. An empirical study showed that even the salespersons in the food retail stores were not able to indicate the differences between organic farming and integrated production (Belz, 1997). The coexistence of different kinds of ecological farming, retail brands and labels led to confusion rather than orientation. The confusion about definitions and standards thus created uncertainty. Existing policies did not help much in this respect. The official agriculture policy subsumed organic farming and integrated production under the generic term of ecological food products.

To provide more clarity, policymakers wanted to make a new law, which would give consumers more guidance. This led to much discussion about the definition of ecological food products. Did ecological food products include organic farming as well as integrated production? Or were ecological food products equivalent to organic food products? Migros and the Swiss union of farmers supported the first, broader definition (ecological food products included products of organic farming and integrated production), whereas the Coop, Bio Suisse, environmental and consumer organizations were in favour of the second, narrower definition (only organic food products were ecological). Eventually, the Swiss government went along with the European regulation on organic farming and defined ecological food products in a narrow sense. The new regulation on organic farming and marking of organic food products was introduced in 1997. As a result, it was no longer possible to promote integrated production with an ecological label. Migros, one of the main protagonists of integrated production, had to give up the M-Sano-brand and stop the promotion of M-Sano as an ecological programme.

The niche of organic farming was stimulated by the strategic involvement from Coop, the second largest retail chain in Switzerland. To position itself Coop launched the Naturaplan in spring 1993 (Belz, 1999: 178–85; Villiger, 2000: 223–47). The Coop Naturaplan was an assortment of organic food products. The marketing manager of Coop announced in the press conference at the start of the Coop Naturaplan: 'We do not plan to introduce some exotic organic food products in areas with marginal revenues. We plan to offer a wide range of organic food products in basic food areas with high revenues.' Thus, Coop did not go for small market niches, but aimed at strong market positions in important product categories such as milk, dairy, bread, vegetables and fruits. To quantify the strategy, Coop announced, that they wanted to reach a revenue of 400 million Swiss francs in 1999 (approximately 260 million euros), which is the equivalent of 20–30 per cent of the relevant product categories of the Coop food range. The announcement and the quantification by the Coop management led to significant changes in perception of the Coop employees in purchasing and marketing. Organic food products were no longer regarded as niche products. Organic farming was recognized by conventional food retailing. From the perspective of Coop, organic food was seen as an important segment with high growth potentials.

The involvement of Coop led to frictions within the organic farming niche. In Bio Suisse, the association of Swiss farming organizations, there were two opposite groups: the fundamentalists and the pragmatists. The fundamentalists were against the partnership with conventional food retail chains such as Coop. They were afraid that organic farmers would become dependent on the large food retail chains and that prices would go down. The pragmatists aimed at the diffusion of organic food products from the eco-niche to the ecological mass market. Consequently, they were in favour of opening up, cooperating with new partners like Coop and further developing the market for organic food products. Eventually, the pragmatists won. The cooperation between Coop and Bio Suisse was fruitful for both actors. Bio Suisse could see the niche grow, by taking advantage of the Coop's sales and distribution network. And Coop could make use of the organic label Bio Suisse had developed, the 'bud', creating more credibility for its products. Coop thus strengthened its ecological image, allowing the firm to better position itself on the market. Coop was able to acquire new customers. The increase in revenues and market shares of Coop during the second half of the 1990s was mainly induced by the growth of the Coop Naturaplan. The niche of organic farming could expand because many Swiss consumers were willing to pay a higher price for organic food products, as long as they met other buying criteria such as high quality, good taste, freshness, and convenience.

The growing success of the Coop Naturaplan, the regulation on organic farming, and the marking of organic food products triggered Migros to introduce M-Bio in 1997, an ecological retail brand of organic food products. In order to avoid a 'me-too' strategy and stay independent, Migros decided against the use of the 'bud' label. Since Migros is one of the best-known and highly reputed brands in Switzerland with an excellent social and ecological record, it was a viable strategy. In the following years Migros extended the product range of M-Bio, pushing the programme in promotion and at the point of sale. During the same period other food retail chains like Primo/Visavis ('Bio Domaine') and Spar ('Natur Pur') also launched ecological retail brands, thus creating a bandwagon effect. In 2002 the total revenue of organic food was over one billion Swiss francs (about 650 million euros), which is between 5 and 6 per cent of the domestic food production and around 3 per cent of the total Swiss food market (including imports). Coop exploited first mover advantages and remained a strong leader in this market sector with a revenue over 500 million Swiss francs (about 325 million euros) in 2002, which is the equivalent of a 50 per cent share in the organic food sector (Coop, 2003).

In sum, by 2000 the established socio-technological regime of industrialized agriculture had fallen apart, and a new one was in the making. Although it is clear that the new regime will be organized around ecological principles, there is not yet final certainty about the exact form of the new regime. At the moment, the great majority of Swiss food products are cultivated using integrated production methods. But organic farming has become a substantial market niche, which receives a lot of attention. Both agricultural practices now receive ecological compensation. But what will happen in the future, if agricultural budgets become tighter? Will organic farming still receive higher ecological compensation than integrated production? Will the compensation to integrated production be cut altogether since it is now regarded as the minimum standard? Organic farming could allow for further market differentiation strategies based on environmental sustainability, whereas this is not the case for integrated production. The regulation on organic farming and marking of organic food products in 1997 decided this battle. This means that organic farming may grow further at the expense of integrated production in the coming years.

Analysis and Discussion

Which insights and lessons can we derive from the case study, which may have wider relevance for other transitions?

A first point is that the case study shows the applicability and fruitfulness of the multi-level perspective. It helps to understand the complexity of the real-world developments, which is the strength and at the same time the weakness of the multi-level perspective (Geels, 2002: 1273). It is truly interdisciplinary. Single disciplines tend to focus on one aspect and explain the transition from that point of view. For example, marketing studies would emphasize the important role of food retail chains as 'ecological gatekeepers' in the agri-food chain. This is just part of the whole story. Using the multi-level perspective it becomes clear that system innovations cannot be pushed by a single actor or be triggered by a single event. Such a transition is the result of linkages between developments at multiple levels. There were several events and changes on the landscape level which put pressure on the socio-technological regime, such as the incidents in Chernobyl and Schweizerhalle, the increasing environmental consciousness of the Swiss population and the GATT negotiations. The internal and external pressures on the regime of industrialized agriculture led to changes in user preferences, and the policy and strategy of retail chains. Taking advantage of the windows of opportunity, the niches of organic farming and integrated production entered mainstream markets, which led to further changes in perceptions and strategies.

A second point is that the transformation of the regime in the second phase of the transition (1990–2000) would not have occurred and cannot be fully understood without the emergence of niches in the first phase of the transition (1970–90). Major societal changes do not 'fall from the sky', but build upon earlier developments (accumulation). The radical innovations had a hard time breaking out of the niche-level in the 1970s and 1980s. The roots of organic farming go back to the beginning of the 20th century, when the anthroposophist Rudolph Steiner and his followers criticized the industrialization of agriculture. However, these critical thoughts did not fit in with developments on the macro level, which were very much in favour of economic growth, material wealth and technological development. That is why organic farmers were hardly recognized. Nevertheless, this 'invisible' niche-period was important, because it allowed stabilization of rules and networks to take place, such as the foundation of the research institute of organic farming in 1973, the establishment of written principles, guidelines and rules, the foundation of Bio Suisse in 1980, and the introduction of the 'bud' in 1981. It was also during this period, that integrated production emerged as a direct response by the largest Swiss food retail chain to the negative side effects of industrialized agriculture. Nevertheless, the new practices remained stuck at the niche level during the 1970s and 1980s and could not break through, because the regime of industrialized agriculture was still stable.

A third point is that the transition involved two niches instead of one. This raises the question of the relationship between organic farming and integrated production. Did the two niches reinforce each other or did they also compete? Was integrated production a stepping-stone (intermediary) on the way towards sustainability and organic farming? Or was it a marginal adaptation of the existing regime? Does integrated production form a barrier to radical change (towards organic farming)? There are no clear-cut answers and since the transition in the Swiss agri-food chain is still going on the raised questions are difficult to answer.

But I think the relationship between organic farming and integrated production is ambivalent. On the one hand, the two niches reinforced each other, stimulating the principle of ecological production. It may be argued that one niche on its own would not have gained enough support and political power to destabilize and substitute the existing socio-technological regime of industrialized agriculture within such a short period of time – less than ten years. In that respect the two niches clearly reinforced each other and joined forces. Both niches are reactions to the negative side effects of industrialized agriculture. Both aim to improve the ecological situation by using the same kinds of technologies (such as soil analysis, mechanical weed control) and less or no agrochemicals. Both qualify for ecological compensation according to article 31b of the agricultural law.

Furthermore, to some degree integrated production has formed a stepping-stone between the two extremes of industrialized agriculture and organic farming. Some conventional farmers switched directly from industrialized agriculture to organic farming, others tried integrated production first before they joined organic farming. However, many chose the latter. For instance, most M-Bio farmers were former M-Sano farmers. During the second half of the 1990s Migros persuaded them to make the move from IP plus to organic farming. To some extent, integrated production formed a locus where conventional farmers could gain experience with new agricultural rules and practices. Building upon these experiences, some of these farmers made a further shift towards organic farming.

On the other hand there are also differences and competition between the two niches. There are different philosophical backgrounds. Organic farming has a different worldview to integrated production. Integrated production tries to reconcile economy and ecology. Organic farming puts nature first, regardless of short-term economic considerations. Furthermore, organic farming and integrated production compete for political and market recognition. Maybe organic farming would have had a larger market share if the niche of integrated production had not existed. Integrated production can be seen as an attempt to upgrade industrialized agriculture and allow the incumbent actors to adapt to the new ecological and social challenges. This may have led to a new lock-in situation, which prevents a more radical change towards organic farming. It is too soon to answer these questions. The relationship between the niches is still in flux. But it highlights the aspect that niches can be both complementary and competitive.

A fourth point is that single actors or social groups cannot bring about transitions. It is the interplay and alignment between social groups, which leads to transitions. In the case study, three social groups were the crucial drivers of the transition: retail shops, consumers and government. National retail chains function as an intermediate actor between farmers and consumers, acting as 'gatekeepers' of sustainability innovations (Belz, 2001; Villiger, 2001). To a large extent, these retail shops determine what consumers can buy. Because of this intermediary function, retail chains are crucial actors for change in the food sector. They gradually became 'product champions' for sustainability innovations: Migros played a crucial role in the set up of integrated production (M-Sano-programme) and the further diffusion of organic farming (M-Bio-programme). Coop was active in the introduction and diffusion of organic food products to conventional retailing and the mainstream market (Coop Naturaplan). The other crucial group were Swiss consumers, who developed a high level of environmental awareness after 1986. And crucially, they were willing to pay a higher price for high quality products with respect to ecological and other criteria such as freshness, taste, convenience and so on. The third social group was the government. In the context of environmental consciousness and liberalization, they put forward the agricultural strategy to switch to high-quality products. The government was willing to back up this strategy with financial encouragement for farmers, who then shifted to ecological production. They helped conventional farmers not only with financial incentives, but also with regulations. The ecological criteria for subsidies were initially formulated at a moderate level (integrated production standard), not as high as IP Suisse. Over time, however, these criteria were made stricter, such as the new regulation of 1997 on organic food products. The mutual reinforcements and alignments between these three social groups provided the internal momentum for this transition.

NOTES

1. First of all, I would like to thank Frank Geels (University of Eindhoven) for critical feedback and substantial help in the revision of the first drafts of this chapter. Moreover, I would like to thank the organizing committee, namely Boelie Elzen, Frank Geels, Ken Green, René Kemp, Johan Schot, Geert Verbong, and Matthias Weber, for the invitation to the international workshop 'Transitions to Sustainability through System Innovations', held at the University of Twente (Netherlands), July 4–6, 2002. The workshop was truly interdisciplinary, interesting and inspiring!
2. The focus on domestic food products means that organic and fair trade products imported from third world countries are not dealt with in the chapter, although they play an important role in Switzerland.
3. From the perspective of information economics 'organic farming' is a credence quality (Nelson, 1970; Darby and Karni, 1973), that is, the customer has to trust the information regarding the sort of agriculture as given by the producer or an independent label organization.
4. 'Sano' is a Latin word and means health. The name indicates the intension of the new programme, which is healthy, residue-free food.
5. Switzerland is a basic democracy. Popular initiatives play an important role in the democratic decision-making process. Every Swiss citizen has the right to launch an initiative in favour or against something. If the initiators are able to gain at least 100 000 supporting signatures within a certain period of time, the initiative can be submitted to the government. If all formal criteria are met, it has to be discussed in the national parliament, which recommends accepting or rejecting the initiative. The final decision is made by the Swiss population in periodical voting.

REFERENCES

Belz, Frank-Martin (1995), *Ökologie und Wettbewerbsfähigkeit in der Lebensmittelbranche*, Bern, Stuttgart, Wien: Paul Haupt.

Belz, Frank-Martin (1997), *Ökologische Sortimentsanalyse im schweizerischen Lebensmittelhandel: Eine explorative Untersuchung*, St. Gallen: Institut für Wirtschaft und Ökologie der Universität St. Gallen (IWÖ-HSG).

Belz, Frank-Martin (1999), 'Integratives Öko-Marketing: Erfolgreiche Vermarktung von ökologischen Produkten im Konsumbereich', in K. Bellmann (ed.), *Betriebliches Umweltmanagement in Deutschland*, Wiesbaden: Gabler, pp. 163–89.

Belz, Frank-Martin (2001), *Integratives Öko-Marketing. Erfolgreiche Vermarktung von ökologischen Produkten und Leistungen*, Wiesbaden: Gabler.

Bundesamt für Statistik (2002), *Umwelt Schweiz: Statistiken und Analysen*, Neuchâtel: Bundespublikationen.

Bundesamt für Umwelt, Wald und Landschaft (2002), *Umwelt Schweiz – Politik und Perspektiven*, Bern: Bundespublikationen.

Carson, Rachel (1962), *Silent Spring*, Boston: Houghton Mifflin.

Coop (2003), *10 Jahre Coop Naturaplan*, Basel: Coop.

Darby, Michael R., and Edi Karni (1973), 'Free competition and the optimal amount of fraud', *Journal of Law and Economics*, **16**, 67–88.

Freeman, Chris, and Carlotta Perez (1988), 'Structural crisis of adjustment, business cycles and investment behaviour', in Giovanni Dosi, Chris Freeman, Richard Nelson, Gerald Silverberg and Luc Soete (eds), *Technical Change and Economic Theory*, London: Pinter, pp. 38–66.

Geels, Frank W. (2002), 'Technological transitions as evolutionary reconfiguration processes: a multi-level perspective and a case-study', *Research Policy*, **31**(8/9), 1257–74.

Gugelmann, Erich (1988), 'Das Marketing der Migros im Spannungsfeld landwirtschaftlicher Produktionstechnologien', *Thexis*, **5**(3), 15–18.

Hansen, Ursula (1988), 'Ökologisches Marketing im Handel', in Arndt Brandt *et al.* (eds), *Ökologisches Marketing*, Frankfurt/Main, New York: Campus.

Jungbluth, Nils (2000), *Umweltfolgen des Nahrungsmittelkonsums: Beurteilung von Produktmerkmalen auf Grundlage einer modularen Ökobilanz*, Berlin: dissertation.de, Verlag im Internet.

Kemp, René, Arie Rip and Johan Schot (2001), 'Constructing transition paths through the management of niches', in Raghu Garud and Peter Karnoe (eds), *Path Dependence and Creation*, Mahwah, NJ: Lawrence Erlbaum Associates Publishers, pp. 269–99.

Nelson, Philip (1970), 'Information and consumer behaviour', *Journal of Political Economy*, **78**, 311–29.

Niggli, Uli, T. Alföldi, P. Mäder, L. Pfiffner, E. Spiess and J.-M. Bessan. (1995), 'DOK-Versuch: vergleichende Langzeituntersuchungen in den drei Anbausystemen biologisch-dynamisch, organisch-biologisch und konventionell, Synthese, 1. und 2. Fruchtperiode', in *Schweizerische Landwirtschaftliche Forschung*, Sonderheft DOK Nr. 4, Bern, pp. 1–34.

Rip, Arie, and René Kemp (1998), 'Technological Change', in Steven Rayner and Elly L. Malone (eds), *Human Choice and Climate Change*, vol. 2, Columbus, OH: Battelle Press, pp. 327–99.

Schweizerischer Bundesrat (1992), *Siebter Landwirtschaftsbericht*, Bern: Eidgenössische Drucksachen- und Materialzentrale.

Villiger, Alex (2000), *Von der Öko-Nische zum ökologischen Massenmarkt*, Wiesbaden: Gabler.

6. The transition from coal to gas: radical change of the Dutch gas system

Aad Correljé and Geert Verbong

INTRODUCTION

From the early 1960s onwards, a new system of gas supply was introduced in the Netherlands, based on the massive amounts of natural gas found in Groningen, in the north of the country. The subsequent construction of a gas transport network made this gas available throughout the country and Western Europe. It provided the Dutch economy with a relatively cheap, reliable and clean source of energy, while households enjoyed the conveniences of gas-fired central heating, cooking and hot water supply. The enormous revenues the state was able to collect permitted the growth and maintenance of the generous Dutch welfare state (Correljé *et al.*, 2003).

At the time of the discovery of Groningen, a significant shift in the Dutch energy economy was already taking place. Figure 6.1 illustrates the evolution of Dutch energy use. The transition from coal to oil had started long before the extraordinary opportunities offered by the Groningen gas accelerated the restructuring of the energy sector. Coal was confronted with competition from increasingly low-cost oil products from the end of the 1950s onwards. Even before the Second World War, the importance of coal had started to fall, and between 1952 and 1962 the share of coal fell from 80 per cent of total energy consumption to below 50 per cent, coal being supplanted by oil. However after 1962 the exponential growth of energy consumption was completely covered by natural gas. Within a decade natural gas had become the major energy feedstock. How could this rapid and remarkable transition occur? We want to address this question in this chapter. We will focus on the radical changes in the system of gas supply, enabling this transition, but we will also point to major societal consequences of this change.

The transition to natural gas was a real system innovation. The institutional framework of the gas industry changed dramatically, the distribution network was greatly expanded and upgraded and new markets were

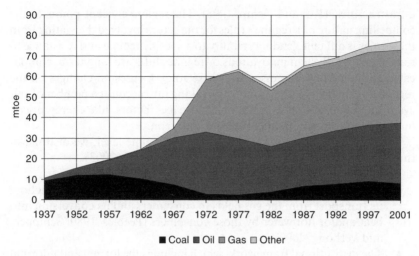

Figure 6.1 The evolution of Dutch energy use

developed with far reaching consequences. According to Rotmans, the transition from one system to another is defined as a multi-stage, multi-level and multi-actor process, that can only be understood in terms of historical coevolutionary processes which link up these actors, factors and levels (Rotmans *et al.*, 2000). We will address the different stages, levels and actors involved in the transition in the Dutch gas system.

Rotmans distinguishes several phases in transition processes: predevelopment, take-off, acceleration and stabilization. The discovery of large amounts of natural gas in 1959 near Slochteren has marked the take-off of a revolution in the field of energy supply and use in the Netherlands and in Europe (Davis, 1984). However the speed of the subsequent transition in the 1960s cannot be understood without taking note of earlier developments that took place in the 1950s. The existing system of gas supply was already changing before Slochteren. Also, the transition took place against the background of the general transition from coal to oil products, as illustrated in Figure 6.1. The transition to natural gas in the Netherlands should be seen as a substantial and integral part of this larger and global transition process, away from coal. The take-off phase has to be understood within this particular context.

For the analysis of the structural changes in the gas system we will use a multi-level model in which the meso level is the level of technological regimes (Geels, 2002). These regimes comprise 'the rule-set or grammar embedded in a complex of engineering practices, production process technologies, product characteristics, ways of handling artefacts and procedures, ways of defining problems; all of them embedded in institutions and infrastructures' (Rip and Kemp, 1998). The regime concept points to the compelling nature of a regime's rules for the actors involved. Deviating from these rules is difficult, lending stability to a specific regime and resistance to radical change. System innovations or regime shifts are long term, complicated and uncertain processes. This case study focuses on changes on the regime level in the Dutch gas industry, taking into account a number of relevant interactions with external or 'landscape' factors, like energy prices, market developments, political culture and so on.

To analyse the processes that occur at the regime level, we distinguish three dimensions of the gas regime (see Correljé *et al.*, 2003).

- The material network (technological system) enabling gas production, its transport from the gas fields to consumers and its conversion into heat and/or hot water by those consumers (Peebles, 1980; Schippers and Verbong, 2000).
- The institutional framework, which includes the formal and informal laws and regulations, the organizational structure, the ownership pattern and other instruments of coordination (North, 1990; Kaijser, 1998).
- The market for energy, connecting gas supply and demand in economic terms. These terms involve market conditions like the development of supply and demand; price setting mechanisms; the allocation of costs, revenues and profits among actors in the supply chain; taxes and subsidies and investments in parts of the supply chain (Adelman, 1962).

The transition to a new system required a process of interrelated changes in these three dimensions. This chapter explores how this happened for the transition to natural gas in the Netherlands. We identify and explain specific patterns in the interplay of institutional, technological and market factors.

We will complement this by an analysis of the role of the actors involved. The Dutch transition to natural gas was a well-coordinated and supervised project. This is often attributed to the dynamic manner in which the exploitation of the gas field in Groningen was undertaken by the owners of the concession – Shell and Exxon – in cooperation with the Dutch government (Lubbers and Lemckert, 1980; Peebles, 1999; Davis, 1984; Estrada, 1988; Kielich, 1988). The impression that emerges from these accounts is that 'all pointers simply stood in the right direction'. This 'whiggish' explanation obscures the conflicts. The negotiations and the power struggles that took place had a major and unexpected impact on the outcome of the process (Correljé *et al.*, 2003). We thus provide a new account of this specific transition.

Our aim is to contribute to the understanding of system innovation and, more specifically, what government agencies and other actors can do to encourage and influence system innovations. We analyse choices made by relevant actors in order to gain insight in the degrees of freedom they have and understand the factors which influence this.

THE GAS REGIME BEFORE SLOCHTEREN

The Dutch gas regime was formed in the 19th century, as the first public utility, when municipalities undertook the supply of gas for public and private gas lighting. This gas was produced through gasification of coal. In the first decades of the 20th century, the emerging competition with electricity forced the gas industry to look for other markets. New applications were found in domestic household cooking and hot water supply, substituting traditional wood or coal fired appliances. Electric cooking was a market niche with a maximum share of about 10 per cent, but particularly during the 1930s Depression, the competition between gas and electricity was fierce. Coal, of course, was the main feedstock for the manufacturing of both city gas as well as electricity. Coal also dominated the market for heating. Until 1960 houses were heated predominantly with coal stoves.

In the 1950s, local city gas factories still dominated the gas market, but there were also firms that produced gas as a by-product in their large coke furnaces. The Dutch steel works, Hoogovens, and the Staatsmijnen (later Dutch State Mines, or DSM) began to expand the sales of this so-called 'long distance' gas. They expanded their networks in the western and in the south-eastern part of the country, respectively. In addition, the rapidly expanding oil refineries in the Rotterdam area started to sell refinery gas, also as a by-product of the refinery process.

Natural gas emerged as a niche in the northern part of the country. In July 1948, gas was found at a depth of nearly 2800 meters in the province of Drente. It was sold to Coevorden, the first city where households started cooking on natural gas. In the 1930s, the Shell subsidiary Bataafse Petroleum Maatschappij (BPM) had acquired the exclusive right to explore oil and gas in the north-eastern part of the country. During the Second World War, an oilfield was found in Schoonebeek, close to Coevorden. In 1947, BPM and the Standard Oil Company of New Jersey, under the name of Esso (later Exxon), established a joint venture for oil and gas exploration and production in the Netherlands, the Nederlandse Aardolie Maatschappij (NAM). The NAM acquired a production permit and started producing oil. Stimulated by this success, NAM continued exploring the Dutch sub-soil. Over the 1950s, a number of moderately sized deposits of oil and gas were found. However gas exploration did not have priority within NAM. Oil was considered more important. A Shell CEO named Bloemgarten stated: 'Stay out of gas, there is no money to be made' (cited in Kielich, 1988, p. 19). Gas supply was generally considered to be a public utility, operated on a low profit, cost-plus basis. Moreover, he foresaw competition between natural gas and, more important for Shell, the rapidly developing sales of oil products to domestic households and industry.

In order to get rid of the cumbersome by-product, the gas was sold to nearby municipalities. Nevertheless, the Dutch government saw advantages in stimulating the exploration and production of natural gas for the country. This was an option to get rid of the small gas factories and to build a national system of gas supply. Therefore, it pressed for an agreement between NAM and the newly founded State Gas Company (SGB). From 1954 onwards, the SGB distributed the natural gas produced by NAM, under the condition that NAM would run all gas fields and that it would sell the gas on a 'cost-plus' basis to the SGB. Until the discovery of Groningen, NAM accepted this because it considered the guaranteed sale of the gas more important than high profits. The high gas price of 33 Dutch cents per cubic metre rendered gas uncompetitive against oil and coal for a wide range of customers. NAM only received 2 to 4 cents.

SGB also took care of the transport and marketing of coke and refinery gas through several regional networks. The final objective of the government was to integrate these networks into one national system. Such attempts failed completely, however, as a consequence of the heterogeneous character of the actors involved and their conflicting interests. Also the variation in quality and energy content of the different gasses posed problems in the system. Natural gas had a higher caloric value than city gas. The gas companies could either mix it with other gases in order to lower the caloric value, or adapt the whole of the infrastructure and appliances. In the urban areas in the western part of the country the first option was chosen. In the north of the country the second option was implemented, providing valuable experience for the national transition to natural gas a few years later. The sudden discovery of large amounts of natural gas in the Netherlands, however, provided unexpected opportunities and problems to the international oil companies involved, as well as to the Dutch gas industry.

A SHOCK TO THE REGIME

Despite Shell's lack of interest in natural gas, its subsidiary NAM continued to explore for gas and on the 22 July 1959 a gas deposit was hit near Slochteren, in the province of Groningen. The gas was of the same composition and pressure as a nearby deposit that been discovered in 1955. NAM estimated the size of the field at about 60 billion cubic metres (Bcm), a huge field at the time. NAM only informed the Minister of Economic Affairs, De Pous, because it preferred to keep other oil companies from exploring in the Netherlands. Moreover, as NAM did not have an exclusive concession for exploration and production, it first wanted to negotiate with the Dutch government about the exploitation of the field. For more than a year, not much happened until, in October 1960, newspapers published the discovery of the enormous gas field in Groningen. Thereafter, following new drillings, the size of the field was readjusted several times: from 150 Bcm to 470 Bcm in 1962, to 1100 Bcm in 1963, and to 1900 Bcm in 1967. It thus became clear that Netherlands soil contained one of the world's largest known gas deposits (Brouwer, 1969).

It was clear to both NAM and the Ministry of Economic Affairs that the large size of the field offered enormous opportunities for the use of gas in the Dutch economy. But it was also evident that the development of such huge resources would put the existing system of energy supply under strong pressure. The prevailing institutional framework was not adequate for a field this size. Indeed NAM would have been forced to sell all gas produced to the SGB. This would create insurmountable problems because of the limited scale of the existing technical infrastructure and the market. From 1960 onwards, the parties started negotiations about a framework for the exploitation of the Groningen field. (Peebles, 1980, 1999; Stern, 1984; Ausems, 1996 and Correljé *et al.*, 2003). These negotiations were difficult because of differing views and interests. They focused on three interrelated dimensions of the new regime: markets, institutional set-up and distribution infrastructure. On each of these dimensions a reorientation was necessary.

A Master Plan

The first issue was the question to which customers the gas would be offered and at what price. Opinions differed greatly. Shell opted for a segmentation of markets, under which small customers would be served through SGB and local distributors, under the prevailing public utility, cost-plus regime. The NAM would supply large Dutch and foreign customers in industry and power production. This plan met strong criticism from the Minister and from Exxon, the former fearing that the Dutch state revenues would be moderate, the latter having bad experiences with similar patterns of exploitation of large gas deposits in the USA (Ellis, 1965). Exxon developed a radically different master plan for a national-scale transition to natural gas. Whereas the Shell plan had assumed that large users would be the most profitable segment to supply, the Exxon approach argued that small users could yield the highest revenues (Correljé, 1998, Heren, 1999).

The latter approach would require substantial changes in the regime. Firstly, the gas should be made available to domestic users on a very large scale through a countrywide high-pressure transmission system that would link all local distribution systems to the Groningen field. Secondly, the consumption of gas should be dramatically increased, by persuading domestic customers to switch from coal or oil to gas, and to start using gas-fired central heating. City gas was only used in cooking and hot water supply, and not for heating. This approach represented a completely new vision on the role of gas in energy markets, pricing strategies and the relationship between public and private activities.

Exxon's plan was not immediately accepted. Shell rejected it, doubting that small users would invest in new equipment and heating systems. Municipalities, the owners of city gas plants and local networks, feared the consequences for the public services they offered. Nevertheless, simulations of a natural gas based system, with data from the Hilversum municipal energy utility, allowed evaluation of different business models, involving combinations of investments, prices and market segments. It showed that the Exxon approach would be advantageous for users, for municipalities and their utilities, for the state, and for gas producers.

The orientation towards small, but high-value users, without alternative fuels at hand once they had converted to natural gas, and, thus, with relatively price-inelastic consumption, became the cornerstone of Dutch gas policy. To attract users, gas costs should be equal to the cost of coal or oil-fired heating, with progressively declining costs at higher levels of consumption. The second group of consumers were the so-called industrial premium markets, in the chemical, metallurgical and ceramic industries. In these sectors, high cost gas did not have to compete with lower-priced fuel oil or coal, because of its technical superiority in production processes.

Creating a New Institutional Framework

Once the parties involved had agreed on the general outline of the market dimension of the new regime, the institutional dimension had to be developed, defining the roles and relations among the several actors involved. Early in 1961, a plan was presented to Minster De Pous. He mandated the Staatsmijnen (DSM) to negotiate on his behalf with Shell and Exxon about the further development of a concessionary regime, the elaboration of the marketing policy and the role of the Dutch state. He passed by SGB because he considered SGB too lightweight to confront the two large international oil companies. DSM was a firm of considerable size, operating in international markets. Moreover, it produced, distributed and marketed manufactured gas in the south of the country. The transition towards natural gas would be at the expense of the coal sector. The involvement of the mining company DSM would be considered as a form of compensation.

Two months later, the three companies presented a brief *Aide Mémoire* to the Minister, outlining the marketing policy and the position of the Dutch State. It proposed to establish a new marketing joint venture for the Dutch market, which would incorporate the SGB through DSM. DSM, Shell and Exxon would participate with an equal share, while DSM should have a right of veto over the strategy of the marketing company. Separately, a second joint venture would be established for production and export in which DSM should have no influence. Yet, DSM would have a 30 per cent share in costs and benefits. Despite the fact that De Pous considered the influence of the state too small, he considered this basic structure appropriate for further negotiations. He wanted a much larger profit share for the state than the usual 10 per cent royalties plus corporate tax.

For the negotiations, the Commissie van der Grinten was installed, involving three members with a representative political and societal background. The commission involved Professor van der Grinten, a Catholic and Chairman of the Mining Council, Dr Tromp, a liberal and member of the Board of Philips and the Dutch Railways, and Mr Vos, a socialist senator and Vice-President of the Mining Council. The commission neatly fitted the Dutch consensus-driven political model. Notwithstanding the functional separation of the main groups in Dutch society (socialists, Protestants, Catholics and liberals) into their own political parties, labour organizations, schools, and so on, intensive contacts existed between the elites of these pillars and the business elite. Sensitive political decisions were discussed and 'pre-cooked' by representative but informal commissions, before discussing them in Parliament. The political culture was pro-business and in favour of gearing agreements towards individual firms (Van Aardenne, 1987).

The Commission consulted the main parties, Shell, Exxon, DSM, SGB, the cooperating electricity producers (Sep), the association of gas companies (VEGIN) and the province of Groningen. Van der Grinten's report of December 1961 signalled a number of important aspects. The oil companies were willing to accept a somewhat higher state share in the profits and in the company boardrooms, but they had serious objections to open state participation in gas production. In their worldwide oil producing activities Exxon and Shell were confronted with other governments that claimed the right for their state to participate.

Shell offered a solution. The Slochteren concession would be given to NAM, which would become the formal 'owner' of the field. In addition, a so-called Maatschap (Society) was founded, in which NAM would include the concession and in which the cost of production and revenues from sales of gas would be accounted for. Shell and Exxon would each receive a 30 per cent share in the profits of the Maatschap, while another 30 per cent would fall to DSM. The Maatschap would transfer the customary 10 per cent royalty to the State. On the profits of the Maatschap the normal corporate tax would be raised. Altogether, the state would collect around 70 per cent of total net revenues. On the board of directors, however, the voting ratio was 50/50 for the state and the oil companies. The Maatschap would sell gas to a national transmission company, later named Gasunie, with the same shareholders as the Maatschap – DSM, Shell and Exxon – that transported the gas to the local, municipally-owned distribution companies. A third company, NAM/Gas Export, would export the gas on account of Gasunie. The Commissie van der Grinten proposed a 50 per cent share for DSM in Gasunie, but Shell and Exxon opted for a similar share as in the Maatschap. Meanwhile De Pous had started negotiations with the main political parties. The Council of Ministers and the Commission for Economic Affairs of Parliament accepted the draft structure without difficulties. Only one member of the socialist party PvdA resisted and proposed nationalization of the Slochteren concession. When the oil companies accepted a 50 per cent state share in Gasunie, 10 per cent direct and 40 per cent through DSM, the PvdA agreed.

Three years after the discovery of the large field in Groningen, the Minister of Economic Affairs was able to lay down the main principles of Dutch gas policy in a White Paper, the *Nota inzake het aardgas* (Ausems, 1996). These principles involved, firstly, that in order to generate maximum revenues the 'market-value' principle was introduced as the basis on which gas should be produced and marketed. The price of gas for the various types of consumers was linked to the price of alternative fuels most likely to be substituted, to gas oil for small-scale users and to fuel oil for large-scale users. Accordingly, consumers would never have to pay *more* for gas than for alternative fuels, but the market value principle also ensured that they would not pay *less*. The application of the principle enabled the concession holders, Shell and Exxon, and the Dutch state to secure much higher revenues than in a pricing process in which the consumer price would be related to the low production costs at the Groningen field. An essential precondition for maintaining the market value principle was, of course, that no alternative supplies of low-priced gas could reach the market – a condition which was fulfilled until recently in the Netherlands and until the early 1970s in Europe (Odell, 1969; Correljé and Odell, 2000). To achieve this, the second main principle in the Nota de Pous stated that the exploitation of the Dutch gas resources should proceed 'in harmony' with the sales of gas achieved, in order to avoid disruptions of the energy market. In the new regime control over the supply of gas was seen as a government responsibility. Yet the Nota stated that the private concession owners, Shell and Exxon, should undertake the exploitation and marketing of the gas reserves in order to enable the country to benefit from their knowledge, experience and financial resources.

The Dutch government and the two companies agreed upon a structure that effectively united these principles. NAM produced gas, while Gasunie sold gas to distribution companies or to large users. From Gasunie's gross revenues, the operating costs of its transmission system plus an annual statutory profit of 80 million guilders were deducted, and the remainder was transferred to the Maatschap, the entity in which the Groningen Concession was embedded. The state's revenues were secured in a number of ways; first, through corporate tax (48 per cent) on profits of the Maatschap, Gasunie and DSM; secondly, through an additional 10 per cent government surcharge on profits of the Maatschap, and thirdly, through dividends and the 'state profit share' paid to the state by, respectively, Gasunie and DSM. From the early 1970s onwards, an additional 'state profit share' was applied to the profits of the Maatschap. The Ministry of Economic Affairs also formally confined its responsibilities to approving decisions taken by DSM and Gasunie in respect of prices, production, national and international trade volume and the construction of transport and storage facilities. In practice, it was always consulted on strategic issues and could initiate discussions for any changes it thought to be necessary in the national interest.

A new institutional structure thus emerged, in which the several interests associated with the old energy supply system were either compensated and 'bought out', or were given favourable new positions. Adequate arrangements were agreed upon regarding the stranded assets in the public city gas supply and in the coal industry. The two main oil companies in the Netherlands, Shell and Exxon, were in the forefront of these new developments. Actually, the main losers were the other oil companies (BP, Chevron, Gulf, Fina) that saw their potential sales in the Netherlands reduced to a share in the market for gasoline and diesel in the transport sector. Indeed the (potential) market for fuel and heating oil was being flooded with natural gas.

The new structure implied a remarkable shift in the role of the state and the private firms in the energy sector. The large state share in the Groningen concession was something new at the time. Only in a few oil and gas producing countries, like Mexico and communist countries, did the state have such a large stake in the oil and gas industry. On the other hand, the role of private firms in the gas industry was also a relatively new phenomenon in this traditional public utility domain. A further important novelty was the way in which coordination of supply and sales was institutionalized, with specific roles for the national state and the producing partners, and the municipalities and their utilities.

Constructing a New Gas Network

When it became clear that there were no major obstacles for the new market strategy and institutional framework, work on the third dimension of the new regime could begin. The preparations and planning for a new gas network, enabling the flow of gas to customers, started in early 1962. A year later, the construction of the high-pressure network that would connect the municipal gas utilities with Slochteren began. Bechtel Engineering, a US firm with a large experience in constructing pipelines, was hired as the main contractor. Four Dutch construction companies took part as sub-contractors. The construction of the system was a complicated task, involving confrontations with agricultural interests, urban expansion plans, road construction, water systems, railroads, archaeological sites and military objects. For landowners and other parties involved, compensation fees had to be negotiated for use of the land during construction of the pipelines and thereafter.

Despite the large scale of the undertaking and the many difficulties the network was constructed rapidly. In December 1963, the first Groningen gas was produced and precisely one year later the DSM plant in the south of the country was supplied with natural gas. In 1966, the system reached the western end of the country and a pipeline was crossing the Ijsselmeer to North Holland. The grids were constructed in such a way that the most densely populated areas were connected first. The rural areas followed later, often in combination with lines to local industrial users. Revenues on sales to the households in the dense areas could be used to finance further rural expansion. This strategy allowed utilities to connect users to their gas network in a profitable way. In 1968, the last municipality in the country was connected. In five years, nearly 1600 kilometres of high-pressure pipes had been constructed, while the total length of the local networks had doubled to more than 5000 kilometres.

Gasunie paid for the construction of the main network. Municipalities had to prepare their local networks for the distribution of the new gas to the consumers. Often municipalities had to negotiate with each other and with Gasunie about the most efficient way to connect to the main grid. Utilities were stimulated to connect as many households as possible, with premiums offered by Gasunie. Some utilities complained and raised doubts over the whole operation. These disputes were solved in the Commission

Cooperation Regional Organizations Gas Supply (SROG). SROG maintained contact between utilities and negotiated on their behalf with Gasunie about the prices, the interconnection of local systems and adjustments to local networks. For Gasunie, this coordination reduced the number of partners they had to deal with.

Local utilities became distributors of Groningen gas. Comfortable arrangements were struck with the municipalities regarding the removal of their city gas manufacturing plants. The utilities played a crucial role in the transformation of the local infrastructure and the end-user's equipment, including the re-fitting of in-house pipelines and the substitution of the old gas boilers, stoves and heaters. For the country as a whole, a strategy was applied that was similar to that used in Coevorden earlier. All equipment was adapted to Groningen quality gas. A big advantage was that the quality of the gas and the characteristics of gas appliances became standardized all over the country.

TAKE-OFF: THE DIFFUSION OF NATURAL GAS

From the moment the new regime was emerging – the institutional changes had been accepted and the network was under construction – the main remaining challenge was to implement the marketing strategy and, in particular, to conquer the domestic market for heating. Since the Second World War the use of coal for home heating had grown only very slowly, as compared to the use of heating oil. Still, by the early 1960s, coal had maintained a share of 55 per cent of total domestic energy use for home heating. A large campaign had to entice domestic customers to switch to gas. Meetings were organized, information leaflets were distributed and publicity appeared in the press and on the radio. To familiarize the public with natural gas, the conveniences of its use in home heating were illustrated widely. Gas was to make the dirty storage of coal in the garden, the cellar or on the balconies redundant. It would terminate moving around coal containers or bags and ashes. In addition, heating up the gas system on a cold winter morning was much quicker than lighting up the coal stove with wood and newspapers. Easily controllable gas systems and central heating actually enlarged the houses, allowing the use of more rooms than the central living room. Indeed, the replacement of coal stoves, mostly placed in the living room, by gas-fired stoves enabled significant progress in terms of comfort and convenience.

The fact that Dutch houses were of relative poor quality became an advantage for the take-off of natural gas. After the Second World War priority was given to the construction of large numbers of new and cheap houses, to fight the shortage of houses for the rapidly growing population. Many new houses had no hot water supply, limited washing facilities and only the central living room was heated. Until 1960 central heating systems were scarce among Dutch households, with the exception of apartment buildings that had oil-fired central heating.

By 1960, the government relaxed the Spartan standards for social housing, while the prosperity of Dutch households started to increase. Because of shortages in the labour market in the early 1960s, wages began to rise. Households were able to improve their living conditions and purchase 'luxury' products like TV sets, furniture and even cars. For a brief period, this did cause a sharp increase in the sales of oil-fired stoves. Yet, this abruptly came to an end when natural gas was introduced. After 1964, coal and oil rapidly gave way to gas-fired stoves. To further enhance comfort, stoves were gradually replaced by central heating systems. This policy was very successful. In 1969 around 80 per cent of Dutch houses were connected to the grid and 60 per cent were heated with gas. By the early 1970s, central heating had become standard for new houses. Both housing corporations and private owners were actively approached to install gas-fired equipment. In the competition between individual central heating and collective heating systems, the individual option prevailed. By the end of the 1970s, 90 per cent of all new houses had their own central heating system, while older houses had been converted too (Van Overbeeke, 2001).

Central heating thus indeed formed a major market niche for the take-off of natural gas, but it was not the only one. In the market niche of cooking

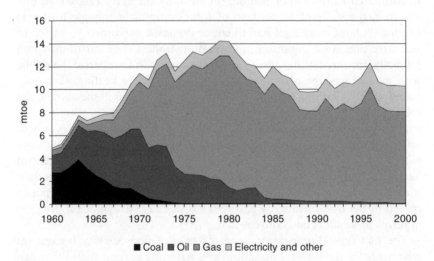

Figure 6.2 The evolution of energy use in domestic households

and hot water supply, natural gas replaced city gas and kerosene and wood in rural areas. Already before natural gas appeared on the scene, more than 80 per cent of households used gas for cooking, publicity campaigns and courses for cooking had to highlight the advantages of natural gas. Users were stimulated to exchange their old equipment, stoves and water heaters – at significant rebates – for new natural gas equipment. The introduction of natural gas also put an end to the competition between electricity and gas with respect to cooking (Van Overbeeke, 2001). When the Gasunie system reached a municipality and local grids had been adjusted, or constructed, all hot water appliances, stoves, heating systems and metre appliances were refitted with new burners or replaced within a few days. This large-scale operation was undertaken and planned with military precision. Many staff of the closed gas works became gas fitters.

To facilitate its introduction, gas was sold to domestic consumers at attractive prices, compared to the fuels traditionally used. But the price at which the gas was sold was not particularly low, in spite of the low production costs at Groningen of less than a cent per cubic metre. Following the 'market value' principle, it was sold at a price just below that of heating oil, anthracite and cokes. The small cost advantage plus the larger convenience of gas firing had to stimulate its use. The utilities were supplied with gas at a price of 6 to 6.5 Dutch cents per cubic metre. The municipalities were forced to apply regressive tariffs; the larger the volume used, the lower the price per cubic metre. For small-scale users, the first 300 cubic metres were sold at 25 cents per cubic metre, the next 300 cubic metres were sold at 20 cents and additional gas would be sold at 10 cents. This implied that users did not reap a large advantage if they only used gas for cooking and hot water supply. When used for heating – particularly central heating – the advantage, however, increased substantially.

As in the domestic sector, gas was also accepted rapidly in industry. In 1969, 65 per cent of the larger firms had converted (partly) to natural gas. The absolute consumption of oil did not decline. Natural gas mainly supplied the additional volumes of energy required by the overall growth of industrial energy consumption. The main reason was that many firms had converted from coal to fuel oil during the 1950s. The relatively new oil-fired installations were not converted to gas immediately, as cost differences were not large. New facilities, however, were generally gas-fired and the growth in industrial gas consumption was associated with the strong expansion of the industry over this period. After 1969, oil use in industry gradually declined. Gas was also increasingly used as raw material in the chemical industry, for example in the production of fertilizers.

Initially, gas was sold only to the premium markets in chemical, metallurgical and ceramic industries, where it would not have to compete with lower priced coal or oil. Yet, the continuous growth in the estimates of remaining gas reserves rendered this orientation to premium markets less relevant. At the time, it was feared that it would be impossible to sell much gas after 2000, because cheap nuclear electricity would have taken over much of the energy supply. Step by step, the premium market principle was set aside and eventually the power sector was also allowed to burn gas. After the Groningen discovery, the electricity sector had shown interest in buying gas, but it was excluded from negotiations. Until 1968 natural gas was used only on a limited scale in the electricity sector, but thereafter new gas fired plants were introduced and the share of natural gas in the electricity sector increased to about 80 per cent in the mid-1970s. This expansion of the power sector caused a significant growth in the consumption of gas.

Societal Impacts

The impacts of the transition to natural gas were manifold and wide-ranging. The massive introduction of natural gas was the deathblow for the Dutch mining industry. This was already under pressure from cheap coal imports from the USA. American coal was produced in open cast mining, allowing for a strong degree of mechanization. The competitive position of the Dutch mines – with a difficult geology and a high labour intensity – was weak. Moreover, it was becoming increasingly difficult to attract miners at reasonable wages in the flourishing Dutch economy, where other more convenient, less dangerous and less dirty jobs were offered widely. The Dutch mines had survived until the early 1960s on the basis of the profitable sales of coal for domestic house heating. As precisely this market segment was threatened by natural gas, the Dutch government decided to avoid growing losses and the need for subsidization, by closing down the mines. Former miners were expected to find jobs easily elsewhere in industry. By 1963 the new Minister of Economic Affairs, Den Uyl, announced the closure of the Dutch mines. The last mine was closed down in the early 1970s.

State revenues from natural gas exploitation facilitated the restructuring of the coal-mining region in the south of the Netherlands. The largest company, DSM, was converted to the manufacturing of chemical products based on natural gas and as part of the new institutional set-up, the other mines had to close. State aid greatly facilitated the transition from coal to gas. However, Hoogovens, another important actor in the old regime, refused to stop its coke gas production and distribution. It was forced out of the distribution sector by the national government. Because no agreement could be reached on compensation, an arbitrator finally had to decide on the (considerable) amount of money to be paid to Hoogovens (Schippers and Verbong, 2000).

The Dutch government also used natural gas as a policy tool. Some industrial sectors and firms were given the right to purchase gas at a rebate. Under this arrangement, a volume of 25 Bcm low-priced gas had been reserved by the government, for regional and sector stimulation policy. This facility had to create jobs in the economic backwaters of the country, by establishing new industries, like for example, the aluminium factory ALDEL in Delfzijl, the Hoechst plant in Vlissingen, and sea water-distillation facilities in Terneuzen. Yet, as none of these industries was labour-intensive, their contribution to the generation of jobs was not impressive. The main effect of this policy was that Dutch industry became rather energy-intensive, reversing an earlier trend of decreasing energy intensity in industry (Schippers and Verbong, 2000).

Not only industry was allowed to reap the advantages of low-priced gas. In 1970, it was decided to boost further the use of natural gas in horticulture and greenhouses. Through a special arrangement these users were supplied with gas, at the low large-scale users' tariff. In a coordinated campaign, the sector was converted to gas and by 1972 the share of gas reached 50 per cent. The reduced use of 'dirty' heavy fuel oil in greenhouses contributed to a substantial decline in the smog produced by these installations.

In addition to growing domestic sales, increasing volumes of gas were committed for export, through contracts signed by NAM/Gasunie-Export with distribution companies in Germany, Belgium and France. An international network of high-pressure pipelines was constructed to connect the areas of consumption with Groningen. In 1964, only 10 million cubic metres were sold to one German utility, just across the border in Oldenburg (Weser-Ems AG). Three years later a hundred times as much gas was exported to other German firms, to Distrigas in Belgium and to Gaz de France. In 1971, contracts were signed with SNAM for Italy and Switzerland. After 10 years of exploitation the annual amount exported was of the same magnitude as domestic consumption: 41 Bcm.

By the early 1970s the new Dutch gas system was well established and had wider effects on the economy and society. A number of developments, like the shifts in relative energy prices following the first energy crisis, the introduction of high calorific off-shore gas into the system, and the consequences of energy saving policies, had an impact on the development of the network, the institutional set-up and the markets for gas. The profitable Dutch gas exports stimulated the activities of other potential suppliers of natural gas; first, in the North Sea, producers became active on the continental shelf of, respectively, the UK, Germany, Denmark and Norway. Other emerging contenders of the Dutch monopoly position in Europe's gas supply were the Soviet Union and Algeria. Particularly through the

1970s, when oil prices rose, these suppliers became increasingly important in the European gas market. Indeed, the linkage of gas prices to those of oil, now provided an enormous boost to exploration and exploitation of gas and justified a further expansion of the trans-European gas network (Odell, 2001, 2002). Yet, whereas adjustments were made to the regime, its essence and the principles that governed gas production, marketing and pricing and the distribution of profits survived into the late 1990s, when the consequences of the EU process of liberalization in the European energy markets began to be felt (Correljé *et al.*, 2003).

CONCLUSIONS

We want to highlight several aspects of the transition, which may have relevance for other transitions.

The first aspect is that the take-off phase of the transition could build upon accumulated experiences from an earlier period. Contrary to common perception, the transition did not begin with the shock of the Slochteren gas field. In the 1950s there were already ongoing dynamics on which the transition could build. A gas network had already been created. This network, while limited to the cooking and water-heating markets, was expanding substantially in the 1950s. The rapid take-off of natural gas in the 1960s could build on the existing infrastructure, technology and users, but the existing gas system provided not just a platform; it was also a barrier, in particular the institutional framework. The discovery of the Groningen gas field not only underlined this problem, but also forced a solution and provided a way out. Although all relevant actors perceived this problem as crucial, the solution was not straightforward. The alignment of all aspects and actors took only a few years, from 1959 to 1962, but this reorientation period was a decisive one in the transition process. In fact the outcome of the transition was to a large degree determined by the negotiations that took place in this period and could not been taken for granted, as the use of the phase model seems to suggest.

Second, many people refer to a smooth transition which seems to have had an abundantly clear logic. This perception seems to be reinforced by the structuralist character of the multi-level model. Although processes at different levels can create windows of opportunity for regime change, the actual linkages have to be made by actors (Geels, 2002). This case study clearly showed how actors struggled and negotiated to use the new opportunity. The transition process may have looked fairly straightforward, but it required the active participation of the many actors involved. This is illustrated by the period of uncertainty, immediately after the discovery of

Groningen. Later on, the actors involved had to take care of all essential ingredients, technical, institutional as well as economic, in a coordinated way. This study clearly shows the importance of an actor perspective. Also, it suggests that the main linkages were created in the short reorientation period, stressing the importance of seizing the opportunities offered. The actors involved actively created the new regime and choices made in this process had major and long-term impacts.

Third, the development of a new vision on how to introduce natural gas was a crucial element in the transition process. After Slochteren, a master plan was designed by Esso engineers, which entailed changes in three dimensions of the socio-technical regime. The development of a new institutional framework was one aspect. Another key ingredient in the development of the gas system was the marketing or pricing strategy, including the economic segmentation of markets; the approaches towards different users, domestic and industrial; development of supply schemes; low-cost equipment supply; special gas prices to specific categories of users and, not least, a well-orchestrated publicity and information campaign, aimed at changing daily habits and routines. The third element was the construction of a new distribution network, enabling the flow of natural gas. The master plan designed by the Esso engineers essentially contained these three key elements, although many details still had to be worked out.

Fourth, there was strong network management. An essential aspect was the fact that two of the major multinational oil companies were involved. This provided the advantages of insight and experience in energy markets. It also enabled relative outsiders – the Esso engineers – to provide the new vision, which became the cornerstone of the new gas regime. These engineers used their experiences in the USA as a starting point for developing the master plan. Another crucial aspect was creating a balance between the public and the private sector. The government carefully selected which actors should be involved, in particular which actor should represent the interests of the Dutch State. The choice of DSM resulted in a small but powerful network. However other actors were deliberately excluded and the government had to take care of the 'losers'. Strong actors such as Hoogovens had to be compensated, others were simply rejected. After the general ideas of the master plan had been accepted and political consensus had been achieved on the institutional framework, the expansion of the gas network by a set of new actors, particularly Gasunie, could take off. The institutional regime granted Gasunie a de facto monopoly in Dutch gas supply and it took charge of the well-planned transition to natural gas in the country. With the emergence of a European gas network in the late 1960s, which was shaped to a high degree by the Dutch example, Gasunie also became a major international player.

Fifth, the national government was one of the key actors in the transition. The motives for the state were diverse and included the objective of a quick and complete exploitation of the Dutch gas reserves, the provision of comfort and luxury to Dutch citizens and the use of gas prices as a valuable instrument for industrial policy. The government pushed the implementation process, but also provided investments through the utilities, compensated the losers, reacted swiftly to emerging problems and convinced the Dutch people of the advantages of natural gas. The effective process of decision-making and planning was possible because the government shrewdly and carefully used the political system to obtain public support, involving relevant representatives and interests, to facilitate political decision-making and to legitimize it. Despite heated discussions, consensus was reached. The representation of all major pillars and interests in the negotiations, secured societal support for the new regime. The important role of the government continued during the take-off phase, although most of the work was delegated to Gasunie.

Sixth, the transition was a coevolutionary process in which a new institutional framework, the gas supply system and its economics coevolved and mutually reinforced each other. This produced a very stable socio-technical configuration, developing its own dynamics, dictated by resources, geopolitics and the characteristics of the technical system on the one hand, and the markets for gas and vested interests on the other. In particular, the shaping and structuration of the market was remarkable. It provided a new public role in hydrocarbon production (with a 70 per cent state share and influence in resource depletion and marketing). Yet, at the same time, it also provided a new role for the private sector in the formerly public system of gas supply. The gas had to be sold according to its market value and this policy essentially has been continued up to this day in form of oil-parity pricing. This was only possible within the setting of the institutional regime, implemented in the 1960s and 1970s. The emergence of a new gas regime had a wider impact on the development of the energy regime, for example in the electricity sector, and on the role and position of the government.

Seventh, the cultural and political context is important for transitions. This allowed actors to behave as they did. But in the subsequent years, the context changed. All kinds of new social movements emerged. These movements themselves were a sign of changing social relations and institutions in the Netherlands and the first step in a social and cultural modernization process. The unravelling of the pillarized society ended the central role the pillars and their organizations played in embedding technological innovations in Dutch society. From about 1970 onwards, innovations and especially large technical projects became much more contested than before. Therefore, the timing of the discovery of Groningen also was important.

The transition would probably not occur in the same way in current times. For current or future transitions, this means that a larger number and variety of actors has to be included in the process. Also, ideas on the role of government have been changing, providing an extra challenge for a transition to a more sustainable system of energy supply.

REFERENCES

Adelman, M.A. (1962), 'The supply and price of natural gas', supplement to the *Journal of Industrial Economics*, Oxford: Basil Blackwell.

Ausems, A.W.M. (1996), 'Nota de Pous 1962 en het aardgasgebouw', in H. 2020, *Handboek Energie en Milieu*, Alphen aan den Rijn: Samsom.

Brouwer, G.C., and M.J. Coenen (1969), *Nederland = Aardgasland, Ratio Reeks*, Amersfoort: A. Roelofs Van Goor.

Correljé, Aad (1998), *Hollands Welvaren: De geschiedenis van een Nederlandse bodemschat*, Hilversum: Teleac/Not.

Correljé, A.F., and P.R. Odell (2000), 'Four decades of Groningen production and pricing policies and a view to the future', *Energy Policy*, **28** (1), 19–27.

Correljé, Aad, Coby van der Linde and Theo Westerwoudt (2003), *Natural Gas in the Netherlands: From Cooperation to Competition?*, The Hague: Oranje Nassau Groep/Clingendael.

Davis, Jerome D. (1984), *Blue Gold: The Political Economy of Natural Gas, World Industries Studies 3*, London: George Allen & Unwin.

Dosi, G. (1988) 'Sources, procedures and microeconomic effects of innovation', *Journal of Economic Literature*, (26), 1120–71.

Ellis, J.H.M. (1965), *Natural Gas Marketing – Commercial Considerations and Economic Criteria*, proceedings of the seminar on the development and utilization of natural gas resources, Mineral Resources Development Series, New York: Economic Commission for Asia and the Far East, United Nations.

Estrada, J., Helge O. Bergensen, A. Moe and A.K. Sydnes (1988), *Natural Gas in Europe: Markets, Organization and Politics*, London and New York: Pinter Publishers.

Geels, F.W. (2002), 'Technological transitions as evolutionary reconfiguration processes; a multi-level perspective and a case study', *Research Policy*, **31** (8/9).

Heren, P. (1999), 'Removing the government from European gas', *Energy Policy*, (27), 3–8.

Kaijser, Arne (1998), 'The helping hand. In search of a Swedish institutional regime for infrastructural systems', in Lena Andersson-Skog and Olle Krantz (eds), *Institutions in the Transport and Communication Industries*, Canton, MA: pp. 223–44.

Kielich, Wolf (1988), *Ondergronds Rijk*, Amsterdam: Uniepers/Gasunie.

Lubbers, Ruud F.M., and C. Lemckert (1980), 'The influence of natural gas on the Dutch economy', in Richard T. Griffiths (ed.), *The Economics and Politics of the Netherlands since 1945*, 's-Gravenhage: Martinus Nijhoff, pp. 87–113.

Nelson, R.R., and B.N. Sampat (2001), 'Making sense of institutions as a factor shaping economic performance', *Journal of Economic Behaviour & Organization*, (44), pp. 31–54.

North, Douglas C. (1990), *Institutions, Institutional Change and Economic Performance*, Cambridge: Cambridge University Press.

Odell, Peter R. (1969), *Natural Gas in Western Europe: A Case Study in the Economic Geography of Resources*, Haarlem: De Erven F. Bohn.

Odell, Peter R. (2001), *Oil and Gas: Crises and Controversies 1961–2000, vol 1, Global Issues*, Brentwood: Multi Science Publishing Company.

Odell, Peter R. (2002), *Oil and Gas: Crises and Controversies 1961–2000, vol 2, Europes's Entanglement*, Brentwood: Multi Science Publishing Company.

Peebles, Malcolm W.H. (1980), *Evolution of the Gas Industry*, London: The Macmillan Press.

Peebles, Malcolm (1999), 'Dutch gas: Its role in the Western European gas markets', in Robert Mabro and Ian Wybrew-Bond (eds), *Gas to Europe*, Oxford: Oxford University Press, The Oxford Institute for Energy Studies.

Portegies, M.J. (1969), 'Marktstrategie van het Nederlandse aardgas', *Economisch Statistische Berichten*, **25** (June), 650–55.

Rip, A., and R. Kemp (1998), 'Technological change', in S. Rayner and L. Malone (eds), *Human Choice and Climate Change, vol 2, Resources and Technology*, Washington, DC: Batelle Press, pp. 327–99.

Rotmans, Jan, René Kemp, Marjolein van Asselt, Frank Geels, Geert Verbong and Kirsten Molendijk (2000), *Transitions and Transition Management: The Case for a Low Emission Energy Supply*, Maastricht: ICIS.

Schippers, Hans W., and Geert P.J. Verbong (2000), 'De revolutie van Slochteren', in Johan W. Schot (ed.), *Techniek in Nederland in de twintigste eeuw, vol II, Delfstoffen, Energie, Chemie*, Walburg: Pers Zutphen, pp. 203–19.

Stern, Jonathan P. (1984), *International Gas Trade in Europe: The Policies of Exporting and Importing Countries*, London: Heinemann Educational Books.

Van Aardenne, G.M.V. (1987), 'De Industrie – politieke slinger beweging', in A. Knoester (ed.), *Lessen uit het Verleden: 125 jaar Vereniging van Staatshuishoudkunde*, Leiden: Sternfert Kroese BV, pp. 319–31.

Van Overbeeke, Peter (2001), *Kachels, Geisers en fornuizen, Keuzeprocessen en energieverbruik in Nederlandse huishoudens 1920–1975*, Amsterdam: Posthumus Instituut/NEHA.

PART III

Transition policy

7. Managing the transition to sustainable mobility

René Kemp and Jan Rotmans

INTRODUCTION

This chapter examines the possibilities for achieving a transition to sustainable transport. It outlines and applies a new policy perspective, called transition management, developed by the authors for the Dutch government for managing the transition process to sustainable transport in a gradual, non-disruptive way. Because current policy has failed adequately to solve the mobility problem, there is a definite need for a new policy perspective that aims to develop structural, long-term solutions that offer user benefits and sustainability benefits. Transition management employs an integrative and multi-scale framework for policy deliberation, choice of instruments and actions by individuals, private and public organizations and NGOs. It aims for long-term change through small steps informed by transition goals and sustainability visions. It is not an instrument but a perspective for government and society as a whole.

The structure of the chapter is as follows. Section 2 offers a discussion of the problems of transport. Section 3 introduces the transition concept and offers a typology of transitions. Section 4 examines the governance aspect of transitions, discussing different coordination methods and modes of governance. Section 5 describes the model of transition management, which is applied to passenger transport in Section 7 after a discussion of the current Dutch transport and mobility policy in Section 6.

PROBLEMS RELATED TO TRANSPORT

Transport suffers from a series of serious problems: congestion, pollution, traffic accidents leading to casualties, noise, fragmentation of landscapes in rural areas and loss of space in urban areas. To these problems we may add the dependence on oil and oil constituencies. Transport is also a major energy consumer and contributor to global warming. In the EU, 28 per cent of CO_2 emissions come from transport and, if nothing is done, CO_2 emissions in 2010 will be 50 per cent above 1990 levels (EC, 2001). The social costs of transport are estimated at 5 per cent of GDP in OECD countries (Quinet, 1994).[1] All countries suffer from the above problems, which suggests that there is no apparent solution to them.

We believe the solution to these problems to lie not in a set of partial fixes but in instigating a transition towards a new system, either a totally new system or some combination of old and new systems. In the Netherlands, the Ministry of Transport, Public Works and Water Management (V&W) has accepted this view, and has set up a transition team to this end. It is currently investigating what to do. Progress in formulating transition policies has been slow, far slower than that at the Ministries of Economic Affairs and Agriculture who advanced much further in thinking about transition policies for the energy transition and the agricultural transition (see www.transitiemanagement.ez.nl).

THE CONCEPT OF TRANSITION

Transitions are transformation processes in which society or a complex subsystem of society changes in a fundamental way over an extended period (more than one generation, that is, 25 years or more) (Rotmans *et al.*, 2000). The term refers to a change in dynamic equilibrium in which an existing equilibrium is superseded by a new one. Transitions are interesting from a sustainability point of view because they offer the prospect of magnitude to environmental benefits through the development of new systems that are inherently more environmentally benign, and improvements of existing systems. Transitions consist of a combination of system improvement and system innovation, involving multiple changes (Rotmans *et al.*, 2000). Examples of new systems offering environmental benefits are: a hydrogen economy, industrial ecology (the closing of material streams through reuse of waste and energy) and customized mobility (as an alternative to auto mobility).[2]

In this chapter we distinguish two types of transitions:[3]

- *evolutionary* transitions, when the outcome is not planned in an important way;
- *goal-oriented* (teleological) transitions, when a (diffuse) goal or vision of the end state is guiding decision-makers, orienting strategic decisions of private decision-makers.

An example of the first is the transition from sailing ships to steam boats (described in Geels, 2002). An example of the second is the development of centralized electricity systems (described in Hughes, 1989).

Within a transition there is multiple causality and coevolution (Rotmans *et al.*, 2000, 2001; Geels, 2002 and this volume). The process of change in a transition is non-linear – slow change is followed by rapid change when concurrent developments reinforce each other, which again is followed by slow change in the stabilization stage. Transitions cannot be planned which is why we do not speak of 'planned transitions'. There are multiple shapes a transition can take but the common shape is that of a sigmoid curve such as that of a logistic. Population size follows an S-curve in a demographic transition. The same is true for the diffusion pattern of technological innovations, where the diffusion reaches a ceiling through an S-shaped pattern. This is a remarkably robust finding from the diffusion literature. It appears that almost all technological diffusion processes are of this form.

Although each transition is unique we believe it is useful to distinguish a number of distinct phases in a transition process:

- The predevelopment phase where there is very little visible change but a great deal of experimentation;
- The take-off phase where the process of change gets under way and the state of the system begins to shift;
- The breakthrough phase in which structural changes occur in a visible way through an accumulation of sociocultural, economic, ecological and institutional changes that react to each other; during the acceleration phase, there are collective learning processes, diffusion and embedding processes;[4]
- the stabilization phase where the speed of societal change decreases and a new dynamic equilibrium is reached.

All transitions contain periods of slow and fast development, caused by processes of positive and negative feedback. A transition consists of a process of gradual change (within which there may be some discontinuities such as a new policy or new institutions) typically spanning one or two generations (25–50 years).[5]

A transition can be accelerated by one-time events, such as a war or large accident (such as Chernobyl) or a crisis (such as the oil crisis) but not be caused by such events. That is due to the coevolution of a set of slow changes, the changes in the stocks that determine the undercurrent for a fundamental change. Superimposed on this undercurrent are events such as calamities that may accelerate the transformation process.

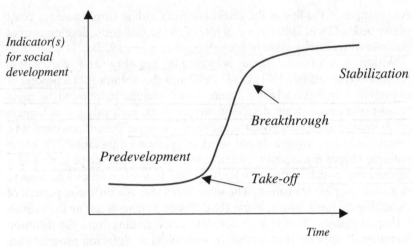

Source: Rotmans *et al.* (2000, 2001).

Figure 7.1   Four phases of transition

A TRANSITION

. . . is the shift from an initial dynamic equilibrium to a new dynamic equilibrium

. . . is characterized by fast and slow developments as a result of interacting processes

. . . involves innovation in an important part of a societal sub-system

---

The concept of transition can be used at different aggregation levels. When analysing transformations in socio-technical systems, it is useful to use the multi-level scheme of Rip and Kemp (1998) and Geels (this volume), which makes a distinction between niches, regimes and the socio-technical landscape.

Regimes are at the heart of the scheme. The term regime refers to dominant practices, rules and ensuing logic of appropriateness that pertain in a domain (either a policy domain or technological domain), giving it stability and guiding decision-making. We have technology regimes, production regimes, user regimes and policy regimes (see Geels, 2003). The second level is that of *niches*, places in which new things are done (possibly tested) or domains for specialized applications.[6] The niche may be a market niche or a niche created by a company (sponsoring a new technology) or government. The third level is the *landscape*, the overall setting in which processes of change occur. The landscape consists of the social values, policy beliefs, worldviews, political coalitions, the built environment (factories, and so on), prices and costs, trade patterns and incomes. The term landscape refers to the socio-technical shape of the land with its gradients, making certain advances easier to do than others (see Rip and Kemp (1998), Geels and Kemp (2000) and Geels (2002)).

The distinction between niches, regimes and socio-technical landscape helps to understand processes of structural change that are seen as the outcome of the interaction of multi-level processes. A common mechanism is landscape factors that put pressure on a regime of production, whose practices and technologies are challenged by new solutions pioneered in niches, with regime actors initially fighting and resisting alternative solutions focusing their attention and money on improving existing technologies, but over time changing course by investing in radical solutions. This is currently happening with fuel cells where Daimler-Chrysler and Ford, long resisting alternative types of propulsion, joined forces with Ballard, a Canadian-based manufacturer of fuel cells. Another example is BP, the UK oil giant which moved into renewables. When this happens, that is, when the belief systems (world views) and management strategies of key actors change, new developments gain momentum and a regime shift may occur.

POSSIBLE WAYS TO MANAGE TRANSITIONS

What are the possibilities for managing transitions? Can transitions really be managed? From what we have said it may be apparent that the easy answer to this question is that transitions cannot be managed for the simple reason that transitions are the result of the interplay of many unlike processes, several of which are beyond the scope of management, such as cultural change which can be considered more as an autonomous process. What one can do, however, is to influence the direction and speed of a transition through various types of steering.

Transitions defy control but they can be influenced. The management of transitions can be done through the (direct and indirect) use of three coordination mechanisms: markets, hierarchy and structure or institutions. Market coordination occurs when prices coordinate economic decisions. In the second, hierarchical case of planning (either state planning or company planning), economic activities are centrally coordinated through a plan or through a set of goals. The third type of coordination is through structure or institutions. By this we mean the coordination that is achieved through standard practices, trust, collective norms, networks and shared expectations and beliefs.[7] Institutions play a coordinating role by limiting the choice set, giving orientation, and reducing uncertainty. Without them the world would be rather unpredictable and the actors without orientation. One important institution is the self-assumed roles of companies (what kind of company they are and want to be). Networks too are an important institution of which the importance is increasingly recognized (Powell, 1990). Institutional change is an element of transition and policy should be concerned with it by facilitating processes of institutionalization.

The idea of institutions as collective properties, shaping further change, is very important for thinking about transitions and transition management. It brings into focus possibilities for intervention at a different level: the level of collective structures and matrices of institutions. Here we are thinking about policies oriented at (i) market structures and networks and (ii) actors' views and beliefs. Examples of the first are policies of market liberalization and privatization. Examples of the second are policies aimed at altering the engineering consensus and assumptions, cluster policies aimed at creating new clusters and product constituencies. What these policies have in common is that they are oriented at creating a structuralist element under which micro-behaviour will proceed.

So far, sustainability goals have been pursued through environmental policy, laying down specific requirements for products and processes, and through subsidies, policies for the use and development of environmental technologies. Past policies led to a considerable greening but progress is often viewed insufficient from a sustainability point of view (Weaver *et al.*, 2000; NMP-4, 2001). The possibilities for gradual improvement should be further exploited but one should also explore the possibilities of system changes that may lead to greater benefits. Support for the latter type of change is warranted because the time scale of system innovation is 25 years or more and beyond the mutual coordination possibilities of individual actors who have a short-term orientation. Economic change and technological progress in a market economy is driven by short-term economic benefits rather than long-term optimality (Kemp and Soete, 1992). System innovation meets several barriers and the environmental problems may be viewed as problems of system coordination besides as problems stemming from the non-internalization of external costs (Smith, 2002). We are often trapped into certain ways of doing things.

Given the institutional barriers to system innovation, policy interventions should be oriented not just at the economic frame conditions (through the use of taxes and regulations) but also towards beliefs, people's outlook on things, expectations, institutional framework and arrangements. Indicative planning through the setting of goals, and the creation of networks and constituencies for alternative systems are ways to do this. These regime policies should complement policies that change the cost structure. Furthermore, apart from a change in policies, we need changes in politics, which should be more oriented towards the long-term and towards sustainability goals. The policy regime has to change too (see Teisman and Edelenbos's chapter in this volume).

The power of the market in efficiently allocating the decisions of millions of actors should be utilized to the largest possible extent, for instance through the use of market-based instruments such as emissions trading, but it should be combined with using the intelligence of people in terms of ideas about alternative systems and institutions. Bottom-up initiatives such as experiments with new technologies should be encouraged and exploited. However, transition management is not limited to bottom-up initiatives but also has top-down elements. Examples are long-term goals, control policies, the establishment and maintenance of portfolios of options and industrial policies. What we need is that people's desire for a better society for themselves and for later generations (which is ill-served by free markets) gets institutionalized in the political system and is used as a guide for policy and economic decision making. Sustainability has to be discovered (created in the act of discovery), which is why we need a great deal of variation. It is not for the government to pick solutions, and their support should be short-term. In our view sustainability is best worked towards in a flexible, forward-looking manner, using all three coordination mechanisms in managing transitions: markets, hierarchy and structure.

TRANSITION MANAGEMENT

This section offers a model for managing transitions to sustainability. The model has been developed and used for the 4th National Environmental Policy Plan of the Netherlands (NEPP4) (VROM 2002). Transition management consists of a deliberate attempt to work towards a transition in what is believed to be a more sustainable direction. There are different ways of trying to achieve a transition. One can opt for the use of economic incentives, rely on a planning and implementation approach or some combination of the two: for example, the use of market-based indicative planning based on visions of sustainability. We opted for the last option, which allows the combination of the best from both worlds: the reliance on markets helps to safeguard user benefits and promotes efficiency, whereas the use of targets informed by long-term visions of sustainability helps to orient socio-technical dynamics to sustainability goals. We thus have efficiency, flexibility, and long-term welfare benefits.

The basic steering philosophy is that of *modulation*, not dictatorship or planning-and-control. Transition management joins in with ongoing dynamics and builds on bottom-up initiatives. Ongoing developments are exploited strategically. Transition management for sustainability tries to orient dynamics to sustainability goals. The long-term goals for functional systems are chosen by society through the political process or in a more direct way in a consultative process. The goals can be quantitative or qualitative. They may refer to the use of a particular solution (fuel cell vehicles, road pricing or multimodal transport) but preferably should refer to performance indicators such as non-congested transport that is safe, accessible and minimizes nuisance. The goals, and policies to further the goals, are not set in stone but should be constantly assessed and periodically adjusted in development rounds.

Existing and possible policy actions are evaluated against two criteria: first, the immediate contribution to policy goals (for example in terms of kilotons of CO_2 reduction and reduced vulnerability through climate change adaptation measures), and second, the contribution of the policies to the overall transition process. Policies thus have a *content goal* and a *process goal*. Learning, maintaining variety and institutional change, are important policy aims, and policy goals are used as means. The use of development rounds brings flexibility to the process, without losing a long-term focus. Transition management is oriented towards achieving structural change in a stepwise manner. A schematic view of transition management is given in Figure 7.2.

Transition management is based on a two-pronged strategy. It is oriented towards both system improvement (improvement of an existing trajectory) and system innovation (representing a new trajectory of development or transformation). The role of government varies in each transition phase. For example, in the predevelopment stage there is a great need for social experimentation and for visioning.[8] In the breakthrough phase there is a special need for controlling the side effects of large-scale application of new technologies. Throughout the entire transition the external costs of technologies (old and new ones) should be reflected in prices. This is not easy. Taxes are disliked by any person who has to pay them. Perhaps it helps if they are introduced as part of a politically-accepted transition endeavour, and when the revenues are used to fund the development of alternatives.

Transition management breaks with the old planning-and-implementation model aimed at achieving particular outcomes. It is based on a

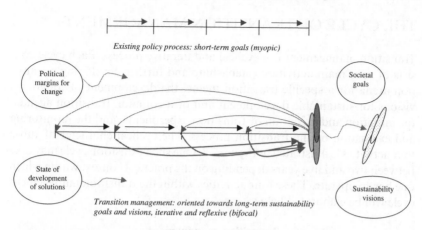

Figure 7.2   Current policy versus transition management

different, more process-oriented philosophy. This helps to deal with complexity and uncertainty in a constructive way. Transition management is a form of process management against a set of goals set by society whose problem-solving capabilities are mobilized and translated into a transition programme, which is legitimized through the political process. It does not consist of a strategy of forced development, going against the grain but uses bottom-up initiatives and business ideas of alternative systems offering sustainability benefits besides user benefits.

Key elements of transition management are:

- Long-term thinking (at least 25 years) as a framework for short-term policy.
- Backcasting: the setting of short-term and longer-term goals based on long-term sustainability visions and short-term possibilities.
- Thinking in terms of more than one domain (multi-domain) and different scale levels (multi-level); how developments in one domain (level) gel with developments in other domains (levels); trying to change the strategic orientation of regime actors.
- A focus on learning and the use of a special learning philosophy of 'learning-by-doing'.
- An orientation towards system innovation.
- Learning about a variety of options (which requires a wide playing field).

THE CYCLE OF TRANSITION MANAGEMENT

Transition management is a cyclical and iterative process. Each cycle consists of four main activities: establishing and further developing a transition arena for a specific transition theme; the development of long-term visions for sustainable development and of a common transition agenda; the initiation and execution of transition experiments; and the monitoring and evaluation of the transition process. The cyclical character of those four activities is illustrated in Figure 7.3. One such transition cycle may take between two and five years depending on the practical context within which one has to operate. These four activities within the transition management cycle will be elaborated below.

Transition management

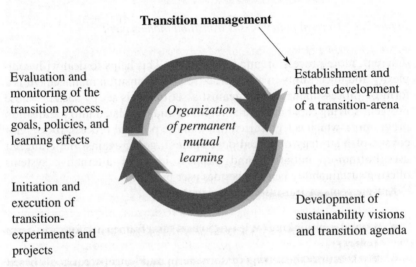

Evaluation and monitoring of the transition process, goals, policies, and learning effects

Organization of permanent mutual learning

Establishment and further development of a transition-arena

Initiation and execution of transition-experiments and projects

Development of sustainability visions and transition agenda

Figure 7.3   The cycle of transition management

The Establishment, Organization and Development of a Transition Arena

A novel and important aspect of transition management is the establishment and organization of a transition arena, in which innovators and imaginative people meet. It would operate in addition to (partly independent from) the normal policymaking networks dominated by incumbent companies having an interest in the status quo. The selection of participants for this transition arena is of vital importance. These participants need to have some basic competences at their disposal: they need to be visionaries, forerunners, able to look beyond their own domain or working area, open-minded thinkers. They must function quite autonomously within their organization but also have the ability to convey the developed vision(s) and set it out within their own organization. They need to be willing to invest a substantial amount of time and energy to play an active role in the transition-arena process.

Government has a task not just in the set-up of a transition arena but also in the facilitation of interactions within the transition-arena, not just in process-terms but also in terms of substance. A continuous process of feeding the participants in the arena with background information and detailed knowledge on a particular topic is necessary, enabling a process of coproduction of knowledge among the participants. This is of vital importance, because arena-experience shows that in most cases arena-participants have insufficient time, specific knowledge or overview to immerse themselves in complex problems. The arena is a novel institution for visionary (out-of-the-box) thinking, feeding into innovation decisions of organizations willing to innovate. The goal is not necessarily to strive for consensus but to discuss problem perceptions, long-term goals and transition paths.

The Development of Sustainability Visions and Transition Agendas

Transition management is based on sustainability visions and the use of transition goals and agendas for functional domains. Examples of goals in the area of energy are clean, cheap and reliable energy. Visions to achieve this are clean coal, renewables and recently, nuclear energy. Organizing an envisioning process aimed at sustainable development is cumbersome. It requires the ability to set aside one's own preferences and the concomitant everyday noise. It also requires insight and imagination to look ahead one or two generations. And last but not least it requires some sort of minimal agreement on what sustainability means for a specific transition theme, while opinions usually diverge. Many sustainability visions are still imposed by the government upon other parties in a top-down manner or originate from a select group of experts who are far from representative of the broad social setting needed.

The long-term visions of sustainability should be used as a guide to formulate programmes and policies and the setting of short-term and long-term objectives. To adumbrate transitional pathways, the transition visions must be appealing and imaginative so as to be supported by a broad range of actors. Inspiring visions are useful for mobilizing social actors, although they should also be realistic about innovation levels within the functional subsystem in question.

There will usually be different sustainability visions and pathways towards achieving them. This is visualized in Figure 7.4 in the form of a

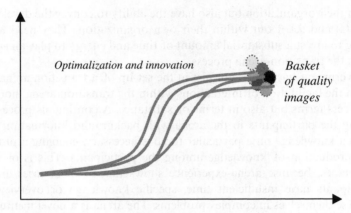

*Figure 7.4   Transition as a goal-seeking process with multiple transition
              images and goals*

basket of images with different paths towards the images. Over time, the
transition visions should be adjusted as a result of what has been learned
by the players in the various transition experiments. Based on a process of
variation and selection new visions emerge, others die out and existing
visions will be adjusted. Only during the course of the transition process
the most innovative, promising and feasible transition visions and images
will be chosen. This evolutionary goal-seeking process means a radical
break with current practice in environmental policy where quantitative
standards are set on the basis of studies of social risk, and adjusted for
political expediency. Risk-based target setting is doomed to fail when many
issues are at stake and when the associated risks cannot easily be expressed
in fixed, purely quantitative objectives. This holds true for climate change
but also for sustainable transport.

Transition management thus differs from so-called 'blueprint' thinking,
which operates from a fixed notion of final goals and corresponding
visions. Figure 7.2 shows the similarities and differences between current
policy-making and transition management. In each case, interim objectives
are used. However, in transition management these are derived from the
long-term objectives (through so-called 'backcasting'), and contain qualitative as well as semi-quantitative measures. Apart from *content* goals or
objectives (which at the start can look like the current policy objectives, but
later will increasingly appear to be different), transition management uses
process objectives (speed and quality of the transition process) and *learning* objectives (what has been learned from the experiments carried out;
what is blocking progress; identification of things that we want to know).
Learning, therefore, is a policy objective in its own right.

Transition-agendas

Based on the common problem perception and the shared sustainability vision(s) a joint transition-agenda can be designed. This is important because all arena-participants take their own agenda into the transition-arena, whereas a joint transition agenda contains common problem perceptions, goals, action points, projects and instruments. The means for realizing an effective execution of the proposed plans are important in order to resolve the problems on the transition-agenda as adequately as possible. Actually, a transition-agenda is a joint action programme for initiating or furthering transitions. It is important to register which party is responsible for which type of activity, project or instrument to be developed or applied. Government would be responsible for certain policies,[9] and industry for certain innovation activities. The monitoring of this joint action programme is important to guarantee that the transition agenda is complied with as well as possible.

An adequate transition agenda forms a binding element in the transition process, in which participants need each other. It coordinates action between mutually dependent actors. Coordination is thus achieved not only through markets but also through collective choice and new institutions. The transition agenda requires a kind of balance between structure and flexibility. Structure is needed to position the scale levels at which the issue in question plays, and to frame the issue in terms of themes and subthemes. The coherence between the various subthemes and scale levels is a separate, important point on the transition-agenda. Structuring the transition-agenda is time-consuming, but pays itself back in the form of increased quality of the transition management process (Dirven *et al.*, 2002). Flexibility is needed because the transition-agenda is dynamic and changes over time. The transition agenda helps to translate long-term thinking into short-term action. Agenda-setting is an iterative and cyclical process and is a learning process in itself.

The Use of Transition-experiments and Programmes for System Innovation

Programmes for system innovation are a key element of transition management. Here one should think of a programme for intermodal transport or decentralized electricity systems. The programmes should be time-limited and be adapted in the light of experience. An important element of these programmes are transition-experiments, that is, strategic experiments designed to learn about system innovation and transition visions. The crucial point is to measure to what extent these experiments and projects contribute to the overall sustainability system goals, and to measure in what way a particular experiment reinforces another experiment. Are there specific niches for experiments that can be identified? What is the attitude of the regime actors towards these niche experiments? The aim is to create a portfolio of transition-experiments which reinforce each other and whose contribution to the sustainability objectives is significant and measurable.

Preferably, these experiments need to link up with ongoing innovation projects and experiments, in such a way that the existing effort put into these innovation experiments can be used as much as possible. Often, many experiments already exist but these are not set up and executed in a systematic manner as a result of which the required cohesion is lacking. Because transition-experiments are often costly and time-consuming, the current infrastructure for innovative experiments should be used as much as possible. This will put some constraints on the feasibility and running time of these experiments, with a possible maximum of five to seven years. The execution mostly runs through the existing networks of the arena-participants to ensure the direct involvement of these forerunners.

The experiments are best undertaken as part of a portfolio-approach. Because transition processes are beset with structural uncertainties of different kinds it is important to keep a number of options open and to explore the nature of these uncertainties through the transition-experiments. Through learning experiences with transition-experiments, the estimation of these uncertainties changes in the course of the transition process. This in turn may lead to adjustment of the transition visions, images and goals. In this search and learning process scenarios play an important role, in particular explorative scenarios (see Elzen *et al.* in this volume), which attempt to explore future possibilities without too many decision-making constraints. Explorative scenarios allow for an investigation of which options and experiments are most promising and feasible, and which ones should drop out. This leads to a necessary variation and selection of options, taking account of possible sustainable futures.

The Monitoring and Evaluation of the Transition Process

Transition management involves monitoring and evaluation as a regular and continuous activity. Two different processes should be monitored: the transition process itself and the cycle of transition management. The monitoring of the transition process itself consists of the monitoring of macro-developments in terms of the slow changes in stocks, of niche-developments in terms of short-term fluctuations of streams, and of regime developments.

The monitoring of the transition management cycle consists of (i) the monitoring of actors within (also 'outside' the arena; just as important) the transition arena: their behaviour, networking activities, alliance forming and responsibilities with regard to activities, projects and instruments; (ii) the monitoring of the transition agenda: the actions, goals, projects and instruments agreed on; and (iii) the monitoring of the actions themselves: the barriers, prospects, points to be improved, and so on. The overall learning philosophy is that of 'learning-by-doing'. Monitoring learning processes, however, is easier said than done. The phenomenon of 'learning' is for many still an abstract notion that cannot be easily translated into components for monitoring.[10] It is therefore important to formulate explicit learning goals for transition experiments which can be monitored.

The evaluation of the above learning processes is a learning process in itself and may lead to an adjustment of the developed transition vision(s), transition-agenda and the transition management process within the transition-arena. The set interim objectives are evaluated to see whether they have been achieved. If this is not the case, they are analysed to see why not. Have there been any unexpected social developments or external factors that were not taken into account? Have the actors involved not complied with the agreements that were made?

Then a new transition management cycle starts which takes another few years. In the second round of this innovation network the proliferation of the required knowledge and insights is central, and this requires a specific strategy for initiating a broad learning process.

Creating and Maintaining Public Support

Because these transition management cycles take several years within a long-term context of 25 to 50 years, the creation and maintenance of public support is a continuous concern. When quick results do not materialize and setbacks are encountered, it is important to keep the transition process going and avoid a backlash. One way to achieve this is through participatory decision-making and the societal choice of goals. But societal support can also be created in a bottom-up manner, by engaging in experiences with technologies in areas in which there is local support. The experience may take away fears elsewhere and give proponents a weapon. With time, solutions may be found for the problems that limit wider application. Education too can allay fears but real experience is probably a more effective strategy. Through the prudent learning on the use of new technologies in niches, societal opposition may be circumvented.

Instrument Choices

Instruments for transition management are in a certain sense endogenous to the process. Transition management does not call for an upheaval in policy instruments but says that different policy fields should be better coordinated. Existing policies could be improved and extended as follows (see Smits and Kuhlmann, 2002):

- *science policy*: sustainability assessments of system innovations, transition road mapping, studies of past and ongoing transitions, focusing on the role of policy and usefulness of various governance models;
- *innovation policy*: the creation of innovation alliances, R&D programmes for sustainable technologies, the use of transition-experiments, and alignment of innovation policies to transition goals;
- *sector policy*: niche policies (through procurement, regulations or the use of economic incentives), the removal of barriers to the development of system innovations, and formulation of long-term goals and visions to give direction to research and innovation;

Smits and Kuhlmann (2002) talk about 'systemic instruments' that combine push with pull and that are not just about incentives but also about strategic intelligence.

Control Policies

A transition to sustainability cannot be achieved without control policies that put pressure on an existing technological regime. The external costs of existing technologies should be internalized, to create a more level playing field. This can be done through taxes and regulations, for example emissions standards. In the case of transport, we are thinking about policies of emission control, road pricing, parking rates and other types of transport management measures to discourage car use. The revenues may be used for investments in multimodal infrastructures.

THE DUTCH TRANSPORT AND MOBILITY POLICY

This section examines the transport and mobility policy in the Netherlands. The Dutch transport and mobility domain is characterized by a corporatist arrangement, in which peak associations play an important role.[11] In the Netherlands these associations include ANWB (representing the interests of car users), RAI and BOVAG (representing the car dealers and garages), 3VO (the traffic safety organization), KNV (freight transport companies), 'Nederland Distributieland' (Holland International Distribution Council) for motorized transport, NS (the national railway company), VSN (regional transport providers) and the large city public transport companies (especially those of Amsterdam and Rotterdam). The Ministry of Traffic and Transport consults with these associations about policy plans on which they have an important influence. Disabled people, cyclists, pedestrians and local actors are weakly represented in the closed policy network which, as far as transport policy is concerned, is dominated by transport engineers. Environmentalists are not very active in the transport domain, although the environmentalist group Milieudefensie (the Dutch branch of Friends of the Earth) has been campaigning against noise from Schiphol, the main airport, and is concerned about CO_2 emissions resulting from air travel and the general burning of fossil fuels.

In the socio-technical transport regime, the government is responsible for the construction and maintenance of the road infrastructure; it seeks to reduce the emissions of pollutants and noise, and it attempts to support public transport, partly through subsidies. These policies have been insufficient for dealing with the growth of transport and for making pubic transport more attractive to users. There are serious problems of accessibility, safety and overall quality of life, and problems related to energy use such as oil dependence and greenhouse gas emissions.[12]

In dealing with emissions, the government has relied heavily upon the use of technical fixes, such as the catalytic converter and use of unleaded petrol. Car traffic flows and volumes are not really controlled; driving speed is controlled only for reasons of safety, not energy consumption. The freedom to drive is accepted by state transport authorities as is people's perceived need for (auto-)mobility. Only within cities and towns is the freedom to drive curtailed through the limited use of car-free zones and one-way streets. A unique feature of the Netherlands are 'woonerven', residential areas where cars are not allowed to drive faster than 30 km per hour.

Within politics and the ministry, changes in technology and behaviour are seen as alternative ways to deal with transport problems which are pursued in parallel but separate from each other. The same is true for private and public transport, which are seen as separate, instead of symbiotic (except for some 'park and ride' facilities). Transport authorities have not yet embraced the new perspective of customized mobility and chain mobility, which tries to integrate public and private transport; they are still locked into the old idea of a modal shift as a strategy for dealing with congestion and pollution. Customized mobility is getting attention but policy-makers do not know how to translate it into concrete action. Progress towards chain mobility has been slow. Some transfer points (called 'transferia') for changing from private car to public transport have been built but these are little used, partly because they have been built at inconvenient locations for potential users. What is lacking is a coordinated attempt to encourage their mobility and discourage car use.

The existing policy in the field of new transport technologies (such as hybrid or electric cars) is very fragmented, being scattered over various stimulation programmes, and is very opportunistic. Experiments are carried out more or less ad hoc. They are not linked to a vision of sustainability or to transition programmes. An exception is the programme *Wegen naar de toekomst* (roads towards the future) which involves a series of experiments with novel road concepts such as flexible infrastructure, automatic vehicle guidance, modular and intelligent roads. This programme started in 1997 and is managed by the ministry who acts as a process manager. It analyses how the existing infrastructure may be better utilized.

There have been various experiments with electric vehicles as a possible means to reduce air pollution and because it constituted an interesting radical product. The experiments, however, are not taking place in a systematic trajectory of experimenting and learning. Very often, the outcome of the experiments is that the particular technology is not yet ready for the (existing) market, which means the (temporal) end of the experiment. Learning *across* experiments (where learning experiences from separate projects are used as input in a new project) hardly takes place.

An interesting initiative in the mid-1990s was *Innovatie in Inland Transporttechnologie* (innovation in national transport technology) which explored new concepts for transport such as intermodal chain mobility, underground city freight transport, fast ships, dynamic traffic management systems, dynamic transit information systems, modular vehicles, automatic vehicle guidance and tele-activities but this never led to concrete programmes and pathway policies pursued as part of a wider transition agenda.

With regard to pollution, especially lead, SO_2 and NO_x problems have been tackled. Lead emissions have been successfully controlled and NO_x emissions have fallen by 21 per cent since 1988. The CO_2 issue has hardly been dealt with, partly because the Dutch government and transport authorities regard CO_2 issues as primarily belonging to the European policy arena. This does not mean that it considers CO_2 unimportant because the Netherlands is quite active in the EU in trying to establish CO_2 levels.

Recently a transport minister, Netelenbos, has fought hard to introduce road pricing in the Randstad metropolitan area where problems of congestion are endemic, but encountered much opposition from the ANWB[13] (a very powerful organization with 3.6 million members, over 20 per cent of the Dutch population, representing the interests of car drivers) and the popular press. It shows that it is hard to press for solutions in a top-down manner. The problems in the Netherlands are of course in no way unique. All countries suffer from problems of congestion, dangerous roads, poor public transport and pollution. The next section will explain what an integrated approach may look like.

The above discussion shows that there are serious problems associated with transport (read: the individual use of cars) in the Netherlands. It has proved very difficult to deal with these problems. At the root of the problems is the growth in car use, which increased 25 per cent between 1986 and 1995 and is still growing. The attempt to introduce road pricing to use the infrastructure more efficiently failed because of societal opposition.

TRANSITION MANAGEMENT FOR SUSTAINABLE MOBILITY

It may be clear that there is no single solution to the problems of transport. Sustainable transport requires a wide array of innovations, technical as well as institutional ones, resulting in systems that offer attractive services for the users while limiting social costs (a list of possible solutions is given in Weber and van Zuylen, 2000). The model of transition management presented above helps to work towards these in a non-disruptive manner. Below, we envisage the elements of transition management described earlier in a transition towards sustainable mobility, focusing on land-based transport.

Transition Goals

The starting point for transition policy is not possible short-term solutions but long-term transition goals. Important goals for the transition are: accessibility, convenience, safety, reduced emissions of pollutants, CO_2 and noise, resulting in better transport and a better quality of life. It may be useful to quantify some of these goals. The goals, rather than the acute problems, should guide national policy and local transport policy. The transition goals should be chosen by society, perhaps as part of societal discussion where transport problems are discussed so that people will see a need for change. People should be directly involved – instead of indirectly (through the political process) – in the choice of transition goals. This constitutes a real break with the past when transport engineers decided on transport policy, and is probably more easily organized at the local level than at the national level. Even when the public does not agree on what kind of transport it wants, there will be areas in which new visions can be tried out and worked towards, with the help of money and support from national authorities. The involvement of the public in transport policy deliberations helps to legitimize programmes of structural change and partially circumvent destructive opposition (NIMBY problems).

Transition Visions

The articulation of transition visions is an important element of transition management. Transition visions, rather than the immediate problems, should guide policy. Transition visions are about solutions that are attractive from a user and societal sustainability point of view. The following elements appear attractive:

- *Customized mobility*: a combination of (individualized) public transport, the selective use of cars and other forms of transport, public as well as private (chain mobility);
- *Mobility management*: the management of traffic streams through road pricing, platooning (automatic vehicle guidance), information services, automatic zone access management using transponders to control access to city centres, parking policy, perhaps the use of tradable kilometre credits where people get mobility rights which they can use or sell;
- *Cleaner cars*: low-emission internal combustion cars, electric vehicles (hybrid vehicles or all-electric vehicles powered by batteries or fuel cells), urban cars, long-distance energy efficient cars with gas turbines (possibly hybrids);
- *Underground transport*: this may take various forms including the radical option of vacuum pipes for transporting capsules;
- *Teleworking*: working from home or a local telecentre, using modern computer communication, and teleconferencing, reducing the need for commuting (but, as a rebound effect, possibly leading to increased travel outside work);
- *Spatial planning limiting the need for transport*: compact cities, the (re)location of office buildings close to (public) transport nodes;
- *Regulation* that strongly favours and encourages customized mobility and discourages car use in specific zones.

Of these visions, cleaner cars and traffic management have received by far the most attention. Little attention has been given to customized mobility, even though it appears to offer the largest potential in the long term. The different visions have to be further articulated, assessed from a sustainability point of view, and discussed within society. Thus far, this has not been attempted in any serious way although recently a 'transition team' has been established at the ministry with this task. Of the visions, the one of customized mobility is the one that is least well articulated and assessed. An attempt to do so is given below.

CUSTOMIZED MOBILITY – THE SUBSTITUTION OF CAR SERVICES BY MOBILITY SERVICES

This consists of the use of mobility services customized to user needs. Car use is combined with other types of transport provided by mobility providers. We will have new types of public transport such as individualized public transport where you are picked up from your home and brought to your destination. Public transport is given preferential treatment through special bus lanes.

Customized mobility involves changes in ownership, infrastructure, car accessibility and behaviour. The trend towards the ownership of more than one car is reversed. People increasingly use cars owned by car-sharing organizations and public transport companies which can be accessed through smart cards and reserved.

Personal travel assistants (PTA) help people find mobility services and to make reservations.

Within such a system, we have mobility agencies and mobility centres where people can shift to other types of transport: light rail, public cars, bicycles etc. Intra and interurban traffic is linked at city mobility stations.

In such a system car accessibility is reduced through zoning policies, making cities more liveable, and we will have a greater variety of cars, for instance (silent) urban cars and (energy efficient) long-distance cars.

Congestion, transport emissions and nuisance are considerably reduced, by a factor 5 (compared to the factor 2–4 improvements that are possible with car-based forms of transport).

We estimate the benefits from customized mobility roughly at a factor of 5,[14] compared to benefits of factor 2 and factor 2–4 associated with transport management and improved car-based forms of transport. The potential for underground transport is hard to assess since the benefits are difficult to establish while the costs are very high, unless cheaper ways of building tunnels are developed.

It should be noted that customized mobility involves many innovations, including enhanced vehicle technology (such as urban cars, long-distance cars, changes in ownership, better public transport, mobility centres where travellers can change from one type of transport to another, and mobility agencies who supervise and manage fleets of cars, buses and bicycles.

These ideas are not new in themselves and can be found in government publications but policy has been oriented towards individual problems rather than towards long-term visions. When asked to think about sustainable mobility in 1995 the chairman of the ANWB, Nouwen, presented the idea of a mobility agency offering information services about possibilities for integrated or customized mobility. He thought the ANWB could become such an agency. But the idea never materialized, probably because an integrated collective effort was needed to pull it off. It is very important to create a business interest in sustainable mobility. Once established, actors can be enrolled into something new, implying they become part of the solution rather than part of the problem.

Transition Experiments

An important objective for policy is to learn about the potential of various visions. To achieve, this we propose to design a variety of social experiments with promising technologies and to create niches for promising technologies through strategic niche management. In transport, governments have supported research on batteries and telematics. Apart from promoting research it is important for society to engage in the real use of new technologies. The real use of new technology fosters interactive learning and institutional adaptation, which is necessary for pushing the transition process forward. Government policy could be used towards this end. Through the utilization of local opportunities for something novel, afforded by special circumstances (a local problem, a unique constituency, special competences), a transition path may be created in a bottom-up, non-disruptive manner.

A key question, of course, is which technologies should be experimented with. The answer, given in the literature on strategic niche management (Schot *et al.*, 1997; Kemp *et al.*, 1997, 1998; Hoogma *et al.*, 2002) is that it is especially important to stimulate pathway technologies, that is technologies that help to bridge the gap between the current regime and a new (sustainable) one, and thus help to escape lock-in.

This is more or less accepted in Dutch transport technology policy. The Dutch *Perspectievennota Verkeer en Vervoer* (the White Paper, 'Perspectives on Traffic and Transport', 1999) talks about *sleuteltechnologieën voor systeemvernieuwing* (key technologies for system innovation) and mentions electronic vehicle identification, automatic vehicle control, interoperability and a global positioning system as key technologies for system innovation. To these we would like to add electric propulsion and, especially, transport information, booking and reservation systems. Both electric propulsion and transport telematics have a great development potential as well as a great potential for achieving environmental sustainability benefits, probably not in the short term but in the long term when they are made part of an integrated mobility system. They are supported by public policies, and there has been investment in these technologies by industry but there is a gap between research and diffusion. Electric propulsion is often dismissed as inefficient because people think it requires batteries, which is not necessarily so. Batteries are one way of providing electricity in a vehicle, primarily suited for vehicles that run short daily distances. For other purposes, fuel cells or hybrid, partial electric propulsion systems are more suited. It is important to explore all kind of electric propulsion systems because they may create varying benefits and because society should not bet on one horse. The fuel cell vehicle is partially viewed as a magical environmental solution because it does not emit any pollutants, but it is also expensive and there is a safety issue because hydrogen is extremely volatile and explosive.

Experiments should be more than demonstration projects. They should be set up in such a way that suppliers as well as users learn about new possibilities. Basic assumptions and existing expectations should be tested through second-order learning (see Brown *et al.* in this volume). For example, car manufacturers should be stimulated to rethink their assumptions about what a car should do whereas users should be stimulated to rethink their mobility needs and how to satisfy these. Of course there is always a chance that the supported technology turns out to be a failure. Failures should be accepted but they could yet become a big problem in the current political system and a serious handicap for system innovation. Transition management helps to confront this by making learning a consideration for policy. Not everything has to be a success in economic terms if learning is a policy objective.

As to the roles of different government levels, local government should be involved in local initiatives, aimed at making local transport more sustainable. National authorities should disseminate the lessons from experiences at the local level, make sure that there is a good portfolio of experiments and facilitate learning across experiments.

The use of learning goals for policy is something novel and radical. Politics traditionally is based on quantitative and qualitative goals for policy outcomes. These still have a role to play but, as we said, should be supplemented by learning goals and goals for making a contribution to system innovation. Substantive goals should be used also for the overall transition and not just for achieving the outcomes.

Policy Programmes for System Innovation

An important part of transition policy are programmes for system innovation, such as programmes for chain mobility (also called 'customized mobility' or 'integrated mobility') and programmes for electric mobility.

These are not just technology programmes but also concern the creation of partnerships. Specific programmes often meet criticism from those who say that the government cannot pick winners. For instance, various government programmes to stimulate battery development have often been criticized because they did not lead to the widespread use of battery vehicles. This does not imply that they failed, however, because they did lead to the use of hybrid vehicles, running partly on batteries, and encouraged companies to investigate lightweight construction and aerodynamic designs that are about to be widely applied. But they have not developed an inexpensive battery with a long range, and after many years of support one should now probably focus attention on developing hybrid vehicles and fuel cell vehicles. It does not mean the programmes were not valuable. As to the nature of the programmes, these should focus on combination of promising options, be time-limited, and the need for support should be frequently assessed. When, after a while, it appears the programme does not yield sufficient learning in view of its costs, then it should be terminated.

In the formulation of these programmes, one should not rely altogether on the solutions favoured by established actors who are likely to be locked into old ways of thinking and have an interest in the status quo. The most innovative electric vehicles, for instance, were developed outside the automobile industry (Hoogma *et al.*, 2001).

On the basis of one of the vision elements presented above, a candidate programme would be a programme for chain mobility. Chain mobility makes a positive contribution to all dimensions of sustainability. It offers benefits in the form of reduced congestion and leads to lower emissions and fewer accidents through a more selective use of cars and trucks. At present there is a gap between individualized and collective transport but various innovations may help to bridge the gap such as:

- *Individual forms of public transport* that make public transport more flexible and more directly tied to the transport needs of the consumer. Examples are 'dial-a-bus' and collective taxis (such as the Dutch 'train-taxis'), using information technology for route planning and vehicle tracking.
- *Collective use of private means of transport*, such as car sharing, bicycle sharing, ride-sharing (e.g. car-pooling), 'stock-market' systems for sharing long-distance trips, or voluntary schemes for transporting disabled or elderly people. The attractiveness of such systems increases with their scope and incorporation of other innovations such as smart cards to access cars and bicycles.
- *Transit information systems and mobility information services* that tell people how they can combine different modes of transport. These

information schemes have to be complemented by 'park and ride' schemes. The existence of such information services may help different transport companies to better align their services and optimize the overall transport system.

The above innovations could help car drivers to move away from the single-vehicle-for-all-time-use paradigm and the individual use of cars. In our view there should be a large programme for integrated mobility because it is attractive from a sustainability *and* user point of view and needs a collaborative effort in terms of infrastructure (transfer places where various mobility services are offered), reorganization of the sector (the creation of mobility agencies and cooperation between transport companies), technology (information and ticketing systems) and the setting of standards of interoperability. In terms of transition it is a serious omission that neither the *Perspectievennota Verkeer en Vervoer* nor the new National Plan for Traffic and Transport (NVVP) have made it a central topic for the whole of transport but merely mention it when talking about public transport.[15] This is an area in which the Netherlands (as well as other countries) can achieve a great deal on its own because it is not dependent on foreign efforts and there are no competitive disadvantages involved. Even the truck sector benefits from it because chain mobility leads to a more efficient use of existing infrastructure.

Transition management does not imply a need to make a choice of one of the visions but recommends exploring several or even all of them simultaneously. Fortunately, several visions sustain each other: green vehicles can be used by car-sharing organizations and public transport companies. High-speed trains and personalized forms of public transport stimulate chain mobility. Whether transport management through road pricing will promote public transport and chain mobility or car use is unclear. If the congestion problem is effectively dealt with, car use becomes more attractive even when people have to pay extra for it. But this should not trouble us. It means that road pricing has benefits either way.

Control Policies

Transition policy should not only stimulate innovation but also use control instruments. We already have control programmes for emissions. What we need on top is policies for *mobility management*, the control of traffic streams. A better use of the road infrastructure leads to reduced congestion and less emission of pollutants. The principle of mobility management has already been officially accepted (as evidenced by the memorandum 'Mobility Management') but is still poorly implemented. Local authorities have an important role to play here since sustainability has local dimensions as well as global implications. Sustainability is about finding locally suitable solutions that are not probably disruptive. Here we are thinking about car-free zones, parking rates, the control of car movement and road pricing. Road pricing should be introduced as widely as possible, not just because it makes economic sense (Verhoef, 1994) and alleviates the problems of congestion but also because it is needed for a transition to alternative mobility and a reduced need for mobility.

It is important that not only the side-effects of the old systems should be contained but that potential side-effects of the new options should also be taken seriously in order not to create new problems. This requires assessment, monitoring and evaluation. Transition management thus relies on a combination of support and control, with the support being based on need. Control policies are an important part of any transition policy for sustainability.

Evaluation and Learning

This is an important element as we have stressed above. Policy should be oriented not just towards achieving particular outcomes but also towards learning. Policy should be adaptive which requires evaluation and learning. Not just instruments should be re-assessed but also goals and transition visions. Past experiments in transport have been too little oriented towards second-order learning (Hoogma *et al.*, 2002). For instance, we have learned very little about the system conditions for the use of transport innovations since the focus usually was on technical and/or economic aspects. Useful lessons may also be learnt from abroad: there is a need to combine lessons learned with experience elsewhere on the same option and a need to evaluate and learn across niches. There should be a transition monitor, which monitors progress and identifies problems.[16]

Creation of Public Support and New Institutions

Transition management implies a need to create social support for transitions in general and specific transition-actions. These are long-term processes with which one should start early. Transport authorities should have started with road pricing at least 10 years ago, as was done in other countries (France, Norway and more recently the UK in the city of London). Differential pricing is already applied in other areas, such as train tickets and in theatres. One can also think about mobility points systems, where people can use or sell mobility rights. The support for new mobility management systems may be created through societal debate and real use. Road pricing was accepted in the countries in which it was introduced after people experienced the benefits.

The Transition Arena and Council

The transition actions should be pursued as part of transition agendas in which there are short-term and long-term transition goals and actions. To stimulate out-of-the-box thinking, outsiders should be involved in the policy formulation process and there should be a commitment to change and clear stakes. This is probably best organized through the set up of a transition arena, and the set up of a transition council with independent experts with a special responsibility for safeguarding the transition process. It should be composed of policy actors (government, business, NGOs) and independent experts. It is important to create a distance between the council and the government because the government is part of the problem and is ill-equipped to deal with innovation issues (Vergragt, 2001).

It should be noted that transition management makes use of the three mechanisms of economic coordination: markets, hierarchy (in the form of planning and control policies), and institutional coordination. It uses markets by relying on decentralized decision-making for making product and service choices. It makes use of (indicative) planning, consisting of a transition goals and policy objectives. And it uses new and old institutions for coordination. The new institutions are: the use of a new model for policy, transition agendas and goals, the fostering of new networks through the transition arena, and perhaps the establishment of a transition council with decision-making responsibilities. Transition policies are also concerned with institutional change. An example is the creation of mobility agencies and new types of cooperation between transport actors. This could be achieved in a direct way through socio-technical alignment policies and in an indirect way through market liberalization policies.

CONCLUDING REMARKS

In this chapter we outlined a model for transition management and applied it to motorized passenger transport, offering practical suggestions for a transition policy, such as programmes for customized mobility, the use of a transition agenda for transport, and the creation of a platform (arena) for innovative actors.

Transition management offers a model for achieving long-term change (a transition) in a gradual, non-disruptive manner. It uses the power of markets and planning and is engaged with the establishment of structuralist elements for transitions (see Grin *et al.*, 2003). Through transition management, a transition path is not chosen but *created in the attempt to traverse*. By creating a little bit of irreversibility in the right direction, the transition process is pushed forward (Rip and Kemp, 1998, p. 391). In our view, transition management not only makes good sense but it is perhaps the only doable way of achieving sustainability benefits while limiting the problems of discomfort. Any other approach is bound to fail in view of the integrated nature of the problems we are facing. In the Netherlands the approach of transition management has been adopted by various ministries, including the ministry responsible for transport, to deal with persistent problems.[17] Hopefully the suggestions will feed into the policy process, but the principal purpose of this chapter was to outline the idea of transition management and give an idea of what it implies in a concrete case.

The model of transition management has been criticized by Berkhout *et al.* (this volume) as relying too much on bottom-up initiatives and expecting too much from solutions grown in niches. In our view, bottom-up initiatives do have an important role to play but unless they are complemented by control policies putting pressure on the existing regime these initiatives will not contribute much. We think that policy should be oriented towards niches as well as regimes and the general conditions. We believe that the commitment of government to a transition, and the institutions being created for transitions will make it easier to introduce control policies. So far this has not happened since transition policy is still in its initial phases, having started with setting up transition arenas with innovative actors.

We want to stress that transition management is not a substitute for control policies (such as pollution taxes or road pricing), which indeed are necessary to bring about transitions towards sustainable energy, transport and agriculture. Transition management does form an important addition, though, notably to improve the coordination of different policies and different policy domains, and to create room for change in a reflexive, adaptive and forward-looking manner.

NOTES

*   We want to thank Boelie Elzen and Derk Loorbach for their helpful comments and suggestions.
1. The European Commission in its communications uses an estimate of 4.1 per cent. This estimate does not include the transport contribution to global warming. The estimates are based on various studies reported in the Communication to the commission 'Towards Fair and Efficient Pricing in Transport' by Neil Kinnock. Ninety per cent of the external costs of transport come from road transport which gives rise to an external cost of 250 billion euros, with cars being responsible for a cost of 164 billion euros.
2. Other examples of system innovation are: biomass-based chemistry, multiple sustainable land-use (the integration of the agricultural function with other functions in rural areas) and flexible, modular manufactured construction (discussed in Ashford *et al.* (2001)).
3. Other typologies are offered by Geels (this volume) and Berkhout *et al.* (this volume).
4. In earlier publications we called this phase the acceleration phase. 'Breakthrough phase'

is probably a better term because it refers to the *absolute* amount of change, which is highest in this stage, rather than the relative amount of change (the speed).

5. The timespan is not a defining characteristic but a result.
6. The place can be a geographic place or refer to a special kind of product or technology used by specialized users.
7. The notion of institution used here is a broad one, which includes interpretative frames and belief systems that colour problem definitions and includes engineering consensus about the relevant problems and appropriate approaches for solving problems in a technical domain (see Parto, 2003).
8. Visioning and experimentation has to continue in the other phases; initial visions should be adapted and new experiments should be set up to learn new things. See Brown *et al.* in this volume.
9. Instrument choices are discussed further on in a separate section.
10. For a discussion of several aspects of learning, see Brown *et al.* in this volume.
11. Corporatism is one of the four ideal types of arrangements identified by Eising and Kohler-Koch (1999). The other three types are: statism, pluralism and network arrangements.
12. The number of traffic deaths in the Netherlands is 1200 and a million traffic accidents of which the total costs are estimated at 11.5 billion guilders (5.2 billion euros). The societal costs of congestion increased by 70 per cent in the 1990/2000 period and are estimated at 1.7 billion guilders (0.3 per cent of GDP) (*Perspectieven nota Verkeer en Vervoer, 1999*). There are no figures for the liveability problem. Not all problems have got worse. The number of traffic deaths is 13 per cent below the 1986 level. NO_x emissions fell 21 per cent since 1988 (figures are for 1998). Currently the focus is on volatile organic compounds, sulphur and particle emissions from diesel engines, and fuel economy.
13. ANWB recently changed its position: it accepts road pricing for special lanes (for commercial transport and for people willing to pay for the use of such lanes).
14. The benefits are greater safety, less congestion and pollution, and less intrusion of social life. Further research is needed on the magnitude of the benefits and on combining the different elements into a single factor.
15. The only noteworthy policy initiative is the Move Programme for Chain Mobility which supported 87 projects in the 1999/2001 period and which is extended to 2006. Under this programme in the 1999/2001 period 8.6 million euros were spent on such things as electronic bicycle racks, park and cycle arrangements, organized car sharing, van pooling, and ICT for transport (Move.02.04 Resultatenboek, 2002). Useful lessons were learnt about the single projects but little has been learnt about chain mobility overall. No attempt was made to institutionalize chain mobility at the local level or national level. It did not lead to a coordinated effort for chain mobility.
16. The details of such a monitor still need to be worked out.
17. Ministry of Housing, Spatial Planning and the Environment (coordination), Ministry of Agriculture (sustainable agriculture), Ministry of Foreign Affairs/Development Aid (biodiversity and natural resources), Ministry of Transport, Public Works and Water Management (sustainable mobility), Ministry of Economic Affairs (sustainable energy).

REFERENCES

Banister, David, Dominic Stead, Peter Steen, Jonas Akerman, Karl Dreborg, Peter Nijkamp and Ruggero Schleichter-Tappeser (2000), *European Transport Policy and Sustainable Mobility*, London and New York: Spon Press.

Eising, R., and B. Kohler-Koch (1999), 'Introduction', in B. Kohler-Koch and R. Eising (eds), *The Transformation of Governance in the European Union*, London: Routledge.

Elzen, B., R. Hoogma and J. Schot (1996), '*Mobiliteit met Toekomst – Naar een vraaggericht technologiebeleid*' (Mobility with a future-towards a demand-oriented technology policy), report to the Dutch Ministry of Traffic and Transport.

Elzen, Boelie, Remco Hoogma and René Kemp (2001), '*Managing the transition to sustainable transport through strategic niche management*', paper for conference 'Managing Transitions in the Transportation Sector: How Fast and How Far?', 11–14, September 2001, Asilomar, CA, published in Dan Sperling and Ken Kurani (eds) *Transportation, Energy and Environmental Policy. Managing Transitions* (2003), Washington, DC: Transportation Resource Board of the National Academies, pp. 175–203.

European Conference of Ministers of Transport (ECMT) (1995), *Urban Travel and Sustainable Development*, Paris: OECD.

European Commission (2001), white paper European Transport Policy for 2010. Time to Decide, Brussels: TREN.

Geels, F.W. (2002), 'Technological transitions as evolutionary reconfiguration processes: a multi-level perspective and a case-study', *Research Policy*, **31** (8/9), 1257–74.

Geels, F.W. (2003), 'Going beyond the sectoral systems of innovation approach: making use of insights from sociology and institutional theory', paper submitted for publication in *Research Policy*.

Geels, Frank, and René Kemp (2000), *Transities vanuit sociotechnisch perspectief*, achtergrondrapport voor de studie 'Transities en Transitiemanagement' van ICIS en MERIT ten behoeve van NMP-4, November 2000, UT, Enschede en MERIT, Maastricht.

Grin, John, Henk van de Graaf and Philip Vergragt (2003), 'Een derde generatie milieubeleid: een sociologisch perspectief en een beleidswetenschappelijk programma', *Beleidswetenschap*, **17** (1).

Hoogma, R. (2000), *Exploiting Technological Niches. Strategies for Experimental Introduction of Electric Vehicles*, Enschede: Twente University Press.

Hoogma, Remco, René Kemp, Johan Schot and Bernhard Truffer (2002), *Experimenting for Sustainable Transport Futures. The Approach of Strategic Niche Management*, London: Spon.

Kemp, René (2000), 'Technology and Environmental Policy – Innovation effects of past policies and suggestions for improvement', OECD proceedings *Innovation and the Environment*, Paris: OECD, pp. 35–61.

Kemp, René, and Benoît Simon (2001), 'Electric vehicles. A socio-technical scenario study', in Eran Feitelson and Erik T. Verhoef (eds), *Transport and the Environment. In Search of Sustainable Solutions*, Cheltenham: Edward Elgar, pp. 103–35.

Kemp, René, and Jan Rotmans (2001), 'The management of the co-evolution of technological, environmental and social systems', paper for conference Towards Environmental Innovation Systems, Eibsee, 27–9 September, 2001 forthcoming in Matthias Weber and Jens Hemmelskamp (eds), *Towards Environmental Innovation Systems*, Springer Verlag.

Kemp, René, Arie Rip and Johan Schot (1997), 'Constructing transition paths through the management of niches', paper for workshop 'Path Creation and Dependence', Copenhagen, 19–22 August, 1997, (published in Raghu Garud and Peter Karnoe (eds) (2001), *Path Creation and Dependence*, Lawrence Erlbaum Associates Publishers.

Kemp, René, Bernhard Truffer and Sylvia Harms (1998), 'Strategic niche management as a tool for transition to a sustainable transportation system', in K. Rennings, O. Hohmeier and R.L. Ottinger (eds), *Social Costs and Sustainable Mobility – Strategies and Experiences in Europe and the United States*, Heidelberg, New York: Physica Verlag (Springer), pp. 167–87.

Kinnock, Neil, 'Towards fair and efficient pricing in transport', communication to the European Commission, COM(95)691.

Move.02.04 (2002), Resultatenboek, June, accessed at www.move-mobiliteit.nl.

Ministry of Transport, Public Works and Water Management (1999), 'New national plan for traffic and transport (NVVP)', the Hague.

Ministry of Transport, Public Works and Water Management (1999), 'Perspectievennota Verkeer en Vervoer', The Hague.

Ministry of Transport, Public Works and Water Management (2002), 'Nota mobility management', The Hague.

Nouwen, P.A. (1995), 'Ontsnapping uit de 20ste eeuwse vervoersdilemma's in Verkeerschaos en vervoershonger – Perspectief op Mobiliteit', SMO, The Hague.

Parto, Saeed (2003), 'Economic activity and institutions: taking stock', MERIT research memorandum 2003–07, Maastricht.

Powell, Walter W. (1990), 'Neither market nor hierarchy, network forms of organisation', *Research in Organizational Behaviour*, **12**, 295–336.

Quinet, E. (1994), 'The social costs of transport: evaluation and links with internalisation Policies', in *Internalising the Social Costs of Transport*, Paris: OECD, pp. 31–76.

Rip, Arie, and René Kemp (1998), 'Technological change', in Steve Rayner and Liz Malone (eds), *Human Choice and Climate Change, vol. 2 Resources and Technology*, Washington DC: Battelle Press, pp. 327–99.

Rip, Arie, Tom Misa and Johan Schot (eds) (1995), *Managing Technology in Society. New Forms for the Control of Technology*, London: Pinter Publishers.

Rotmans, Jan, René Kemp, Marjolein van Asselt, Frank Geels, Geert Verbong en Kirsten Molendijk (2000), 'Transities & Transitiemanagement. De casus van een emissiearme energievoorziening', eindrapport van studie 'Transities en Transitiemanagement' ten behoeve van NMP-4, October 2000, ICIS & MERIT, Maastricht.

Rotmans, Jan, René Kemp and Marjolein van Asselt (2001), 'More evolution than revolution. Transition management in public policy', in *Foresight* 3 (1), 15–31.

Smits, Ruud, and Stefan Kuhlmann (2002), 'The rise of systemic instruments in innovation policy', mimeo.

Vergragt, Philip J. (2001), 'Backcasting for environmental sustainability: from STD and SusHouse towards implementation', paper for conference Towards Environmental Innovation Systems, Eibsee, 27–29 September, 2001.

Verhoef, E. (1994), *The Economics of Regulating Road Transport,* Cheltenham: Edward Elgar.

VROM (2000), 'National Environmental Policy Plan (NEPP)', The Hague.

Weaver, Paul, Leo Jansen, Geert Grootveld and Philip Vergragt (2000), *Sustainable Technology Development*, Sheffield: Greenleaf Publishing.

Weber, Matthias K., and Henk van Zuylen (2000), 'European policy for technology innovation in transport: finding the right role and the right options', IPTS report 48, October, 4–13.

8. Getting through the 'twilight zone': managing transitions through process-based, horizontal and interactive governance

Geert R. Teisman and Jurian Edelenbos

INTRODUCTION

Quality is in the Eye of the Beholder and Requires Combining Above All

Sustainable development is a frequently discussed concept (Palmer *et al.*, 1997). It fits in with the more general quest for quality. This quest appears to become an important point of attention in a network society. There seems to be a broad consensus that quality is needed. In that sense the need for sustainability is universally defined and embraced. The definition has to do with survival and with the ability to develop a society without creating a scarcity of its basic elements and building materials. Although the quest for sustainability may command broad support, effective results will not be realized easily.

The lack of progress in achieving effective results has partly to do with the differences of opinion on the question of what sustainability is and how it is to be achieved. Definitions of sustainable development vary considerably. Various directions to solve the problem are defined. Every direction in itself can be advanced by different implementation schemes. Transitions towards sustainability therefore will have to be achieved within a multiplicity of realities. This insight will serve as a basis assumption for our research on the question of how sustainability can be achieved.

It draws our attention to perceived realities. How sustainability is defined, and how this 'better' situation is to be achieved, is in the eye of the beholder. The meaning of 'sustainable development' is determined by different standards, beliefs, values and interests, but also by different perceptions of what our circumstances are and what these are likely to be in the near future. We assume that the meaning will develop over time and can combine a variety of aspects. Combining will help implementation.

Combining Requires More Complex Methods of Transition Management

To create sustainable development, new methods of transition management are considered. We agree with Robert Flood (1999, p. 1) that 'Traditional management strategies that seemed sufficient as recently as a generation ago are found wanting today'. And we also tend to agree with Elliot and Kiel's idea that 'the best adaptive match for complexity is greater complexity' (Elliot and Kiel 1997, p. 76).

Guiding society towards (much) more sustainability requires transition management that can handle a variety of definitions used by the many actors involved. Transition management is not in the first place an implementation project based on clear goals and planning schemes. Rather, it should be conceptualized as a quest for joint visions on and passable paths towards sustainability.[1] We emphasize the use of the plural form in this statement: the quest should deal with multiplicity and should even use it as a quality in itself. This is what we mean by 'adaptive match for complexity'. Transition management should incorporate the idea that the organizations involved in the transaction process will have and will maintain different definitions of the most desirable result and the most suitable methods to achieve 'their' kind of sustainability.

Long-term Transition in a Network of Nearsighted Organizations

A transition process is inter-organizational and cannot be dedicated just to the position and view held by a single actor. At the same time the actors involved in the processes will normally think in terms of their own positions and viewpoints. In general this leads not just to an overestimation of their own position and the effectiveness of their own methods, but also to an underestimation of the importance of other organizations and the effectiveness of the methods they use. Another consequence of nearsighted organizations is that they tend to expect others to change their viewpoints and management methods in order to create transitions and at the same time assume that they themselves can go on acting in the same way as they have been doing. This applies particularly to government organizations. They tend to adhere to their own organizational habits, and in fact this is one of problems that need to be addressed by transitions.

Transition is Above All Ongoing Interaction

Because of the multiplicity of the 'sustainable development' concept, transition processes have to be organized and managed in terms of ongoing interaction (Baxter *et al.*, 1999; DeSario and Langton, 1987; Kickert *et al.*, 1997;

Pelletier *et al.*, 1999; Renn *et al.*, 1995; Edelenbos, 2001). Inter-organizational interaction should enable stakeholders to find temporary balances between economic, social, spatial and ecological goals in order to develop joint or at least mutually supportive actions. A balance will be temporary and only be held as long as the first results satisfy the actors. This makes any balance unstable. Roads and destinations are under discussion at the same time.

The roads to a more sustainable society are open ones, which pursue important changes towards sustainability, but also deal with a variety of definitions regarding specific goals and the effectiveness of the means applied, including definitions of the entire situation. The main management dilemma will be that while progress has to be made, at the same time there should also be a discussion about what such progress really entails.

Interaction as a Means for Transition and a Transition in Itself

A wide range of interactive processes has recently been developed and examined in the public domain (Teisman and Klijn, 2002). Interactive processes are well-known in the relationship between government and citizens. However, interaction in transition processes should be far more comprehensive, since this also involves interaction between various levels of government. Intergovernmental interaction is particularly problematic here. Because of their strongly organization-oriented way of thinking and organizing, governments are not well equipped for cooperation. The paradox seems to be that it is precisely because competition is denied within governments, and precisely because a formal illusion of unity is upheld, that competition tends to flourish and becomes difficult to handle (because it is rejected).

A third dimension of interaction processes is public–private partnership. In the traditional government approach, an important difference is assumed to exist between market and government. Here, processes normally take the form of government steering of the function of the market on the one hand and the contracting out of schemes on the other. Transitions, however, require more than this: they should, to a considerable extent, constitute a joint undertaking in which interaction is the norm.

The experiences with recent attempts to develop interactive practices have been only partly successful (Edelenbos, 2000; Klijn and Koppenjan, 2000; Edelenbos and Monnikhof, 2001; Teisman, 2001; Tops *et al.*, 1999). The mixed results make clear that transition management has to take place in a context of simultaneous changes: the subject matter (sustainability implies multiple goals and combination) and the management methods are under (re)construction. It seems to be extremely difficult for organizations to accomplish both these changes simultaneously. Sometimes it is even seen as a guarantee of failure if an organization attempts to change its goals and its methods at the same time. Transition management, however, does require this combination of changes. The traditional organization-based, hierarchic management paradigm has to be transformed into or combined with a process-based, horizontal interaction paradigm.

Getting Through The Twilight Zone

Periods of transition can be conceptualized as 'twilight zones', in which old institutions, identities and habits exist next to new ones, and struggle with each other for dominance. The new identity tries to take over, whereas the old one tries to resist take-over. Attempts to restore hierarchy and the importance of political parties are accompanied by experiments with interactive arrangements. The struggle in the 'twilight zone' of institutional change will probably take time and will create a rather ambiguous situation.

In a twilight zone reality and unreality merge. The twilight zone is '. . . the no-man's land between the old reality and the new. It's the limbo between the old sense of identity and the new' (Bridges, 1995, p. 5)[2]. Different realities exist side by side with alternately one or the other gaining the upper hand. It is not a crossing from one side of the street to the other. It is a journey from an existing identity to a developing one. People need to recognize that it is natural to feel somewhat frightened and confused in this no-man's land. As the old patterns are extinguished in their minds and the new ones begin to take shape, people in this neutral zone are assailed by self-doubt (Bridges, 1995).

What Will Follow

The next section will explore the concept of 'transition'. A subsequent section will discuss the development of a process-based horizontal interactive management approach to transitions. Next, we will address institutional barriers that are likely to undermine this approach. We will consider methods to bypass these barriers and will end the chapter with the presentation of three different democratic systems as combinations of organization-based and process-based public management approaches.

TRANSITIONS: FURTHER CONCEPTUAL EXPLORATION

Introduction

Various concepts exist that address aspects of the term 'transition': transformation, innovation, change, evolution, revolution and breakthrough.

The term transition specifically emphasizes the dynamic aspects, from an initial situation to a different situation with characteristics that did not exist in the initial situation. Something new has to be created (see Chapter 1 in this volume).

Transition and Change

Some authors make an explicit distinction between change and transition. 'Change is situational: the new site, the new boss, the new team roles, the new policy. Transition is the psychological process people go through to come to terms with the new situation. Change is external, transition is internal' (Bridges, 1995, p. 3). Bridges even goes one step further by stating that change will not occur unless a transition has taken place: 'There can be any number of changes, but unless there are transitions, nothing will be different when the dust clears. (. . .) Transition depends on letting go of the old reality and the old identity you had before the change took place. (. . .) Transition starts with an ending' (*ibid.*, p. 4).

Transition and Recursiveness

In the literature on transition (more specifically that on organizational change) a distinction is made between changes *within* and changes *of* existing repertoires. Here the word 'repertoires' refers to routines, existing patterns of behaviour and action, and institutions. There is widespread agreement that recursiveness is sustained by standard operating procedures, by sagas, myths and ideologies, by the interests of political coalitions, and by single-loop learning (Clark and Starkey, 1988).

The term 'recursiveness'[3] can be used to describe change within existing repertoires, while the term 'transition' refers to changes of existing repertoires (*ibid.*, p. 50). 'Attention to recursiveness strongly suggests that a distinction should be drawn between two kinds of change; recursiveness – reproduction from the repertoire or structural poses; and transitions in which there are alterations to the repertoire and/or their deployment to events' (*ibid.*, p. 60). Thus, recursiveness means the reproduction of existing processes, structures and systems, while transition, on the other hand, implies that a change is taking place from an existing structure or existing system into a new structure or system.

Transitions: Rapid and Slow

The distinction between recursiveness and transition leads to another distinction: that between rapid (revolutionary) and slow or gradual (evolutionary) transitions. In the perspective of rapid transitions, consciously initiated transitions are emphasized (Beckhard and Harris, 1987; Hammer and Champy, 1993). This perspective sees transitions as revolutions that are capable of being manipulated and realized quickly. The perspective of gradual transitions focuses on revolutions that are difficult to manage and control, and that are often of a coincidental and unintentional nature.

Those who see transitions mainly as slow and cumbersome processes emphasize the principle of structuring, or *structuration* (Giddens, 1984). 'Slow change models implicitly show (. . .) events as bound by multiple networks of habits and unreflective practices legitimated by ideologies and by rules' (Clark and Starkey, 1998, p. 62). Structuration means that habits, routines, hidden (and often unspoken) rules, agreements, language and moral codes provide a certain regularity, repetition and order to human intentions and activities. In other words: existing structures and institutions provide repetition and therefore recursiveness rather than transitions. Structuration provides stability, which is often maintained over a very long period. Structuration is retained and continues to accumulate problems until the system is ready to explode; an explosive change, that is to say, a transition, is the final result.

Miller and Friessen (1984) have shown that transitions do have different origins and routes.[4] In their opinion, organizations tend to retain and elaborate existing configurations over a relatively long period. Any configurations are likely to be both recursive and (as they emphasize) to attain a high degree of momentum towards an archetypal consistency. They argue that all configurations imply a theoretical fit between the structural form and three arrays of elements: (i) the system of meaning; (ii) its most powerful sub-units; and (iii) its key contingencies. The fit between structural form and the three arrays will be the result of a socioevolutionary process by which inappropriate enterprises are removed. Consequently, the momentum of the configurations will continue until either the enterprise is eliminated (a possibility that is not examined by them) or there is a quantum leap to a totally new configuration.

Transitions: Quantum Leaps Only?

Miller and Friessen (1984) explored transitions by postulating two basic assumptions on episodes of change. Firstly, that these episodes will be of two distinct kinds. The first kind of episode will occur when the existing configuration is carried forward in a slightly modified format rather than altered in any significant manner. This is labelled *momentum*. The second kind of episode is defined by a sharp difference between the starting and closing scores. This difference will indicate that packages of variables are moving in dissimilar directions: this type of episode is labelled a *transition*. It is expected, firstly, that instances of momentum will outnumber instances of transition, and secondly, that transitions will and should be very rare occasions on which there will be a dramatic alteration in the entire configuration of the organization – its strategy, its structuration and its system of meaning.

In their work Miller and Friessen propagate the 'quantum leap thesis', which is part of the debate on the best approach to transitions. Should transitions occur in the manner of logical incrementalism as suggested by Lindblom (1959, 1993 with Woodhouse) or in the manner of very extensive and dramatic transformations? Miller and Friessen argue that transitions should generally take the form of dramatic alterations or quantum leaps: 'Eventual changes in structure must often be dramatic and revolutionary' (Miller and Friessen, 1984, p. 217).

So, in addressing the issue of transitional change, they contend that such change should be dramatic and that it ought to involve the creative destruction of the existing repertoires. Their reasoning is that organizational symbolism and the meaning systems are tightly linked into organization-specific paradigms whose major form of alteration is single-loop learning. They argue that it would be impossible for organizations to keep shifting their meaning systems and structural forms in a fine-tuned adjustment to each fluctuation in the states of key contingency variables as implied in the organization-design theories proposed by Galbraith (1977). Instead, it may be anticipated that organizations will retain and refine an archetypal design over a long period.

Others (like Lindblom, 1959) have emphasized the possibility of a more gradual change: the more radical the restructuring required to introduce a new energy technology, the more likely that this will lead to conflicts, particularly with those who have a vested interest in the existing structures, that is in:

- established material conditions, conventional technologies, physical plant and physical infrastructure;
- existing knowledge, expertise, educational and research systems and in the status and privileges of particular professional and occupational groupings;
- certain social organizational conditions: authority and control, rules and procedures, and institutional arrangements in general (Baumgartner and Burns, 1984, p. 16).

The contrast between rapid and gradual transition can be depicted as a contrast between design and development. The table below summarizes

Table 8.1 ⟨*Transitions seen as revolutions and evolutions*⟩

	Transitions as revolutions (the design perspective)	Transitions as evolutions (the development perspective)
Transition strategy	is the implementation of a system design intended to achieve a stable final situation. The emphasis is mainly on the product; here the aim is to achieve immediate success	is action-oriented system development aimed at enhancing the capacity for change. The emphasis is mainly on the process, the intention here is to build on minor successes
Transition object	is the formal structure; the emphasis is on structures	is the informal organization; the emphasis is on human behaviour and processes
Transition form	is revolutionary: by short but effective dramatic quantum jumps	is evolutionary: by gradual, slow but sure, incremental, piecemeal changes
Transition method	is based on principles of architecture, as when building a house: tight standards and planning, think first, act afterwards, 'planned change': predictability, all in good time, restrictiveness, with a clear distinction between design and implementation	is based on growth principles, as when designing a garden: attention to the capacity for change, learning while acting, bringing and keeping things in motion: infinity, irregularity, fickleness, with liquid changes between the various phases
Transition logic	is based on analytical-rational considerations; changes are forced from the top, the process of change is controlled top-down, contacts with members of the organization is in the form of directives: informing, instructing, teaching, where it is attempted to break any resistance: 'tell and sell' and conflicts are settled unilaterally or simply denied	is based on social-emotional considerations; changes are supported by the stakeholders; this bottom-up approach shapes the process of change, i.e. participation and interaction is the key to success: consultation, learning, whereby impasses are converted into compromises and conflicts are discussed and worked through

the differences between rapid and slow transitions (Edelenbos and Van Twist, 1996).

Our View on Transitions and Systems

Exploration of the concept of transition has resulted in a distinction between two different perspectives. The first is that of transitions in the form of design, the second is that of transitions in the form of development. The first perspective is a more advanced way of planning. The second emphasizes the need for interaction among stakeholders and shows awareness of the recursiveness of behaviour and the resistance against transition that is embedded in existing institutions (behaviour, rules and roles). These institutions complicate any transition.

We have a development perspective on transitions and see them as evolutionary processes. We conceptualize a transition as a complex and dynamic process around a package of different (sustainability) issues, in which different actors and stakeholders have different institutional backgrounds and therefore play different roles and try to realize different objectives (see also Geels in this volume). We do not agree with Geels that transitions come in phases. Transitions result from unordered and chaotic processes, partly created through management but also born from coincidences.

Transitions take place in systems. We see systems as complex interplays of many interdependent factors and actors (see Chapter 1 of this book). Interdependency is an important aspect of complex systems and makes the non-linear dynamics of the systems hard to predict (De Rosnay, 1998). Complex systems are sets of interconnected parts. Each part is a system itself, and the whole system may be regarded as part of a larger system (McLoughlin, 1969). Interaction in these systems is crucial and should get more attention in the management debate.

INTERACTION AND THE NEED FOR INTERACTIVE GOVERNANCE IN A HIERARCHICAL ORDER

The Troublesome Coexistence of Two Steering Paradigms

Traditionally, improvement of steering in both public and business administration has been sought through an increase of the control of processes from a central steering unit, particularly by means of standardized planning systems and regulation. This form of steering has indeed generated impressive results. To increase the interaction and support transitions, however, new arrangements are developed which create the twilight zone.

While forms of vertical steering and associated justification structures will remain, more horizontal forms of steering are developed (alliances, partnerships). This combination will probably change the position of vertical steering. If self-directing alliances become the important arrangements for transition, central steering will lose its traditional role of controlling processes.

Instead it could become an effective form of intervention and rewarding horizontal steering and management mechanism. This idea has been elaborated in various scientific publications (*see, inter alia*, Castells, 1996; Hamel and Prahalad, 1994; Jarillo, 1993). Interactive policymaking, intergovernmental cooperation and public–private partnerships are forms of governance that fit the horizontal steering paradigm.

The vertical steering paradigm assumes that each problem has an owner, and that this owner usually also has the (best) solution. Policymaking in this case is a matter of directing the behaviour and attitudes of stakeholders towards the known solution. The horizontal steering paradigm, however, proceeds from the assumption that policy issues can affect many actors and that they will all have their own definition of the policy problem and solutions (Kickert *et al.*, 1997). Therefore, the horizontal steering paradigm is directed towards the management of a process which allows these actors as well as their problems and solutions to interact, to learn from one another, and to derive from this new, shared problems and solutions.

Politicians, civil servants and governors will have to operate increasingly in an insecure decision-making environment, in which different actor networks constitute the platforms for debates with different groups of interested parties, and less in a stable constellation of ideologically like-minded groups or homogeneous citizens (Renn *et al.*, 1995). The horizontal steering paradigm does justice to the constellations of interest and administrative reality in modern society. After all, the various actors in contemporary society have diverse but also shared interests, and while their perceptions may differ, they are condemned to live together.

The Need for Process-based, Horizontal and Interactive Governance

The process-based, horizontal interaction paradigm implies early involvement of stakeholders in the transition process (Barker and Wood, 1999; Edelenbos, 1999; Rothman and Robinson, 1997). A process of joint fact-finding is generated in which actors interactively develop a picture of what sustainability should look like. Interactive processes are not self-executive and therefore need careful governance (Edelenbos, 2000; Teisman, 2001). Instead of focusing on organizations, transition managers should design and manage (parts of) processes in such a way that the wide range of views does not lead to inertia and deadlocks. Governance then consists of three elements (Teisman, 2001): (i) the facilitation of debate and negotiation among stakeholders, (ii) creating links and (iii) embedding short-term processes in long-term processes.

Facilitation means that managers must try to organize events and create places where stakeholders can interact with each other. Through interaction, ambitions and expectations of different stakeholders can be communicated and negotiated. To facilitate this interaction managers should establish rules and roles in the interactive game. The stakeholders must accept these in order to guarantee its legitimacy. The actual design varies from one process to another depending on the unique dynamics of each individual process and its specific institutional conditions.

In the second place, governance implies the linking of the different actor networks and interactions between actors in the interactive process. If parallel processes become dissociated, it may become very difficult to develop workable solutions. Linking means, for example, that outcomes of different interactive networks have to be consolidated and integrated in plans that gain the support of the stakeholders.

In the third place, process-based governance concerns the embeddedness of interactive processes in existing processes and institutions. New roles have to be fit in with existing behaviour patterns. New interaction rules have to fit in with existing decision making procedures.

We Know What is Important, but can we do it?: Institutional Implications of Interaction

At present, however, interactive management methods do not fit in well with existing institutions. Existing institutions are difficult to change and create path dependency (Krasner, 1988). This means that the trajectories of future developments are strongly determined by historical trajectories. We can therefore expect that existing institutional systems may frustrate the effectiveness of experimental process-oriented management methods.

BARRIERS TO JOINT TRANSITION PROCESSES

Introduction

The phrase 'The best way to kill a new idea is to put it in an old organization' illustrates the difficult task involved in realizing system innovation and institutional change. The existing roles played by the actors, the existing rules that are in use, procedures, routines, patterns and repertoires often kill new processes and institutions such as interactive processes. Institutional innovation is a difficult assignment, with many obstacles. We will elaborate the following institutional barriers:

1. the missing link between interactive processes and formal decision-making;
2. the way departmental structures of public organizations frustrate interaction;
3. the reluctance of public actors to share responsibility and account-ability with each other and with private actors or societal actors.

The Missing Link Between Interactive Processes and Formal Decision-making

As we have seen, one of the major pitfalls of interactive processes is disso-ciation from the existing institutional environment. Interactive governance is often organized as an informal process, which runs parallel to, or prior to, the formal processes of negotiation and decision-making. As such, interactive processes can be seen as an extra phase or stage before the real decision-making process begins. The formal processes often do not adapt themselves to the informal games of interactive governance, and vice versa. This often leads to 'cherry-picking' behaviour on the part of decision-makers, because they do not feel committed to the variety created by the interactive process. As a result, the rich variation evaporates as soon as the informal interactive process has ended and formal policymaking has begun (Edelenbos and Van Eeten, 2001).

Evaluations of interactive processes (Edelenbos and Monnikhof, 2001; Teisman, 2001; Van Eeten, 1999; Klijn and Koppenjan, 2000) have empha-sized that while these processes are well equipped to generate a wide range of ideas, plans and suggestions, they are often ill equipped to draw this variety out of interactive processes and use it for subsequent – often formal – (policy) processes.

Because of this, ideas and plans from interactive processes are often badly incorporated into decision-making (Edelenbos, 2000; Teisman, 2001). It is difficult to capitalize on variety in administrative and political processes. One reason for this is that interactive processes often become dissociated from formal administrative and political processes.

To give an illustration, we mention the interactive process in the munici-pality of the middle-sized Dutch city of Zwolle, where the municipality tried to solve social, physical and economic problems using a district-oriented approach. We observed that the council 'committees' and the municipal administration maintained a large distance from the district-oriented working process. Decision-making within the municipal administration and the council was insufficiently linked with the outcomes of the interactive process at the district level. In other words, there was an enormous gap between political-administrative decision-making and planning within the district. As a consequence, the administrators were located at a great distance from the district-oriented process, and lost sight of actual developments within the interactive process. This made it impossible for administrative and political incorporation of district-oriented activities to take place in an adequate manner. The lack of feedback to the council committees on the events and outcomes of the pilots reflected this. In addition, the district-oriented approach was rarely placed on the administrative agenda within the municipal administration. Furthermore, the distance between politics and government on the one hand and the district-oriented approach on the other was expressed by the absence of in-depth boundary conditions and frameworks, and by the fact that administrative and political reference points failed to develop.

We conclude from this example that the link between interactive processes and formal decision-making is often missing. This generally leads to an immediate loss of variety in decision-making. Research into the program of transition management will have to pay more attention to this missing link. The paradox that needs to be addressed is that variety is needed in long-term transitions and that this can only be maintained by way of more interactive arrangements and not through existing formal decision-making processes. If these formal processes cannot be adjusted to interaction, transitions will fail.

Departmentalization

Organizations are often highly departmentalized (Kanter Moss, 1983, p. 28). This means that organizations are made up of sub-units, each of which has its own tasks and responsibilities. As such, an organization is concerned with the departmentalization of actions, events, and problems, and aims to keep each of its elements separate from the others. The departmentalized approach sees problems as narrowly as possible, independent from their context and independent from their connections with other problems. An organization with a departmentalized culture is likely to have a segmented structure: a large number of compartments separated from each other – one department from the other, the upper level from the lower level, the branch office from the main office, labour from management, men from women. Only a minimum number of exchanges take place at the boundaries between these segments; after all, each department is presumed to stand or fall more or less independently from the other in any case, so why should cooperation be needed at all? Departmentalism assumes that problems can be solved when they are carved into pieces that are assigned to specialists who work in isolation. Even innovation itself can become a speciality in such a compartmentalized system – something that is assigned to the R&D department so that no one else needs to worry about it.

Interactive processes not only imply cooperation with private actors, citizens and societal organizations, but also an integral approach for the internal government organization. In our research we have seen that the departmentalized structure and culture of public organizations is often the cause of poor internal cooperation between units and layers and external cooperation with stakeholders. In other words, public organizations are often unable to perform any 'boundary-crossing' activities, because of their internal organizational problems.

Interactive processes can accomplish renewed contacts between policy sectors which have become strongly departmentalized over time (Teisman, 2001). In such a case, interactive processes become meaningful in that they accomplish more horizontal interaction between the various governments and between organizational elements of these institutions.

The departmentalization of public organizations tends to hamper rather than facilitate internal and external cooperation. For decades, the relationship between the Ministry of Housing, Spatial Planning and the Environment (in Dutch: the Ministry of VROM) and the Ministry of Transport, Public Works and Water Management (in Dutch: the Ministry of V&W) could be mainly characterized in terms of interdepartmental quarrels and bureaucratic politics. The Ministry of VROM was of the opinion that other ministries like V&W contributed to diffusion and segmentation and as such it saw these ministries as enemies that had to be restrained rather than as potential partners. On the other hand, the Ministry of V&W saw VROM as a ministry that imposed additional demands on the infrastructure without being prepared to pay for them. The consequence of all this has been uncoordinated policy development: city districts were built without creating a better use of space and/or a reduction of car traffic. Decision-making on the infrastructure lags behind or runs parallel to construction activities. Due to the lack of any adjustment at the state level, public organizations use not only their own arguments, but also their own time paths (Teisman, 2001).

We conclude that initiatives of interactive processes often perish in interdepartmental squabbling and disputes in public organizations. These fights about demarcation absorb far too much time and energy from civil servants. Time and energy could be spent more effectively in achieving cooperative interaction with external stakeholders. More research should be done on the question under what circumstances can the dedication to organization and positions be combined with or converted into dedication to processes.

Responsibility and Accountability

New modes of interactive processes have introduced elements or methods of direct democracy into the Dutch political system of representative democracy, which has been largely immune to any pressures of institutional innovation (Andeweg, 1989). In our view, the extent to which interactive processes can be introduced into the representative system depends largely on questions regarding the allotment of responsibility and accountability: how much of it should be transferred, to whom, how, and are power-holders prepared to share or even transfer some of their responsibilities and accountabilities?

If interactive processes are introduced, the accountability structure for management executives (such as the Cabinet or the Mayor and aldermen) will inevitably change. 'Upward' accountability has always dominated in public organizations. Interactive processes, however, stress the need for 'outward' accountability, that is, accountability to clients using instruments such as performance agreements and contracts, and accountability to stakeholders through, for instance, performance reporting (Corbett, 1996; Stewart, 2002).

To give an illustration, in an interactive process of policymaking organized by the municipality of De Bilt in the Netherlands the rule was imposed that members of the municipal management executive should present proposals to the municipal council for formal decision-making on the basis of a reasoned choice from the ideas and plans offered by the stakeholders in the interactive process. The municipal management executive had to explain carefully why they adopted certain proposals in their official viewpoint and rejected other proposals. This form of outward accountability was not realized in actual practice. While the Mayor and aldermen did enter into a debate with the stakeholders during the last interactive sessions, they refused to provide any substantive motives for their viewpoints during these sessions. The members of the administration kept their opinions vague and obscure, and expressed them more clearly only in the written municipal administration proposal. Many participants experienced the opinions of the administration as a jack-in-the-box. The municipal administration adhered to its classic accountability to the municipal council, that is, upward accountability, while rejecting the concept of any outward accountability to the stakeholders in the interactive process.

We conclude that an effective introduction of interactive processes requires a re-evaluation and repositioning of existing lines of accountability.

It necessitates changes in political accountability (Van Montfoort, 2001). According to the representative system, members of an administration are accountable to elected politicians. But with the interactive process a second line of accountability emerges, directly to the people (the stakeholders). Stakeholders want to hear directly from the management executive (Cabinet or Mayor and aldermen) why certain proposals made by them were or were not adopted in administrative viewpoints. Politicians are less able to make political choices on the basis of the fact that they were after all chosen by the citizens (procedural legitimacy) but they are increasingly held accountable by the public for why they did or did not adopt certain ideas or plans from the interactive process (policy-substantive legitimacy). In many interactive processes, such public and substantive justification towards the stakeholders is lacking, because government organizations are reluctant to share responsibility with other governments, with private parties and with stakeholders from society or citizens. They are dedicated to internal and hierarchical methods of responsibility and accountability (upward accountability). They assume that it is impossible to share and transfer responsibility to others (outward accountability). In this basic belief they are supported by politicians. Responsibility and accountability are defined in an organization-oriented way while what we need is a 'network-oriented' type of accountability.

Indeed, the sharing and allotting of responsibility is needed in transition processes. Methods to link new participation-oriented schemes of governance to traditional ones, which have been lacking so far, will have to be developed. Research should focus on cases where combinations of both do occur, and under which conditions such combinations can work.

TRANSITION MANAGEMENT SEEN AS THE MANAGEMENT OF INSTITUTIONAL CHANGE

Introduction

In this section we will present some thoughts on how to overcome the three institutional barriers. We stress that interactive processes on sustainability do not take place in an institutional emptiness, that institutional contexts change only slowly, and that institutional adaptation is an important aspect of transition management.

In this section we will deal with the possibilities of process-based, horizontal interactive governance in overcoming the barriers. We will do this by introducing three different democracy systems in which joint transition processes have different meanings and structures.

Three Democracy Systems

Interactive processes and joint transition processes can be seen as 'injections' of direct or participatory democracy elements into an existing indirect or representative democracy arrangement (Edelenbos, 2000). Direct democracy generally involves that the citizens can either accept or reject a project or law, while in a representative democracy the electorate votes for parties or individuals on the basis of policy packages and programmes. In most democracies, a representative system is used, since the involvement of all individual citizens in every political decision would be impractical. Nevertheless, almost all existing democracies possess certain features that may be regarded as manifestations of direct democracy, such as citizens' initiatives and referenda in parliamentary systems.

Along the continuum of representative – participatory democracy, three possible democratic system innovations of transition management are seen to emerge in practice (Figure 8.1).

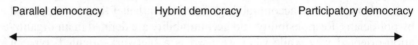

Parallel democracy   Hybrid democracy   Participatory democracy

Figure 8.1   Three democratic systems

These three forms can be briefly characterized as follows:

1. Innovation through the creation of dual democracy systems (parallel democracy): a kind of 'living apart together' form of interaction in which results are 'thrown over' from one system to the other, and vice versa;
2. Innovation through the creation of hybrid democracy systems (hybrid democracy): a type of dynamic interaction in which a system deals with an unstable combination of values and procedures;
3. Innovation through the creation of symbiotic democracy systems (participatory democracy): a type of participatory democracy with private involvement on the basis of partnerships.

These three forms are elaborated in the following sections.

Parallel Democracy

In a parallel democracy, no real institutional change takes place, although in current practice parallel democracy is often put forward as a model to deal with system innovation. The two systems, that is, the interactive process on the one hand and the representative democracy system on the other, exist next to each other, but are not completely separated. The existing representative democratic system is loosely linked to the interactive process, and thus to the participatory democracy principles associated with it.

In such a democratic system, a separation exists between the network of the interactive process of societal, environmental and economic interest groups, and the network in which politicians and civil servants are active. But these two networks are not completely disconnected. The links between the two systems can be established in a number of different ways, which we will illustrate in the following case study.

An example of the organization of links between two more or less independent systems is the interactive process in the Dutch city of Enschede, where the issue at stake was the redevelopment of an inner-city area (the Stadserf). Although administrators and politicians had been given a passive and distant role in this interactive process, they were kept frequently informed of in-depth developments through public meetings and information transfer meetings. In addition, a consultative group was set up, in which consultations were held about the design of the subsequent steps of the interactive process, the progress that was made, and the preparation of larger meetings for all participants in the process. In addition to the process manager, this consultative body consisted of representatives from social interest groups in Enschede, aldermen, council members of the Committee for General Administrative Matters, and individual citizens. In this way they were kept continuously informed of developments in the interactive process.

The link between the interactive process and the existing representative democracy system is in Dutch practice often very weak or loose. As a consequence, the representative system is dominant over the interactive process and parallel democracy is mainly a reproduction of the existing institutional features of the representative democracy system. This type of transition can be labelled as 'recursiveness'.

Hybrid Democracy

A hybrid democracy combines institutional elements of the two different democratic systems (representative and direct democracy). In this democratic system the interactive process lives in close harmony with the system of representative democracy. Institutional elements of participatory democracy are 'transplanted' in the representative democracy system. The representative system evolves more in the direction of participatory democracy – the existing institutional configuration carries forward in slightly modified manner. This is what we called earlier momentum in an earlier section (Miller and Friessen, 1984).

This hybrid democratic system differs from a parallel democracy to the extent that the links between the existing representative democratic system and the interactive process are 'firmer'. The firm links between the two systems can be organized in different ways, as will be illustrated in the case study below.

In the interactive process in the Dutch municipality of Doetinchem, where the issue was the realization of a civil plan for a sustainable residential area 'Wijnbergen', the council members took an active attitude throughout the interactive process. They entered into discussions with the other participants, openly adopted certain viewpoints, answered questions, and took part in designing the Wijnbergen area.

Towards the end of the interactive process, at the request of the process manager, the council members openly stated their views on certain results of the interactive process, such as the relocation of the high-voltage wires in the Wijnbergen area, the green area 'the Kapperskolk', and so on. This was done not just by the participating council members but also by the other members of the municipal council. These viewpoints were expounded during the meetings of the fractions of the various political parties. They were pronounced at various public meetings, in which the opinions of the participants, the council and the Mayor and aldermen were presented next to each other. After this, council members who were active in the workshop entered into discussions with members of the administration and other participants about the positions adopted by them. They motivated their positions and interim choices and listened to those of the other participants. The Mayor and the aldermen and the council members openly chose their position on various results of the workshop and explained in a motivated way why their opinions differed or coincided. Moreover, the Mayor and the alderman for Spatial Planning entered into discussion with the council members and other participants and tried to convince each other. After these public meetings the members of the municipal administration readopted their usual role by drawing up a council proposal (with the cooperation of the civil servants) which was then discussed at a spatial planning committee meeting.

Participatory Democracy

In such a democratic system, elements of the two different democratic systems merge to form completely new institutional elements. Elements of a direct democratic system, which accompanies the introduction of interactive processes, dominate the existing representative democratic system while the interactive process is continuing. The old 'identity' of the representative democracy system disappears and the new 'identity' of the interactive process takes over. 'Transition starts with an ending' (Bridges, 1995, p. 4).

For example, to realize a certain project politicians transfer decision-making power to the stakeholders in the interactive process. This institutional revolution can take different shapes in practice. We will illustrate this in the following case study.

At the beginning of the interactive process in the Dutch municipality of Leerdam, concerning the development of a square in the city centre, the administration had expressed its commitment to the outcome of the process in advance. The members of the administration thus gave a decisive voice to the stakeholders in the interactive process. Thus, the interactive process became leading and the existing political-administrative system followed the process and outcomes of the interactive process. A participatory democracy system emerged and the existing representative democracy system disappeared for the duration of the interactive process. The outcome of the process was seen as 'substantial strong advice' which would be difficult for politicians to ignore. Eventually, the outcome of the interactive process indeed had the nature of such substantial advice, and was adopted in full by the Mayor and aldermen as well as the council.

The administration did indicate certain boundary conditions in advance. These conditions were of a substantive nature (taking existing policies into account), of a financial nature (allocating a certain budget), and of a temporal nature (observing a certain time period). Although the role of the council in having to give final go-ahead remained intact, the council did commit itself strongly – provided certain conditions were met – to the process and to the results it would generate.

CONCLUSION

In this chapter we stated that the transition towards a sustainable society also necessitates a transition in the way transitions are managed. Or to put in other words: 'management of transitions requires a transition of management'. A more process-based, interactive approach has to be established. Intergovernmental cooperation, public–private partnerships and interactive governance requires a transition in itself – from a vertical one-way steering paradigm to a horizontal two-sided (and often multiple-sided) development process paradigm.

This transition takes place in a 'twilight zone' in which the organization-based, hierarchical steering paradigm and the process-based, horizontal and interaction paradigm will have to exist next to each other and are struggling for dominance. As a consequence the transition towards a sustainable society is not a straightforward one dedicated to change concerning the contents only. Institutional innovations are needed and have to be managed carefully. The twilight zone is the 'heart' of the transition process, in which existing institutions change or persevere.

The process-based, horizontal interaction paradigm meets a lot of institutional barriers. We have discussed three barriers: (i) missing links between interactive processes and formal decision-making; (ii) fragmented departmental structures of governmental organizations frustrating productive and innovative interactions; and (iii) the reluctance of public actors to share responsibility and accountability with each other and with private actors or societal actors.

We distinguished three ways in which institutional innovators try to overcome these barriers. We have presented several experiments as possible forerunners for new democratic systems in which the vertical steering paradigm that dominates the representative democratic system and the horizontal development process paradigm that could be a dominant perspective in participatory democratic system are somehow combined: (i) parallel democracy; (ii) hybrid democracy; and (iii) participatory democracy.

We argued that parallel democracy is in current Dutch practice pushed forward as a model for system innovation. But the link between interactive processes and existing political-administrative processes is very loose and the existing representative democracy system dominates at the expense of the interactive process, so that we can hardly speak of a system innovation or a transition. We can label this development as 'recursiveness'. We conclude that this model is unsuitable for realizing transitions.

This implies a need for a change towards a hybrid democracy or participatory democracy. These models have to be further developed, tested and improved in order to get through the 'twilight zone' towards a type of sustainable society that can fulfil many of the presented ambitions. It can be expected that developing, testing and improving such methods will meet a lot of resistance which may frustrate transitions towards sustainability for a long time. But the only way forward is to try and in a process of 'learning by doing' gain experience of what is possible in practice.

NOTES

1. As opposed to 'the quest for control' that still dominates governmental policies (see van Gunsteren, 1976, for an extensive elaboration of this quest).
2. Bridges (1995) describes the same period as the 'neutral zone'.
3. 'Recursiveness means that events occur serially and that the events define time' (Clark and Starkey, 1988, p. 55).
4. They examined 36 longitudinal accounts of companies from which they extracted 135 episodes when the organization experienced one or more of the following: a new product, plan or technology; the replacement of the chief executive; change in the environment arising form the actions of competitors; modification of the organization

structure and power; a change in administration; an acquisition or merger or addition of new functions.

REFERENCES

Andeweg, R.B. (1989), 'Institutional conservatism in the Netherlands: proposals for and resistance to change', in H. Daalder and G.A. Irwin (eds), *Politics in the Netherlands: How Much Change?*, London: Frank Cass, pp. 12–29.

Barker, A., and C. Wood (1999), 'An evaluation of EIA system performance in eight EU countries', *Environmental Impact Assessment Review*, **19** (4), 387–404.

Baumgartner, T., and T.R. Burns (eds) (1984), *Transitions to Alternative Energy Systems. Entrepreneurs, New Technologies, and Social Change*, Boulder and London: Westview Press.

Baxter, J.W., J.D. Eyles and S.J. Elliot (1999), 'From siting principles to siting practices: a case study of discord among trust, equity and community participation', *Journal of Environmental Planning and Management*, **42** (4), 501–25.

Beckhard, R., and R.T. Harris (1987), *Organizational Transitions. Managing Complex Change*, Reading, MA: Addison-Wesley.

Bridges, W. (1995), *Managing Transitions. Making the Most of Change*, London: Nicholas Brealey.

Castells, M. (1996), *The Network Society*, Cambridge, MA: Blackwell.

Clark, P., and K. Starkey (1988), *Organization Transitions and Innovation-Design*, London: Pinter.

Corbett, D. (1996), *Australian Public Sector Management*, Sydney: Allen & Unwin.

de Rosnay, J. (1998), *The Symbiotic Human Being* (in Dutch), Addison Wesley Longman.

DeSario, J., and S. Langton (1987), 'Toward a metapolicy for social planning', in J. DeSario and S. Langton (eds), *Citizen Participation in Public Decision Making*, Westport, CT: Greenwood Press, pp. 205–21.

Edelenbos, J. (1999), 'Design and management of participatory public policy-making', *Public Management*, **1** (4), 569–78.

Edelenbos, J. (2000), 'Process management of interactive governance (in Dutch)', PhD thesis, Utrecht.

Edelenbos, J. (2001), 'Interactive and communicative planning', in R. Zarnic (ed.), *The 2nd COST UCE Conference The Future of the City. New Quality of Life*, Bled, Slovenia, pp. 48–52.

Edelenbos, J., and M.J.W. van Twist (1996), *Management of Change* (in Dutch), Delft: University of Technology.

Edelenbos, J., and R.A.H. Monnikhof (eds) (2001), *Local Interactive Governance* (in Dutch), Utrecht: Lemma.

Edelenbos, J., and M. van Eeten (2001), 'The missing link. processing variation in dialogical evaluation', *Evaluation*, **7** (2), 211–17.

Elliot E., and D. Kiel (1997), 'Nonlinear dynamics, complexity and public policy: use, misuse, and applicability', in R.A. Eve, S. Horsfall and M.E. Lee (eds), *Chaos, Complexity and Sociology; Myths, Models and Theories*, Thousand Oaks: Sage, pp. 64–78.

Flood, R.L. (1999), *Rethinking the Fifth Discipline; Learning Within the Unknowable*, London: Routledge.

Galbraith, J. (1977), *Organization Design*, Reading, MA: Addison-Wesley.

Giddens, A. (1984), *The Constitution of Society; Outline of the Theory of Structuration*, Los Angeles: Berkeley.

Hamel, G., and C.K. Prahalad (1994), *Competing for the Future*, Boston: Harvard Business School Press.

Hammer, H., and J. Champy (1993), *Reengineering the Corporation. A Manifesto for Business Revolution*, London: Nicholas Brealey.

Jarillo, J.C. (1993), *Strategic Networks. Creating Borderless Organization*, Oxford: Butterworth-Heinemann.

Kickert, W.J.M., E-H. Klijn and J.F.M. Koppenjan (eds) (1997), *Managing Complex Networks. Strategies for the Public Sector*, London: Sage Publications.

Klijn, E.H., and J.F.M. Koppenjan (2000), 'Politicians and interactive decision making: institutional spoilsports or playmakers?', *Public Administration*, **78** (2), 365–88.

Krasner, S.D. (1988), 'Sovereignty. An institutional perspective', *Comparative Political Studies*, **21** (1), 66–94.

Lindblom, C.E. (1959), 'The science of muddling through', *Public Administration Review*, 79–88.

Lindblom. C.E., and E.J. Woodhouse (1993), *The Policy-making Process*, London: Prentice-Hall.

McLoughlin, J.B. (1969), *Urban and Regional Planning: A Systems Approach*, London: Faber and Faber.

Miller, D., and P.H. Friesen (1984), *Organizations. A Quantum View*, Englewood Cliffs, NJ: Prentice-Hall.

Palmer, J., I. Cooper and R. van der Vorst (1997), 'Mapping out fuzzy buzzwords – who sits where on sustainability and sustainable development', *Sustainable Development*, **5** (3), 87–93.

Pelletier, D., V. Kraak, C. McCullum, U. Uusitalo and R. Rich (1999), 'The shaping of collective values through deliberative democracy: an empirical study from New York's North Country', *Policy Sciences*, **32** (4), 103–31.

Renn, O., T. Webler and P. Wiedemann (1995), *Fairness and Competence in Citizen Participation. Evaluating Models for Environmental Discourse*, Dordrecht: Kluwer Academic Publishers.

Rothman, D.S., and J.B. Robinson (1997), 'Growing pains: A conceptual framework for considering integrated assessments', *Environmental Monitoring and Assessment*, **46** (3), 23–43.

Stewart, J. (2002), 'Turning organizations into policy: how far have we gone and how far can we go?', paper for IRSPM VI conference, Edinburgh.

Teisman, G.R. (2001), *Mobilising Co-opetitive Governance* (in Dutch), Rotterdam: Erasmus University.

Teisman, G.R., and E-H. Klijn (2002), 'Partnership arrangements: governmental rhetoric or governance scheme?', *Public Administration Review*, **62** (2), 197–205.

Tops, P.W., M. Boogers, F. Hendriks and R. Weterings (1999), 'On interactive decision-making', study for the state commission on Dualism and Local Democracy, The Hague.

van Eeten, M. (1999), *Dialogues of the Deaf. Defining New Agendas for Environmental Deadlocks*, Delft: Eburon.

van Montfoort, C.J. (2001), 'Dimensions of political accountability' (in Dutch), *Bestuurskunde*, **4**, 152–60.

van Gunsteren, H.R. (1976), *The Quest for Control. A Critique of the Rational-Central-Rule Approach in Public Affairs*, London: John Wiley.

9. Bounded socio-technical experiments (BSTEs): higher order learning for transitions towards sustainable mobility[1]

Halina Szejnwald Brown, Philip J. Vergragt, Ken Green, Luca Berchicci

INTRODUCTION

A bounded socio-technical experiment (BSTE) attempts to introduce a new technology, service, or a social arrangement on a small scale. Many such experiments are ongoing worldwide. They are carried out by coalitions of diverse actors and are driven by long-term and large-scale visions of advancing society's sustainability agenda. This chapter analyses two such experiments from the domain of personal mobility, focusing on the processes of higher order learning that occur through BSTEs. Based on the conceptual frameworks from theories of organizational learning, policy-oriented learning and diffusion of innovation, we identify two types of learning: the first type occurs among the participants in the experiment and their immediate professional networks; the second type occurs in society at large. Both types play a key role in the potential or envisaged societal transition towards sustainable mobility systems.

Two Dutch case studies, in which the Design for Sustainability Group at the Technical University of Delft has participated, provide empirical data for the analysis. One case consists of the development of a three-wheeled, bike-plus vehicle (Mitka); the second case seeks to solve mobility problems on the island of Texel. We find that higher-order learning of the first type occurs among the BSTE participants and beyond. Learning can be facilitated by the deployment of structured visioning exercises, by the diffusion of ideas among related BSTEs, by innovative couplings of problems and solutions, and by creating links among related experiments. Government agencies, universities and other intellectual entrepreneurs have key roles to play in making that happen. The cases provide much less insight about the second type of learning. Research on the latter is necessary.

The search for sustainable personal mobility solutions looms large on the policy, research and business agendas. Some of the approaches include: less polluting and more efficient cars, greater reliance on mass transport and bicycles, traffic controls, redesigned mobility services and technological innovation in human-powered vehicles. In the Netherlands, the government actively supports these efforts through subsidies for research and development, for infrastructure and for promising local efforts in reconfiguring mobility services. Much of what we might call 'socio-technical experimentation' on a small scale is taking place in sustainable mobility.

This chapter focuses on the processes of social learning in these types of small-scale socio-technical experiments. Its objectives are to explore the mechanisms by which social learning occurs; to question the methods that are appropriate for studying and monitoring the learning processes; to consider factors and techniques for enhancing social learning processes (for instance, visioning exercises); to reflect on how to define success in these experiments; and to contribute to the development of theory on social learning and institutional change occurring through such experiments. The chapter builds on research in *Strategic Niche Management* (Kemp *et al.*, 1998), *Social Management of Environmental Change* (the SMEC project) (Irwin *et al.*, 1994) and *Social Niche Management* (Verheul and Vergragt, 1995).

We introduce the term *bounded socio-technical experiment* (BSTE) to denote a process exhibiting several characteristics. It is an attempt to develop and introduce a new technology or service on a scale bounded in space and time. The time dimension is around five years, while the space dimension is defined either geographically (a community) or by a number of users (small). BSTE is a collective endeavour, carried out by a coalition of diverse actors, including business, government, technical experts, educational and research institutions, NGOs and others. There is a cognitive component to BSTE in that at least some (but not all) of the participants explicitly recognize the effort to be an experiment, in which learning-by-doing, doing-while-learning, trying out new strategies and new technological solutions, and continuous course correction, are standard features.

BSTE is driven by a long-term and large-scale vision of advancing society's sustainability agenda, though the vision does not need to be shared equally by its participants. Its goal is to try out innovative approaches for solving larger societal problems of unsustainable technologies and services. This latter characteristic distinguishes BSTE from, for example, solving a particular environmental problem in a community, or from a strictly market-driven introduction of a new mode of transportation. A successful

BSTE creates a functioning, socially-embedded new configuration of technology or service that then serves as a starting point for further innovation or for diffusion, or that can inform the policymaking process. An obvious indication of a BSTE's success is when this new configuration diffuses beyond the experimental boundaries and is widely adopted. To serve the goal of a sustainability transition, changes in societal institutions, infrastructures and relationships among societal actors should accompany such wide-scale adoption.

BSTEs are necessary components of a transition to a sustainable society. This is because a BSTE may provide an opportunity for testing the feasibility of a radically new technology before it is ready to enter the open market. Similarly, a BSTE allows for development of new social arrangements among actors and to consider them as templates for other societal contexts. Finally, BSTEs are a way to include actors who would otherwise not see a place for themselves in the types of projects in technological and system innovation that are often sponsored by powerful corporate, governmental, or NGO entities.

Strategic Niche Management (SNM) is another school of thought that, like the BSTE framework, recognizes the key role of small-scale experimenting in promoting a socio-technical change towards sustainability. However, while the BSTE perspective views experimentation primarily as an incubator of ideas, an accumulation of empirical experience with technologies and services, and a place for social learning, the basic premise of SNM is that the direction of the coevolution of technology and society can, and should, be modulated by strategic policy interventions in experiments. The interventions consist of creating protective technological niches for promising new technologies, where they can be tested and developed (Kemp *et al.*, 1998; Hoogma *et al.*, 2002). SNM is a policy tool and a method of advancing the society in a specific direction, that of a technological regime shift (Kemp and Rotmans, 2003).

Both SNM and BSTE are highly relevant for transition management. The crucial difference is that, while SNM is mainly seen as a policy tool for a transition into a direction that is already more or less specified, BSTE is a more open process of learning and experimenting. Although it is driven by a vision of sustainability, its quintessence is that actors in the process 'learn' about viable solutions in the process. Thus even if a BSTE does not lead to a commercial or otherwise viable solution for sustainable mobility, it still contributes through higher-order learning.

The collective archives of recent experiments with alternative personal mobility indeed abound in examples of technologies and services that have not grown beyond experimental level. Our own incomplete inventory includes several dozen recent technological innovations with two- and three-wheeled human- and mechanical-powered vehicles. Schwartz (2002) has assembled a riveting case study of the rise and demise of the carefully nurtured Think electric car project. Hoogma *et al.* (2002) and Weber *et al.* (1999) analysed over a dozen cases, drawing lessons on how to improve the chances of large-scale adoption and diffusion of the experimental technologies and services. Since the majority of the experiments analysed by Schwartz, Weber and Hoogma involved strategic nurturing (through subsidies, partnerships and policy interventions) one might question the effectiveness of strategic niche management as a tool for widespread adoption of more sustainable mobility systems. Alternatively, one might attribute the lack of diffusion to inappropriate application of the tool.

While highly relevant, these questions are not the subject of our inquiry. Instead, in this chapter we ask a different question: what social benefits, if any, accrue from experiments that do not diffuse into the society at large? We explore this question by drawing on detailed analyses of two ongoing Dutch experiments in mobility as well as on our own experience in visioning and project management. One of the experiments is a development of a three-wheeled 'bike-plus' vehicle; the second is an effort to improve the overall mobility and tourism on the island of Texel while halting the growth in automobile traffic.

The chapter advances two propositions: first, a BSTE serves as a nucleus for higher-order social learning about sustainable mobility. Second, monitoring and better understanding of the learning processes in BSTEs is necessary for advancing the theory of transition to a sustainable society. Our analysis of the cases proceeds from three perspectives: behaviours of the actors, ongoing learning processes, and horizontal diffusion of ideas from the experiments into other experiments.

SUCCESS IN BSTEs

Each experiment, diffusing or not, can serve as a source of knowledge about how to avoid repeating mistakes and how to build on good experiences. This is a challenging proposition because each experiment represents a complex problem, in which variables are interconnected, uncertainty is high and where causal relationships between the variables are impossible to establish. Each succeeds or fails for its own unique combination of reasons. Terms such as *problem set* (Trist, 1983) or *wicked problem* (Rittel and Webber, 1973) have been applied to such cases. For example, in recent reviews of experiments in mobility, Weber *et al.* (1999) and Hoogma *et al.* (2002) identified a wide range of reasons for unsuccessful adoption and diffusion, from technical problems, to infrastructure, to consumer and business attitudes, to various shortcomings in project design and management, to short-term investment horizons. Although the list of lessons from each experiment was long, no particular pattern emerged. Further experimentation will be likely to increase the list of lessons learned, without, however, producing guidance for designing mobility experiments that lead to adoption and diffusion.

This is not to say that experiments cannot be conducted in ways that increase the likelihood of adoption and diffusion of the new technology and of societal learning. In order to do so, De Bruijn and Ten Heuvelhof (2000) argue that one has to treat an experiment as a process rather than as an objective-driven project and its participants should be viewed as learning networks.

Another perspective on bounded socio-technical experiments in mobility treats them as the means for societal learning about technology and social arrangements, for changing the prevalent perspectives on mobility and access, and for changing norms, values and institutions. In this respect, the definition of BSTE success is more comprehensive than in the other perspective, including such outcomes as diffusion of ideas to other problems or BSTEs, or higher-order learning among the BSTE participants and within the society at large. Numerous authors refer to the importance of higher-order learning in experiments and often note its absence (Hoogma *et al.*, 2003; 2002). Yet, with a few exceptions (Hoogma *et al.*, 2003), little systematic study has been done on defining and monitoring the learning processes.

Based on the preceding discussion and following Hoogma's classification (2002), we propose the following criteria for evaluating success in bounded socio-technical experiments:

1. Diffusion of the results of an experiment, in the form of a new technology, product, or service, to a larger scale where it is a commercial as well as an environmental success;
2. Capturing the interest of consumers, businesses and societal institutions, which leads to further experimentation in the same type of technology and social arrangements, and additional investments;
3. Branching out into a new application, or nucleating a new, different experiment;
4. Occurrence of higher-order learning within the BSTE-oriented coalition and beyond it, and in society at large.

As stated earlier, many BSTEs have failed by the first criterion. With regard to the second and third criteria, considerable research needs to be done to reveal the extent to which the new applications or experiments have taken place.

We know even less about the higher-order learning taking place in BSTEs (part of criterion 4). To reflect on the role of learning in BSTE, let us consider the typical goings-on in the conduct of an experiment in scientific research and to then translate those to the BSTE case. Although the comparison with a scientific experiment is risky (because here we analyse a problem set), something may still be learned from it. One of the key characteristics of a scientific experiment is its openness to unexpected developments. Surprising results are the key source of new ideas and hypotheses. The experimenter is prepared to evaluate the new data continuously *vis-à-vis* the initial plan or inquiry and to plan the next steps of the inquiry accordingly. Translated to BSTE, this means that throughout its duration, the experimenter must be open to the idea of reassessing the problem definition driving the experiment, its objectives, approaches and tools used in its execution.

The second characteristic of a scientific experiment is that it entails hypothesis testing. In translation to a socio-technical experiment, this means that BSTE starts with a particular combination of problem definition and a perceived solution, but both are likely to be replaced in response to new evidence and new developments in the experiment's context. The third relevant characteristic is that new knowledge from other experiments in a related or sometimes unrelated scientific area often provides crucial insights into interpretation of data and the choice of direction of the scientific inquiry.

The above characteristics imply that societal actors who embark on an experiment in technological or system innovation need to retain a great deal of openness and flexibility in defining its objectives and expected outcomes and to be prepared to change them in mid-course. They also need to be outwardly oriented and intellectually entrepreneurial, as manifested by active scanning of related ongoing experiments, identifying new links between problems and solutions (especially problems for which their own experimental approach may be a good solution), and by identifying new potential partnerships.

Creating an atmosphere that is conducive to such openness and flexibility is a matter of appropriate design of an experiment and of choosing the right actors. These features are especially important because BSTEs are more messy and harder to analyse than controlled laboratory experiments in the conduct of science. In short, champions of bounded socio-technical experiments in mobility must be flexible, adventurous, intellectually entrepreneurial and have high tolerance for uncertainty. They also must have a high capacity for self-assessment, reflection and change of objectives in response to new developments. Stated differently, they need to have a capacity for learning.

LEARNING IN BSTEs

We define learning in BSTEs as three interrelated shifts: (i) a shift in the framing of the mobility problem and of the perceived solution (or a menu of solutions), (ii) a shift in the principal approaches to solving the problem and in the weighing of choices between desirable yet competing objectives; (iii) a shift in the relationship among the participants in the experiment, including mutual convergence of goals and problem definitions. These shifts can occur among the participants of an experiment and their professional networks as well as in the broader social sphere.

This definition of learning emerges from three distinct areas of research: organizational learning; policy-oriented learning; and diffusion of techno-logical innovation. In general, the learning theories make a distinction between lower order and higher-order forms of learning (Argyris and Schön, 1994; Senge, 1990; Keohane and Nye, 1989; Hall, 1993; Sabatier, 1999). In the lower order category, the so called 'technical', 'adaptive' or 'single-loop' learning consists of searching for new policy instruments in the context of fixed policy objectives (as applied to policy) or of fixing new problems within the same problem definition and procedures (as applied to organization). Examples related to the introduction of electric vehicles include improve-ments in technological design or better marketing and pricing.

In contrast, higher-order 'conceptual' policy-oriented learning involves redefining policy goals and adjusting problem definition and strategies. In the organizational learning perspective, higher-order 'generative' or 'double-loop' learning involves changes in the norms, values, goals and operating procedures that govern the decision making process and actions of organizations. Drawing on a recent review of the experiment with elec-tric vehicles in La Rochelle, France, higher-order learning occurred when users reconfigured their personal mobility patterns (Hoogma *et al.*, 2002). Table 9.1 lists some examples of what might count as higher-order learn-ing among the BSTE participants or in society at large.

Both organizational learning and policy-oriented learning fields assume that higher-order learning is a gradual process occurring over time and that it occurs through self-examination and reflection. In organizations, major failure is seen by many scholars as the primary driver of learning because it often challenges the fundamental organizational assumptions and their core identity, and thus induces self-examination and conceptual change (Lant and Mezias, 1990; Argyris and Schön, 1994; Bolman, 1978; Sitkin and Weingart, 1995). Other researches (Cook and Yanow, 1993; Senge, 1990) postulate that new information or new organizational strategies can also trigger learning, even in the absence of overt failures. Senge in part-icular emphasizes the role of a shared vision, system thinking and group

Table 9.1 *Illustrations of higher-order learning of the first type and the
             second type through BSTEs in personal mobility*

	Learning of the first type
Organization	• Redefines its core business or functions in relation to mobility
	• Redefines the role of mobility in relation to its other main organizational functions
	• Discovers new business opportunities in mobility services
	• Defines new mutually beneficial collaborations and strategic partnerships in mobility
Government agency	• Formulates a new policy approach with regard to mobility systems

	Learning of the second type
Consumers	• Discover new ways to define and satisfy mobility needs and wants
	• Discover new couplings between problems and solutions
Various actors	• Find new ways to organize mobility around work, recreation, and daily functions

commitment as the key attributes of teams in which higher-order learning occurs. This author proposes structured exercises in communication and creativity, deployment of mental models and trust building as some of the ways to induce organizational learning.

The organizational learning framework is useful in two ways for thinking about learning in BSTEs: it makes a distinction between lower- and higher-order learning; and it draws attention to reflection, self-evaluation and interaction among members of an organization as the key paths for achieving higher-order learning. A limitation of the organizational learning framework for BSTEs is that BSTE-oriented coalitions lack some of the key characteristics that play a role in organizational learning: shared culture, goals, norms, procedures and routines. On the other hand, the attributes of learning teams identified by Senge and others, while derived from their observations in business organizations, need not necessarily be limited to those. Our own experience with visioning exercises (see the next section) points in that direction.

The literature on policy-oriented learning addresses the limitation of the organizational learning theory by concerning itself with learning processes occurring among numerous, often competing, actors (government, industry, NGOs, expert communities, the media and others). From this field of study we draw three observations relevant to BSTEs. First, higher-order learning can indeed take place within such coalitions. Second, failure or the threat of failure are powerful and common triggers of policy-oriented learning. Third, in addition to failure, new information is an effective facilitator of policy-oriented learning, especially when the information acquires urgency and focus through the media attention and public engagement (Keohane and Nye, 1989; Sabatier, 1999; Lee, 1993; van Eijndhoven *et at.*, 2001).

Glasbergen (1996) stresses interaction as a key factor in facilitating policy-oriented learning by distinguishing between two types of higher-order learning: social and conceptual. Social learning concerns itself with interactions and communications between actors, the relations among them, the quality of dialogue and the congruency in the collective problem definition and identification of solutions. In that view, technical, conceptual and social learning evolve progressively from one another. In landmark studies of diffusion of technologies Rogers (1985) takes another perspective on social learning. In this framework, derived from the work of Bandura (1977), Hamblin (1979) and others, higher-order social learning is at the heart of diffusion of innovations within society, which Rogers defines as 'a process by which an innovation is communicated through certain channels over time among the members of a social system' (Rogers, 1985, p. 10). The central idea of social learning in diffusion of innovations is that an individual learns by observing the behaviour of others and then decides to do (or not do) something similar.

Based on the above discussion, we can thus identify two types of higher-order learning associated with bounded socio-technical experiments. The first type occurs among the participants in an experiment and their immediate professional networks (business partners, members of the organizations that employ them, other organizations with which they routinely interact). The second type of learning consists of diffusion of new ideas about mobility solutions into the society. The diffusion manifests itself overtly when members of the society adopt the novel technology and services. It occurs less visibly when members of the society change their conceptions of different ways to satisfy the need for access, for individual freedom, for convenience and for other physical and cultural attributes of personal mobility.

For the first type of learning, the literatures on organizational learning and policy learning suggest that failure, surprises, public and media attention, and various adverse events or threats of such events (and the sense of urgency they create) are effective drivers of higher-order learning. Interactions among actors around a shared goal or problem are also effective drivers. Studies of organizations also suggest that this type of learning can be strategically induced through structured exercises in visioning, system thinking, mental model building and other techniques. To the extent that many of the above factors are central features of BSTEs, experiments in mobility can be fertile grounds for the first type of learning.

On the other hand, BSTEs often lack the crucial sense of urgency. This is because the risks are spread out among numerous actors and because individual commitments vary. In contrast to policy-oriented learning, BSTE-oriented coalitions are often a collection of individual interests attracted by the prospect of a new technology or to a new social arrangement (Irwin *et al.*, 1994). These interests may range from seeking commercial success to gaining visibility, to improving corporate image and social legitimacy, to contributing to long-term sustainability.

Champions of bounded socio-technical experiments must also contend with two inherent dilemmas. It is not uncommon for these individuals to pursue their vision in the absence of strong backing from the organization they represent. This 'actors' dilemma – an individual versus an organization – can lead to risk-avoiding behaviour in individual decisions on the part of the project leadership, which translates, in turn, into higher risks for the project. Another 'actors' dilemma inherent to BSTEs (congruency of vision versus breadth of support) derives from the tension between the need to build broad base of support for the project and the need to create a common vision among the actors. The larger the number of actors, the more difficult it is to create such a vision.

The higher-order learning of the second type occurs incrementally when information about the innovation travels among the members of the society through various channels, leading to a collective change in the perceptions of mobility solutions. On an individual level it may involve the act of adoption, rejection, or simply observation and evaluation. We envision two scenarios of how such a collective change might occur: in one, the innovation is widely adopted; in another, information about numerous related innovations in mobility, each with a limited degree of adoption, diffuses through the society until it reaches some kind of 'critical mass' of collective consciousness.

VISIONING: EXPERIENCE FROM THE SUSHOUSE PROJECT

Learning is most effective in the presence of adverse outcomes or threats of such outcomes. However, we submit that structured exercises, braided into the experiment at key points, are also likely to be effective in inducing learning, embedding it into the practice of the participants and offering some 'breathing spaces' for explicit identification and review of the options for further development. 'Visioning' is an example of structured exercises with which the authors are familiar through the SusHouse Project (Vergragt, 2003; Green and Vergragt, 2002). Its methodology involved the construction of imaginative, 'micro normative' scenarios ('visions' of how the household functions could be fulfilled in the year 2050) that suggested new ways of fulfilling various household functions in more sustainable ways. The scenarios are intended to generate visions of sustainable household function fulfilment that differ radically from the present, breaching current trends. Such visions may open new ways of thinking, researching, designing and acting in the present (or at least in the next few years). Sustainability would be achieved by radical combinations of both technological and social innovations, leading to 'factor improvements', it was hoped, up to 20-fold.

The researchers were keen to develop a method that would enable companies, governmental policy organizations and NGOs to carry out their own analyses of any household function. Such analyses would lead to the identification of possible products, systems and social innovations that could offer business opportunities and policy initiatives *now* to start the transition to sustainable economies and societies.

To maximize the action aspect of visioning, one of the central features of the SusHouse methodology is the involvement of a wide range of 'stakeholders' in the generation of the scenarios, as well as in their assessment and the development of innovative and policy initiatives that the scenarios suggest. The stakeholders that took part were chosen to represent the full 'supply chain' of each household function (see Quist *et al.*, 2002). It also sought to include people who might be representative of future stakeholders (such as small firms or young people).

The SusHouse method thus favours a more participative and interactive way of devising policy and identifying new innovations than is usually employed in more traditional policymaking (Grin and van de Graaf, 1996). The methodology is also concerned with leading to designs of products, systems of provision, social arrangements and cultural attitudes rather than just an orientation to policy. The SusHouse methodology can be seen as a structured way to induce higher-order learning both in the outcomes of new scenarios and in the kinds of social outcomes that are necessary to such radical innovation: the building and maintaining of new network coalitions. We see these visioning exercises as an avenue for introducing learning into the types of BSTEs where threat of failure is high, such as the Mitka case described below.

ONGOING EXPERIMENTS IN MOBILITY AT DELFT UNIVERSITY OF TECHNOLOGY

The two case studies described in this section have been developed through joint efforts between the Design for Sustainability (DfS) Group at Technical University of Delft (TU Delft), TNO Industry (TNO) and several other actors. TNO is a major Dutch organization for applied research in technological innovation in industry. These and several other projects in product–service innovation have been carried out through a cooperative agreement between TU Delft and TNO under the umbrella of the Kathalys Project (Brezet *et al.*, 2001), with funding from the Dutch ministries of the environment and economic affairs. The case studies are in various stages of development.

Case One. Bicycle-Plus: Mitka

Mitka (an acronym derived from 'mobility solution for individual transportation on short distances', in Dutch) is a roofed three-wheel human-powered vehicle with an electric engine that doubles human pedalling power. It has a maximum speed of 30–40 km/hour and tilts automatically during steering. Mitka has an innovative shape with a natural position of a driver's body (Figure 9.1). It is intended as an alternative to a car for commuting distances up to 25 kilometres. Its environmental impact (especially CO_2, local emissions and resource use) is estimated to be one-third of that of a car (Luiten *et al.*, 2001).

Figure 9.1   Mitka, May 2002

Stage one: visioning and coalition building

The idea of Mitka emerged through the discussions between members of the Design for Sustainability group at TU Delft and a TNO manager who sometime in 1996–7 developed a shared vision of a mobility system for daily commuting that would radically differ from the unsustainable dependence on an automobile.

A product vision was developed, using future conditioning and visioning as design tools (Maas, 1997). The key characteristics of the new vehicle, selected by the initial participants (TNO, TU Delft, a bicycle manufacturer) through several creativity visioning workshops, included: speed higher than a bicycle, power assistance, youthfully athletic appearance, resemblance to a bicycle yet innovative, safety and comfort, and low environmental impact (although few calculations were made at that time). A flexible modular system was desirable, such as interchangeable modules for frame, steering mechanisms and brakes, which could be customized to individual preferences.

While the ideas for the features of the new vehicle were brewing, the TNO manager, whose enthusiasm, commitment and energy kept this initiative alive, pursued two essential objectives: funding for the project and links with viable business partners with high potential for production and marketing. The way out would be to find an immediate mobility problem that Mitka could solve. In short, the sustainability solution was searching for an immediate problem to solve.

It was therefore fortuitous when the environmental manager of Nike Europe became interested in the project. In addition to the recognizable 'big name', Nike offered a valuable opportunity to test the new vehicle among the employees at its European headquarters in Hilversum: the company was running out of car-parking space and welcomed alternative solutions. In short succession, Gazelle, a bicycle manufacturer, joined the project and funding was obtained from the Ecology, Economy and Technology Program of the Dutch Government. The coalition that emerged from that stage consisted of the TNO manager, the environmental director of Nike Europe, DfS director at TU Delft, Peter van der Veer, a bicycle designer, and the Gazelle company managing director. We list them as individuals, rather than as organizations, to underscore the power of individual entrepreneurship that drove the project at this stage and the dilemma faced by these individuals (Berchicci *et al.*, 2002). By and large, they followed their own individual interests and values more than those of their respective organization's actors (the Gazelle director was the exception). This created a tension – a dilemma – for each, as summarized in Table 9.2.

Another dilemma, largely internalized by the project champion, was that of a tension between the need to create broad support and the need to create

Table 9.2   Actors' dilemmas: individual versus organization

Individual interest	Organizational interest
Nike manager: Interested in sustainability initiatives	Manufacturer of youthful, innovative, sleek, 'winning' athletic products. Sustainability a strategic asset for corporate image. Transportation solutions not part of corporate environmental strategy
TNO manager: Committed to innovating in product-service for sustainability	Assists industrial clients in product development and technological innovation. Sustainability not on the agenda
Gazelle director: Interested in business opportunities	Seeks to enlarge markets for its bicycles through innovation
DfS director: Committed to innovating in product-service for sustainability, teaching through empirical problem solving, attracting funds to support research	Traditional engineering education. Design for sustainability not a mainstream activity. Social experimentation not in the engineering tradition

a common vision among the actors. The participation of Nike and Gazelle were crucial to the survival and the success of the project. But that meant that facing up to some fundamental differences in problem definitions and expected solutions among the participants were set aside during that stage, only to emerge later. Table 9.3 summarizes the differences among the actors.

The tension between the individuals and their institutions affected the behaviours of the Nike and Gazelle representatives in a particular way: they avoided taking radical steps within their organizations, especially by not making major institutional commitments of resources. Other coalition members carried only somewhat higher risks (reputation and future funding opportunities) but they, too, were not taking financial risks for their organizations (see Table 9.3).

In short, the sense of urgency was lacking. These attitudes were not a major impediment to progress of the project so long as the government funding continued. But it had other consequences for the project: no self-correcting mechanisms were put in place at that early stage for robust separation of viable from less viable design ideas and for the reality checks of the emerging artefact *vis-à-vis* the societal context in which it would have to function.

Table 9.3 Actors' dilemmas: broad support versus congruency of goals

Roles of actors	Problem definition	Solution to problem	Risks taken	Contribution and attitude
TNO Project leader	People drive cars for short distances because bicycles are slow, too much effort, and weather-dependent. People reject bike-pluses because of image, poor marketing, conservatism.	New vehicle: faster, power assisted, weather protective. New vehicle: sleek, bicycle-look-alike. Partner: high marketing potential.	Medium: reputation, prestige.	Active in finding financial support. Assembling project team, visioning, design, networking and publicity.
Nike Company Client	Insufficient environmental image. Insufficient parking for employees. Protect company image.	Participate in the project while using Nike logo on new vehicle. Offer new vehicle to employees. New vehicle: fast, attractive, innovative, sleek.	Low: financial.	Wait-and-see. Surveyed attitudes.
Gazelle Company Business developer	Bicycle market saturated. Need new features.	New vehicle: bicycle with extra features. Avoid radical changes. Join Nike in a project.	None.	'Wait-and-see.' Passive participant. Brought product designer and engineering designer into the coalition.
DfS Knowledge keeper. Strong project supporter	Current trends in car use for home-work commuting not sustainable. Alternative product-service needed in mobility.	New product service system combination for sustainability transition.	Medium: reputation, prestige.	Involved in all stages. Students involved. Networking and publicity seeking.
Governmental Programme Financial support	Niches needed for development of radical ideas in sustainable mobility.	Promoting experiments in development and testing of new product-service.	Medium: financial (diffused), reputation, prestige.	Long-term support without interference.

Stage two: from a vision to a design concept
Early in 2000, after more than three years of incubation, the parameters of
a flexible modular bike-plus vehicle emerged, along with a coalition of actors
poised to develop it and pilot in a specific 'real-life' context. In March 2000,
Nike conducted an internet-based exercise among its employees in
Hilversum, in which they were asked to 'build' on a computer screen, out of
individual components, a vehicle that would meet the general set of specifications earlier defined by the Mitka coalition as well as their own preferences
as the future users of Mitka. One of the central findings from this exercise was
the users' preference for a two-wheeled vehicle over a three-wheeled version.
Nevertheless, in May 2000 the coalition chose a three-wheeled Mitka.

Two factors explain this: the appeal of the sleek innovative appearance;
and the absence of opposition to it. This behaviour was a clear illustration
of a high-risk behaviour with regard to the project. Furthermore, the
imperative of maintaining a unified coalition produced a counterincentive
for revisiting the initial vision for the project. Thus the project entered the
development phase with many open questions.

Stage three: from a design choice to a working model
For the next two years, with the continuation of the government subsidies,
efforts were directed in three directions: (i) soliciting users' feedback;
(ii) generating publicity; (iii) refining the design of Mitka and solving the
engineering and construction problems. This stage was dominated by interests and inclinations of the project champion, TNO. Any problems arising
from the users' response or the infrastructure were dealt with strictly by
consecutive changes in the technical design, without revisiting either the
design choices or the mobility concept the Mitka represented.

Here, the story of Mitka takes a new turn. Sometime in 2000, the DfS
director became aware of another case of transportation problems and
searches for solutions. On the island of Texel, the tension between the desire
to promote tourism while holding back the number of cars on the island
reached a crescendo. An idea emerged that Mitka might be part of the solution to Texel's problem. This was an opening to the second case study
described below.

By early 2002, Mitka has evolved into a working vehicle, ready for testing
with Nike employees in September 2002. As the project approaches the
pilot stage, several unresolved issues loom large. The most acute of those
are summarized in Table 9.4.

The table shows that many of the unresolved issues are related to the
three-wheel design, the radically different sleek appearance and the practi-
calities of daily life with Mitka. Notably, there were numerous opportunities during the preceding two years to foresee these problem areas. As

Table 9.4   Unresolved barriers to Mitka adoption

Type of barrier	Unresolved issues
Technical design	Several unresolved issues
Infrastructure	The two-front-wheels-one-back-wheel design imposes 90 cm width on vehicle that exceeds permitted 75 cm
	Two Mitkas cannot pass on bicycle path
	In pedestrianized cities (i.e. Amsterdam) Mitka can be seen as too wide for the small roads
	Residential storage difficult; an obstacle to widespread adoption
	Facilities for battery recharging and technical assistance for maintenance and repairs problematic
Regulations	A paradox: attainable speed above 25 km/h requires use of helmets but human-powered vehicles do not require helmets
User acceptance	Sleek form attractive to some potential users, but liability to others, for whom Mitka departs radically from their accepted meanings and routines of daily life
Market factors	Price a deterrent to individual users, although alternatives to private ownership exist
	Nike likes sleek and innovative design, including three wheels, while Gazelle seeks to avoid radical departure from a bicycle

summarized in Table 9.5, Nike's studies of consumers' views identified many of the current obstacles.

Meanwhile, the publicity generating activities for the Mitka project included photo opportunities with the crown prince and his consort sitting in the Mitka. The high publicity raised the stakes for all the participants. While the financial risks continued to be low for all the actors, the heightened public expectations increased the reputational and prestige risks for all the participants. The commercial failure of the project, should it occur, would now carry a price. Partly in response to this development, the

Table 9.5   Results of surveys in Mitka development

Time	Event	Result
March 2000	Nike employees were asked, via internet, to 'design' a vehicle from individual parts	Majority preferred two-wheeled version over a three-wheeled
		15-kilometre distance was the maximum; more luggage storage space was preferred
Key decision: May 2000	Choice of three wheels, two in front	
September 2000	Coalition members and Nike employees evaluated a 1/3 scale model of Mitka	The response was positive
February 2001	Visioning exercise with 9 Nike employees focused on 'imagining' life with Mitka	Potential users have difficulty envisioning the daily life with the new artifact
		The three-wheel vehicle seen as a problem of manoeuvering
		Mixed reaction to the radically in design
		Strong preference for leasing over ownership
March 2001	Interviews with bicyclists at a bicycle fair, where a prototype of Mitka was displayed	Mixed reactions towards Mitka Concerns about the infrastructure – technical service and parking
		Not appropriate for transporting children
		Strong preference for non-ownership
April and May 2001	In-depth interviews with 12 Nike employees, who were presented with the prototype	Hesitance about the radicalness of the design
		Seen as a substitution for the second family car
		Strong preference for non-ownership

Table 9.5   (continued)

Time	Event	Result
		Mixed reactions to rain protection
		Preference for two-wheel version
		Potential users have difficulty envisioning the daily life with Mitka

coalition brought in a new actor, a consulting firm whose assignment was to commercialize the new vehicle.

This was a turning point in the project. After a long period of low risk-taking and of keeping the social context secondary to the engineering and product design, the new actor introduced a sense of urgency into the coalition. By reopening the questions of consumer needs, marketing and business opportunities, the incoming partner brought a new reality into the project. First, the rapidly approaching pilot stage has raised the Mitka project to a higher level of corporate attention. Second, new actors became interested in the project: Brabant Development Corporation (BOM in a Dutch acronym) and a major Dutch insurance company. The latter is currently in the process of expanding its core business to providing employers with complete mobility solutions for their employees. It became interested in including Mitka in its range of transportation alternatives.

BOM is a semi-private development agency for the province of Brabant in the Netherlands that has been pushing hard towards innovation in transportation services. Brabant plans to build a 13 km demonstration route that is intended to become a testing ground for innovative ideas in transportation including fast no-stopping bicycle lanes. In another development, Gazelle Company has most recently initiated development of a two-wheeled variant of Mitka, using many of the engineering and design concepts of its predecessor (Figure 9.2). Gazelle has thus joined several other enterprises seeking to exploit the market potential created by the societal interest in sustainable personal mobility solutions.

Analysis
Has this BSTE led to a horizontal diffusion of ideas, to new couplings between problems and solutions or to new BSTEs? Has higher-order learning – and by whom – taken place in this experiment? Could these processes

have been enhanced? At the time of this writing the project continues to evolve and it is too soon to predict Mitka's prospects of diffusing to a larger scale, giving rise to a new generation of bike-plus vehicles or its commercial success.[2] Mitka has, however, advanced another experiment in mobility on Texel Island through a horizontal diffusion of ideas (see Case Two below).

With regard to the second question, the answer is mixed. Stage one was by definition a learning experience. Consecutive generations of students and faculty at TU Delft together with the TNO manager turned a broad vision of a societal problem into a specific solution, in the form of a bike-plus vehicle. Reflection, self-assessment and consideration of the actors' roles took place. On the other hand, the BSTE coalition, once formed, did not clarify one another's goals and interests and did not attempt to create a shared vision. Neither was the project plan assessed against the accumulated experience from previous social experiments in mobility, either domestically or abroad.

In stage two, the coalition narrowed down its design options rather rapidly. While the design ideas converged, the individual problem definitions held by the coalition members did not. Reflection, self-assessment, critical evaluation of goals and objectives and of problem definition, played a minor role in the coalition's decisions at that point. What learning took place in that stage was primarily of the first order.

In the first part of stage three, the coalition continued the stage two behaviour. The dominant mode of learning at this stage was technical. In the second part of stage three, the emergence of new actors and growing sense of urgency triggered higher-order learning within the alliance. In a

Figure 9.2   Mitka two-wheel concept by Van der Veer Design, September 2002

significant turnaround in problem definition, Mitka, rather than being a solution to the Nike parking problem or to the bigger problem of unsustainable dependence on cars, has become a placeholder, a generic element among many in designing new mobility solutions. Regardless of whether or not we shall see Mitkas on bicycle routes of Holland, the executives of Nike, Gazelle, the insurance company, Brabant Development Corporation, TNO, and the engineering and design partners have entered the social discourse about sustainable mobility, mobility services and product–service combination. They have, some for the first time, considered the possibility of having their respective companies invest in mobility solutions far removed from the core businesses. Each has seen their individual problem redefined and each has considered its role in relation to the other actors in the coalition.

In summary, the Mitka coalition missed opportunities for higher-order learning at several key junctures. We believe that visioning exercises in all stages and especially with new partners could have alleviated that problem. Such exercises might have introduced more flexibility for both the design of the Mitka and for the supporting infrastructures.

Case Two: Mobility Solutions on the Island of Texel

Texel is a 9 km by 30 km Dutch Island off the coast of North Holland, reachable by a ferry from Den Helder. Its permanent population of 14 000 swells in the summer to approximately 60 000. Tourists come to Texel for its unspoiled nature, cycling, the sea, beaches and the cultural ambiance of the six quaint villages. The original population of the island is a close-knit community with its own culture, traditions and dialect. They accept tourists because tourism is the mainstay of Texel's economy and cycle hire is an important part of it (there are about 15 bicycle-hiring companies).

By the end of the 1990s, the use of cars on Texel created a dilemma for future economic growth. The ferry could not accommodate the demand for the growing car transport during the peak season and the parking space at food markets and other businesses was becoming scarce. Expansion would, in the long run, undermine the main attraction of the island as a tourist centre: its unspoiled natural environment and unhurried lifestyle. Something needed to be done.

Stage one: problem definition

In the late 1990s, leading citizens of the island, including the manager of the ferryboat, the bicycle hire companies, the taxi company and others established Sustainable Texel Foundation (STF). STF's mission was to promote the economic growth of Texel through tourism while protecting its main cultural and environmental assets. The issue of cars figured prominently on the STF's agenda. During the next two years STF and the local government debated the island's development plan. The Mayor advanced the idea of free bus transportation, but vigorous resistance led to his resignation in 1999. One positive outcome of the increasingly heated debate was that the bicycle hire companies organized themselves into a single umbrella organization.

Despite the polarization, by 2000 the key actors shared a common problem definition, namely that future increase in tourism would have to go hand in hand with a diminishing intensity in individual car usage. Any solution would have to protect the short-term economic interests of the existing businesses.

Stage two: search for solutions through future visions

The director of the DfS program at TU Delft, who has a vacation house on Texel, had been following the debate over the island's development plan for a while and established a dialogue with the Sustainable Texel Foundation about developing an integrated mobility plan. Sometime in 2000, the STF and DfS directors jointly presented an initial plan to all the actors outside STF. The plan included introducing Mitka to the island as well as other elements of a chain mobility system using high-tech communication technologies. It received uniformly positive reactions. Thus encouraged, the DfS director invited a group of TU Delft students to further investigate the mobility solutions on the island as part of the regular teaching activities. The TU Delft group brought with them considerable experience in mobility solutions, including the techniques of future visioning and scenario building, the Mitka project and a Shell study on the opportunities for information and communication technology in personal transportation. After interviewing the key stakeholders on the island and mapping their individual interests, students came up with a vision of the future transportation system and an implementation plan.

At the core of that vision was a chain mobility system consisting of Mitka (and its analogues), taxis, bicycles and a redesigned environmentally-friendly ferryboat with capability for accommodating new transportation modalities such as Mitka. Every vehicle in the chain mobility system would be equipped with a computer. Utilization of state-of-the-art information and communication technology (ICT), including a global positioning system (GPS) formed the backbone of this plan. The implementation plan sought to realize this future vision incrementally, starting with improving the bicycle services on the island and with creating a new business organization.

The Sustainable Texel Foundation organized several seminars for its membership and for the local government to discuss the Delft proposal. This event increased the interest of the local authorities in continuing with the process. However, other actors were less enthusiastic. These actors interpreted the vision to be the plan of action, rather than a possible option for the future, intended to serve as a source of inspiration for further planning. Viewed as such, the vision appeared too innovative (possibly radical).

However, the vision presented by the TU Delft group was in fact significant in advancing the planning process. First, its innovativeness disturbed the status quo and thus mobilized the key parties to become active participants. Second, their mental range of options for Texel's mobility widened through exposure to the Delft ideas. They were therefore receptive to the proposal from the DfS director to hire an independent party to write a business plan acceptable to all parties.

Stage three: emergence of an incremental solution
An independent consultant was hired with financial support from the local municipality, the province of North Holland and the Ministry of Transportation. His task was to write a business plan, which would be endorsed by all stakeholders on the island. The consultant's approach was to synthesize the existing ideas offered by the Texel's key individual economic and civic interests.

The underlying premise of the plan was to enhance and to build on the activity that is central to the enjoyment of the island by the tourists: cycling. It was based on three elements: innovation, service and information. The innovation part consisted of cycling on solar power with new types of 'power-assisted' bi- and tricycles, starting with the introduction of the Mitka. The service part was to provide for the take-back bicycle retrieval from any point on the island to its origins. The information element consisted of installation of fixed and mobile ICT stations for Texel to inform tourists about their location and the possibilities for transportation, food services and other available amenities.

Each actor, including the Delft group, could recognize some of its own ideas in the plan. At the same time, the radical elements of the Delft visions – promoting Mitka, installing ICT technologies on all vehicles, employing the GPS system – occupied a distant second stage. Moreover, the idea of a new business has been replaced with a proposal for a foundation, Texel Own Mobility Organization, TEMO in Dutch. TEMO would gain support from the local businesses by assisting them in marketing, fundraising (subsidies and sponsoring), sourcing (lease contracts for innovative bicycles, and so on), and offering opportunities to participate in and influence present and future decisions about the island.

The stated mission of TEMO reflects the evolution of the shared problem definition among the islanders. It replaces the earlier version 'Texel can only grow in tourism if people leave their cars at their hotel or home', which focused on a car as the negative force needing taming with: 'reduction in car use will support growth of tourism on Texel', and 'TEMO's goal is to encourage people to leave cars at their island residences and to increase bicycle riding instead' (Vogtlander, 2003). Part of the toning down of the language about cars reflects the influence of the ferryboat company, which is pursuing a plan for a new vessel with a greater capacity for cars.

The business plan is under consideration at the time of this writing. In the meantime, the Texel's initiatives in mobility have attracted the attention of the Tourist Information Services at the neighbouring island of Ameland, which seeks to adopt it. If that should happen, the cautious Texel community might be mobilized to act sooner and more boldly than it has so far, stimulated by competition.

Analysis

This case is different from the Mitka case on several fundamental counts. First, the key actors were available from the outset. Second, all key actors but one (TU Delft) had serious financial stakes in the project. Third, the key actors shared a common problem definition: how to stop the growing car congestion on the island so as not to affect the local economy in any negative way. Fourth, the sense of urgency was present.

These circumstances produced different tensions from those in Case One. The dilemma of an individual versus an organization did not arise. Similarly, the dilemma of gaining broad support and commitment versus pursuing a congruent clear vision was minor in this case. Everybody was deeply invested in finding a way to grow economically through tourism without undercutting the source of this growth: the natural environment, lifestyle and the cultural heritage of Texel. This created an atmosphere in which differences in opinions could be openly voiced and worked through. However, there were other consequences: the parties acted in a risk-averse manner both with regard to their own interests and with regard to the interests of the project (in contrast with the Mitka case). These attitudes were not receptive to radical solutions.

This case illustrates how an intellectual entrepreneurship of an experiment participant can induce horizontal diffusion of elements of one bounded socio-technical experiment to another, where they can in turn have major impacts on the trajectory and outcome. The import of the Mitka idea brought about by outsiders facilitated the emergence of a radical, highly technological vision of mobility on Texel, if only for a short time before it was scaled down. This entrepreneurship turned a common problem of planning for economic growth into a BSTE in mobility solutions. While Mitka's future is highly uncertain, these efforts created a conceptual space for a bike-plus vehicle and similar sustainable mobility concepts on the island, which are now accepted by the conservative island society. In short, higher-order learning took place.

The problem redefinition is another manifestation of higher-order learning in this case. Initially, car transportation was perceived as the major threat to Texel's future. By the end of the process, the actors defined the problem, positively and outwardly looking, as maximizing the island's principal asset, cycling, as one of the key forms of recreation. Framed this way, the problem facilitated the emergence of a wide range of incremental solutions at present, and created an opportunity for future experimentation.

Another manifestation of the presence of higher-order learning among the participants in the experiment is that the key actors are now more willing to cooperate than three years ago. In particular, the employment of ICT and photovoltaic technologies is a major shift in the mental range of approaches ever contemplated by the traditional Texel society. In the future, Texel may become testing grounds for innovative ideas in alternative mobility that will be implemented at a rate that is comfortable for its stakeholders. The businesses on the island have learned that business opportunities may emerge from such experiments in the future.

Visioning exercises were instrumental for arriving at this point. The initial vision presented by the Delft group at local seminars, although initially received with scepticism, nonetheless left an indelible mark on the future process and its participants. It mobilized participation and creative processes, gave a direction and a focal point to the debate, enlarged the range of possibilities and ultimately contributed both to the problem redefinition and the solutions.

CONCLUSIONS AND DISCUSSION

In this chapter we postulate that experimenting and higher-order learning are essential for transitions towards a sustainable society. BSTEs may or may not be set up explicitly with the aim of learning; however without that the experiments often remain isolated and lack follow up. Necessary conditions for learning appear to be a shared sense of urgency; actors that are intellectually open for new ideas and for collaboration, and are risk-taking with respect to established practices. Visioning exercises appear to be necessary during all phases of the project, not just in the start-up phase. If they are not deployed, there is a risk that BSTEs degenerate into product development without taking into account the aim of solving societal problems that is at the heart of BSTEs.

The two case studies highlight the structural dilemmas occurring in BSTEs. The dilemmas are particularly pronounced in those BSTEs that are driven by an attempt to introduce new technology. This is because activist visionaries frequently initiate such technological experiments and they must build heterogeneous coalitions. Incongruent visions and interests, low commitments and levels of risk-taking by key actors are likely to emerge in such experiments. In contrast, in BSTEs where an existing local problem is collectively recognized and where an innovative technology is one of several approaches to solving the problem, the two dilemmas are less pronounced.

One of the most significant outcomes of the two experiments is what they reveal about higher-order learning of the first type and the conditions under which it occurs. First, they confirm that higher-order learning of the first type requires the presence of particular drivers. A sense of urgency is the most effective driver, in the form of risk-taking, financial stakes, preserving reputations or a mounting of the problem in need of a solution. Its magnitude fluctuates in the course of an experiment.

Second, the cases suggest that deployment of structured visioning exercises is necessary for inducing higher-order learning of the first type. These structured vision exercises should open up new types of solutions challenging the existing paradigm. Moreover, it appears that visioning in the first phases of BSTEs is not enough; repeated visioning exercises, especially when new partners enter the process or in order to open up new alternatives, is necessary. From the SusHouse project we learned that visioning could be done with a broad range of stakeholders; iterative learning can take place if it is repeated with the narrower group of participants in the BSTE process.

The third observation from the case analyses is that branching out of ideas among related bounded socio-technical experiments may be a key agent for inducing higher-order learning. The two case studies show the mechanisms by which such branching out of ideas from one BSTE to another might occur.

The case studies have much less to say about the second type of learning: diffusion of ideas about different ways of satisfying individual mobility needs. This is partly because neither innovation has not yet come to fruition. But they do highlight the relative isolation of BSTEs in mobility from one another.

The two types of learning are necessary ingredients in attaining a critical mass of societal intelligence for a transition towards sustainability. We can expect that more experiments in the future will be set up within the BSTE or SNM frameworks. In our view, substantial social value can be extracted from such experiments by monitoring and, where appropriate, management of social learning. One challenge in designing bounded socio-technical experiments is to find ways of linking them in a more planned way to one another. Governments, as well as various intellectually entrepreneurial societal agents have pivotal roles to play in making that happen (Hoogma *et al.*, 2003; Vergragt, 2003). Another challenge is to monitor and better understand the diffusion of social learning about innovative mobility solutions that occurs as a result of the experiments. The substantial body of previous research on social learning (Rogers, 1985; Hamblin, 1979; Bandura, 1977; and others) can provide a starting point for addressing this challenge.

ACKNOWLEDGEMENTS

We thank Dr Joost Vogtländer for information on Case Two, Professor Han Brezet for information on both cases and Professor John Grin for illuminating discussions.

NOTES

1. This chapter was first published in 'Learning for Sustainability Transition through Bounded Socio-Technical Experiments in Personal Mobility' by Halina Brown, *Technology Analysis and Strategic Management*, (2003) **15** (3), http://www.tandf.co.uk/journals/carfax/09537325.html.
2. At the time of writing (August 2003), more than one year after the paper was initially written, the situation is as follows: 'The experiment with the new prototype has been successfully conducted at Nike Europe (July 2003). A company is being set up to manufacture the first 100 supertrikes, which will then be subjected to further testing in a series of new experiments' (Van der Horst *et al.*, 2003).

REFERENCES

Argyris, C., and M. Schön (1994), *Organizational Learning: A Theory of Action Perspective*, Reading, MA: Addison-Wesley.
Bandura, Albert (1977), *Social Learning Theory*, Englewood Cliffs, NJ: Prentice Hall.
Berchicci L., S. Silvester and M. Knot (2002), 'Innovative artefacts for sustainable mobility systems – the example of the Mitka', paper for the *10th Conference of the Greening of Industry Network*, 23–6 June, Gothenburg.
Bolman, L. (1978), 'Organizational learning', in Argyris, C. (eds), *Increasing Leadership Effectiveness*, New York: Wiley.
Brezet, H., P.J. Vergragt and T. van der Horst (2001), *Vision on Sustainable Product Innovation*, Amsterdam: BIS Publishers.

de Bruijn, Hans, and Ernst ten Heuvelhof (2000), *Networks and Decision Making*, Utrecht: Lemma Publishers.

Cook, Scott, and Dvora Yanow (1993), 'Culture and organizational learning', *Journal of Management Inquiry*, December: 273–390.

Glasbergen, Pieter (1996), 'Learning to manage the environment' in William M. Lafferty and James Meadowcroft (eds), *Democracy and the Environment: Problems and Prospects*, Cheltenham, UK: Edward Elgar, pp. 175–212.

Green, K., and P.J. Vergragt (2002), 'Towards sustainable households: a methodology for developing sustainable technological and social innovations', *Futures*, **34**, 381–400.

Grin, J., and H. van de Graaf (1996), 'Technology assessment as learning', *Science, Technology and Human Values*, **20** (1), 72–99.

Hall, P. (1993), 'Policy paradigms, social learning, and the state', *Comparative Politics*, **25** (3), 275–96.

Hamblin, Robert L., R.B. Jacobson and J.L. Miller (1979), 'Modelling use diffusion', *Social Forces*, **57**, 799–811.

Hoogma, R., R. Kemp, J. Schot and B. Truffer (2002), *Experimenting for Sustainable Transport. The Approach of Strategic Niche Management*. London: Spon Press.

Hoogma, R., M. Weber and B. Elzen (2003), 'Integrated long-term strategies to induce regime shifts to sustainability. The approach of Strategic Niche Management', to be published as chapter in Hemmelskamp, J. and M. Weber (eds), *Innovation Systems Towards Sustainability*, Heidelberg: Springer.

Irwin, A., S. Georg and P.J. Vergragt (1994), 'The social management of environmental change', *Futures*, **26** (3), 323–34.

Kemp, R., J. Schot and R. Hoogma (1998), 'Regime shifts to sustainability through processes of niche formation: the approach of strategic niche management', *Technology Analysis and Strategic Management*, **10** (2), 175–95.

Kemp R., and J. Rotmans (2003), 'The management of the co-evolution of technical, environmental and social systems', to be published as chapter in Hemmelskamp, J. and M. Weber (eds), *Innovation Systems Towards Sustainability*, Heidelberg: Springer.

Keohane, R.O., and J.S. Nye (1989), *Power and Interdependence*, 2nd edn, Boston: Scott, Forsman.

Lant, T.K., and S.J. Mezias (1990), 'Managing discontinuous change: a simulation study of organizational learning and entrepreneurship', *Strategic Management Journal*, **11**, 147–79.

Lee, K.N. (1993), *Compass and Gyroscope. Integrating Science and Politics for the Environment*, Washington, DC: Island Press.

Luiten, H., M. Knot and T. van der Horst (2001), 'Sustainable product-service-systems: the Kathalys method', paper for EcoDesign Conference 2001, Tokyo.

Maas, T. (1997), *Bewegend leven in 2005*, master's thesis, Faculty of Industrial Design Engineering, Delft University of Technology, the Netherlands.

Quist, J., K. Green, K. Toth and W. Young (2002), 'Stakeholder involvement and alliances for sustainable households: the case of shopping, cooking and eating', in J.N.M. De Bruijn and A. Tukker (eds), *Partnership and Leadership: Building Alliances for a Sustainable Future*, Amsterdam: Kluwer Academic.

Rittel, H.W.J., and M.M. Webber (1973), 'Dilemmas in a general theory of planning', *Policy Sciences*, **4**, 155–69.

Rogers, Everett M. (1985), *Diffusion of Innovations*, 4th edn, New York: The Free Press.

Sabatier, P. (ed.) (1999), *Theories of the Policy Process*, Boulder: Westview Press.

Schwartz, B. (2002), 'Strategies for developing new environmentally adapted cars: on the example of the electric car TH!NK City', paper presented at the EGOS 18th colloquium 'Organizational Politics and the Politics of Organizations', 4–6 July, Barcelona.

Senge P.M. (1990), 'Building learning organizations', *Sloan Management Review*, **32** (1), 7–23.

Sitkin S.B., and L.R. Weingart (1995), 'Determinants of risky decision-making behavior: a test of the mediating role of risk perceptions and propensity', *Academy of Management Journal*, **38** (6), 1573–92.

Trist E. (1983), 'Referent organizations and the development of inter-organizational domains', *Human Relations*, **36** (3), 269–84.

van der Horst, Tom, P.J. Vergragt and E.H.D. van Sandick (2003), 'The seven characteristics of successful sustainable system innovations', paper for 11th Greening of Industry Conference, 12–15 October, San Francisco, USA.

van Eijndhoven, J., W. Clark and J. Jager (2001), 'The long-term development of global environmental risk management: conclusions and implications for the future', in *The Social Learning Group, Learning to Manage Global Environmental Risks*, Boston, MA: MIT Press, pp. 181–97.

Vergragt, P.J. (2000) 'Strategies towards the sustainable household', *Final Report of the SusHouse Project*, Delft University of Technology, the Netherlands.

Vergragt, P.J. (2003), 'Back-casting for environmental sustainability: from STD and SusHouse towards implementation', to be published as chapter in Hemmelskamp, J. and M. Weber (eds), *Innovation Systems towards Sustainability*, Heidelberg: Springer.

Verheul, H., and P.J. Vergragt (1995), 'Social experiments in the development of environmental technology: a bottom-up perspective', *Technology Analysis & Strategic Management*, **7** (3), 315–26.

Vogtlander, J. (2003), '*TEMO business Plan 2003*', TEMO organization, Texel, the Netherlands.

Weber M., R. Hoogma, B. Lane and J. Schot (1999), *Experimenting for Sustainable Transport Innovations. A Workbook for Strategic Niche Management*, Twente: University of Twente, the Netherlands.

PART IV

Tools for transition policy and empirical illustrations

10. Managing experiments for transition: examples of societal embedding in energy and health care sectors

Sirkku Kivisaari, Raimo Lovio, Erja Väyrynen

INTRODUCTION

It has been increasingly accepted that climate change poses a world-wide threat to the environment, human life and economic development. Human activity increases the concentrations of greenhouse gas emissions which raise the average global temperature. The change of temperature can vary to a great extent in different parts of the world. The change is estimated to lead to higher amounts of rainfall, to a rising sea level, and to a reduction of snow cover. The climate change issue and the need to curb an increase in the environmental impacts of energy production and consumption create a strong force for major changes in the energy sector.

To take a sustainability issue from another societal sector, health care systems in all Western countries are struggling to find ways to meet the new challenges related to ageing of the population. More care services for the elderly will be needed but also the quality of services calls for change in the ageing society. Emphasis in health care will transfer from external causes of diseases to biological ageing and degenerative diseases. Chronic diseases like diabetes and hypertension are increasing among elderly people. The need to renew the intertwined system of services and technologies to meet the growing and changing needs is presently considered urgent.

These examples show that transition to sustainability requires system innovations in many spheres of society. System innovation is a term that refers to major changes in the way societal functions are fulfilled (Schot et al., 2001). Such changes typically involve a coevolution of technological solutions, infrastructures, social practices, regulation and industry structures. Concern for sustainable development has raised the question whether it is possible to speed up and manage these change processes.

Experiments with alternatives to an existing system can play a crucial role in broader transition processes because they provide the seeds for change. This standpoint relates to a dynamic multi-level perspective on transitions (Geels, 2004, Figure 2.5). From this perspective, regimes tend to generate incremental innovations while radically new innovations are generated in experiments which are protected from 'normal' market selection. Radically new innovations need protection because they may have relatively low technical performance and they may be cumbersome and expensive to buy and use. The crucial role for experiments is to provide locations for learning processes and space to build the social networks that support innovation (Kemp *et al.*, 1998, Hoogma *et al.*, 2002). This implies that experiments can be used as tools in transition policy.

This chapter assesses the role and usefulness of experiments for broader transition and, more specifically, the relevance of 'societal embedding of innovations' as a management tool for experiments. The societal embedding approach has been designed to enhance commercialization of innovations that both yield financial profit and contribute to sustainable development (Kivisaari *et al.*, 1999, Väyrynen *et al.*, 2002). It has been geared especially towards supporting collaboration between public and private actors in cases where there is a considerable public interest in finding innovative solutions to societal issues.

This chapter is based on analysis of two Finnish experiments which can be perceived as pilots of system innovations. The experiments should contribute to the realization of two policy goals, notably energy conservation and seamless[1] health care. The former experiment deals with enhancing business based on a new energy service company concept in Finnish municipalities, called ESCO, and the latter with development and diffusion of a novel diabetes self-management system. Meeting environmental challenges in energy production and consumption on the one hand, and health care service delivery for ageing societies on the other, are distinct examples of societal goals that can only be realized through innovative public–private partnerships.

The chapter is structured as follows. The next section introduces transition management as a general framework and societal embedding as a tool for managing experiments. Sections 3 and 4 describe the experiments related to ESCO and the diabetes self-management concepts. Both sections are structured in a similar way. They start with a description of the prevailing system, its problems and the solution that the piloted system aims to bring. Subsequently, the sections give a brief historical account of activities contributing to experimentation, a description of the experiment and a description of developments following experimentation. The sections end by assessing the experiment as an instrument in transition management.

Section 5 summarizes the findings, discusses the role of experiments in transition and makes suggestions for improved tools for managing experiments.

THE FRAMEWORK

Experiments as Tools for Transition

The role of experiments in transition processes is an important topic in the literature on transition management. This literature emphasizes the interaction between technical and social change. It describes transition as an interactive process between three levels: landscape developments, socio-technical regimes, and technological niches (Geels, 2004, Kemp and Rotmans, 2002, Elzen *et al.*, 2002, Hoogma *et al.*, 2002). In this literature, experiments are regarded as necessary components of broader transition processes. They help to create a pathway to a new socio-technical regime.

Regimes tend to generate incremental innovations, while radically new innovations are generated in niches which are protected from 'normal' market selection. Radically new innovations need protection because their cost efficiencies, technical performance and usability often need improving. Niches provide locations for experiments and learning processes and they provide space to build the social networks which support innovation (Geels, 2004). These niche processes have been analysed and described in studies on strategic niche management (SNM) (Kemp *et al.*, 1998, Weber and Dorda, 1999).

Diffusion and breakthrough of radical innovations has been suggested to take place as the outcome of linkages between developments at multiple levels. Geels (2004) claims that innovations can break from the niche level when the external circumstances are favourable to them. The ongoing processes at the regime and landscape level may create a 'window of opportunity' for a radical innovation. The windows are opened by tensions in the socio-technical regime. For instance, landscape level changes may lead to pressures on the regime, like climate change putting pressure on energy and transport sectors. Pressure on an existing regime may also come from technical problems, negative externalities or changing user preferences. In this multi-level perspective, internal drivers, like improvement of the price–performance ratio, also play an important role and may stimulate diffusion of a radical innovation.

The Approach of Societal Embedding

Strategic niche management has been offered as a tool to introduce new technology in a probe-and-learn manner, benefiting from special circumstances

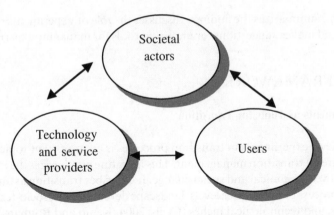

Figure 10.1   The key actors in societal embedding

offered by the local context. Societal embedding, used in managing the experiments under study here, is a somewhat similar approach and will be described below.

Societal embedding seeks to add momentum to the introduction and diffusion of sustainable solutions. It is characterized by activating and sustaining dialogue among actors who set conditions for the development and diffusion of innovation. Dialogue is the means by which the solution is shaped to meet the needs and requirements of key actors (Figure 10.1), that is, a case-specific combination of producers, users and societal actors. The latter refers to a variety of actors, like public authorities or interest groups, who take part in setting the context for producers and users to act. For instance, the Finnish Diabetes Association, insurance institutions, various regulative bodies and professional unions turned out to play critical roles as societal actors in market construction for diabetes self-management systems.

At the heart of societal embedding is a simultaneous striving to build a support network for innovation and to promote changes in the environment to facilitate innovation diffusion. The approach aims to enhance and facilitate learning-by-doing, learning–by-using and learning-by-interacting. These characteristics relate it closely to the approach of strategic niche management (Kemp *et al.,* 1998). Development of the societal embedding approach has, indeed, been inspired by the SNM studies. While the approaches are similar in many ways, they stress different aspects. SNM identifies distinctive tensions related to different stages of the commercialization process. Societal embedding, in turn, is based on a cyclic view of innovation and emphasizes certain fundamental questions requiring continuous reconsideration (see Figure 10.2) . . . The approaches are based on complementary, rather than conflicting, perceptions of innovation.

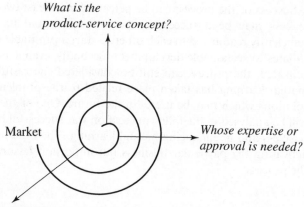

Figure 10.2 Societal embedding as a learning loop

The spiral in Figure 10.2 starts from the middle and it represents the time from idea generation to diffusion of the innovation. Three fundamental questions arise on this development path:

1. What are the desired characteristics of the innovation?
2. Whose expertise or approval is needed for development and diffusion?
3. What are the interests of the key actors and how can their commitment be gained?

During the process, these questions need to be reconsidered repeatedly. Initially, there is usually a more or less vague idea of the concept to be developed, a team will be nominated to advance the concept and its commitment must be guaranteed. During the process a more thorough understanding of the targeted concept develops which may necessitate reconsideration of the composition of the development team or network. If new actors will be included in the network it is important to make sure that they will be committed. For that reason different needs and interests should be articulated in the network. As it is important that each key actor, including the new ones, perceives the target as desirable, readjustment of the concept may be needed. And so the cyclical process continues.

By enhancing dialogue between producers, users and societal actors, societal embedding seeks mutual adjustment of the innovation and its environment. Dialogue is advanced through means of thematic interviews and multi-voiced seminars.

Success of the process can be perceived in at least two ways. Firstly, the process may be a success if the innovation and its environment are sufficiently readjusted to each other to start a profitable business that contributes to sustainable development. Secondly, even if new business is not activated, the process can still be considered successful when important mutual learning has taken place related to the problem and its possible solutions which may be useful in the future. One of the experiments that will be analysed in the following section was successful both in starting up business and in enhancing mutual learning. The other did not succeed in activating the particular business but important lessons were learned in the process.

EXPERIMENTS WITH ENERGY SAVING INNOVATION

The Prevailing System and its Problems: Insufficient Progress in Energy Saving

In 2002, total energy consumption in Finland reached an all-time high, almost twice the consumption in 1973 during the first oil crisis. Total consumption of electricity also reached a record, almost three times the consumption of the early 1970s (*Energy Review*, 1/2003). The steady growth of energy use makes it difficult for Finland to meet the policy goals related to climate change. The Finnish government has agreed to the Kyoto Protocol and the related EU agreement on targets for different EU countries. According to these agreements, Finland's greenhouse gas emissions should be back at the 1990 level by 2010. However, in 2002 Finland's CO_2 emissions were 63 million tonnes, an all-time high which exceeds the target level by 17 per cent (*Energy Review*, 1/2003).

Improving efficiency in the use and production of energy has been part of Finnish energy and environmental policies for decades. Nevertheless, energy conservation has not progressed as fast as needed. In the 1980s, energy intensity (energy consumption/GDP) in Finland showed an average annual decrease of 1.1 per cent, which dropped to 0.8 per cent in the 1990s. According to the goals set by Kyoto Protocol, the annual decrease in energy intensity should be at least 2 per cent in the next few years (Lovio, 2001).

The slow progress in energy conservation in the 1990s was due to many factors. One major reason is that economic incentives have not been strong enough. Energy prices in the world market were low in the late 1990s. Increases in energy taxes were supported by a minority of political parties in Finland and in the EU. In addition, the liberalization of the electricity market implied a shift from a top-down steering model towards market-based competition and a temporary reduction in the energy price level. This resulted in decreasing governmental influence, which was emphasized by the growing privatization of public energy companies. As for direct regulation, there have been no radical changes in standards in recent years. Thus, emphasis in governmental policy was on voluntary agreements and other network-based instruments to promote energy savings.

The energy conservation programme was first launched in 1992 and it was revised and intensified in 1995 and 2000. The revision of 2000 was made as a part of preparations for the National Climate Strategy. The Ministry for Trade and Industry (MTI) monitors developments and reports on them as part of the National Climate Strategy. In practice, an organization called Motiva Oy has been the tool of the MTI to enhance implementation of its policy.

Motiva was established as an Information Centre for Energy Efficiency in 1993 by the MTI. As of 2000 Motiva has been an impartial and state-owned joint stock company with some 25 employees. It is a service organization activating the market for energy efficiency and renewable energy sources. Its forms of operation are:

- to prepare, support and monitor voluntary energy conservation agreements;
- to develop and market energy audits and analyses;
- to boost the introduction of advanced energy-saving technologies;
- to influence people's attitudes in favour of energy conservation and permanently change their habits of using energy.

In recent years, Motiva has especially tried to find new, innovative ways to boost the introduction of energy-saving technologies. The new tools are aimed, first, at creating markets for new energy-efficient technologies, for instance through innovative procurement procedures. Second, Motiva has promoted new, innovative ways to finance energy saving investments. Enhancing of energy service company business is one of the new ways. In the following, we will describe efforts to promote ESCO.

ESCO's Solution

ESCO service is based on the idea that energy service companies (ESCOs) offer their customers the service of taking responsibility for the outcome of energy saving investments by financing, designing and installing the equipment, and that they gain their returns by receiving a share of the energy costs saved (Figure 10.3, see also for example Heiskanen *et al.*, 2001).

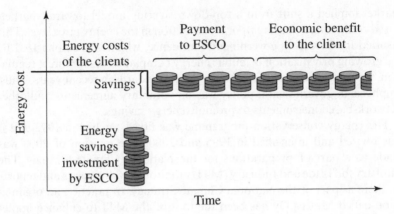

Figure 10.3   The principle of the ESCO concept

The ESCO concept can be considered a radical innovation in the sense that it leads to outsourcing of energy saving activities. Outsourcing incorporates an advantage because companies and public organizations do not always have enough time, expertise or other resources to realize energy saving potentials internally, even if this would be profitable. Meanwhile, ESCOs have the expertise and the strong financial incentive to induce energy saving.

Historical Description of Events and the Experiment

Events before the experiment
The ESCO concept was transferred to Finland from the USA and Canada where it had been successfully used for energy saving purposes in the public sector. However, owing to differences in legislation and practices between North America and Finland, the ESCO concept could not be adopted as such. As a result of a collaborative effort organized by Motiva, a contract model was designed to facilitate the use of the ESCO concept in Finland (Kilpeläinen *et al.*, 2000). A few ESCO contracts were concluded but diffusion of the concept was slower than expected.

The experimental phase
ESCO promotion activities were continued within the experiment, which was carried out by VTT Technology Studies in 2001 to 2002 as part of a national technology programme to control climate change (Climtech). The experiment was funded by the National Technology Agency of Finland (Tekes). The aim of the experiment was to shape the ESCO concept to

better meet the needs of Finnish municipalities regarding energy conservation and to examine the possibilities for implementing the ESCO service concept in Finnish municipalities via societal embedding. The significance of this experiment arises from the fact that municipalities own numerous buildings and consequently, are major consumers of energy for heating and electricity. Provided that municipalities would start to apply the ESCO concept, the volume of the energy-saving market would expand considerably. This would also create favourable conditions for technological innovations in this field.

VTT Technology Studies managed the experiment in close cooperation with Motiva. Based on Motiva's know-how and contacts, three municipalities, three ESCO candidates and three financing institutions were identified as potential partners for experimentation as they were known to be interested in cooperation with each other in energy conservation. The objective was to get the three 'local working groups' to agree on concrete local piloting sites for ESCO experimentation while VTT would support network construction and learning processes and further develop the ESCO concept in the process. While the local partners were working to find appropriate pilot sites, researchers facilitated their work by preparing a list of suggested modifications for the ESCO concept. The Association of Finnish Local and Regional Authorities provided expert assistance to make the concept better fit the needs of municipalities.

The societal embedding of the ESCO concept was carried out by conducting a series of thematic interviews and through organizing workshops. By interviewing professionals in different positions, the key actors of the market network were identified and their needs, visions, and expectations were examined. On the basis of this information, a series of interactive dialogues with the key actors were organized. They were encouraged to express their needs and interests, to listen to those of others, and to identify common ground for action. During this process, the major barriers for the business were identified and action was taken to remove them.

Figure 10.4 illustrates the flow of the process. The column on the left indicates the local bilateral activities between the cities and ESCOs that focused on finding suitable objects for ESCO projects among city-owned buildings that had been energy audited. The column in the middle illustrates the interactive networking that has been generated by societal embedding. This was the core process of the intervention which involved conducting interviews, working in seminars, workshops and local groups. The right-hand column illustrates the activities of researchers as network managers, 'messengers' and critical intermediaries. They were responsible for building the needed-actor network, for increasing mutual

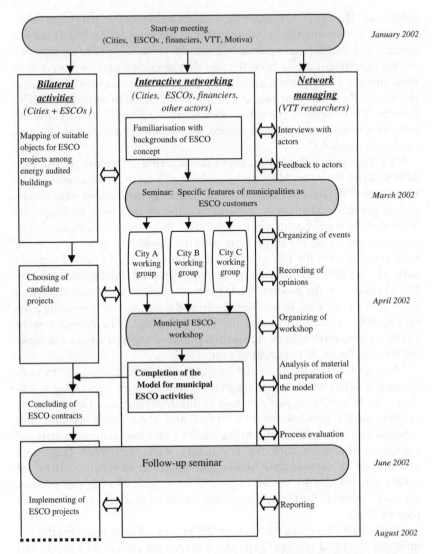

| | | January 2002 |
| Start-up meeting (Cities, ESCOs, financiers, VTT, Motiva) | | |

Bilateral activities *(Cities + ESCOs)*

Mapping of suitable objects for ESCO projects among energy audited buildings

Interactive networking *(Cities, ESCOs, financiers, other actors)*

Familiarisation with backgrounds of ESCO concept

Network managing *(VTT researchers)*

Interviews with actors

Feedback to actors

Seminar: Specific features of municipalities as ESCO customers — *March 2002*

Choosing of candidate projects

City A working group | City B working group | City C working group

Organizing of events

Recording of opinions — *April 2002*

Municipal ESCO-workshop

Organizing of workshop

Completion of the Model for municipal ESCO activities

Analysis of material and preparation of the model

Concluding of ESCO contracts

Process evaluation

Follow-up seminar — *June 2002*

Implementing of ESCO projects

Reporting

August 2002

Figure 10.4   Process description: societal embedding of ESCO concept in municipalities

understanding and for supporting the learning of all actors in the process. The double-sided arrows in Figure 10.4 indicate collaboration between the three different types of activities.

Towards the end of the nine-month experiment, the differences in the case cities took the following shape:

- *City A* (200 000 inhabitants): The city has a large department for internal services. The department has strong expertise in engineering and it appeared that they did not see any benefits in outsourcing energy saving investments. 'If the energy saving investment is profitable we'll plan and carry it out by ourselves.' The city did not continue with the ESCO concept after the experiment.
- *City B* (50 000 inhabitants): The municipality was interested in outsourcing the energy saving investment but, after preliminary planning, it seemed that the estimated pay-back time was too long for the ESCO candidate. The intended ESCO was a consulting engineering firm. The consulting firm also considered potential balance sheet problems caused by the ESCO investment as a threat to its basic consulting activities and, as a result, decided to withdraw from the project. The city still considers the ESCO model an attractive alternative and has started to look for a new ESCO partner.
- *City C* (90 000 inhabitants): The city was interested in the two main features of the ESCO concept, outsourcing both human resources and the investment itself. The ESCO candidate was a consulting engineering firm and it faced the same problems as the firm in city B. The problem was solved by inclusion of another ESCO that would concentrate on financing. Thus, ESCO's roles (financing and technical implementation) were divided between two companies. After this procedure, a suitable site for an ESCO project was found, the ESCO agreement was signed between the city and the new ESCO, and the engineering firm entered into the agreement as a sub-contractor responsible for technical implementation. The energy saving investment of this pilot case was granted a 20 per cent subsidy by the Ministry of Trade and Industry. As a result, the project was started and carried out successfully. The new ESCO company has gained credibility through this agreement and has since been able to expand its ESCO business significantly.

During experimentation, the major barriers to implementation of the ESCO concept were identified. The measures taken to remove or lower the barriers are described below.

1. *Uncertainty in the face of a new concept.* Municipal decision making may prove bureaucratic and slow when an unknown business concept enters the procedure. The principles of the ESCO model are not easy to understand, and the win-win nature of the concept is not easily recognized. To make the concept more lucid and better fit the needs of municipalities, a reviewed model for the process of ESCO activities was

developed by VTT, with expert assistance from the Association of
Finnish Local and Regional Authorities and in cooperation with the
selected local groups. A written report was produced to describe
aspects that need to be dealt with when applying ESCO practices in
municipalities.

2. *Unclarity in the roles of various actors in the ESCO process*. The roles
   of different actors were clarified during the experimentation. The most
   significant change took place in the role of engineering firms. These
   firms no longer aim at taking on the role of ESCOs; they prefer to act
   as sub-contractors for the ESCO which only takes care of financing.
   One reason was that the magnitude of the ESCO investment could
   have caused too heavy a load on the balance sheet of the engineering
   firm and thus weakened its financial position in the future.

3. *Complexity of agreement*. The agreements needed in ESCO projects
   are rather complex which is mainly due to the concept itself. To help
   ESCO partners, Motiva has designed a model contract. However, the
   circumstances for different ESCO cases can vary so much that the
   model can only be partially applied. In addition, ESCOs are founded
   on diverse backgrounds and have developed their own terms for agreements. At the moment, there are three types of ESCO companies on
   the market:

   - existing heating service companies exploiting existing customer
     connections; in their ESCO projects only the payment method is
     new to them;
   - new companies built around the new concept by traditional
     actors in the energy and financing sectors; customers are found
     via their existing business network;
   - new companies with an idealistic orientation who seek new cus-
     tomers and strive to finance environmentally sound projects.

   The experiment increased awareness of the diversity of ESCO companies and the need to enhance business for different types of them.

4. *Long pay-back time*. When the pay-back time of the energy saving
   investment exceeds four to five years, which is not uncommon in typical
   ESCO projects, the interest of ESCO candidates starts to fade. During
   the experiment, a new type of ESCO was introduced to the market.
   This ESCO, concentrating on the financing issues, has proved to be
   more patient and willing to enter into agreements with a duration of
   five to ten years.

5. *Competition in public procurement*. One of the most difficult issues concerning regulations turned out to be the legislation that necessitates the

use of competitive bidding in public procurement, which also applied to ESCO projects. It became apparent that in a project of the ESCO nature, municipalities are in need of a well thought-out set of criteria to compare the total value of different tenders. The final report on the experiment proposed a more diversified set of appropriate criteria to assess ESCO tenders than mere economic efficiency.

6. *Need for public support.* Energy-saving investments are still in need of public support. In its energy subsidy policy, the Finnish Ministry of Trade and Industry stresses the introduction of new technology which contributes either to energy conservation or to using renewable sources of energy. ESCO projects often include conventional energy conservation technologies which would receive a lower subsidy percentage. In 2002, during the experiment, the MTI decided to treat investment subsidies for ESCO projects as comparable to subsidies for new technology. In practice, this means an investment subsidy of 20 per cent instead of the earlier 10 per cent. This seems to have a substantial speeding-up effect on the market.

Events after the experimentation
The number of ESCO projects in Finnish municipalities remained modest up to 2001 but rose considerably in 2002 (Figure 10.5). The experiment described above was carried out in 2001–2. The volume of energy savings is still rather low due to the small size of the projects, which are mainly perceived as pilot projects. A comparison of ESCO activities in Finnish industry with those in municipalities indicates that the number of projects is comparable but that the volume of energy savings in the industry exceeds 50 000 MWh/a, that is more than five times the figure for municipalities.

Assessment of the Experiment

When assessing the role of experiments in transitions we need to consider developments on different levels. These are depicted in Figure 10.6.

Niche-level developments
Three main developments took place on the technological niche level. First, the experiment in City C was carried out successfully and it provides a workable model for other municipalities. Second, the experiment resulted in the creation of a new type of ESCO and this company has expanded its business since the experiment. Third, the model developed for the ESCO contracts for municipal use is expected to facilitate market building in the future as it can be applied in all municipalities.

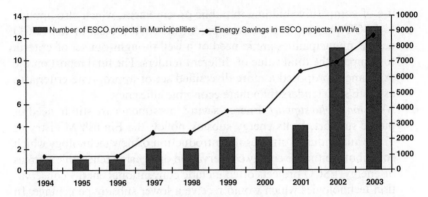

*Figure 10.5   The development of ESCO operations in 1994–2003 (Motiva
project record)*

Contribution to regime-level developments

In addition, the experiment has contributed to the building of a 'bridge'
that may enable changes in the socio-technical regime. This has happened
in two ways. First, collaboration with Motiva has provided inspiration and
enhanced Motiva's learning. During the project, Motiva familiarized itself
with societal embedding and the conceptual tools connected to it. The
approach proved a useful tool for clarifying and developing Motiva's networking activities.

This was strongly manifested in Motiva's annual report of 2002. Its editorial states: 'We are active as a network influencer and have good references
regarding the societal embedding of new technology'. When describing
Motiva's operations the annual report mentions this experiment:

> The networking operating model used by Motiva was developed in Tekes'
> Climtech Programme in the Societal Embedding of climate-friendly inno-
> vations. The concept is used to combine the views and objectives of official
> decision-makers, research, and methods and service producers. Motiva provided
> its skills at interpreting and supplying information on the potential afforded to
> end-users by technologies and methods.

And finally the report suggests that 'good results encourage those involved
to continue developing the societal embedding concept.'

Motiva's overall mode of operation was characterized, even beforehand,
by network building and target-oriented implementation of joint projects.
However, the above citations from its annual report of 2002 suggest that the
experimentation gave additional inspiration and support for its role as

network manager in the field of energy conservation and the use of energy-efficient solutions.

A second influence of the experiment on regime level can be observed in the government's new action plan for energy efficiency for 2003 to 2006. The preparation of the plan was carried out in autumn 2002, right after the experiment. There was interaction between researchers and representatives of the Ministry of Trade and Industry in the project. The MTI representative in VTT's project management was involved in the task force preparing the action plan. Some of the proposals made by the VTT researchers were taken into consideration in preparation of the plan and became manifest in its provisions.

The ESCO concept was first introduced in the government's energy conservation programme in 2000. The action plan states that ESCO activities have begun well, but reaching the targets and establishing the activities calls for additional support measures. It identifies various problematic issues, including guarantee arrangements, activation of local financiers and application of public and private procurement practices. The action plan recommends that various guarantee arrangements will be explored and tested

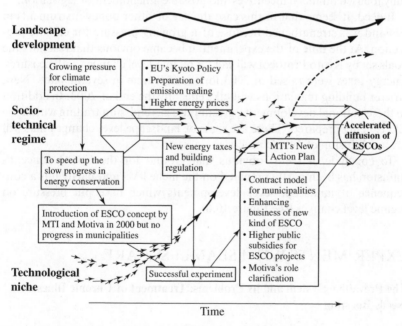

Figure 10.6　Driving forces for diffusion of ESCO practices in municipalities

from the point of view of their usability and expansion possibilities for ESCO activities.

A longer time perspective will have to reveal the role of these developments in the creation of a pathway to a possible new regime. At this point in time, despite the implications of niche and regime-level developments, the total effect of the experiment on the transition seems to be modest. This takes us to another aspect to be considered, namely the parallel developments on the landscape level.

Parallel development on landscape and regime levels
In the course of the experiment, network management, regulation and the use of economic incentives were closely linked. The experiment was supported by adjustment of regulations and financial incentives. All key actors had a positive attitude towards implementation of the ESCO concept but in the beginning none of them was interested enough to take a leading position. The public financial support that was offered provided a necessary incentive to start a pilot project. Additionally, further adjustment of the regulatory framework may be needed for further enhancement of ESCO contracts. Thus, the case revealed the need to integrate network management with carefully focused financial incentives and possible amendment of legislation.

Indeed, it seems that in this case the use of other policy instruments in Finland was strengthened because of a growing pressure for climate protection. At the time of the experiment, it became obvious that reaching the goals set by Kyoto Protocol will call for regime-level changes and measures. Energy taxes were raised in 2003 for the first time in several years. New, stricter building regulations will take effect by the end of 2003. In addition to these national developments, greenhouse gas emission trading within the EU is being prepared. These are signs of landscape level changes that will favour diffusion of ESCO practices.

To conclude, it seems obvious that ground for the ESCO concept's diffusion has been partly prepared on the niche level and partly it is a consequence of landscape level developments which have put pressure on regime level changes (see Figure 10.6).

EXPERIMENTS WITH SEAMLESS CARE

The Prevailing System and its Problems: Treatment of Chronic Illnesses Needs Boosting

Compared with many other sectors in Finnish society, the health sector has long been characterized by strong and diverse government influence and great public interest. The strong emphasis on equal access, equal public services and income transfer systems, sufficiency of social welfare and decentralization of service provision have been and still are characteristic of the system. The provision of primary health care for all citizens and increasing equal access to services are major responsibilities of the government.

Major new challenges were foreseen in the early 1990s. One of them was that growing numbers of elderly people were expected to increase the demand for health care services dramatically and to demand different types of health care services in the future. As the increase in health care expenditure had exceeded the rate of economic growth during the preceding two decades, a political debate had started concerning the limits on public funding of health care. Meeting the growing demand and, simultaneously, limiting expansion in public funding was seen to require a higher cost-efficiency of the health system. Exploitation of information technology was identified as key to solving the problem.

In the mid 1990s a structural change in the Finnish health system was started towards preventive and out-patient care and to support independent living. In 1996, the Ministry of Social Affairs and Health prepared a strategy for exploitation of information technology. Among the major definitions of the strategy were development towards seamless care, empowerment of citizens, increasing integration with information systems and strengthening of the wellbeing cluster. Within these strategic guidelines, the ministry started to finance various pilot projects to search for new modes of operation. These projects initially focused on IT applications mainly to support healthcare personnel and governmental institutions. Telemedicine, expert systems and databases for patient records were examples of applications to improve the infrastructure and to facilitate better cooperation between the various stakeholders within healthcare.

These concepts, however, did not contribute to empowering the citizens. Especially in treating some chronic illnesses, a need was recognized for IT-based services to support and activate the individual patient. Empowering the patient was expected to result in reductions in healthcare demand and, thereby, in the need for public funds.

Chronic illnesses like diabetes and hypertension are responsible for a considerable part of national health care costs. For instance, the costs caused directly by diabetes represent 11–12 per cent of the total Finnish annual health care budget. The cost is especially high in cases where the disease is not adequately treated. Chronic diseases are particularly common among elderly people and it can be anticipated that their treatment will pose an increasing challenge with an ageing population. The role of the patient is particularly crucial in management of diabetes because the patient's wellbeing depends closely on her or his lifestyle (for example, in the areas of nutrition, physical exercise).

The existing system of diabetes care is based on self-monitoring, periodic checkups in primary health care and in diabetes clinics for special health care. Although the Finnish diabetes care is placed fairly well in international rankings, there is evidence that diabetes management of a considerable number of citizens is poor or very poor.

The Diabetes Self-management System

Developing self-management is one recommendation in the latest national diabetes prevention and care development program (DEHKO, 2000). The system supporting diabetics' self-management, to be analysed here, is a tool that aims to improve management of diabetes by empowering the patient. The interactive system consists of a central database which the patient and the healthcare personnel can access with a web browser or a mobile phone. The service provider is responsible for the database, and the patient wanting to use the service must sign a contract which allows the provider to gather and file her or his diabetes data. The patient also authorizes the healthcare personnel to use the gathered data (Söderlund *et al.*, 2000).

The web together with wireless communication allows diabetics to record and access essential personal disease-related data. The system also gives health care personnel access to more detailed, long-term and up-to-date data on their patients' health status and the opportunity to give immediate feedback. Better management decreases the risk of complications and the need to see a doctor, thus saving public funds and resources. However, successful implementation of such a system requires changes in job descriptions, responsibilities and work division among health specialists and reorganization in health units: a systemic change within the existing regime.

The Historical Description of Events and the Experiment

Events before the experiment
As part of the Finnish government's arrangements to strengthen the national innovation system, the well-being cluster received public funding for activities that were related to technology programmes and to a major regional experiment for seamless care (called Macropilot). Tekes launched a technology program called Digital Media for Health Care from 1996 to 1999 to develop technologies for self-maintenance, independent living and home care. One line of activities, organized by VTT, was to support market development for the new technologies that received R&D funding from the programme.

Two Finnish companies developing diabetes self-management systems with competing concepts received R&D funding from the program. One of them was a major IT-company (company A) that was searching for new application areas for their technologies. The other was a small company (company B) which started to develop a diabetes-related database for health care professionals but later extended the concept to include eHealth services for citizens with diabetes.

The IT company had made efforts to increase its credibility as a technology provider for the health care sector and to incorporate health-related skills and expertise into the development process. For these purposes it had concluded partnership arrangements with prominent physicians and well-known health care companies. It had also organized piloting of the concept with the patients of the physicians. The small company was working closely with Finnish health district professionals and piloting their system in domestic hospitals.

The IT company was highly experienced in developing and marketing consumer products and found it hard to understand that the diabetes self-management system differed from a consumer product. The company was in a rush to pilot and commercialize its innovation but its speed was slowed down by the prudent pace of public health care decision-makers and professionals in accepting the system for use.

The experimental phase
As part of 'Digital Media for Health Care' programme, VTT started to organize experiments dealing with societal embedding of four seamless care concepts. These were related to orthopaedic teleconsultation, self-management of hypertension, electronic prescription, and diabetes self-management. In this section, we focus on the experiment with the diabetes self-management system. As a partly unsuccessful experiment it provides useful insight into barriers of societal embedding.

Negotiations with both above-mentioned companies were held in order to involve them both in the societal embedding process. Participation implied the companies had to provide some funds for the process. Both companies were motivated to take part in the experiment, but only the IT company had the required financial resources; so, it was the only company included in the process. The major difference between the concepts of these companies was that the IT company (A) viewed their product more as a consumer product while the small company (B) was more familiar with the health-care system and worked to develop a tool for health professionals.

The experiment started with the IT company was confined to a period of one year in the early piloting phase. One of the problems that became clear already at the beginning of the process was that the company had created a complete technology-push situation by accepting as partners only the physicians whose opinions supported company ideas. The company rejected the involvement of opposing actors.

A number of professionals were interviewed to identify critical stakeholders who would be setting conditions for development and implementation of the disease management system. Another aim of the interviews was the articulation of the needs and interests of these actors. The interviews resulted in construction of a more elaborate conception of the necessary market network. The interviews indicated that the company had too simplistic and optimistic a view of applying its concept to the health care system. They also suggested that lack of clinical evidence on the effectiveness of the new system was considered a problem among professionals.

Evidence of a product's usefulness is crucial in the field of medical technologies. Although it is intuitively clear that the web together with wireless technologies gives a patient better control of her or his chronic condition as well as better communication links with the clinical team, it also requires a rather large and well-designed clinical trial to demonstrate that the technology really makes a difference. A possible additional challenge is the usability and availability of the product to all diabetic patients. Setting up a clinical trial is not in itself so difficult. What makes it difficult in this case is the fact that the trial would have to run for several years to reveal whether better overall control and a reduction of secondary complications are achieved. Although the company became aware of these issues, overall, it underestimated them.

The interviews also indicated the lack of development resources in public health-care organizations. The already over-burdened personnel was not well compensated for the piloting of new concepts and perceived it as an extra workload.

Another obvious problem related to difficulties in defining the service to be provided and the customer to whom it should be offered. The disease management system was designed to work as a communication link between citizens and health care specialists. One problem was that it fitted neither the conventional professional market segments where systems are used by health care professionals nor the consumer market where they are used by citizens with limited training. The new concept was to be offered to an emerging market segment where the customer was simultaneously a professional and a citizen.

Mapping the existing regulatory environment and determining what kind of prospects it offered for implementation of disease management systems was started. The researchers and the company negotiated with regulators, lawyers specializing in the health system and distinguished physicians. The major problem turned out to be privacy protection regulations that prevented private companies from keeping registers of personal health data in the public health-care system.

A multi-voiced seminar was organized for key actors representing different areas of clinical, medical, administrative, technical and business expertise. There appeared to be wide consensus on the need to develop and implement disease management systems such as the diabetes self-management concept. The problem was that there was a lack of understanding on how the change process could be managed in public health care.

Events after the experiment
The IT company had been overly optimistic about its ability to control its environment and influence opinion leaders and decision-makers. When faced with reality, instead of learning and adjusting the product, the provider opted for a solution that fitted the corporate strategy, that is they targeted the diabetic patient as the customer who would buy (pay for) the service. Hence, they completely overlooked the fact that diabetic patients are under the care of a physician and that his or her decision is required for use of the product.

In 1999 a joint venture was set up by the Finnish IT company and an American health technology company to commercialize the new system. The new company was located in California. Later, the company revised its strategy but at the time its technology (wireless, GSM, text messages), although in wide use in Finland, was too advanced for California. And the Finnish market, obviously, did not provide a large enough market for business. The company went bankrupt in 2001.

Simultaneously with the developments described above, the company B that dropped out of the societal embedding process, had continued piloting its competitive diabetes concept in Finnish municipalities. The company has been able to sell its system to most Finnish hospital districts and has also extended its web-based systems to incorporate coronary heart disease management and eye-screening management. Its web-based diabetes self-management system is in wide use in Finland and the company has also found an entry to the British market as the system is currently being implemented in two British hospitals. The company emphasizes that in its concept a patient's self-management relates to management of chronic illnesses in a team of various actors. The team incorporates primary health care, special health care, private health care and the patient.

The pilots that have explored these disease management concepts thus far have indicated the diabetics' satisfaction with the self-management system's reliability and usefulness. They have also shown considerable cost savings that have resulted from diminished need to treat patients inside hospital walls when using self-management system (Söderlund *et al.*, 2000; Eerola and Kivisaari, 2001).

Assessment of the Experiment

Limited development on niche level

The described experiment did not succeed in contributing to profitable business in the specific case. However, it did provide some useful lessons on the necessary market network for diabetes self-management systems although the company was not inclined to take it seriously. In this section we will discuss two major barriers for learning. The first is that imbalance of the network of actors hinders dialogue, the second that collaboration between public and private actors seems to be especially problematic in the field of health care.

All four experiments that VTT organized for the societal embedding of seamless care concepts resulted in deeper insight into the composition of the network needed to commercialize different seamless care concepts, and to articulate the different needs and interests of key actors. In the diabetes self-management experiment, however, the IT company was not responsive to the interests of health care professionals and regulating bodies but rather perceived itself as a self-sufficient and strong player. It was eager to push a change process forward but did not understand the market network and the roles of key actors. Meanwhile, the small companies in the other three experiments were extremely motivated to listen to opposing views and willing to take part in dialogue and to learn. This underlines the importance of a balanced network. Collaboration and dialogue do not work if actors do not have respect for one another and if they do not see the importance of creating win-win situations.

Developing system innovation in health care calls for interactive development of new services and novel technologies to support them. The services and technologies are closely intertwined: potential new technologies need to support the provision of the new service while also supporting a customer's operational needs. This is why system innovation necessitates collaboration between public health specialists, who are responsible for developing services, and the private companies which develop technologies to support the services. Collaboration of public and private actors, however, has proven to be very hard in health care. The market is strongly regulated and controlled by public bodies. Health professionals have powerful unions to protect their interests. The public actors do not consider private companies, with their profit orientation, as 'legitimate' players in the health system's development activities; and companies expect public organizations

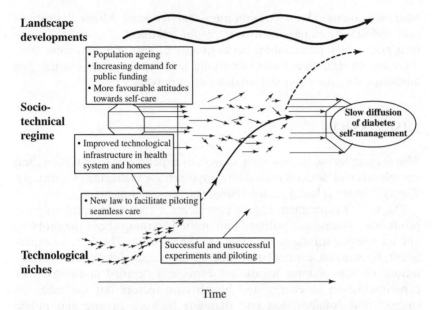

Landscape developments

Socio-technical regime

Technological niches

• Population ageing
• Increasing demand for public funding
• More favourable attitudes towards self-care

• Improved technological infrastructure in health system and homes

• New law to facilitate piloting seamless care

Successful and unsuccessful experiments and piloting

Slow diffusion of diabetes self-management

Time

Figure 10.7   Driving forces for diffusion of diabetes self-management systems

to act like private companies and do not understand their slow and complex decision-making processes. All in all, there is neither mutual respect nor trust among these actors. This was well indicated by the major Macropilot regional experiment for seamless care (Kivisaari *et al.*, 2002).

Limited support from regime or landscape level
On the regime level some changes supporting seamless care can be observed (Figure 10.7). A new, temporal law was enacted in 2000 to facilitate and enable the piloting of seamless care concepts in specified regions in Finland. The initial validity of the law was three years but it has been extended. This change in the infrastructure is an important step towards adapting the environment to exploiting disease management systems.

Also the technological infrastructure has been upgraded and the ability of staff in primary health care and hospitals to use web-based tools has improved. Cultural changes towards motivation and citizens' capability to maintain and enhance their own health and wellbeing tend to support change as well.

On the landscape level, however, there are no recent new developments. Population ageing and problems of public funding for increasing demand have been common knowledge for more than ten years. Although seamless care and disease management concepts for treatment of chronic illnesses incorporate high potential for better quality of care at a reasonable cost, there are no clear time limits that would modify the rate of change. The landscape does not open real windows of opportunity.

DISCUSSION

This chapter focuses on assessing the role of experiments in transitions and the relevance of societal embedding approach for managing experiments. The assessment is based on the analysis of two experiments.

The ESCO experiment can be considered a success in many ways. A profitable business was initiated and mutual learning about the problem and its possible solutions took place in the network. The diabetes experiment, by contrast, cannot be considered very successful. Within the limitations of this chapter we cannot provide a detailed comparison of experimentation in energy and health care sectors but the cases do suggest that collaboration and dialogue between private and public actors is far more difficult to initiate and maintain in health than in energy issues. In health care, not only are professional unions and associations powerful public players, but so are regulators. The profit orientation of private companies arouses suspicion among them. Private companies, on their part, consider public practices very bureaucratic and odd. In the energy sector problems related to public–private partnership are not great: most players are private companies and unions are not in powerful positions.

The Role of Experiments in Transition

The dynamic multi-level model of transitions helps interpreting developments in energy conservation and seamless care. The empirical analysis supports Geels's ideas about the diffusion of radical innovation as an interplay of developments at multiple levels.

The successful ESCO experiment increased the credibility of the concept and encouraged political and other actors to make incremental changes in the regime. Simultaneously, landscape level changes exerted pressure in the same direction. Thus, regime-level changes were pushed forward by the interplay between landscape pressure and successful experiments. We can expect that changes in the regime tend to create further space for new experiments and developments which may create additional pressure towards regime changes.

The multi-level perspective also helps interpretation of slow develop-ments in health care. Some conditions for wider diffusion of diabetes self-management systems on the regime level are slowly changing. However, these developments are not speeded up by obvious niche-level successes, concrete pressing time limits, or sanctions from the landscape level. On the niche level the analysed experiment taught lessons on the necessary com-position of a market network for diabetes management systems, but in terms of business start-up the experiment failed. On the landscape level the trends causing general pressure have not turned into concrete requirements for regime-level changes.

Management of Societal Embedding

The analysis gave new insight in the management of experiments. It indi-cated that making good decisions about timing the experiment, providing the experiment with sufficient public resources, and securing a convenor with the required qualifications, are important to be able to draw practically useful conclusions from it. This is important because these niche-level learning processes may yield seeds for change.

Timing and time frame

Diffusion of radical innovations are typically long-term processes because innovation and its environment need to be adapted to each other. For the adaptation to happen, the ground for collaboration between producers, users, and societal actors needs to be smoothed and mutual trust needs to be built. The societal embedding approach is designed for these purposes but the process is necessarily slow and it calls for resources and skills on the part of the process manager as well as all the key actors involved. Therefore, it is important to consider the best timing and the needed time frame for societal embedding in each case.

Two basic variations of the process can be distinguished (Figure 10.8). The intensive societal embedding (A type) concerns periods in which new concepts have to be defined and/or experimented with. The ESCO experi-ment was an example of intensive societal embedding in an early piloting phase. This kind of societal embedding is effective, and when it is applied only periodically, it does not require too much financial and time resources from those involved.

The lighter long-term (B type) intervention in the course of the develop-ment process may be an interesting alternative because it provides a sufficient time frame for learning. It also provides ease and flexibility in coping with resource needs because money and time investments are spread

(A) Intensive, periodic

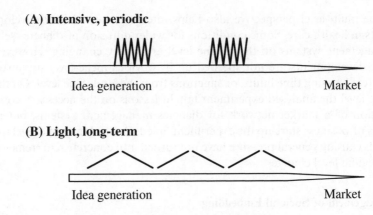

Idea generation   Market

(B) Light, long-term

Idea generation   Market

Figure 10.8   Two basic modes of societal embedding

more evenly over a longer time span. Long-term public financing for process management is needed for carrying out this kind of experiment.

Providing the experiment with enough resources
It is vital for successful experimentation that the key actors are committed to reaching the target and that they have resources to carry out their tasks in the process. The availability of public funding to manage the societal embedding process is obviously an important success factor. If funding has to come from private sources, only large companies with major financial resources can participate in these processes and small innovative companies will be excluded.

However, it is equally important that users are provided with sufficient resources. In the experiments analysed here, the users were public organizations. The public sector is not well prepared to carry out experimentation related to innovation processes and typically there are no funds to compensate personnel for experimentation. Experiments thus become an extra burden to take care of along with normal responsibilities. So it is not enough that the users perceive the target as desirable for them. If the financial resources supporting participation are missing, their commitment will decline and the experiment will be weakened.

Skills of the convenor
Management of the societal embedding process calls for behaviour that is independent from the interests of key stakeholders. The actor responsible for managing the process can represent neither technology companies, their customers nor organizations responsible for regulating the market. The convenor must be independent but it is important that the convenor also

perceives the target of the process as valuable and favourable and is committed to reaching it.

According to the experience gained, it is important that the convenor has competence in process management as well as credibility in understanding substantial issues. These competencies do not always go hand in hand and, therefore, it may be advisable to engage two convenors, one responsible for process management and one with competence in the subject matter who can provide credibility to the process.

To conclude, the multi-level perspective of transition increases public understanding of the role of experiments. Perceiving experiments as possible stimulants of changes at the regime level highlights the importance of mutual learning in the process. The increased understanding of timing, resources and convenor competencies will contribute to improve societal embedding as a tool for managing experiments.

NOTE

1. Seamless care is a relatively new term in the health care literature. It usually refers to the desirable continuity of care delivered to a patient in the health care system across the spectrum of caregivers and their environments (Canadian Society of Hospital Pharmacists, Seamless Care Workshop 1998, Executive summary.) Care is carried out without interruption so that when one caregiver ceases to be responsible for the patient's care, another caregiver or health care professional accepts responsibility for it.

REFERENCES

Diabetes prevention and care development program 2000–2001(DEHKO) (2000), The Finnish Diabetes Association (in Finnish).

Eerola, Annele, and Kivisaari Sirkku (2001), 'Challenges of parliamentary technology assessment – the case of internet-based disease management systems', paper for the congress Innovation for an E-Society: Challenges for Technology Assessment, Berlin, 17–19 October, Congress Pre-prints, ISBN 3-89750-097-3.

Elzen, Boelie, Frank Geels, Peter Hofman and Ken Green (2002), 'Socio-technical scenarios as a tool for transition policy, an example from the traffic and transport domain', paper for workshop on Transitions to Sustainability through System Innovations, University of Twente, Enschede, 4–6 July.

Energy Review (2003), Ministry of Trade and Industry, January.

Geels, Frank (2004), 'Understanding technological transitions: a critical literature review and a conceptual synthesis', Chapter 2 this volume.

Heiskanen, Eva, Halme Minna, Jalas Mikko, Kärnä Anna and Lovio Raimo (2001), 'Dematerialization: the potential of ICT and services', The Finnish Environment Publications Series 533, Ministry of the Environment.

Hoogma, Remco, René Kemp, Johan Schot and Bernhard Truffer (2002), *Experimenting for Sustainable Transport. The Approach of Strategic Niche Management*, London: Spon Press.

Kemp, René, Johan Schot and Remco Hoogma (1998), 'Regime shifts to sustainability through processes of niche formation: the approach of strategic niche management', *Technology Analysis and Strategic Management* **10** (2), 175–194.

Kemp, René, and Jan Rotmans (2002), 'Managing the transition to sustainable mobility', paper for workshop on Transitions to Sustainability Through System Innovations, University of Twente, Enschede, 4–6 July.

Kilpeläinen, Heikki, Hannu Valkonen and Heikki Väisänen (2000), *The General Principles in ESCO Activities and MotivaESCO Concept*, in Finnish, Motiva Publications, March.

Kivisaari, Sirkku, Sami Kortelainen and Niilo Saranummi (1999), 'Societal embedding of innovation in health care', in Finnish, Tekes Digital Media Report, July.

Kivisaari, Sirkku, Petri Rouvinen and Pekka Ylä-Anttila (2002), 'Assessment of Macro Pilot cluster effects', in Finnish, Helsinki: The Research Institute of the Finnish Economy C79.

Lovio, Raimo (2001), 'The role of dematerialization in achieving environmental goals in the energy sector: the Finnish evidence from 1980 to 2002, in Eva Heiskanen, Minna Halme, Mikko Jalas, Anna Kärnä and Raimo Lovio (2001), *Dematerialization: the Potential of ICT and Services*, The Finnish Environment Publications Series 533, Ministry of the Environment, pp. 111–20.

Schot, Johan, Geer Verbong, Frank Geels, Ken Green, René Kemp, Boelie Elzen and Matthias Weber (2001), 'Transitions to sustainability through system innovations', keynote paper for the international expert meeting, University of Twente, July 2002.

Söderlund, Riitta, Pekka Reijonen and Malin Brännback (2000), 'A web-based solution for enhancing diabetic well-being', in Lauren B. Eder (ed.), *Managing Healthcare Information Systems with Web-enabled Technologies*, Hershey, PA: Idea Group Publishing.

Weber, Matthias, and Dorda Andreas (1999), 'Strategic niche management: a tool for the market introduction of new transport concepts and technologies', IPTS report 31, pp. 20–8.

Väyrynen, Erja, Sirkku Kivisaari and Raimo Lovio (2002), 'Societal embedding of innovations related to renewable energies and energy saving', in S. Soimakallio and I. Savolainen (eds), *Technology and Climate Change Climtech 1999–2002*, technology programme final report, December, Helsinki: National Technology Agency of Finland (Tekes), pp. 235–44.

11. Socio-technical scenarios as a tool for transition policy: an example from the traffic and transport domain

Boelie Elzen, Frank W. Geels, Peter S. Hofman and Ken Green

INTRODUCTION

Modern societies face huge challenges related to existing socio-technical systems which are difficult to tackle without fundamental change. An example is in agriculture which exhibits various unsustainable features like BSE, foot and mouth disease, high nitrogen emissions, and so on. Another example is water supply, with symptoms like flooding, soil dehydration and quality problems. Also the transport system faces structural problems like congestion, atmospheric pollution (NO_x and particulates), and CO_2 emissions. Such problems are deeply rooted in societal structures and institutions and are closely related to societal processes. To solve such problems fundamentally requires transitions or system innovations as is argued in the fourth Dutch National Environmental Policy Plan (VROM 2001).

A transition in this sense denotes a long-term development process in an encompassing system that fulfils a basic societal function like food production, mobility, energy, communication, and so on. A transition implies a drastic change of the technical as well as the societal and cultural dimensions of such a system. This emphasis on the coevolution of technical and societal change distinguishes transitions from more incremental processes of innovation which are primarily characterized by technical development (successive generations of technologies) with the societal embedding of these technologies changing relatively little (see Geels in this volume).

From the sustainability perspective, an important question is whether transitions can be induced or stimulated. In the strict sense the answer is 'no', given the complex nature of transitions. What is possible, though, is to try and stimulate developments in specific, more sustainable directions over a longer period of time (Rotmans *et al.*, 2000 and 2001). This requires a vision as to which directions that might be, that is, which combination(s) of technologies and their societal embedding might produce a sustainable system. To help develop such visions, scenario studies or other foresight methods are used.

There exists a variety of scenario and foresight methodologies, each of which has its own strengths and limitations, especially in exploring the complex and convoluted processes that characterize a transition. To remedy these limitations we have developed a new scenario method based on a scientifically-supported theory of transitions. We call this method 'Socio-Technical Scenarios' (STSc).

In this chapter, we will describe the method briefly and illustrate it by describing two short scenarios for the passenger mobility domain.[1] We have chosen this domain because we are familiar with it due to our work over the past decade (Elzen *et al.*, 1996a; Achterhuis and Elzen, 1998; Geels, 2002b). In the final section, we will use the two scenarios to draw some conclusions for transition policy in this domain and argue that these conclusions have broader applicability than just for the mobility system.

The chapter discusses many topics: the need for a new scenario methodology although a wide variety of methods already exists, the theoretical underpinning of the methodology, the methodology itself, its illustration and conclusions for transition policy. It is impossible to elaborate all those points extensively. Therefore, our main goal here is to demonstrate and argue the potential of the method as a tool in transition policy.

TRANSITION THEORY

The so-called 'multi-level perspective' has been developed to analyse and explain transitions and system innovations (see Geels in this volume). This perspective distinguishes three levels (Kemp, 1994; Schot *et al.*, 1994; Rip and Kemp, 1998, Kemp *et al.*, 2001; Geels, 2002a,b):

1. The meso level of 'socio-technical regimes' (S-T regimes) which denotes an existing socio-technical system that is embedded in society and carried by a variety of societal actors (such as companies, public authorities, users). These actors have vested interests in the existing system and invest in incremental innovations to improve its performance.

   In the domain of passenger mobility, for which scenarios will be described later in this chapter, the S-T regime consists of the following elements and actors: (i) technical artefacts such as cars, buses, bicycles and so on, manufactured by companies and their parts-suppliers;

(ii) infrastructures (road, rail) for which public authorities are largely responsible; (iii) fuel infrastructure with a large role for oil companies; (iv) regulations and standards (such as on vehicle emissions, parking rates, taxes, traffic rules); (v) cultural and symbolic meanings related to cars (such as the freedom to move, individuality) that have emerged in an interplay between various actors, partly via media and advertising campaigns; (vi) markets, user preferences and user practices (such as the preference for high-performance cars, their use for various purposes, sufficient space, long range); (vii) maintenance and parts-supply networks (such as garages), and so on.

2. The micro level of 'technological niches'. This denotes protected spaces in which radical innovations are developed. In their initial stage, these innovations cannot compete with existing technologies and need to be protected against regular market forces. They have the potential to solve certain problems in the regime when fully developed. Innovations in niches are supported by a network of actors who expect or have a strategic vision that the innovation can be developed as a viable market product. Niches are important as a learning space on issues like technology, user preferences and practices, regulation, and so on.

    In the passenger mobility domain, a large number of niches is and has been developed in recent years, such as cars with alternative propulsion (battery electric, hybrid electric, fuel cells, and natural gas vehicles), 'transferia' (transfer points between private cars and public transport), car-sharing, chain mobility, chipcards, individualized public transport. Some of these niches are close to broad application while others are still far from it.

3. The macro-level of 'socio-technical landscape'. This denotes the 'external environment' that is only partly influenced by actors in the regime under analysis but mostly results from the juxtaposition of the dynamic in a variety of regimes.

    Relevant factors in relation to mobility include commuting patterns, patterns of recreation, concern about climate change, oil prices, broad cultural changes (such as public concern about the state of the environment, concern about the urban and natural landscape), demographic changes (greying of society possibly leading to changing mobility requirements), generic new technologies like ICT that also penetrate the mobility system.

Radical innovations in niches cannot easily break through an existing regime because the latter is very resilient (Elzen *et al.*, 1996b). In many cases, there is a mismatch with existing user preferences and existing regulations. (Freeman and Perez, 1988). Still, radical innovations form the seeds for transitions and their chance of breaking through can increase when the existing regime becomes less stable, through internal problems or negative externalities that cannot be solved adequately. Usually, such breakthroughs take place through mutual reinforcement of several technologies – high-capacity batteries, lightweight car bodies and more efficient electric drive trains – that, in combination, can stimulate the uptake of electric vehicles. Interactions, hybridizations and cross-links between technologies are important in making this happen. Typically, such breakthroughs do not happen suddenly but result from successive small steps, also called 'niche-accumulation' (first application in small market A, then small market B, and only then mass market C (see Geels, 2002a)).

In this framework, four phases can de distinguished in a transition: (i) pre-development, in which radical innovations are developed at the niche-level; (ii) take-off, in which innovations conquer market niches with specific selection criteria; (iii) breakthrough, in which innovations start to conquer mass markets, partly facilitated by destabilization of the existing regime; and (iv) substitution and stabilization of a new socio-technical regime (Rotmans *et al.*, 2000).

From the policy perspective, the relevant issue is whether and to what extent transitions can be induced or stimulated. Transitions have two main characteristics that make it impossible to steer their course in the strict sense, namely complexity and uncertainty. Transitions are complex because of the multitude of relevant interactions between a wide range of actors, such as companies and their suppliers, public authorities at local, national and supranational levels, users, knowledge institutes and societal groups. Thus, public authorities are just one actor among many and may influence the 'rules of the game' but cannot control the development. They only have limited knowledge of the relevant developments in the regime and the effect of policy instruments is also limited. All actors operate in a collective game, all of whom have their own strategies and means and try to realize their goals by operating in various networks and making moves as they see fit. For instance, when new technologies become available, public authorities may adapt emission standards or give subsidies to users to buy it. Companies may react by building new coalitions or adapting strategies. Because each player has its own goals, no actor can oversee the game as a whole and control it. Outcomes will be partly unintended (at least for some players) and unforeseen. There may be periods of relative ease and stability but also periods of relatively rapid change. Thus, transition processes are far from linear; they are uncontrolled and have uncertain outcomes.

The characteristics of complexity and uncertainty carry a warning concerning the possible ambitions of transition policies. This does not mean that such policies are futile but it does suggest that policy instruments should be used and combined in a way that differs from current practice. This does not imply that present instruments should be altogether replaced (although there will be a need for new instruments) but that the choice of type of instrument, their combination and tuning should be embedded in an overall perspective on transitions.

Suggestions on how to do this have been recently developed in the so-called 'modulation approach' of transition policy (Kemp *et al.*, 2001; Rotmans *et al.*, 2000, 2001; Geels, 2002b; Kemp and Rotmans in this volume). The basic idea is that transition policy should not go against the tide but should hook on to ongoing processes and attempt to influence those a bit. An intervention at the right point and time may influence the direction of technological trajectories and may have a substantial effect on later results by making use of path-dependencies (Arthur, 1988; David, 1985).

The general strategy for transition policy is to influence two of the levels described above at the same time (see Geels in this volume). On the one hand the pressure on the existing regime should be increased, by using generic tools like tradable emission permits, pollution taxes and emission standards. On the other hand, alternatives in niches should be stimulated via technology policy, targeting innovation in concrete domains. The choice of instruments should be tuned to 'windows of opportunity' that may result from landscape-level developments like increasing societal concerns in relation to climate change or regime-level concerns like traffic jams.

This general strategy needs to be differentiated, depending upon the phase of the transition process. In the early phases, niche-level policies should emphasize vision-development, learning processes, experimentation, building social networks. Regime-level policies should increase the pressure for specific improvements but this has to be tuned with niche-level developments since increasing the pressure without stimulating concrete alternatives in niches has only limited effect. In later phases, economic competition in regular markets becomes important. This requires policy approaches that stimulate or force the use of new technologies like regulation, taxation and/or purchase subsidies. Furthermore, policies may be needed to stimulate broader adaptation and transformation such as building new infrastructures, monitoring of (side) effects and adjustments to counter negative effects. Figure 11.1 gives an impression of the types of policies needed for different phases.

This general transition policy needs to be further specified and this raises new questions. One problem is that at the niche-level a wide variety of alternatives is usually developed. Each of these holds a specific promise but it is unclear which alternative can be made to work in practice. There is thus a need to select and focus and to assess which innovation should be stimulated in what way. A vision is needed of possible or likely future developments,

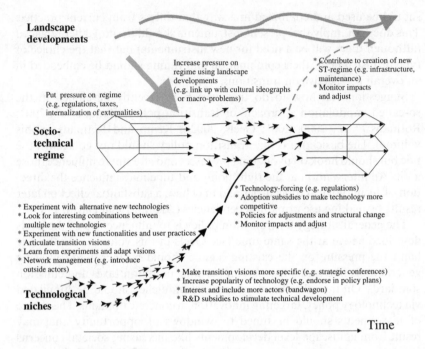

Landscape developments

Increase pressure on
regime using landscape
developments
(e.g. link up with cultural ideographs
or macro-problems)

* Contribute to creation of new
  ST-regime (e.g. infrastructure,
  maintenance)
* Monitor impacts
  and adjust

Put pressure on regime
(e.g. regulations, taxes,
internalization of externalities)

**Socio-
technical
regime**

* Technology-forcing (e.g. regulations)
* Adoption subsidies to make technology more
  competitive
* Policies for adjustments and structural change
* Monitor impacts and adjust

* Experiment with alternative new technologies
* Look for interesting combinations between
  multiple new technologies
* Experiment with new functionalities and user practices
* Articulate transition visions
* Learn from experiments and adapt visions
* Network management (e.g. introduce
  outside actors)

* Make transition visions more specific (e.g. strategic conferences)
* Increase popularity of technology (e.g. endorse in policy plans)
* Interest and include more actors (bandwagon)
* R&D subsidies to stimulate technical development

**Technological
niches**

Time

Source: Geels, 2002c, p. 363.

Figure 11.1   Different transition policies in different phases

especially within the socio-technical regime. The vision should concern not
only technology but also the possibilities and effects of policy, markets and
user preferences. A further crucial question is how promising niches can be
stimulated to hook on to the regime, possibly through synergy and linkages
between niches. Scenarios and foresight studies can be an important tool to
make this possible.

SOCIO-TECHNICAL SCENARIOS

To be useful as in instrument in transition policy, a scenario should describe
a true transition. In view of the basic characteristics and elements of transitions, and transition policy, this implies that a scenario should have at
least the following features:

1.   Transition scenarios should show socio-technical development, that is,
     the coevolution of technology and its societal embedding ('leapfrog'

dynamic). This implies attention to different types of actors, their goals, strategies and resources. Concrete features like technologies, investments and infrastructures should not appear automatically but must be made plausible as the result of interactions between actors. Thus, transition paths do not come out of the blue but it becomes clear *why* they develop.

2. Learning processes and niche dynamic should be visible in the scenarios. Important questions to deal with are: What happens in niches? Which innovations are developed? What are the problems and possibilities? In which direction are solutions sought? What learning takes place on technology, new user practices, regulation, and so forth? Which actors are involved in the learning processes?

3. Spread of novelties should not only describe diffusion of individual innovations but also pay attention to their development and the interaction between niches, such as in linking individual technologies (hybridizations) and synergistic effects.

3. Market take-up should also address the development of innovations through successive niches (niche-accumulation).

A broad range of scenario methods exists, each with its own strengths and weaknesses: trend-extrapolation via learning curves, computer simulations, Delphi-exercises, interactive technology assessment. These methods are particularly suited to explore relatively stable patterns of development, assuming that various functions remain the same and users do not change preferences. Transitions and system innovations, however, imply structural change in which functions, user practices, policy and infrastructure also change. Existing methods are less suited to explore such 'radical' changes.[2] Simulations with computer models, for instance, are well suited to explore the market penetration of technologies but do not explore possible societal changes that may coevolve with these technologies. In such models, market diffusion is determined only by price–performance assumptions. There is little attention to the activities of actors such as strategic games and coalition, learning processes and expectations.

These shortcomings in existing exploratory methods are recognized and various recent studies have sought to remedy them. In the Dutch 'Sustainable Technology Development' (STD) programme, a 'backcasting' method was developed in which an attempt was made to translate desirable future visions back into short-term actions (DTO, 2003). Another example is the 'SusHouse' project in which an attempt was made to broaden participants' cognitive frames by sketching radically different futures, not only in terms of new technologies but also with new user practices, infrastructures and societal embedding (Green and Vergragt, 2002, Vergragt, 2000). Such

scenarios, however, primarily sketch end situations rather than the convoluted development paths that may lead to these ends which are characterized by cross-links between various options and by leapfrog effects. The
specific strength of the STSc method is that it does explore transition *paths*,
taking into consideration the requirements described above.

The multi-level perspective emphasizes complexity, non-linearity and the
uncertainty of transition processes. It recognizes that transitions may
follow a variety of courses. To be able to develop scenarios, however, this
variety needs to be reduced but we should take care not to end up with a
model in which outcomes are completely determined by 'driving forces' and
'factors'. What we are looking for is the middle course between 'chance' and
'necessity', in line with a longstanding debate within evolutionary theories.
A possible middle course is the use of patterns and mechanisms. (Geels,
2002c) These describe 'partial dynamics' that have been identified in a
variety of historical studies. This structures the complexity of the multi-
level perspective to some extent without becoming deterministic. The frame
below gives some examples of patterns and mechanisms.

PATTERNS AND MECHANISMS IN TRANSITIONS

Geels (2002b, pp. 124–28) distinguishes two general patterns or
routes in transitions: technical substitution and broad transformation. In the *substitution* route the existing regime is relatively stable
while radical innovations are developed in niches. When niche
innovations have stabilized in terms of price/performance they can
(often quite suddenly) break through in regular markets where they
push aside existing companies and lead to Schumpeter's 'gales of
destruction'. In this route, the existing technologies are substituted
by new innovations after which broader changes may occur. In the
transformation route the regime starts to change in an earlier
stage, because of persistent problems that may lead to changing
user preferences, policy and culture. The destabilization of the
existing regime leads to a broad search for alternatives. There is a
long period of uncertainty as to which alternative may be the best,
connected with the fact that the selection criteria in the regime are
changing. There may be a range of technical options that influence
each other in various ways. Eventually, one of these (or a combination) emerges as a winner after which the new regime gradually
stabilizes.

Other patterns, describing partial dynamics include: (i) the
process of niche accumulation mentioned before in the

break-through of radical innovations; (ii) pressure on the regime to create room for niches; (iii) niche proliferation, that is, the spread of niches to other domains (other regimes) or other geographical areas; (iv) the linkage of separate niches and synergy between niche developments.

Some mechanisms are: (i) the so-called 'sailing ship effect' (when the existing regime defends itself against radical innovations by improving performance, like sailing ships starting to use more masts and sail when steamships emerged; (ii) add-on and hybridization: two initially separate technical options merge to a new form (such as electric propulsion and internal combustion engines merging in hybrid cars); (iii) coevolution of technology and behaviour: through hands-on experience with new technologies users may change their patterns of behaviour; this usually starts with 'lead users' and may later spread; (iv) coevolution of technology and society (leapfrog effects).

The various steps necessary to actually construct an STSc have been described elsewhere (Elzen *et al.*, 2002; Geels, 2002c). In this chapter, we will only present some general guidelines and minimal requirements for constructing a STSc.

- An STSc starts with a pre-history. This sketches the recent dynamics of the regime under analysis because a scenario cannot just go in any direction from the present; recent directions of development will continue into the near future at least.
- STScs are based on the multi-level perspective described above. The crucial requirement is that the developments are plausible and should not come out of the blue as a *deus ex machina*. The scenario should describe continuity in developments that build further upon one another.
- The story should contain developments at all three levels. The regime level constitutes the thread in the story since this is the level at which transitions are analysed. Developments in relevant niches should also be described as well as landscape-level developments that influence perceptions and strategies of actors in the regime and in niches.
- Make clear the role of various societal groups (companies, users, public authorities) and describe how they operate in the game. Describe their goals, strategies, and means to make the moves they make in the game plausible.

- At the niche level, pay attention to learning and articulation processes (not just on technology but also on user preferences, policy and so on). When a niche breaks through, show how various barriers have been conquered.
- STSc use socio-technical patterns and mechanisms in transitions. One should take care not to focus merely on technology, and to show the coevolution of technology and society.
- Beware of linear patterns of development. Theoretical insights in trajectories and path dependencies leave room to 'play' with hybridizations, bifurcations (an option finding different domains of application with subsequent separate development paths), cross-linkages (links between niches; links between niche and regime), and so on. This non-linearity allows for changes of direction and accelerations or slowing down of developments.

ILLUSTRATION: TWO SCENARIOS FOR THE MOBILITY DOMAIN

The two scenarios below are meant to illustrate the important characteristics of the approach and its usefulness. The main contrast between the scenarios is that they feature the two general patters described in the frame above, the first scenario illustrating a *substitution* route, the second a *transformation* route. The scenarios show that these differences can largely result from different government policies. They can hardly be called radical, but a consistent application of historically-founded patterns in the transition dynamic shows that small initial differences can lead to very different outcomes in the long term. By assessing these different outcomes in terms of sustainability we will draw some conclusions on possible and promising policy interventions to realize sustainable mobility.

The scenarios have been divided into four phases which largely reflect the four phases in the transition process described earlier. We have not used these phases too rigidly since, in some periods, some alternatives may be in a pre-development phase while others may already be deployed in markets.

The scenarios have been described as a 'history of the future', that is in the past tense. This is to prevent the reader from thinking too easily that something else might also happen (which is always the case) and instead draw attention to the plausibility of the story as it develops.

In accordance with the requirements for an STSc presented above, we first describe the most important characteristics of the dynamic of the mobility regime in the recent past, called the 'pre-future'. Subsequently both scenarios will be described.

1990–2000: The Pre-Future – A Regime Under Pressure

At the beginning of the 21st century, the traffic and transport regime was gradually changing. There were two main sets of driving forces for these changes, one linked to an internal regime dynamic, the other related to the broader societal embedding of the regime. The internal dynamic largely concerned innovation of cars and other vehicles. When the car market became more competitive in the second half of the 20th century, car manufacturers developed new products and accessories in order to gain new markets. One of the effects was that a broader range of vehicles was developed. In the 1960s and 70s, the four-person car (sedan and station wagon) was by far the most common type of passenger vehicle. By the late 1990s, however, the range of vehicles included city-cars, space wagons, sports utility vehicles, and so on. Although the all-purpose car was still the most popular vehicle, the notion of using a different type of vehicle for different purposes started to gain ground.

The second set of driving forces was related to a range of societal problems (partially) associated with traffic and transport. These included:

- polluting emissions;
- CO_2 emissions;
- congestion.

To tackle these problems, a range of policy approaches was developed and tried. This resulted in more room for various new technologies and concepts that were developed and tinkered with in niches. The range included different propulsion concepts for vehicles (electric, natural gas, hybrid, fuel cells, and so on), stimulation of modal shift, new concepts like chain mobility and intermodality, new ownership concepts like car-sharing, and so on.

In theoretical terms, the variation process in industry led towards a diversification of vehicle types while the selection environment was also changing, partly because the regime was in trouble (congestion) and partly under influence of the socio-technical landscape that exerted pressure to counter pollution and greenhouse gas emissions. The pressure on the regime created room for development of a variety of niches that tried to link up to the regime.

Scenario 1: High-Tech Individual Mobility

2000–10: Linking niches to a regime under pressure
In this period, the problems of traffic and transport were primarily tackled by creating new infrastructure (roads, bridges, and tunnels),

regulation (for example on emissions) and financial instruments (e.g. taxing CO_2 emissions and various forms of road pricing). Following the motto 'pay for nuisance', levies became dependent upon the kind and magnitude of nuisance. Around 2010, the following measures were widely applied:

- substantial CO_2 tax on fossil fuels;
- road-use fee related to certified emissions for each vehicle;
- rush-hour fees on the most congested highways;
- pay lanes on highways (people willing to pay could choose a less congested lane).

In terms of marginal cost per kilometre, public transport became increasingly competitive with cars, especially during rush hour and for busy road connections, but this hardly affected the behaviour of travellers. Overall, the level of mobility increased but so did congestion and its associated problems. Pricing mechanisms had some effect in spreading congestion peaks on main roads but average congestion remained and especially in cities the problems got worse.

Thus, the regime as a whole hardly changed. At the fringes of the regime, however, there were noticeable effects. One innovation was small electric vehicles, known as city EVs (CEVs). At the turn of the century such vehicles were on offer but they were not marketed seriously until some European cities with narrow streets and medieval centres started stimulating their use through various measures. Initial owners were affluent city dwellers but increased demand led to economies of scale and lower prices which enlarged the market. International imitation of city policy and competition led to niche markets across Europe.

Regime pressure also stimulated the hybrid electric vehicle (HEV) niche. They were available at the turn of the century and each car manufacturer had a development programme, but they were hardly sold. The breakthrough came in California through legislation that mandated car manufacturers to sell a certain number of zero-emission vehicles. The manufacturers had opposed this rule for over a decade and in 2005 an agreement was concluded with the state that sales of large numbers of HEVs was an alternative. The European manufacturers soon followed, fearing that the American and Japanese vehicles would penetrate European markets. HEVs were initially bought by rather wealthy people but around 2010 their prices had dropped considerably and the general picture was that the double fuel efficiency made an HEV cheaper over its lifetime. It was expected that in the future the balance would shift further to the advantage of the HEV.

2010–20: the growth of market niches

By 2010, problems seemed to increase rather than decrease. At the land-scape level pressure to curb CO_2 emissions became stronger and taxes on fossil fuels were further increased which was accepted on the basis of the argument that people could also buy fuel-efficient hybrids. Fees within the pay-for-use and pay-for-nuisance philosophies were increased but became differentiated to be lower for the upcoming cleaner vehicles. More specific pressure came from cities that imposed an increasing variety of measures to enhance the quality of life, including:

- new and enlarged limited access zones, including zero-emission zones;
- increased parking rates, differentiated according to various nuisance criteria;
- various forms of preferential treatment for public transport.

The higher fuel costs increased demand for fuel-efficient vehicles and stimulated their development. Overall numbers of vehicles continued to grow, partly because of the popularity of CEVs as a second or third vehicle. They were cheap and permitted to run where other vehicles were not. In terms of life-cycle costs, including fuel, HEVs had become considerably cheaper than conventional vehicles. Still, the latter kept a considerable market-share since they accelerated faster and were considered more sporty. In cities, however, they were largely replaced by CEVs. As a result, by 2020 CO_2 emissions had dropped about 20 per cent compared to 2000.

To tackle congestion, especially in cities, public transport was stimulated through measures like priority bus lanes, traffic priority rules and a better supply of service. The result was that in many cases public transport became swifter than self-driving while relative costs rapidly decreased due to the increased cost of owning and using cars.

From the perspective of the traveller, the regime had somewhat changed in this period, not so much in terms of the supply of vehicles and services but in terms of the relation between cost and functionality. The number and area of zones where conventional vehicles were not allowed increased. Except for public transport, the costs of mobility increased rapidly. The reason was not fuel costs, despite the 35 per cent increase compared to 2000, because fuel efficiency had also increased through HEVs. The most significant cost items were road-use fees and parking fees following the pay-for-nuisance philosophy. Still, the vast majority preferred their private vehicle to a bus, tram or subway. The overall share of public transport hardly changed except in a few cities with strong policies to discourage car-use.

At the fringes of the regime new developments took place including fuel cell buses (FCBs), biofuels and a transformation of the CEV-niche. Until 2015, work on FCBs was limited to demonstration projects due to the high cost and lack of fuel-infrastructure. Under pressure from the need to curb CO_2 emissions the EU and various national governments decided to stimulate development of a hydrogen economy, initially for generating electricity. Some technologies thus developed also stimulated FCB development and led to economies of scale. The public liked these buses a lot, largely because they were so silent, and around 2020 bus companies started to purchase them in increasing numbers, to stimulate bus use.

The regime pressure also provided an impetus for the biofuels niche. With the prospect of a drastic reduction of fuel consumption (through HEVs) the potential of biofuels considerably increased, encouraging public authorities to stimulate their wider use. Around 2010 their share started to increase significantly, initially by mixing them with fossil fuels.

The regime pressure also induced qualitative change, e.g. in connection with CEVs. In the preceding decade they had become popular as a second vehicle but some owners sold their first car which they used too little, making the cost too high. Parking was very expensive, for instance, especially in comparison with a CEV which had a much lower 'nuisance rate'. People started using different options for longer trips, including trains and car rental.

2020–35: dominance of the HEV
CO_2 emissions had dropped some 20 per cent since the turn of the century but to achieve sustainability an 80–90 per cent reduction was deemed necessary. To realize this, stimulating HEV use became a priority. Plans were announced to double fuel prices over a ten-year period. This would not need to make driving more expensive since car users could limit fuel use by using HEVs. Because of the ten-year period they could adapt smoothly to the new situation.

Total mobility had increased significantly making congestion problems ever more pressing. On highways, various forms of pay-for-nuisance had spread traffic jams rather than decreased them. In urban areas, parts of cities had been made more pleasant by limited access zones but congestion in other parts and on main arteries had increased. Although public transport was mostly cheaper in terms of direct costs, people continued to prefer private means of transport.

Because citizens valued highly the pedestrian and limited access zones and because good alternatives had become available, the costs of driving private cars were increased further. Parking and road-use fees were increased drastically, sometimes doubled over a decade. This stimulated some modal shift but only on the busiest routes with the highest fees.

Concerning vehicle types, by the end of the period HEVs gained the majority share. Despite their fuel efficiency the cost of driving them were still high due to the high fuel prices. In the Netherlands, this legitimized conversion to an LPG variant by the existing industry that also converted conventional vehicles. Car manufacturers took over this strategy but instead chose a natural gas version since this fuel was more widely available across Europe. This was extra attractive since methane could be produced from organic feedstocks which was cheap for the user due to the low CO_2 tax. Around 2030 these gas-hybrids were sold in small niches.

This created the prospect that fuel stations would have to provide an ever-increasing range of fuels which triggered increasing protests from fuel companies. After several years of discussion between car manufacturers, fuel providers and public authorities a voluntary agreement was reached to phase out liquid fuels in the next one to two decades and stimulate the use of gaseous fuels. This meant an enormous impetus for the HEV and especially the gaseous version. By 2035, annual sales of conventional vehicles became a small minority and as a result the CO_2 emissions from passenger transport decreased further to about half the 2000 level.

Because of the increasing popularity of CEVs as a first car, conventional car manufacturers started to lose market shares. CEVs used a simple technology that could be made cost-effectively in relatively small series and they were produced by a large number of companies. Looking for new markets, the manufacturers developed a new type of vehicle, the 'long distance vehicle' (LDV) which was sold as the ideal supplement to a CEV. An LDV was very comfortable, featured all kinds of gadgets and was equipped with a fuel cell propulsion to make it very clean. This increased demand for a hydrogen infrastructure that was already high because of fuel cell buses and fuel cells for electricity generation. In the early 2020s, the first FC-LDVs were introduced to the market. Their high-tech image initially appealed to the top segment of the market but gradually they became more widely used by people who drove a lot. When limited access zones grew in numbers and size they also became commonly used as taxis leading to a 10 per cent market share in 2035.

The persisting congestion problem created new possibilities for an old niche that had existed for half a century – automatic vehicle guidance (AVG). For decades, the technology had been considered 'ready' but the enormous costs of infrastructures and implementation barriers had prevented application. Since the turn of the century, pricing measures had spread congestion peaks but the overall growth of mobility and freight traffic had had the effect that various stretches of road were congested virtually 24 hours per day, seven days per week.

In the mid-2030s, a new linking-opportunity for the niche emerged. The government income from various transport fees was enormous. The ICT industry, that was facing a downturn after several decades of growth, mobilized the car lobby to stress that car drivers' taxes were not used to relieve congestion while there was a perfect opportunity to do so via AVG. This resulted in a national 'Deltaplan traffic flow' aimed at boosting traffic flow in the next decade or two, partly by introducing AVG.

2035–50: further technical improvement

Around 2035, CO_2 emissions were reduced to half the 2000 level but this was still far from a sustainable level. Still, with the increased share of renewable fuels (methane from organic sources; sustainably-produced hydrogen), and increasing shares of fuel-efficient vehicles (HEV, LDV, FCB) the trend was in the right direction. The general belief was that further pricing measures should suffice to achieve the overall reduction goal.

Congestion, however, continued to be an elusive problem. Pricing measures had led to some modal shift, especially in cities, but the average level was comparable to or even worse than that at the turn of the century. More stringent methods like banning cars further, however, were considered unacceptable. The problem seemed insoluble.

Highway congestion was attacked though through the 'Deltaplan'. The first AVG lanes became available around 2040 and in the following decade the major part of the highway system was equipped with such lanes. They were initially used by more affluent people and business traffic. By the end of the 2040s about half the highways were equipped with AVG lanes which were used by about one-quarter of total traffic. This share remained relatively stable since a lower number of vehicles on the other lanes had also reduced congestion there.

Due to reduced congestion, the total number of vehicles started to grow again, partly at the expense of public transport. Many of these vehicles were LDVs, most of which equipped with AVG technology, leading to a 20 per cent market share in 2050. The CEV share remained fairly constant while the remainder were HEVs. LDVs used hydrogen, most of which was sustainably produced, like the electricity for CEVs. Most of the HEVs used gas, a considerable portion of which was produced sustainably from biofuels. With the average fuel efficiency of HEVs between two and three times that of the average year-2000 conventional vehicle, the overall effect was that the desired CO_2 reduction of 80–90 per cent could be achieved.

Scenario 2: Customized Mobility

2000–10: opening up of a regime under pressure
Congestion was the most persistent problem in the traffic and transport domain. At the turn of the millennium the main approach was to use technical and pricing measures to spread peaks across the day. Many cities worried about quality of life which was not just a matter of lowering pollution but also of abating noise and making cities more pleasant and safe. The concept of the sustainable city gained popularity and zoning measures (low-speed zones, limited-access zones, pedestrian zones) were one of several approaches to try and achieve it. At the landscape level, the concern about CO_2 emissions exerted pressure on the regime. Formally, this was a concern for the European and national authorities but many local actors were also inspired by it under the adage 'think globally, act locally'.

During the period, the private car remained dominant and congestion increased with overall pkt (passenger kilometres travelled). Some bottlenecks were removed through new infrastructure which gave some, albeit only temporary, relief. Pursuing the approach started at the turn of the century, and road pricing became common after 2005. These systems became more and more refined in that the rates were made dependent upon the nuisance caused. This relieved congestion on highways but the underlying road network became more jammed.

Concerning CO_2 emissions it became clear by 2005 that the various measures taken had no effect. Taxes on fossil fuels were raised by 20 per cent at the end of the decade but, as had been the experience in previous decades, this hardly affected pkt. It did, however, have an effect on the manufacturers' strategies. The demand for cleaner and more fuel efficient vehicles increased and in the second part of the decade car manufacturers also started to seriously market HEVs which led to a small market share by 2010.

Congestion in cities continued to get worse. Local authorities got more and more fed up with this and took stronger measures to discourage car-use, including higher parking rates, zoning measures, improved public transport services, and prioritizing public transport. By 2015, a noticeable modal shift started to take place in major cities. In many cases, public transport had become a cheaper as well as a quicker alternative to car-use.

The pressure on the regime stimulated the growth of various niches, including CEVs. They were primarily sold in southern Europe to affluent city residents. In the period 2005–10 tens of thousands were sold, especially as a second vehicle and high-tech 'gadget'. They were also functional, though, because they were allowed in zones where conventional vehicles were not and parking rates for them were considerably lower. After 2005, a variety of cities across Europe used them in self-service experiments in connection with train journeys.

The regime pressure to curb CO_2 emissions also provided opportunities for the biofuels niche. Backed by the EU, national authorities imposed low taxes on biofuels while taxes on fossil fuels went up to stimulate reduction of CO_2 emissions. Fuel producers liaised with the agro-industry and various processors of organic waste to ensure they would not lose their market share. By 2010, the biofuels share was a few per cent but it was growing.

Common travel behaviour hardly changed during this decade but a growing group of city dwellers started to realize that there was an increasing tension between their role as traveller, wanting 'right of way', and their role as city resident, wanting less traffic.

2010–20: the take-off of intermodal travel

Although emission of pollutants had been reduced considerably (gross emitters had virtually disappeared) pollution remained a problem in cities. The main reason for the reduction was that residents attached more value to the quality of city life. In accordance, city authorities tried to push back the role of the car and create alternatives instead. They were supported by national authorities that used the increasing revenues from fossil fuel taxes and road pricing to support experiments with alternatives. The general 'pay-for-nuisance' approach was continued to stimulate breakthrough of alternatives like biofuels and fuel efficient vehicles.

Growing HEV use (see previous period) was stimulated further by lower road-use fees. Fuel cost savings made the demand for HEVs rise sharply and it quickly became a subject of fierce competition between the car manufactures. In the second half of the 2010s, sales of new HEVs overtook those of conventional cars.

City policy to ban conventional cars from (parts of) cities made the CEV market grow rapidly. Increasing numbers of city residents bought one as a second vehicle and used their first vehicle (increasingly an HEV) only for long-distance trips.

The regime pressure for clean vehicles also increased the potential of fuel cell electric vehicles (FCEVs). The initial focus was on heavy duty vehicles where higher purchase costs were less important and which could be refuelled more easily at a central depot. Since 2005 various experiments were carried out in which hydrogen was produced from organic feedstocks. The low tax on biofuels made such schemes close to being competitive which stimulated demand from bus companies. Economies of scale made prices go down and, as a result, most of the new buses bought in the second half of the 2010s ran on fuel cells.

With increased congestion and increased cost of driving, public transport became ever more attractive. Train services were improved and made more frequent which stimulated demand for better travel options to and from stations. This encouraged city authorities in their quest for the 'sustainable city' and their efforts to improve public transport and discourage car use. Choosing a transport option at a station was facilitated by pocket computers with an internet link. In 2020, public transport use in cities was usually quicker than a private car and also cheaper in terms of marginal costs.

Cities pursued very active mobility policies and across Europe, a wave of projects was carried out in the 2010s, using or combining a wide variety of options, including:

- A range of (public) transport services, such as:
  - individual public transport (CEVs as well as energy-efficient conventional vehicles)
  - on-demand services (first conventional vans but increasingly hybrids)
  - direct shuttle services to hospitals, shopping centres, business centres, and so on.
- Priority for public transport (dedicated bus lanes; priority signalling)
- Zoning policies:
  - barriers between neighbouring zones to make through traffic impossible
  - zero-emission zones
  - no-car zones
- High parking rates (lower for EVs, HEVs and shared cars)
- Transfer points with a variety of transport services and vehicles to rent.

Many of these experiments had a strong local flavour but there was a lot of exchange of experience between cities. Gradually a general concept developed characterized by a layered structure of transfer points. At the city level, there were so-called city mobility stations (CMS) which linked intra- and inter-urban traffic. Many of these had developed from park and ride facilities (or 'transferia', in Dutch) where an increasing number of local services were offered. At the neighbourhood level experiments were carried out with mobility centres (MC) which linked a variety of high-speed urban transport networks and services with diffuse streams to and from nearby specific destinations. Some car-sharing organizations established their depots at these MCs. This layered structure became known as the City Transfer System (Citrans).

Around 2020, Citrans became generally accepted as the conceptual way to think about sustainable transport in cities. As a complete system, it existed hardly anywhere but various cities had realized bits and pieces. In most cities, the car was still the dominant means of transport but the Citrans concept did create a focus in attempts to tackle transport challenges.

The high cost of car use made residents increasingly assess their travel needs in functional terms and by 2020 the private car was no longer the automatic choice. The majority of people based the choice for a travel option on cost, ease of use and travel time. In many cases, public transport was better in all dimensions.

2020–35: Citrans challenges car dominance

The regime pressure to curb CO_2 emissions continued to increase and despite promising signs (increasing use of biofuels, HEVs) further pricing measures were considered necessary. Congestion problems on main roads had slightly increased but since there were good alternatives this was seen as a private problem. The quest for the sustainable city became stronger in the 2010s implying increased pressure to reduce the role of the car.

The Citrans concept provided a lead in choosing concrete measures. Financed from car-use revenues, large cities invested heavily in city mobility stations (CMS). Depending upon the local situation, services offered included train, bus, metro, tram, shuttle services, 'individual public transport' (CEVs offered for short-term rent), long-distance rental cars, bicycles, etc.

Interestingly, some of these new combinations induced changes in travel behaviour. Various citizens sold their regular car and just kept a CEV for local trips. There was a sound financial rationale for this: it was very expensive to own a conventional car that could be ever less used in cities. The CMS offered a very functional alternative that was also flexible. Although these groups were initially small, they did suggest potential for radical change eventually.

Some cities started to develop transfer points at the neighbourhood level (mobility centres, or MC). They offered the same services as the CMS (although initially on a smaller scale) with the exception of long-distance trains. The forerunners became widely recognized as examples of good practice by policymakers as well as the general public (who learned about them via TV programmes). As of 2030, an increasing number of cities started to follow their example.

Around 2020 the large majority of new cars sold were HEVs but even a 100 per cent share would not realize the necessary reduction of CO_2 emissions. Further stimulation of biofuels would not fill the gap either. This stimulated new interest in fuel cell cars running on sustainably produced hydrogen. Car manufacturers saw this as a new long-term business opportunity, and public authorities stimulated development of a hydrogen infrastructure.

During the period, the privately-owned car kept its dominant position in terms of market but its dominance started to become smaller. Of the alternatives, new HEVs running on gaseous fuels were offered (attracting lower fuel tax), including a high-tech variant with a gas turbine, as well as FCEVs. When occasional car rental became more common, many took the opportunity to try out these 'futuristic' vehicles which stimulated much interest in them.

Through taxation measures it became more attractive to use biofuels to produce hydrogen than to mix them with conventional fuels. This made the prices of liquid fuels at the pump go up which raised awareness of the increasing cost of self-driving a hybrid. The process of doing away with the privately-owned all-purpose car was thus reinforced.

The rise of the Citrans system with various services offered at CMS and MC redefined the role of public transport. In cities where it had been realized the public transport service system became dominant. It offered far more flexibility and ease of use than the private car, making it more attractive to do away with the latter. It became common to use a combination of services tuned to specific travel needs, sometimes using a privately-owned vehicle for part of the trip.

2035–50: Citrans victory–demise of the private car
By 2035, the Citrans system became seen as a key characteristic of the sustainable city. Local authorities were determined to realize it by a combination of infrastructural planning and a variety of measures to stimulate its use and discourage the possession and use of private cars.

National authorities, joining forces at the EU level, sought to further reduce fossil fuel use. In 2035 they announced that liquid fuel tax (for the typical mix of fossil and biofuels) would be gradually increased in the period 2038–45. At the end of the period, the fuel cost for a liquid fuel HEV could be three times as high as for the biogas type.

European cities concentrated on realizing their own Citrans variant. Acceptance was very high: television-programmes on examples of good practice enthused residents with the idea of living in low-car-use neighbourhoods, and they valued the choice from a variety of travel options, including self-drive. As a result, Citrans made its way across Europe.

This was not only a matter of technical change but travellers, transport operators, policymakers, as well as industrialists started to think in a new way about mobility and transport. The central issue for policymakers was how to improve Citrans and how to further discourage private car use. For travellers, the value of using a combination of modes was self-evident and for any trip one could easily select the optimal combination on the basis of needs and preferences.

As a result, private car ownership and use went down rapidly in the period 2035–50. Self-drive vehicles were usually rented rather than owned (except CEVs). Since FCEVs and gas-turbine HEVs on biofuels were far cheaper in use (lower fuel taxes) than other types, they became the most used by the late 2040s. Forecasts indicated that by 2060 fossil fuels would be virtually abandoned, and this would symbolize the demise of the old regime.

REFLECTION UPON AND COMPARISON OF THE SCENARIOS

In this section, we will compare both scenarios in a general sense as a stepping stone for policy recommendations. The second scenario describes a more fundamental transition than the first. It features more substantial changes in behaviour and mobility patterns, while the first scenario keeps closer to current behaviour, filled in with high-tech options. Still, the first also shows a considerable change, in technology, regulation and infrastructure.

The seeds for the large changes in the second scenario are the preparedness and determination to experiment with new options in niches. Cities especially play an important role in the quest for alternatives to increase quality of life, also trying to learn from experiences elsewhere. The focus on quality of life implies a broader problem definition then in the first scenario, leading to explicit attempts to develop new systems rather than individual technologies.

Concerning policy, economic instruments and regulation at the regime level play an important role in both scenarios, albeit in a different way. In the first scenario the focus is on influencing the selection environment rather than on stimulating radical innovation in niches. The selection thus only affects existing technologies and concepts, leading to high-tech variants. The principal effect of increasing pressure is that industry develops innovations to relieve the pressure. Travellers, who do not have an alternative, grudgingly accept the more strict rules but do not change their travel patterns. An attempt is made to solve each problem separately via a range of technical measures which leads to a wider variety of mobility options. This may reduce CO_2 emissions significantly but it hardly affects congestion. Traffic jams may be relieved via dynamic traffic management and ICT (automatic vehicle control, and so on) but congestion in cities will remain a large problem.

In the second scenario, economic instruments and regulation are not applied until several alternatives have been articulated in niches and are widely known. This strategy encourages the building of new networks with new actors that facilitates the generation of new ideas. Regime measures are combined with experimentation in niches which eventually results in a drastic transformation of the mobility regime.

In the second scenario, there is a more integral approach to problems, addressing CO_2 emissions, congestion and quality of life at the same time. Large cities form the seeds from which this new mobility system develops. They thus constitute promising locations to try out new concepts and new routes towards sustainability. A combination of learning experiences from different sites may reveal the contours of a new system. Such a vision helps to identify its necessary elements, introduction of which can then be stimulated by strict measures. Various alternatives can gradually grow while some of these are combined to new forms of chain mobility. The continuation of this pattern of development leads to range of mobility services and new forms of car ownership. Many people own a city electric vehicle for inner-city use but few own a car for long-distance, inter-city use.

The contrast between the scenarios shows that (i) learning in experiments and (ii) timing and optimal combination of policy instruments make the crucial difference (see Figure 11.1).

STRATEGIES FOR TRANSITION POLICY

The scenarios show that a transition is possible and even plausible by using historically-founded patterns and mechanisms from transition theory. Both scenarios have advantages and disadvantages in terms of effects, costs and risks. In both scenarios, the following economic instruments are used to put pressure on the regime to reduce CO_2 emissions and congestions:

- higher taxes for fossil fuels, doubling in the course of a few decades;
- differentiated road pricing, depending upon forms of nuisance;
- high parking rates.

As described in the preceding section, however, these measures play a different role. They are used in different ways with different timing. In general, the first scenario describes a type of 'pressure-cooker' strategy. Only when problems become unbearable, do public authorities take firm measures to (partly) release the pressure. A considerable risk of this strategy is that it may trigger large societal opposition. Various groups are likely not to accept the measures, especially when they see no clear alternatives. An example is the 2001 European-wide uproar among truck drivers and truck companies when diesel prices were increased significantly. Another risk is that problems will not be solved, especially congestion, which may lead to a long trajectory of substituting one problem with another. An advantage of the first scenario is that the costs of the transition are borne by industry and car drivers. The government primarily tightens regulation, invests hardly anything in niches and leaves it to the market to make choices.

In the second scenario, public authorities try to prevent societal resistance by an explicit strategy of developing alternatives, by stimulating a broad transformation process in which various actors participate in experiments. Thus they can play an active role and get used to new systems which may increase acceptance. A disadvantage of this strategy is the large use of public funds. Various experiments will certainly fail and this runs the risk that opponents will exploit failures by presenting them as a waste of taxpayers' money. Furthermore, new infrastructure (such as transferia) will require huge investments. An advantage is that problems are approached in an integral way, reducing environmental pollution as well as congestion considerably.

STIMULATING NICHE DEVELOPMENT

In terms of sustainability, the outcome of the second scenario is more attractive than the first. It features a transition with desirable outcomes on a broader range of dimensions. Current mobility policy, however, is closer to the strategy in the first scenario thus risking resulting in less sustainable outcomes. There is some experimentation with alternatives, but half-heartedly because 'you never can tell'. Budgets are accordingly meagre. To orient policy more towards transition, it should incorporate more elements from the second strategy. This, first of all, implies a significant increase in budgets for experimentation. This begs the question whether the STSc approach can help making choices for short-term action, that is, to help suggest which niches should be stimulated and how.

Although the scenarios sketched in this chapter are very brief they do suggest some important conclusions.[3] Concerning possible changes of behaviour and mobility patterns three niches seem particularly relevant: CEVs, multimodal transfer points as a stepping stone towards the later Citrans system, and car-sharing.

Stimulating CEVs runs against the current wisdom that they cannot compete with conventional cars and can only become an additional vehicle in the household. This may initially be true but after some time CEVs may link with other developments and trigger new mobility patterns. In the scenario, CEVs are initially only affordable for the affluent as an additional vehicle. In the current situation this is used as an argument against such vehicles since it would affect sustainability negatively. The scenario, however, illustrates that such a first 'germ' may lead to leapfrog effects between CEVs and policy. Links may develop with, for example, car-sharing and the new combination may provide a stepping stone towards a greater and more attractive supply of mobility services.

The STSc method thus facilitates the exploration of unpredictable processes. When certain outcomes are subsequently assessed as desirable, policy intervention may attempt to stimulate various developments required to realize it. This is not to say that the path in the scenario can be easily realized. Transformation processes remain unpredictable, depend upon the moves of a variety of actors and external circumstances, and take decades. Consistent policies, however, can help to stimulate some directions more than others and thus encourage movement towards desirable outcomes. Thus, the STS method does support the conclusion that CEVs should be taken more seriously as a stepping stone towards sustainable mobility than in current policy.

The same is true for multimodal transfer points. In the Netherlands, most mobility experts and policy makers are sceptical about this concept based on the experience with transferia. These experiences, however, concern isolated attempts to combine an existing car system with an existing public transport system. The scenario, however, shows that the potential can be significant when the concept is made part of wider attempts to increase quality of life in cities. They may link to limited-access zones, car sharing, CEVs, public transport priority policy, high parking rates, and so on. The central issue is the need for a consistent long-term policy strategy to realize this. This also implies a risk because policy and politics tend to be haphazard, aiming for short-term results. Nonetheless, the central conclusion from this scenario is that multimodal transfer points can be important in a transition, provided they are considered in combination with other options.

Comparable considerations are valid for car sharing which is also not taken seriously in current policy. By seeing this concept as part of a more encompassing mobility system and mobility chains, new linkage options emerge. This may result in a process in which travel behaviour can change, making it more common to choose from various combinations of vehicles and services depending upon actual travel need. The STSc exploration shows that such a change can be quite plausible as the result of various small steps in a consistent direction.

The scenarios thus lead to the conclusion that these three options, CEVs, multimodal transfer points and car-sharing, hold a promise of stimulating different mobility behaviour. The scenarios suggest that no individual option is likely to realize this but that synergies can be expected when combining them.

To tackle environmental problems, two niches in particular seem interesting: hybrid electric vehicles (HEVs) and biofuels. These options play a role in both scenarios, lending them a certain robustness, but they can also reinforce each other. This offers the possibility of taking a more critical stance towards car manufacturers who argue that it is wasteful to invest in HEVs now because fuel cell electric vehicles (FCEVs) have a much larger potential to reduce emissions. Their argument implies that conventional vehicles will remain dominant for several decades to come (which is beneficial for the manufacturers in view of sunk investments) and that during this period CO_2 emissions from transport can only go down slowly, if at all. The scenarios, however, show that HEVs can play an important role as a stepping stone in a transition, possibly towards FCEVs.

The crucial question then becomes whether HEV introduction can be stimulated. In the first scenario this is more or less forced by the Californian authorities and accelerated by the world-wide competition between car manufacturers. In the second scenario the political determination to increase fuel prices convinces manufacturers that demand for hybrids will increase. The issue then becomes either to force or convince manufacturers. In the European context, the first route does not seem to fit the political culture and the more feasible strategy would be to make clear to manufacturers that hybrids are in demand and that public authorities are prepared to use price instruments to stimulate market development.

Biofuels have considerable policy attention since they offer the possibility of a closed carbon-cycle. This made the European Commission formulate the target of a 6 per cent share of biofuels in 2010 (EU, 2001, p. 87). Many are sceptical about the feasibility of biofuels since an important limitation will be the availability of feedstocks given the enormous magnitude of overall fuel consumption. This limitation, however, can be reduced significantly by considering the use of biofuels in combination with HEVs. Because of their high fuel efficiency far less fuel will be needed per kilometre. Furthermore, efficient HEVs make it possible to drive longer distances on cleaner gaseous fuels[4] which can also be made from organic feedstocks. A combination with HEVs can thus increase the potential of biofuels enormously. It therefore makes sense to first focus on this combination, since the basic technologies have been proven, and later, say in one to two decades, assess whether there is a need to stimulate FCEV uptake and invest in the necessary fuel infrastructure.

The 'strategic niche management' (SNM) approach emphasizes that niches can form the seeds for a transition and that their development should be stimulated. Various recommendations have been made on how to achieve this. (Hoogma *et al.*, 2002, Moon and Elzen, 2000). SNM, however, does not provide a method to choose which niches should be emphasized. The analysis above illustrates that the STSc method can help to make such choices. The combination of SNM and STSc, therefore, provides a powerful tool for transition policy.

CONCLUSION

In this section we will draw some general conclusions on the socio-technical scenario method. We will focus on two issues, notably a comparison with other scenario and foresight methods, and an evaluation as a tool in transition policy.

Comparison with Other Methods

The STSc method is based on a scientific theory on transitions which acknowledges the complexity of such processes. This makes it possible, as the scenarios above illustrate, to satisfy the criteria formulated in an earlier section, notably:

- attention to coevolution of technical and social (including behavioural) development;
- attention to dynamic and linking of niches;
- attention to linkages between niches;
- attention to broad breakthrough resulting from such linkages and leapfrog dynamics.

The scenarios show this can indeed render explorations of the future that sketch a transition path. These paths do not appear as a *deus ex machina* but result from plausible new links in specific circumstances, as in a game in which actors make moves and react to one another. Since no one can oversee the game as a whole the outcomes can be different from what actors expect. This is true, for instance, for travel behaviour. Most experts think it is futile to make people abandon their cars. The scenarios, however, illustrate that this is possible, not as a result of an improbable turn in thought and behaviour but as the result of new choices in changing circumstances. Since the method is based on a general theory of transitions it can also be used to explore such options in other domains, like energy, water and food.

In this brief chapter we cannot sufficiently acknowledge the richness of various other methods to explore possible futures but we can still claim that in comparison to these the STSc method has at least two strong features, notably:

- The method is based on a scientific theory of transitions. The patterns and mechanisms used in the method thus provide an insight into why certain linkages and developments occur. This renders better clues for policy intervention than more deterministic methods.
- The method not only pays attention to outcomes but focuses on transition *paths*. In contrast with most other methods this does not render simple diffusion paths but the scenarios show a variety of linking options and pay attention to qualitative change and leapfrog effects.

Compared to other methods, the STSc method has also less developed sides and disadvantages. In its present shape, the method is not suited to compute the effects of (combinations of) policy instruments. For instance, it does not render suggestions for the level of parking rates, ecotaxes, and so on. Other methods may be better suited for that.

Furthermore, there is a subjective element in the scenarios presented. This partly results from the nature of transitions which are complex and undetermined which leaves room for subjectivity. In the scenarios above, for instance, we had to choose a limited number of niches in view of the limited overall length. A policymaker who is interested in another niche may still use the method to explore its possibilities which may refine or amend the conclusions we have drawn here.

An improvement we will develop in future work is to pay more attention to the notions of development paths and bifurcations. Focusing on such forks helps to make more explicit how small initial changes can have large effects on later outcomes.

Instruments in Transition Policy

We have developed the STSc method as a tool for transition policy. From our analysis, we can draw the conclusion that the method can be used as a tool to make strategic choices. It can help to develop a general transition strategy which not only looks at separate instruments but pays specific attention to the relations between instruments and the timing of using various instruments (see Figure 11.1). This facilitates the evaluation of various policy strategies in terms of effects, desirable as well as undesirable, and risks. The STSc method is not an automaton that provides a detailed prescription of instruments but it can be used as a strategic framework to make explicit and compare political and policy considerations.

The approach can also provide a focus on content in general transition policy, especially by helping select promising niches. This not only leads to a plea for more experimentation but also allows the exploration more precisely of what the potential of various options might be. It is crucial not to assess these options individually but to explore how a combination of options may open up a different course. The exploration of linkages between niches can be especially fruitful in identifying promising options as the scenarios illustrate. The STSc method thus provides a useful supplement to the strategic niche management approach.

This chapter illustrates the method applied to the domain of passenger mobility. Elsewhere, (Elzen *et al.*, 2002) we have described scenarios for the domain of electricity. Application of the method to this as well as other domains is possible since it is based on a general theory of transitions. We can therefore claim that the method is useful as a general tool in transition policy.

NOTES

The research on which this chapter is based was funded by the Ovtch National Research Council from the Programme on Environment and Economy and the Programme on Energy Research.
1. An elaboration can be found in Elzen *et al.* (2002) which also contains an example of a STSc in the electricity domain.
2. For a more elaborate discussion of the suitability of these methods to explore transitions, see Elzen *et al.*, 2002.
3. In Elzen *et al.* (2002) we have described two longer scenarios of 25 pages each which largely support these conclusions.
4. In the Netherlands, the limited driving range on a tank of gaseous fuel (usually LPG) is seen as an important drawback. Since gaseous fuels are cleaner than liquid fuels this limits the use of cleaner vehicles. Energy efficient hybrids lift this limitation.

REFERENCES

Achterhuis, Hans, and Boelie Elzen (1998), *Cultuur en Mobiliteit* (Culture and Mobility), The Hague: Rathenau Instituut.
Arthur, W.B. (1988), 'Competing technologies: an overview', in G. Dosi, C. Freeman, R. Nelson, G. Silverberg and L. Soete (eds), *Technical Change and Economic Theory*, London: Pinter, pp. 590–607.
David, P.A. (1985), 'Clio and the Economics of QWERTY', *American Economic Review*, **75**, 332–37.
DTO (2003), DTO website: http://www.dto-kov.nl/.
Elzen, Boelie, Remco Hoogma and Johan Schot (1996a), *Mobiliteit met Toekomst – Naar een vraaggericht Technologiebeleid*, (Mobility with a Future – Towards a Demand-oriented Technology Policy, The Hague: Ministerie van Verkeer en Waterstaat.

Elzen, Boelie, Bert Enserink and Wim A. Smit (1996b), 'Socio-technical networks: how a technology studies approach may help to solve problems related to technical change', *Social Studies of Science*, **26** (1), 95–141.

Elzen, B., F.W. Geels, R. Hoogma, J.W. Schot and R. Te Velde (1998), 'Strategieën voor innovatie: Experimenten met elektrische voertuigen als opstap naar marktontwikkeling' (Strategies for Innovation: Experiments with Electric Vehicles as a Stepping Stone for Market Development), report for the Dutch Electricity Utilities (SEP).

Elzen, Boelie, Peter Hofman and Frank Geels (2002), *Sociotechnical Scenarios (STSc) – A New Methodology to Explore Technological Transitions*, PRET project final report, Enschede: Universiteit Twente.

EU (2001), *European Transport Policy for 2010: Time to Decide*, white paper.

Freeman, C., and C. Perez (1988), 'Structural crisis of adjustment, business cycles and investment behaviour', in G. Dosi, C. Freeman, R. Nelson, G. Silverberg and L. Soete (eds), *Technical Change and Economic Theory*, London: Pinter, pp. 38–66.

Geels, F.W. (2002a), 'Technological transitions as evolutionary reconfiguration processes: a multi-level perspective and a case-study', *Research Policy*, **31** 8/9 (forthcoming).

Geels, F.W. (2002b), 'Understanding the dynamics of technological transitions', PhD thesis, Universiteit Twente, Enschede.

Geels, F.W. (2002c), 'Towards sociotechnical scenarios and reflexive anticipation: using patterns and regularities in technology dynamics', in R. Williams and K.H. Sorensen (eds), *Shaping Technology, Guiding Policy: Concepts, Spaces and Tools*, Cheltenham: Edward Elgar, pp. 355–81.

Green, K., and P. Vergragt (2002), 'Towards sustainable households: a methodology for developing sustainable technological and social innovations', *Futures*, **34**, 381–400.

Hoogma, R., R. Kemp, J. Schot and B. Truffer (2002), *Experimenting for Sustainable Transport: The Approach of Strategic Niche Management*, London and New York: Spon Press.

Kemp, R. (1994), 'Technology and the transition to environmental sustainability. The problem of technological regime shifts', *Futures*, **26** (10), 1023–46.

Kemp, R., J. Schot and R. Hoogma (1998), 'Regime shifts to sustainability through processes of niche formation: the approach of strategic niche management', *Technology Analysis and Strategic Management*, **10**, 175–96.

Kemp, René, Arie Rip and Johan Schot (2001), 'Constructing transition paths through the management of niches', in Raghu Garud and Peter Karnøe (eds), *Path Dependence and Creation*, London: Lawrence Erlbaum Associates, pp. 269–99.

Moon, D., and B. Elzen (2000), *Demonstrating Cleaner Vehicles – Guidelines for Success*, final report of EU Project UTOPIA (contract no. UR-97-SC-2076), http://utopia.jrc.it/.

Rip, A., and R. Kemp (1998), 'Technological change', in S. Rayner and E.L. Malone (eds), *Human Choice and Climate Change*, vol 2, Columbus, OH: Battelle Press, pp. 327–99.

Rotmans, Jan, René Kemp, Marjolein van Asselt, Frank Geels, Geert Verbong and Kirsten Molendijk (2000), 'Transities en Transitiemanagement: De casus van een emissiearme energievoorziening', 'Transitions and transition management: the case of a low-emission energy supply', concept eindrapport voor studie 'Transities en Transitiemanagement' van ICIS en MERIT t.b.v. NMP-4.

Rotmans, J., R. Kemp and M. van Asselt (2001), 'More evolution than revolution: transition management in public policy', *Foresight*, **3** (1), 15–31.

Schot, J., R. Hoogma and B. Elzen (1994), 'Strategies for shifting technological systems. The case of the automobile system', *Futures*, **26**, 1060–76.

Schot, J.W. (1998), 'The usefulness of evolutionary models for explaining innovation. The case of the Netherlands in the nineteenth century', *History of Technology*, **14**, 173–200.

Vergragt, P.J. (2000), 'Strategies towards the Sustainable Household', SusHouse Project final report, ISBN: 90-5638-056-7.

VROM (2001), *Een wereld en een wil, werken aan duurzaamheid, Nationaal Milieubeleidsplan 4*, (National Environmental Policy Plan 4) The Hague: Ministry of Housing, Spatial Planning and Environment (VROM).

12. Conclusion. Transitions to sustainability: lessons learned and remaining challenges

Boelie Elzen, Frank W. Geels and Ken Green

In Chapter 1, we argued that system innovations are necessary to achieve sustainability, a scale of change that is much larger than that implied in the incremental paths of innovation that are currently being pursued. Based on this, we raised two research questions, notably:

1. How do system innovations (for transitions) develop? What theories can be used to conceptualize (part of) their dynamics and what gaps exist in those theories? What can we learn from historical examples of transitions?
2. Can system innovations be influenced by actors, in particular public authorities and, if so, how? What instruments and tools are available, are additional tools needed and how should they be used?

In this final chapter, we will review the answers that have been suggested in this book to these two questions. Given the embryonic stage of transition research, our aim is to tease out interesting insights and reflect on the strengths and weaknesses of these findings. We conclude by presenting an agenda for future research.

UNDERSTANDING TRANSITIONS – LESSONS LEARNED

Grasping Heterogeneity – the Multi-level Perspective

In Chapter 1, we defined system innovations (for transitions) requiring changes in those socio-technical systems that meet human needs. Such systems are characterized by a range of technologies, infrastructures, patterns of behaviour, cultural values and policies. A transition implies a process of change that affects all or a large proportion of these dimensions; that is, they are characterized by a combination of technical and societal/behavioural change, in a process of 'coevolution'. Changes take place in the spheres of production, distribution and, crucially consumption and ways of life.

The chapters in this book treat various aspects of the transition process from a number of angles, highlighting economic, social, technical, and political as well as many other factors. It illustrates that transition processes cannot be understood by relying on a single discipline. Belz, for instance, in his Swiss agri-food case, argues that single disciplines tend to focus on one aspect of a transition and explain it from that point of view. For example, marketing studies emphasize the important role of food retail chains as 'diffusion agents' in the agri-food chain. This, however, is just part of the whole story. Belz shows that system innovations in the Swiss case were pushed through interactions between a variety of actors and triggered by various events. The transition was the result of linkages between developments at multiple levels.

Other chapters corroborate the points made by Belz. Analysing a variety of concrete cases and phenomena, the chapters illustrate the main characteristics of system innovations highlighted in Chapter 1, namely that these processes must at least display the following general features:

- *multi-actor*: they involve a wide range of actors, including firms, consumers, NGOs, research institutes and governments;
- *multi-factor*: they are not caused by a change in a single factor but are the result of the interplay of many factors that influence each other; they are a combination of technical, regulatory, societal and behavioural change;
- *multi-level*: they imply change at various levels – the micro-level of niches (new developments that initially do not fit an existing system), the meso-level of structuring paradigms and rules (regimes or systems), and the macro-level comprising wider societal and cultural characteristics and trends such as individualization and globalization;
- these types of multidimensional changes take a very long time to develop.

In summary, the chapters illustrate that system innovations are not caused by a change in a single factor but are the result of the interplay of many factors that influence each other on varying levels. One of the main challenges is to grasp the dynamic of such complicated processes in a coherent analytical framework.

To this end, Geels proposed the 'multi-level perspective' in Chapter 2. This perspective can indeed cope with the multi-actor, multi-factor and multi-level aspects of transitions. Several other chapters in this book use this perspective as well, propose additions to it or discuss their own findings in relation to it. For that reason, it is appropriate to recapture some of these proposals and findings.

Geels builds upon insights from sociology of technology and innovation studies. His chapter offers an overview of various sources from these disciplines which analyse relevant aspects of transitions but do not add up to a coherent perspective. He then offers a pragmatic integration of various literatures into the multi-level perspective in which he distinguishes different levels and different phases. While early sociology of technology studies often had a micro-focus on actors, Geels's perspective aims to add structural contexts within which actors act. The multi-level perspective thus provides a framework to integrate and position several existing theories and insights.

Various empirical chapters in this book illustrate the usefulness of the multi-level perspective to describe and analyse transitions. They also show that actors can be integrated into the perspective. Geels characterized his model as a structuralist-process approach but the case studies illustrate that actual linkages always need to be made by actors within their activities and constructions of cognition. The case studies show that the multi-level perspective is flexible enough to accommodate the contribution of actors. While the perspective gives an 'outside in' explanation of system innovations, including actors provides a complementary 'inside out' account.

The empirical studies make clear that actors do not need to make multi-level linkages on purpose but that such linkages can also be the *unintended* effect of their actions. There is no overall rationality to guide a transition. Instead, actors navigate system innovations through probing and learning, finding their way through searching and (re-)acting, through trial and error. Yet, interactions and struggles may add up to aggregated patterns.

Various chapters in the book illustrate that the multi-level perspective has both strengths and weaknesses. A first strength of the perspective is its scope and generality. It is an encompassing perspective which can combine insights from sociological, economic and socio-technical theories. Another strength is that it can accommodate empirical reality, acknowledging several main features of its complexity. A weakness of such appreciative theorizing is the use of metaphors and loose concepts (e.g. 'landscape'). Furthermore, the perspective is fairly complex since it focuses attention on dynamics at multiple levels and on multiple dimensions.

The chapter by Berkhout, Smith and Stirling provides a critical discussion of the multi-level perspective. The predominantly descriptive nature of this approach, they argue, runs the risk of treating future transitions teleologically since it is based on past examples of socio-technical transformations and the development of historical narratives of systems change. This may create the impression that there is a degree of inevitability about the process whereby niches that are initially fledgling ones unavoidably lead to lasting and increasingly large-scale changes in a socio-technical system. In practice, they argue, very few local configurations developed in niches are successful in seeding system innovation. This raises the question why and how some niches set in motion transformational change at wider scales while others fail. In terms of the multi-level perspective this question transforms to why and how some niches are able to link up to an existing regime and why and how they are able to grow further afterwards. This issue indeed seems to touch the core of transition analysis since many chapters in this volume deal with it in one way or another.

With these warnings in mind, the multi-level perspective can still be seen as a useful perspective to analyse transitions and system innovations. The fact that various chapters in this volume use the perspective or parts of it is itself an indication that it provides a powerful tool to deal with a variety of issues in understanding transitions as well as to develop suggestions on how to induce and stimulate them as will be discussed further below.

General Features of System Innovations

A drawback of the multi-level perspective is that it is a very aggregated approach, covering entire transition processes at several scales and over long periods of time. This should be supplemented with a more differentiated view on transitions. A step in that direction is to develop typologies of transitions. Berkhout, Smith and Stirling make this step by suggesting four types of transitions, depending on (i) the degree of coordination of regime change between actors, networks and institutions, and (ii) the locus of resources required to respond to selection pressures acting on the regime. The four types are called: 'purposive transitions', 'endogenous renewal', 're-orientation of trajectories' and 'emergent transformations'. Such work on typologies and transition routes provides a promising direction for future research. This conceptual work should be supplemented with historical case studies as a way to test typologies or to use them as inductive inspiration to develop ideas about transition routes.

An important general pattern in transition processes highlighted in several chapters is that the course of a transition is shaped to a considerable extent by the vicissitudes of the development of novelties in their early phases when most actors in a system tend to see them as irrelevant. By definition, transitions imply drastic changes on many dimensions. The developments that trigger those changes (technological, social as well as political) will initially encounter resistance from the regime. They need to go through a process of adaptation and learning in niches to the point that they are able to link up to an existing system.

Several chapters illustrate how transitions are at least in part shaped by these niche processes. Belz, for instance, argues that in the Swiss agri-food case the transformation of the regime in the second phase of the transition (1990–2000) would not have occurred and cannot be fully understood without the emergence of niches in the first phase of the transition (1970–90). Major societal changes do not 'fall from the sky', but build upon other pre-developments by accumulation. The roots of organic farming go back to the beginning of the 20th century but then did not succeed in linking up with developments at the macro level. Nevertheless, Belz continues, this 'invisible' niche-period was important, because it facilitated stabilization of rules and networks. It was also during this period that integrated production emerged as a direct response by the largest Swiss food retail chain to the negative side effects of industrialized agriculture. Nevertheless, the new practices remained stuck at the niche level during the 1970s and 1980s and could not break through, partly because the regime of industrialized agriculture was still stable. When, subsequently, the regime opened up, creating a 'window opportunity', all of the elements were already in place to facilitate the niche to break through.

Although niches are indeed important as the locus for 'seeds for transitions', several chapters also provide a warning not to look exclusively at niches because the majority of the seedlings will die before they can survive and grow on their own. Niches indeed are crucial as the breeders for transitions but whether they can survive and eventually break through depends upon the links between developments at multiple levels. Correljé and Verbong, for instance, in their study of the Dutch gas transition explain that the take-off phase of the transition was built upon accumulated experiences from an earlier period. Contrary to common perception, the transition did not begin with the find of the Slochteren gas field because, in the preceding years, several developments had already started on which the transition could build. This implies that empirical studies of transitions should look at not just promising novelties but also at ongoing processes at the regime and landscape levels.

Therefore, to understand transition processes a focus on niches is necessary but by no means sufficient. We also need to analyse how existing systems (or regimes) react to counter the 'threat' of niches and how linkage processes overcome the resistance. Furthermore, the regime and landscape levels not only throw up barriers for niches, they may also provide possibilities to link up in the form of 'windows of opportunity' as is illustrated by several case studies in this book.

Next to these general-level patterns in the dynamic of transitions, it is useful to distinguish a variety of more specific typical processes that can be seen as 'sub-dynamics' which may occur under specific circumstances. The chapters provide a number of examples on issues like the role of visions, networks, niches, and specific actors. They highlight patterns like certain actors functioning as 'gatekeepers', the 'sailing ship effect', the importance of outsiders in introducing challenging aspects in future visions, the compensation of losers, hypes and bandwagon effects, strategic games and so on. These findings and proposals provide stepping stones for more focused concrete follow-on work for researchers interested in those specific topics.

One final issue we want to emphasize is the active role of users in transition processes. Shove's chapter argues, in particular, that that change of user behaviour is a prerequisite for a transition. Also the Dutch gas-transition case shows that the diffusion of natural gas required wider changes in user practices. It is important to acknowledge this active role of users because most work on innovation and diffusion hardly acknowledges it. Users on the one hand may form a barrier to a transition since they do not easily change their ways and adopt new patterns of behaviour. On the other hand, as Shove argues, it is clear that firmly-held concepts of normal practice are immensely malleable. The cases in this book show that users can be found who are willing to change their behaviour and that a transition only occurs when larger groups subsequently follow them. Thus, users can either make or break a transition. It is therefore crucial to gain a better understanding of (the potential of) their role under different circumstances.

INDUCING TRANSITIONS – LESSONS LEARNED

Modest Ambitions for Transition Policy

In Chapter 1, we argued that transitions or system innovations have a high potential to help to achieve sustainability. An important issue then becomes how insights into the dynamic of these processes can be used to induce and stimulate system innovations. More specifically, this poses the challenge of exploring possibilities and developing suggestions for 'transition policy' or 'transition management', as it is also called (Rotmans *et al.*, 2000, 2001).

Is this a useful question at all? Given the complexity of transition processes there are good reasons to argue that transition management is merely a contradiction in terms! Far simpler processes have proven to be impossible to manage so how could it ever be achieved for encompassing processes like transitions and system innovations?

We can start modestly by acknowledging that it is impossible to manage transitions in the sense that a central actor like a government can set a specific objective and realize that objective by using the right instruments under the right circumstances. It will never work that way because transitions are the result of unpredictable interactions between different stakeholders, power games, new developments that cannot be foreseen, as well as unanticipated catastrophes or opportunities.

Several chapters in this book provide a number of suggestions for possible ambitions, strategies and tools for transition policy but how they work out remains to be seen. The best we can say is that these proposals are interesting and merit further exploration. They hold promise if only for the reason that they address the shortcomings in existing policies to address the challenges of achieving sustainability. Several chapters provide good reasons to assume that alternative proposals might work better, though they also illustrate this may trigger new problems. Whether these proposals actually help to induce and realize a particular transition is something we can only establish after a considerable period of experience.

General steering philosophy

Transitions or system innovation cannot be managed in the strict sense. For that reason, several authors have suggested that the policy objective should be to find ways to 'modulate on-going dynamics' so that it bends slightly in the direction of desired objectives (see Kemp and Rotmans in this volume). This may still be significant since a slight initial bend can lead to drastically different outcomes in the longer term which, after all, is what transitions are about. This approach is like Charles Lindblom's notion of 'muddling through' (Lindblom and Woodhouse, 1993) but with an added element: understanding the dynamics of development allows one to identify opportunities for intervention and specify how such interventions can be productive. This 'muddling through' implies that at the very heart of transition policy is the notion of 'learning-by-doing' as also argued in various chapters in this book. It is impossible to steer them towards specific goals using specific strategies so the only alternative is to take initial steps on the basis of limited knowledge and insights, after some time evaluate the effects of these steps, adjust strategies when needed and continue in a cyclical process of action and evaluation.

A first question then becomes what 'limited knowledge and insights' are needed to identify these first steps. We have already stated that the general objective for transition policy is to modulate ongoing dynamics. This implies a need to assess these dynamics for a concrete case where a transition is deemed desirable and to take into account the strategies and objectives of the various actors involved. To realize this, public authorities have to interact with other players in innovation processes (producers, users, intermediaries) to assess their desired (longer term) objectives.

This then raises several questions, the most important of which are (i) how can we assess other stakeholders' objectives and (ii) how can we use this knowledge in choosing concrete policy measures? These questions also raise the issue of the role of governments in transition processes. Teisman and Edelenbos argue in their chapter that a top-down steering model is not consistent with the objective of steering transitions. 'Management of transitions requires a transition of management', as they state. A more horizontal steering model would be needed and policy objectives should be established in interaction with various stakeholders rather than unilaterally by governments. The same point is raised in the chapter by Kemp and Rotmans. They also argue, however, that this 'interactiveness' in policy making is only part of the story. It should be supplemented by more traditional command-and-control policies. It is evident that there is a tension here: on the one hand government would act on equal footing with other actors, on the other it would 'stand above them' and use control instruments.

How to deal with this tension in practice is an open question and is likely to depend upon the specifics of a concrete case. Government strategies would need to be based on an assessment of the dynamics of that case which is partly influenced by the strategies and objectives of a variety of actors. How to take these into account is very unclear and a matter of much debate. Seeking to tackle this issue, several chapters in this book use the notion of 'visions' and 'vision-building'. The idea is that heterogeneous actors discuss desired long-term objectives and, in the process, reach some sort of agreement on this. These visions should then be used to identify next steps en route to the realization of these objectives.

Vision-building, however, is a very messy type of endeavour as various chapters illustrate. The result will rarely, if ever, be a broad consensus on where we should go. There may be some elements on which all actors agree but there will probably be far more elements where only some actors agree while there are probably also elements where all actors disagree. In the book *Contested Futures*, it is argued that competition and strategic games are also played out in the definition of future visions (Brown *et al.*, 2000).

Still, knowing the objectives of crucial stakeholders will probably be a better foundation for subsequent action than 'just throwing a stone in the pond'. The chapter by Brown, Vergragt, Green and Berchicci goes a step further by arguing that a process of visioning is a necessity when the objective is to induce a transition rather than incremental innovation. In the latter case, the longer-term development path is the result of opportunistic attempts to develop short-term solutions to pressing problems. As historical evidence shows, this is likely to lead to a very crooked course of development and it is very questionable that it will lead to sustainability in the broad sense. When striving for a transition, by contrast, an explicit attempt should be made to identify a longer-term sustainability objective, however vague, and to try and develop a course (or courses) towards the realization of that objective.

The chapter by Elzen, Geels, Hofman and Green hooks on to this. It also argues for the importance of vision-building and subsequently provides a method for the identification of possible courses towards the realization of such visions. It illustrates that such visions can be used to evaluate whether ongoing developments are 'on course' and to inspire an adaptation of strategies when this appears no longer to be the case. These observations lead to the conclusion that visions and vision-building need to be an element in transition policy but how they should be fitted in is still unclear.

One point we would like to stress here is that 'building visions' should not be confused with 'reaching consensus'. Visions created in interaction between heterogeneous stakeholders will have elements of consensus as well as elements of dissensus as various chapters in this book clearly illustrate. A critical issue for further research is how to acknowledge this dual character and yet use them as 'signposts' in transition policy.

All this implies that transition policy or transition management in the strict sense is not possible but that we do have various suggestions for 'explorative transition policies' that are worthwhile thinking further about. The points discussed imply these explorative policies have the following characteristics:

- The ambition is to realize long-term 'fundamental' changes. The goal is not to solve today's problems by tomorrow but to induce and stimulate the development of longer term but more fundamental and more effective solutions. This may even imply having to accept that problems initially get worse.
- Transitions cannot be managed in the strict sense; that is, they cannot be steered by a central actor (government or other) to realize specific objectives.
- By implication, transition management is, at least partly, an interactive process that needs to take place between a heterogeneous set of actors, each acting on the basis of their own vital interests and expectations.
- Transition management requires anticipation methods and (interactive) vision-building processes. Some notion is needed on the direction in which to move to be able to identify 'promising next steps' and to facilitate evaluation of the results of these steps.

- It combines interactive instruments and strategies with command and control instruments.
- Transition management implies a cyclic process of vision-building, taking action, evaluating the response to this and subsequently taking new action. In its very essence it is a process of 'learning-by-doing'.

This list, of course, raises more questions then it answers. Most importantly, it talks about taking action but says nothing about what types of action. We will address this issue briefly in the next section.

Stimulating Learning: Experiments and Niches

Concerning the types of actions to be taken we are on slippery ground since there is virtually no empirical evidence. Historical case studies of transition management may partly serve as empirical tests but this raises the problem of generalizability. Do lessons from one domain also hold for other domains? And do lessons from a particular era (with its particular political culture and actor-constellation) also hold for other periods (with other political cultures and actor-constellations)?

An alternative starting point is to infer suggestions from general insights in transition processes. As a general pattern we can say that novelties that induce a transition go through two main stages, notably a niche stage in which the emphasis is on 'probing and learning' and a breakthrough stage in which the emphasis is on economic issues. Transition policy should take this into account, seeking to stimulate probing and learning for those novelties that need it and stimulating market take-up when learning has sufficiently progressed.

With respect to learning in niches, several chapters in this volume highlight the importance of experiments and niches as a breeding ground for radical alternatives or novelties. They also show, however, that niche developments themselves are not sufficient for transitions. Learning effects may remain limited to local experiments, or learning may be more about technical matters than social aspects. There may be difficulty in achieving second-order learning (or higher learning as Brown, Vergragt, Green and Berchicci put it). Berkhout, Smith and Stirling even question whether the multi-level perspective places far too much emphasis on niches. They argue that many niches never break through and make any progress. One can only agree with them on the latter point. Just as in any evolutionary process, possibly nine out of ten variations do not make it; but does this diminish the importance of variation? Studies of successful transitions illustrate this is not the case either. In all cases, radical novelties need to go through a typically very long probing and learning process before they could link up to an existing system and make a breakthrough possible. Furthermore, although the multi-level perspective highlights the importance of niches, it explicitly argues that niches alone are not enough. Breakthrough also depends upon ongoing processes in regimes and landscapes.

Thus, learning processes in connection with novelties provide a crucial first step en route to a transition and transition policy should therefore stimulate this.[1] To be able to specify how such stimulation could take place, let us briefly recapture the main aspects of niche dynamic and niche-regime interaction.

Initially, novelties with transformation potential have difficulty linking up to an existing system. This raises a range of issues concerning how they may survive, how they can develop further so that linking up does occur and how it is possible that from this point on it is not the small novelty that adapts to the regime but it is the regime that transforms to fit the novelty. In general, such a qualitative transformation is unlikely because existing systems tend to defend themselves against the perceived threats of novelties. In such a situation, novelties require actors who believe in their potential and who are prepared to work against the odds. A crucial question then becomes which strategies they (can) use to change the odds. In an extreme case, they may be just a few tinkerers working from a shed but to make the novelty grow they will have to liaise with others who should also be prepared to work against the odds. They can thus build a network of different types of actors, including technology developers who are willing to invest time, effort and money (the entrepreneurs). The network also requires users who deviate from the mainstream and who are prepared or interested in using a technology with clear disadvantages[2] as well as investors who are willing to take considerable risks (venture capitalists). Finally, there is a need for regulators who are willing to stick their necks out and give preferential treatment to the novelty.

What can policy do to stimulate such niche processes? Firstly, policy has to be rooted in insights into these processes; this still leaves a lot to be desired. It implies a clear policy need to further these insights by stimulating research. One important issue, for instance, is to provide an overview of which potential novelties there are in a specific field that merit further development and exploration. For each of these, research should also suggest promising issues for further development and learning. But research cannot provide all the answers. Transition policy implies 'learning-by-doing' as does a transition process itself. An important objective of policy should therefore be to stimulate and optimize the conditions for learning, such as by providing funds for experimentation, stimulating network-building and vision-building processes between actors. Again, research could help to provide information to base such decisions upon but the results from such research will never be straightforward. Thus, there will always remain an element of tentativeness in exploratory transition policies.

Stimulating Breakthrough

Stimulating niche development is crucial as it allows the possible seeds for a transition (the novelties) to germinate. To continue the metaphor, one may say they are initially grown in a greenhouse. To induce a transition, however, they need to go outside the greenhouse, survive under 'real world conditions' and grow further. This means the novelties need to grow in an environment that may be partially friendly to them (by offering 'windows of opportunity') but that will also have hostile elements because an existing regime tends to defend itself against upcoming novelties in various ways, by throwing up barriers to the novelty, by improving performance of the regime or by absorbing elements of the novelty.

This volume has chapters that focus on learning and niches (Kivisaari, Lovio and Väyrynen; Brown, Vergragt, Green and Berchicci) as well as chapters on the wider breakthrough of novelties (Belz; Correljé and Verbong). These latter studies could tell us something on how to stimulate such breakthroughs but the problem is that the cases they present might be too atypical to allow general conclusions. In the Dutch gas transition case there was a considerable degree of consensus; this is far from typical for other domains. In the Swiss agriculture case, the government developed a vision for a transition that received broad public support, a situation which is not typical for various other domains either. Current domains which face sustainability challenges (such as energy, mobility, food/agriculture) are typically characterized by a large degree of dissensus.

On the basis of existing innovation and market diffusion studies it is clear that there exists a variety of policy instruments that can stimulate market take-up, including financial instruments (subsidies and taxes), standards (such as emission standards) or direct regulation (for example, car-free zones). These, of course, could also play a role to stimulate the breakthrough of novelties with transformation potential. The transition objective, however, poses a number of additional challenges. On the one hand, there is a need to stimulate learning in niches (as discussed in the section above), on the other the need to stimulate breakthrough. This already suggests a need for tuning and paying attention to timing. This issue becomes even more complex because there are usually several niches, each of which holds certain promises while having problems as well. So, what does one stimulate when? Based on a scenario study (rather than an empirical study) the chapter by Elzen *et al.* argues that this tuning of policy instruments can have crucial impacts on the course of a transition path. More research as well as policy experience is needed to be able to make more precise recommendations on what combination of instruments to use under what circumstances.

In conclusion, the chapters in this book do allow us to identify various important and necessary elements of transition management (such as processes of vision building and the need to build networks) but there are also important elements missing. A main gap in this book is that we have no cases where the need for a transition or a desired transition path is heavily contested. The main reason for this is that, where this is the case (such as in mobility or energy supply), the lack of consensus results in incrementalism, trying to solve small problems without explicitly attempting to work towards a long-term vision. Attempts to target system innovation are not on the policy agenda for such cases so there simply is no empirical evidence. This is a major shortcoming since these are the cases that we eventually seek to target.

The points just made are rather general and to be practically useful they should be specified further on the basis of further research on transitions, including findings discussed in several chapters in this book. Furthermore, concrete policy recommendations need to be tuned to the state-of-affairs in concrete domains. As a result, concrete transition policy for the energy domain may contain a different mix of approaches than, for instance, for the traffic and transport domain. This will need to be explored in detail in further research for which the findings in this book could provide a starting point.

RESEARCH AGENDA

Transitions or system innovations are heterogeneous phenomena with many aspects and dimensions. Disciplinary perspectives, however useful, often approach from a specific viewpoint, highlighting particular aspects, but ignoring others. To obtain a more fully developed view, we need to relate multiple perspectives to each other, to try and create synergy from interdisciplinary and transdisciplinary work. This is difficult in practice. As editors of this book and coorganizers of the workshop from which the book came, we sought such an integration but this proved difficult. Although most of the chapters do take a view beyond a single discipline, they typically only cover a limited set of relevant aspects.

Still, we do think that this book can be seen as a fruitful first attempt at an interdisciplinary analysis of transitions. Several disciplines are represented but several others could make useful contributions as well. Given the range of multi-dimensional phenomena that characterize a transition we think at least the following fields should be represented: innovation studies, (socio)economic research, history of (socio)technical change, policy studies, science and technology studies, user-related studies and cultural studies. All of these disciplines analyse specific aspects of transition processes but in an actual transition these aspects occur concurrently. The challenge therefore is to integrate findings from different disciplines to grasp the process as a whole.

On the basis of the first section of this chapter we can highlight the following research challenges:

- develop typologies of transitions;
- further develop 'heterogeneous' analytical frameworks such as the multi-level perspective;
- understand why and how some niches set in motion transformational change at wider scales while others fail; this is at least partially related to the dynamic of regimes and landscapes;
- distinguish a variety of more specific typical processes that can be seen as 'sub-dynamics' that may occur under specific circumstances;
- explore the role of various types of actors, especially users.

These topics define the major tasks for the years ahead. A wide variety of studies will be needed in different domains and socio-technical systems to analyse (the interplay between) different levels, analyse the importance of different 'environments', confront findings from different studies and generalize beyond the individual analyses. This implies a need to carry out a wide range of case studies to inspire the development of theories and test them. By combining insights from several case studies we may be able to identify general and/or broad patterns in transitions.

Such findings and patterns, however, cannot simply be translated to the present and future, because socio-technical systems and the constellation of societal groups can function differently. Nevertheless, such historical findings can provide a useful stepping stone as well as provide empirical material to aid theory development.

In many existing historical studies of transitions and system innovations, the question of boundaries pops up. Where does a system begin and where does it end? This is an inherently problematic issue because it is characteristic of system innovations that boundaries change during the process. System innovations are precisely about structural changes in elements and their relationships. By implication it is not possible to define boundaries of systems and associated networks forever. Boundaries change over time, and they vary between sectors. Transport systems function differently from electricity systems, which, in their turn, differ from agricultural systems. Although these boundaries are fluid, any research in terms of systems should take the issue of boundaries seriously, especially since one of the features of transitions is that novelties initially are developed outside or at the fringes of a system, then link up to it and subsequently transform it.

A further research challenge is to connect insights in system innovations more systematically to sustainability issues. In Chapter 1 we highlighted the promise that system innovations could lead to large jumps in environmental efficiency. But how can the promise be fulfilled for different sectors? How necessary is it to target system innovations? Despite their potential, in some sectors large improvements might also be gained with incremental innovations. Another issue is how system innovations can be related to other dimensions of sustainability, not just ecological but also economic and societal aspects like equity. If structural change implies that some companies or sectors may be wiped out this has considerable negative societal effects, including uncertainty, job loss and social instability. An open question and research challenge then is whether transitions can be managed in such a way that major upheavals do not occur.

This brings us to the general issue of translating insights in the dynamics of transition processes into suggestions for transition management. Chapters in the second part of the book have mainly worked from one of the policy perspectives we mentioned in the introduction: the policy networks governance paradigm. This policy paradigm has certain characteristics that fit very well with insights in transition dynamics, especially in the concepts of learning, adaptive visions and networks. The transition tools proposed in Chapters 9, 10 and 11 further articulate dimensions of this paradigm. Although more should be done on this promising route, it has the disadvantage that the other two policy paradigms have received less attention. More work should be done to find out which roles the three policy paradigms (and their instruments) can play in transition management. Different (combinations) of instruments will probably have to play a different role in different phases or different types of transitions so the main issue is to investigate the conditions for an optimal tuning of the various instruments. More concretely, this leads to the following questions:

- What new instruments might emerge from a consideration of the third paradigm for transitions? Because this paradigm is rather new, its possibilities and effectiveness have not been entirely elaborated.
- If all paradigms have a role to play in managing transitions, which is most appropriate under which circumstances? Can this be related to different phases in transitions (e.g. invention and generation of new options, the linking of novelties to existing regimes, the wider

diffusion of the novelties and transformation of the regime) which may require different policy interventions?

- How can we organize and optimize learning? The chapter by Brown, Vergragt, Green and Berchicci distinguishes two types of learning, first and second order, as necessary ingredients in attaining a critical mass of societal intelligence for a transition towards sustainability. They argue that a substantial social value can be extracted from experiments by the monitoring and, where appropriate, the management of social learning. A major challenge in designing experiments is to find ways of linking them in a more planned way to one another. Governments, as well as various intellectually entrepreneurial societal agents, have pivotal roles to play in making that happen (Hoogma *et al.*, 2004; Vergragt, 2003).
- How can we monitor and better understand the diffusion of social learning about radical novelties that occurs as a result of the experiments? The substantial body of previous research on social learning (including Rogers, 1985; Hamblin, 1979; Bandura, 1977) can provide a starting point for addressing this challenge.
- What do the different policy paradigms imply for the role of different actors in supporting management of transition, especially the balance between 'private' action and 'public' intervention/support?

Relying on the third policy paradigm, if only partly, requires taking the role and interests of different stakeholders seriously. If we look at the three major groups of stakeholders – producers, governments and users/ consumers – the latter have been largely underplayed in research on innovation and transition processes. Shove has illustrated in this book that they play a crucial role. Existing literature on innovation that does look at users mostly focuses on their role as adopters of new technologies and products. Research in the field of STS, however, has demonstrated that users play a much more active role (see Oudshoorn and Pinch, 2003; Lie and Sørensen,1996). The role of users therefore requires much more systematic investigation.

NECESSARY LINKS BETWEEN TRANSITION RESEARCH AND TRANSITION POLICY

Above, we have stressed several times that transitions cannot be planned and that they can only develop in a process of 'learning-by-doing'. The same is true for transition management: on the basis of some of the chapters in this book we can formulate some general recommendations for 'exploratory transition policies' but their value can only be established in practice and results need to be used to adapt policies when needed, another aspect of 'learning-by-doing'.

We are in a situation that our understanding of transition processes and transition policy are both limited, possibly even extremely limited. One way forward is to first develop a better understanding of transitions on the basis of historical research. This will render better knowledge of the dynamic of transition processes and should allow the analysis of the role of various factors in inducing, stimulating or impeding transitions under different circumstances. A better understanding of the dynamic could subsequently help to develop better founded policy suggestions on (im)possibilities of inducing and stimulating transitions.

Still, however useful and necessary, the better understanding of transitions will not provide a sufficiently solid basis for transition policy for two reasons. Firstly, past transitions were rarely the result of dedicated attempts to realize them. Suggestions for transition policy based on their analysis will of necessity be hypothetical and their value will have to be assessed by trying them out in practice. Secondly, transitions are so complex with so many uncontrollable factors playing a role that attempts to steer or guide their course will always have an element of tentativeness and continuous feedback and adjustment will be necessary as time goes on.

Therefore, it is neither useful nor necessary to make attempts to induce transitions (or transition policy) until we have developed a better understanding of the dynamic of transitions. We can distinguish three types of activity that need to go on concurrently and that need to influence each other continuously, notably:

1. The analysis of past transitions on the basis of historical research: this should render a better and more refined theory (or theories) on the dynamic of transitions which can be used to refine and specify suggestions on (im)possibilities for transition policy.
2. Transition policy (or management) in practice: governments in various countries are already trying to stimulate innovation but several chapters in this book as well as other sources suggest changes are needed if the objective is to induce transitions. On the basis of these suggestions 'exploratory transition policies' should be started in various domains (such as in food, water, energy, mobility).
3. Learning-by-doing: the attempts at transition management should be closely monitored and subsequent developments evaluated. Results can be used to enhance the understanding of transition processes (in combination with historical analyses) and be fed back into the development of better suggestions for transition management or policy.

This combined approach will require a closer and more continuous interaction between policy and research than is common. To realize this may itself constitute a challenge but is a necessary requirement given the complexity of the issue we are dealing with. It can be seen as a first go at realizing the interactivity that is required in transition policy.

Thus, the challenge to realize transitions towards sustainability in a variety of domains can only be fruitfully tackled when short-term attempts to induce them are carried out in close interaction with work on furthering the understanding of the dynamic of transitions. Still, given that so much work still needs to done on both the understanding and the inducement side it makes sense to define separate projects for each area as long as the results are frequently related to each other.

NOTES

1. The policy strategy to stimulate learning in niches is also called 'strategic niche management' (see Hoogma *et al.*, 2002).
2. In innovation studies and economics these are sometimes called the 'leading edge consumers' or 'first users'.

REFERENCES

Bandura, Albert (1977), *Social Learning Theory*, Englewood Cliffs, NJ: Prentice Hall.

Brown, N., B. Rappert and A. Webster (eds) (2000), *Contested Futures: A Sociology of Prospective Technoscience*, Aldershot: Ashgate.

Hamblin, Robert L., R.B. Jacobson, and J.L. Miller (1979), 'Modelling use diffusion', *Social Forces*, **57**, 799–811.

Hoogma, R., R. Kemp, J. Schot and B. Truffer (2002), *Experimenting for Sustainable Transport: The Approach of Strategic Niche Management*, London and New York: Spon Press

Hoogma, R., K.M. Weber and B. Elzen (2004), 'Integrated long-term strategies to induce regime shifts to sustainability: the approach of strategic niche management', in K.M. Weber and J. Hemmelskamp (eds), *Towards Environmental Innovation Systems*, Heidelberg: Springer.

Lie, Merete, and Knut H. Sørensen (eds) (1996), *Making Technology Our Own: Domesticating Technology into Everyday Life*, Oslo: Scandinavian University Press.

Lindblom, Charles E., and Edward J. Woodhouse (1993), *The Policy-making Process*, Englewood Cliffs, NJ: Prentice Hall.

Oudshoorn, Nelly, and Trevor Pinch (eds) (2003), *How Users Matter: The Co-Construction of Users and Technology*, Cambridge, MA: MIT Press.

Rogers, Everett M. (1985), *Diffusion of Innovations*, 4th edn, New York: The Free Press.

Rotmans, Jan, René Kemp, Marjolein van Asselt, Frank Geels, Geert Verbong, Kirsten Molendijk (2000), 'Transities en Transitiemanagement: de casus van een emissiearme energievoorziening' (Transitions and transition management: the case of a low-emission energy supply), study for Dutch National Environmental Policy Plan, Maastricht: ICIS.

Rotmans, J., R. Kemp and M. van Asselt (2001), 'More Evolution than Revolution: Transition Management in Public Policy', *Foresight*, **3** (1), 15–31.

Vergragt, P.J. (2004), 'Back-casting for environmental sustainability: from STD and SusHouse towards implementation', in K.M.Weber and J. Hemmelskamp (eds), *Towards Environmental Innovation Systems*, Heidelberg: Springer.

Index